NONLINEAR PREFERENCE AND UTILITY THEORY

JOHNS HOPKINS SERIES IN THE MATHEMATICAL SCIENCES

Nonlinear Preference and Utility Theory

PETER C. FISHBURN

AT&T Bell Laboratories

THE JOHNS HOPKINS UNIVERSITY PRESS   BALTIMORE AND LONDON

The Johns Hopkins University Press, 701 West 40th Street, Baltimore, Maryland 21211
The Johns Hopkins Press Ltd., London

Library of Congress Cataloging-in-Publication Data
Fishburn, Peter C.
  Nonlinear preference and utility theory.
  (Johns Hopkins series in the mathematical sciences; 5)
  Bibliography: p.
  Includes index.
  1. Utility theory. 2. Game theory. 3. Uncertainty.
4. Decision-making. I. Title. II. Series.
HB203.F57 1988   658.4′033   87-29729
ISBN 0-8018-3598-4 (alk. paper)

The paper used in this publication meets the minimum requirements of American National Standard for Information Sciences—Permanence of Paper for Printed Library Materials, ANSI Z39.48-1984.

TO TOM AND WEST AND RUSS

Contents

Preface

The theories of John von Neumann and Oskar Morgenstern for preference comparisons under risk and of Frank P. Ramsey and Leonard J. Savage for preference comparisons under uncertainty have been widely adopted as the quintessential paradigms for rational decision making in the face of uncertainty. Their expected (linear) utility models have profoundly affected economic analysis, risk assessment, and statistical decision theory over the past 35 years.

During this period there has been a growing awareness—stimulated in large part by Maurice Allais's work in the early 1950s—that people's reasoned judgments often violate the basic assumptions of expected utility. Numerous studies have demonstrated that such violations tend to follow systematic and predictable patterns. Investigators have therefore proposed alternative theories of rational preference that accommodate systematic departures from expected utility while retaining much of its mathematical elegance and computational convenience. With the notable exception of Allais's own theory from the early 1950s, most of the alternatives have emerged during the past decade.

This book attempts to make sense of recent and not so recent developments in preference theory for risky and uncertain decisions. It is arranged in two main parts: Chapters 1 through 6 focus on decision under risk, Chapters 7 through 9 on decision under uncertainty. Each main part answers three questions:

1. What is expected utility theory?
2. What is wrong with it from a rational preference perspective?
3. What has been proposed to correct the problems?

Question 1 is dealt with in Chapter 1 for decision under risk (von Neumann and Morgenstern) and in Chapter 7 for decision under uncertainty (Savage). Chapter 2 and the first part of Chapter 8 address question 2. Question 3 is partly answered by surveys of alternative theories of preference in risky situations (Chapter 3) and in uncertain situations (Chapter 8). These five chapters (1-3, 7-8) comprise a book within the book whose purpose is to provide an up-to-date view of expected utility and its alternatives that aims for organizational clarity and inclusiveness.

The other four chapters expand on question 3 by detailing new theories that I have had some role in developing. These chapters form a second book within the book that organizes material previously available only in a scattered set of journal articles.

The book is intended for graduate students and research workers in mathematics, economics, statistics, operations research, psychology, and related fields that are interested in the foundations and potential applications of decision making under risk and uncertainty.

Acknowledgments

This book was written in conjunction with the 1986 Mathematical Sciences Lecture Series at the Johns Hopkins University. It owes a great deal to three people at the university: Alan Goldman of the Mathematical Sciences Department, who elicited my interest in their annual series soon after I joined Bell Telephone Laboratories in 1978; Alan Karr, who organized the 1986 Series as the then head of the department; and Anders Richter, Editorial Director of the Johns Hopkins University Press. Their encouragement and cooperation have been extraordinary and are deeply appreciated. It is also a pleasure to thank Marilyn Karr for her gracious hospitality and the participants of the 1986 Series for their support and stimulation.

My mathematical research for Chapters 4–6 and 9 was done at AT&T Bell Laboratories between 1979 and the fall of 1986. I am indebted to many people there for their encouragement and support of this work. Special thanks go to Ed Zajac, former director of the Economics Research Center; Ronald Graham, present director of the Mathematical Sciences Research Center; and to Susan Tarczynski, Cynthia Martin, and Janice Preckwinkle for their superb typing of the manuscript and the journal articles that converged in its preparation.

I am indebted also to the publishers, editors, and referees of journals in which those articles appeared, the *Journal of Mathematical Psychology,* the *Journal of Economic Theory, The Annals of Statistics, Mathematical Social Sciences, The Review of Economic Studies, Econometrica, Management Science, INFOR (Canadian Journal of Operational Research and Information Processing),* the *Journal of Mathematical Economics,* the *International Review of Economics and Business,* and *Economics Letters.*

It is a distinct pleasure to acknowledge and thank teachers and colleagues who have shared their interest and expertise in decision theory with me during the past three decades. Russ Ackoff and Jimmie Savage were my two great teachers in the subject. In more recent years I have been strongly influenced by the careful experimental research and incisive thinking of Duncan Luce and Amos Tversky. Younger colleagues who deserve credit and thanks for their research in nonlinear utility theory and the excitement it has generated include Mark Machina and Chew Soo Hong. Among my coauthors, Irving LaValle, William Gehrlein, and Robert Rosenthal have my appreciation and thanks for their collaboration on topics in nonlinear utility. The material in Sections 6.4 and 9.4–9.6 was developed jointly with Irving LaValle, and that in Section 6.5 with Robert Rosenthal.

NONLINEAR PREFERENCE AND UTILITY THEORY

1 Historical Background: Expected Utility

Expected utility has served for more than a generation as the preeminent model of rational preferences in decision making under conditions of risk. During this time, and especially in the past decade, the assumptions of expected utility have come under attack as principles that any reasonable person's preferences ought to satisfy. New theories have recently been developed to accommodate some of the more persistent violations of expected utility without giving up too much of its mathematical elegance. This chapter reviews the fundamentals of expected utility theory to set the stage for a critique of its axioms and a discussion of alternative theories in ensuing chapters.

1.1 DANIEL BERNOULLI AND GABRIEL CRAMER

It was widely held in the early years of the development of probability theory that risky monetary ventures ought to be evaluated by their expected returns—the more the better. Thus, suppose p and q are probability distributions on a set X of monetary gains ($x \geq 0$) and losses ($x < 0$) that correspond to two risky ventures. Then, with

$$E(x, p) = \sum_{x \in X} xp(x),$$

p is more desirable than q precisely when $E(x, p) > E(x, q)$.

The first major challenge to this principle of expected return maximization appeared in 1738 at the hand of Daniel Bernoulli, a member of the Swiss family of distinguished mathematicians. Bernoulli proposed two theses. His first thesis does not involve risk or probability. It says that a person's subjective value $v(w)$ of wealth w does not increase linearly in w but rather increases at a decreasing rate, a proposition known later in economics as the principle of diminishing marginal utility of wealth. Bernoulli argued further that the rate of increase in $v(w)$ is inversely proportional to w and, hence, that v is a logarithmic function of wealth.

Bernoulli's second thesis, set forth in opposition to maximization of expected return or expected wealth, says that a risky prospect p' on levels of wealth ought to be evaluated by its expected subjective value $\Sigma \, v(w)p'(w)$. Alternatively, if w_0 is present wealth and $p(x) = p'(w_0 + x)$, so that p is the probability distribution induced by p' on increments to present wealth, then the expected subjective value of p is

$$E(v, p) = \sum_{x \in X} v(w_0 + x)p(x),$$

with p more desirable than q when $E(v, p) > E(v, q)$.

Bernoulli defended his theses with examples from games of chance and insurance. Would you engage in a one-time not-to-be-repeated wager that yields gain \$21,000 or loss \$20,000 each with probability $\frac{1}{2}$? If you refuse, you violate the principle of maximum expected return, which is \$500 for the wager (versus \$0 otherwise). According to Bernoulli's principle, your refusal simply means that $[v(w_0 + 21,000) + v(w_0 - 20,000)]/2 < v(w_0)$ and that you are acting prudently in accord with your subjective values. In another instance, merchants insure seabound cargoes against loss even though they know that the insurer expects to gain at their expense from the transaction. Nevertheless, the merchants are simply acting in their own best interests by maximizing their expected subjective value.

A prime motivator for Bernoulli's work on the evaluation of risky ventures was the famous St. Petersburg game, devised by his cousin Nicholas Bernoulli in 1713. In current terms, a fair coin is tossed until a head appears. If the first head occurs at the nth toss, the payoff is 2^n dollars. Suppose you own title to one play of the game; that is, you can engage in it without cost. What is the least amount you would sell your title for? According to the Bernoullis, this least amount is your equivalent monetary value of the game.

Nicholas observed that the expected payoff

$$(\tfrac{1}{2})2 + (\tfrac{1}{4})2^2 + (\tfrac{1}{8})2^3 + \cdots = 1 + 1 + 1 + \cdots$$

is infinite, but most people would sell title for a relatively small sum, and he asked for an explanation of such a flagrant violation of maximum expected return. Daniel showed how his theory resolves the issue by providing a unique solution s to the equation

$$\sum_n v(w_0 + 2^n)2^{-n} = v(w_0 + s)$$

for any finite w_0, where s is the minimum selling price or equivalent monetary value. Moreover, except for the very rich, a person would gladly sell title for about \$25 or \$30. The effect of w_0 can be seen indirectly by estimating your minimum selling price when the payoff at n is 2^n cents instead of 2^n dollars and comparing 100 times this estimate to your answer from the preceding paragraph.

In a postscript to his 1738 paper, Daniel said that Nicholas told him that another Swiss mathematician, Gabriel Cramer, developed a theory to explain the St. Petersburg game that is remarkably similar to Daniel's own theory. Moreover, Cramer did so in 1728, several years before Daniel wrote his paper. The postscript quotes extensively from the letter to Nicholas in which Cramer describes his resolution of the issue, and includes the following passage:

You asked for an explanation of the discrepancy between the mathematical calculation and the vulgar evaluation. I believe that it results from the fact that, *in their theory*, mathematicians evaluate money in proportion to its quantity while, *in practice*, people with common sense evaluate money in proportion to the utility they can obtain from it. (Translated from the French by L. Sommer in Bernoulli [1954], p. 33.)

Unlike Bernoulli, Cramer pays little attention to initial wealth, and for $x \geq 0$ sets $v(x) = \sqrt{x}$. In his terms, the minimum selling price is the value of s that satisfies

$$(\tfrac{1}{2})\sqrt{2} + (\tfrac{1}{4})\sqrt{4} + (\tfrac{1}{8})\sqrt{8} + \cdots = \sqrt{s},$$

which is a little under \$6.

Later reviews and discussion of the St. Petersburg game are available in Menger (1967) and Samuelson (1977).

1.2 RISKLESS UTILITY IN ECONOMICS

Bernoulli's notion of the diminishing marginal utility of wealth became a centerpiece of the riskless theory of consumer economics during the second half of the nineteenth century, especially in the works of Gossen (1854), Jevons (1871), Menger (1871), Walras (1874), and Marshall (1890). See Stigler (1950) and Kauder (1965) for historical details.

During this period, *utility* was adopted as the standard term for what otherwise might be referred to as subjective value, moral worth, or psychic satisfaction. Utility was predominantly viewed "as a psychological entity measurable in its own right" (Strotz, 1953, p. 84), and there was active debate about the extent to which utility was measurable in any precise sense. However, interest in the measurability issue waned under the ordinalist revolution of Edgeworth (1881), Fisher (1892), Pareto (1906), and Slutsky (1915), which insisted that utility represented nothing more than an individual's preference ordering over consumption bundles or alternative riskless futures. In particular, it makes no sense to measure gradations in utility apart from a simple ordering, not to mention the impossibility of interpersonal comparisons of utility.

Despite the popularity of the ordinal position, a modest revival of interest in the measurability of intensive utility occurred during the 1920s and 1930s, aided in part by the emerging use of axiomatic theory in mathematics. The proponents of measurability included Frisch (1926), Lange (1934), and Alt (1936), each of whom axiomatized the notion of comparable preference differences or intensities of preference in somewhat different ways. Their basic argument was that we do in fact make intensity or strength-of-preference comparisons all the time, and that it was possible to be precise about such comparisons. Consider, for example, monetary gains. Surely you prefer \$100 to \$0, so set $v(\$100) = v_1$ and $v(\$0) = v_0$, subject only to $v_1 > v_0$. Now vary x over the interval between \$0 and \$100 to determine the point at which the intensity of your preference for \$100 over x equals the intensity of your preference for x over \$0. Suppose the answer is $x = \$40$. Then \$40 lies midway in preference between \$0 and \$100, so $v(\$40) = (v_0 + v_1)/2$. By ascertaining additional preference midpoints between \$0 and \$40, between \$40 and \$100, and so forth, you can obtain a good picture of your utility function on the interval from \$0 to \$100. Moreover, this function is "measurable" in the sense that it is fully determined once v_0 and v_1 are specified. In particular, if v and v' are any two such functions, then they are related by the equation $[v(x) - v_0]/[v_1 - v_0] = [v'(x) - v_0']/[v_1' - v_0']$ for all x; that is,

(1.1) $$v'(x) = av(x) + b$$

for all x in [\$0, \$100], where a and b are real numbers with $a > 0$.

This approach to measurable, or "cardinal" (Hicks and Allen, 1934; Fishburn, 1976a) utility can be made precise by a set of assumptions or axioms about a binary relation $\succ^*$ on $X \times X$, where X is a set of things to be evaluated and $(x, y) \succ^* (z, w)$ is interpreted to mean that the individual's strength of preference for x over y exceeds his or her strength of preference for z over w. Equal intensity can then be defined by

$(x, y) \sim^* (z, w)$ if neither $(x, y) \succ^* (z, w)$ nor $(z, w) \succ^* (x, y)$,

and the underlying preference relation $\succ$ on X can be defined from $\succ^*$ by

$$x \succ y \quad \text{if } (x, y) \succ^* (y, y).$$

Under a sufficiently strong set of axioms, examples of which appear in Fishburn (1970a, Chapter 6) and Krantz et al. (1971, Chapter 4), we can derive the utility representation for comparable differences,

$$(x, y) \succ^* (z, w) \Leftrightarrow v(x) - v(y) > v(z) - v(w),$$

with v unique up to the type of transformation noted at the end of the preceding paragraph.

The importance of this for our study of preference between risky decisions is that it put Bernoulli's theory of maximum expected utility on a more rigorous foundation by providing an axiomatic basis for the value function v used in his expectation operation. Moreover, by rendering v unique up to *positive linear transformations*, or positive affine transformations, as in (1.1), it endows his type of riskless utility function with the properties that are needed to preserve expected utility order under admissible transformations of that function.

To be more precise about this, let X be an arbitrary nonempty set, and let P_X denote the set of all *simple* probability measures on X so that p is in P_X if and only if $p(x) \geq 0$ for all x, $p(x) > 0$ for at most a finite number of $x \in X$, and $\Sigma_X\, p(x) = 1$.

THEOREM 1.1. *Suppose v and v' are two real-valued functions on X. Then, for all $p, q \in P_X$,*

$$(1.2) \quad \sum v(x)p(x) > \sum v(x)q(x) \Leftrightarrow \sum v'(x)p(x) > \sum v'(x)q(x)$$

if and only if there are real numbers a and b, with $a > 0$, such that

$$(1.1) \qquad v'(x) = av(x) + b \qquad \text{for all } x \in X.$$

Proof. Let v be given. If $v' = av + b$, $a > 0$, then (1.2) clearly holds. Conversely, suppose (1.2) holds. If v is constant, so equality holds on both sides of (1.2) at all p and q, then v' must also be constant and $v' = v + b$ for some real number b. Suppose henceforth that v is not constant. For definiteness take $v(x_0) > v(y_0)$. Since v' must preserve the ordering of v on X, $v'(x_0) > v'(y_0)$. Then, for each $z \in X$, exactly one of the following obtains:

(i) $v(z) > v(x_0) > v(y_0)$ and there is a unique $0 < \lambda < 1$ such that $v(x_0) = \lambda v(z) + (1 - \lambda)v(y_0)$; hence also $v'(x_0) = \lambda v'(z) + (1 - \lambda)v'(y_0)$ by (1.2) [take $p(x_0) = 1$, $q(z) = \lambda$, $q(y_0) = 1 - \lambda$].

(ii) $v(x_0) \geq v(z) \geq v(y_0)$ and there is a unique $0 \leq \lambda \leq 1$ such that $v(z) = \lambda v(x_0) + (1 - \lambda)v(y_0)$; hence also $v'(z) = \lambda v'(x_0) + (1 - \lambda)v'(y_0)$ by (1.2).

(iii) $v(x_0) > v(y_0) > v(z)$ and there is a unique $0 < \lambda < 1$ such that $v(y_0) = \lambda v(x_0) + (1 - \lambda)v(z)$; hence also $v'(y_0) = \lambda v'(x_0) + (1 - \lambda)\, v'(z)$ by (1.2).

Regardless of which of (i), (ii), or (iii) holds, we have

$$v'(z) = av(z) + b,$$

where

$$a = [v'(x_0) - v'(y_0)]/[v(x_0) - v(y_0)] > 0$$

and

$$b = [v(x_0)v'(y_0) - v'(x_0)v(y_0)]/[v(x_0) - v(y_0)]. \quad \blacksquare$$

If the set of probability distributions on which expected utilities are computed is not as rich as supposed in Theorem 1.1, then it may be possible to transform v in ways other than (1.1) without violating (1.2). However, we are assured of consistency in (1.2) ·in all circumstances only when the admissible transformations of the utility function do not go beyond (1.1) with $a > 0$. However, it might be noted that when X is finite, there is a problem in ensuring (1.1) with the comparable preference differences approach unless utilities are evenly spaced (Davidson and Suppes, 1956) or X is embedded in a richer structure.

For later reference we say that a theory of choice among risky decisions is a *Bernoullian expected utility theory* when it consists of

1. A set X of outcomes and a set P of probability distributions or measures on X
2. A utility function v on X based on a notion of riskless comparable preference differences, usually presumed unique up to positive linear transformations
3. The principle of choice which says that the most desirable distributions, or their corresponding risky alternatives, are those that maximize expected utility $\Sigma \, v(x)p(x)$

The third element is sometimes stated as an injunction: Some distribution from a feasible set that maximizes $\Sigma \, v(x)p(x)$ over the p in the feasible set ought to be chosen when such a maximizing distribution exists.

1.3   VON NEUMANN AND MORGENSTERN

In Bernoullian expected utility theory, preference between probability distributions, if considered at all, is *defined* by expected utilities, so p is said to be preferred to q just when $\Sigma \, v(x)p(x) > \Sigma \, v(x)q(x)$. The expected utility theory introduced in 1944 by von Neumann and Morgenstern differs radically from the Bernoullian theory despite the fact that their mathematical *forms* of expected utility are identical. To distinguish notationally between them, we write $\Sigma \, u(x)p(x)$ for the von Neumann–Morgenstern context, reserving

$\Sigma\ v(x)p(x)$ for the Bernoullian context. The difference between u and v lies in their interpretations and the ways they are assessed. We note these shortly.

There are also similarities. Both u and v preserve the individual's preference order on outcomes in X, so for all $x, y \in X, u(x) > u(y) \Leftrightarrow v(x) > v(y)$. Moreover u, like v in (1.1), is unique up to positive linear transformations, so if u is a von Neumann–Morgenstern utility function on outcomes in a particular situation then so is u' if and only if $u' = au + b$ for numbers $a > 0$ and b. The similarities end here. In particular, u need not be a positive linear transformation of v, and, consequently, the orderings of P by expected utility magnitudes under u and under v can be quite different.

The theory of von Neumann and Morgenstern *begins* with a binary relation $>$ on a convex set P. It then makes assumptions about the behavior of $>$ on P, which are stated formally as axioms. The axioms are then shown to imply the existence of a real-valued function u on P that preserves the order of $>$ on P and is linear in the convexity operation. That is, for all $p, q \in P$ and all $0 \leqslant \lambda \leqslant 1$,

(1.3) $$p > q \Leftrightarrow u(p) > u(q),$$

(1.4) $$u(\lambda p + (1 - \lambda)q) = \lambda u(p) + (1 - \lambda)u(q),$$

where (1.3) is the *order-preserving property* and (1.4) is the *linearity property*. Henceforth, we refer to a real-valued function on a convex set that satisfies (1.4) for all $0 \leqslant \lambda \leqslant 1$ and all p and q in the set as a *linear functional*. If (1.3) holds, it is an *order-preserving linear functional*.

Interpretations are in order before we consider the mathematical structure of the von Neumann–Morgenstern theory in detail. Although $>$ is an undefined primitive in their system, it is natural to interpret it as a preference relation and to read $p > q$ as "p is preferred to q." The set P need not be a set of probability distributions or measures, but we shall interpret it in this way. Generalizations that treat P axiomatically as a "mixture set" are discussed by Herstein and Milnor (1953) and Fishburn (1970a, 1982a). In the probability setting, the convex combination $\lambda p + (1 - \lambda)q$ is defined pointwise as the usual convex combination of real-valued functions p and q. Thus, when p and q are simple measures on X, $\lambda p + (1 - \lambda)q$ assigns probability $\lambda p(x) + (1 - \lambda)q(x)$ to each $x \in X$, so $\lambda p + (1 - \lambda)q$ is also a simple measure on X. More generally, if p and q are probability measures on an algebra $\mathcal{Q}$ of events, then $(\lambda p + (1 - \lambda)q)(A) = \lambda p(A) + (1 - \lambda)q(A)$ for each $A \in \mathcal{Q}$, and $\lambda p + (1 - \lambda)q$ is also a probability measure on $\mathcal{Q}$.

The axioms of the von Neumann–Morgenstern theory apply simply and solely to $>$ on P. Unlike Bernoullian theory, preference applies immediately to comparisons of risky alternatives, not just to outcomes. Moreover, their *axioms* involve no notion of comparable preference differences or strength of preference, since they use only "ordinal" preference comparisons. In a manner of speaking, the role of strength of preference in Bernoulli's approach, which guarantees preservation of the Bernoullian expected utility order under admissible transformations of v as in Theorem 1.1, is replaced by the global application of $>$ to P in conjunction with the linearity property (1.4).

The fact that u is unique up to positive linear transformations when it is an order-preserving linear functional on P, even though it is based solely on simple preference comparisons, led Baumol (1958) to describe it as "the cardinal utility which is ordinal." There are other examples of this. In the riskless setting, if $>$ is a preference relation on a commodity space or multiattribute space $X = X_1 \times X_2 \times \cdots \times X_n$ that is representable additively as

$$(x_1, \ldots, x_n) > (y_1, \ldots, y_n) \Leftrightarrow f(x_1, \ldots, x_n) > f(y_1, \ldots, y_n),$$

$$(1.5) \qquad f(x_1, x_2, \ldots, x_n) = f_1(x_1) + f_2(x_2) + \cdots + f_n(x_n)$$

for all $x, y \in X$, then suitably strong structural assumptions (Debreu, 1960; Fishburn, 1970a, Chapter 5; Krantz et al., 1971, Chapter 6) imply that f is unique up to positive linear transformations. Here the additivity property (1.5) rather than the linearity property (1.4) induces uniqueness.

This section began with remarks about u on X, then switched to u on P with no mention of X. The reason is that X plays no role in the formal theory of von Neumann and Morgenstern, but enters, almost as an afterthought, when P is interpreted as a set of probability distributions on X. This interpretation customarily assumes that P contains each measure that assigns probability 1 to some outcome, and it *defines* u on X from u on P by

$$(1.6) \qquad u(x) = u(p) \qquad \text{when } p(x) = 1.$$

The anticipated expected utility form follows from this definition and linearity.

THEOREM 1.2. *Suppose u is a linear functional on a convex set P of probability measures on X that contains every one-point measure, and u is extended to X by (1.6). Then for every simple measure p in P_X,*

$$(1.7) \qquad u(p) = \sum u(x)p(x).$$

Proof. Let n be the number of points in X assigned positive probability by p in P_X. Then (1.7) follows from (1.6) for $n = 1$, from (1.4) for $n = 2$, and from (1.4) by a straightforward induction on n when $n \geqslant 3$. ∎

Theorem 1.2 highlights another distinction between the two approaches to expected utility. Bernoulli invokes the expectational form at the outset, whereas von Neumann and Morgenstern deduce it from their axioms.

The difference between the two approaches can also be seen in their assessment procedures for v or u on X. Consider again the determination of an amount x whose utility is midway between the utilities of $0 and $100. In Bernoulli's approach, x is the amount at which your strength of preference for $100 over x equals your strength of preference for x over $0. For von Neumann and Morgenstern, x is the amount at which you are indifferent between receiving x as a sure thing and playing out the lottery that pays either $0 or $100, each with probability $\frac{1}{2}$. Indifference between x and the lottery translates to

$$u(x) = u(\$100 \text{ with probability } \tfrac{1}{2} \text{ or } \$0 \text{ with probability } \tfrac{1}{2})$$

$$= [u(\$100) + u(\$0)]/2.$$

We conclude this section with a few historical remarks before turning to the von Neumann–Morgenstern axioms and theorem in the next section. When it was introduced, their theory was widely misunderstood and it took about a decade, with considerable help from expositors such as Marschak (1950), Strotz (1953), Luce and Raiffa (1957), and Baumol (1958), to set matters straight. One cause for confusion was the long-established use of utility as a measure of psychic satisfaction with strength-of-preference connotations whenever it was measurable, that is, unique up to positive linear transformations. Several writers have wished that von Neumann and Morgenstern had used a term other than *utility* for their value function to avoid entanglement with prior uses of the term in economics, but the usage stuck.

Another cause for confusion was the terse and somewhat enigmatic style used by von Neumann and Morgenstern to express their axioms. One of their axiomatic curiosities is their treatment of the indifference relation. They divided out indifference without warning and proceeded to axiomatize strict preference between indifference classes, but this was not clarified until the appearance of their second edition (1947), which for the first time presented their proof of the linear utility representation. The proof itself is rather hard to follow and was substantially improved by later writers.

The axioms stated in the next section differ slightly from the originals and are due to Jensen (1967). Other axiom sets that are equivalent to Jensen's set will be noted in Section 1.5.

1.4   THE LINEAR UTILITY THEOREM

We assume throughout this section that P is a nonempty set of probability measures $p, q, \ldots$ defined on a Boolean algebra $\mathcal{C}$ of subsets of X. Thus for each $p \in P$, $p(A) \geqslant 0$ for every $A \in \mathcal{C}$, $p(A \cup B) = p(A) + p(B)$ whenever A and B are disjoint events in $\mathcal{C}$, and $p = 1$ on the universal event X in $\mathcal{Q}$. By definition, $\mathcal{Q}$ is closed under complementation and finite unions. We assume also that P is convex; that is, $\lambda p + (1 - \lambda)q$ is in P whenever $0 \leqslant \lambda \leqslant 1$ and $p, q \in P$.

Given this structure for P, let $>$ be a binary relation on P, interpreted as strict preference. The *indifference relation* $\sim$ on P and the *preference-or-indifference relation* $\gtrsim$ on P are defined from $>$ by

$$p \sim q \text{ if neither } p > q \text{ nor } q > p,$$

$$p \gtrsim q \text{ if either } p > q \text{ or } p \sim q.$$

It is natural to assume that $>$ is *asymmetric*; that is, for all $p, q \in P, p > q$ $\Rightarrow$ not $(q > p)$. When $>$ is asymmetric, $\sim$ is both *reflexive* $(p \sim p)$ and *symmetric* $(p \sim q \Rightarrow q \sim p)$.

We say that a binary relation R on P is *transitive* if, for all $p, q, r \in P$,

$$\{p \ R \ q, q \ R \ r\} \Rightarrow p \ R \ r,$$

and that it is *negatively transitive* if, for all $p, q, r \in P$,

$$\{\text{not } (p \ R \ q), \text{not } (q \ R \ r)\} \Rightarrow \text{not } (p \ R \ r)$$

or, equivalently,

$$p \ R \ r \Rightarrow (p \ R \ q \text{ or } q \ R \ r).$$

When R is both asymmetric and negatively transitive, it is a *weak order* (asymmetric sense).

We shall assume that $>$ on P is a weak order. This implies that each of $>$, $\sim$, and $\gtrsim$ is transitive and that $\{p \sim q, q > r\} \Rightarrow p > r$ and $\{p > q, q \sim r\} \Rightarrow p > r$. The proofs are easy and are omitted. Under the weak-order assumption, $\sim$ is an *equivalence relation* (i.e., reflexive, symmetric, and transitive) on P, and the indifference classes in the quotient set $P/\sim$, each of which consists of all measures indifferent to one another, are totally ordered by the natural extension of $>$ from P to $P/\sim$. As mentioned in the preceding section, this is the point at which von Neumann and Morgenstern begin their axiomatization.

We consider three axioms for $>$ on P. They are to be understood as applying to all $p, q, r \in P$ and all $0 < \lambda < 1$:

A1. Order: $>$ *on P is a weak order.*
A2. Independence: $p > q \Rightarrow \lambda p + (1 - \lambda)r > \lambda q + (1 - \lambda)r.$
A3. Continuity: $\{p > q, q > r\} \Rightarrow (\alpha p + (1 - \alpha)r > q \text{ and } q > \beta p + (1 - \beta)r \text{ for some } \alpha \text{ and } \beta \text{ in } (0, 1)).$

The ordering axiom A1 has been a mainstay of the economic conception of rationality at least since the time of Bernoulli and Cramer. Violations of

A1, and especially of its implication that $>$ is transitive, are usually viewed as aberrations that any reasonable person would gladly "correct" if informed of his or her "error."

Axiom A2 is also known as a linearity assumption and is closely associated with similar axioms that are referred to as substitution principles, cancellation conditions, additivity axioms, and sure-thing principles. It simply says that if p is preferred to q, then a nontrivial convex combination of p and r is preferred to the similar combination of q and r. It is usually defended as a criterion of consistent and coherent preferences by imaging $\lambda p + (1 - \lambda)r$ as a two-stage lottery that yields either p with probability λ or r with probability $1 - \lambda$ in the first stage and then makes the final choice according to the one of p and r that obtains in the first stage. Under a similar interpretation for $\lambda q + (1 - \lambda)r$, it is argued that since both mixtures lead to r with identical probabilities $1 - \lambda$ in the first stage, and since you are equally well off in these cases, your preference between the mixtures ought to depend solely on your preference between p and q.

The continuity or Archimedean axiom A3 is designed to prevent one measure from being infinitely preferred to another and is more a concession to our system of real numbers than to an intuitive notion of rationality. Without A3 in the presence of A1 and A2, there is no guarantee that the entities in P can be mapped into real numbers whose order preserves $>$ on P. Nevertheless, A3 does embody a degree of common sense, since it seems reasonable that, if p is preferred to q and q is preferred to r, then there ought to be a probability $\alpha < 1$ at which $\alpha p + (1 - \alpha)r$ is preferred to q and another probability $\beta > 0$ at which q is preferred to $\beta p + (1 - \beta)r$.

Criticisms of the axioms are deferred to Chapter 2. For the time being we shall be content to explore their technical implications.

THEOREM 1.3. *Suppose P is a nonempty convex set of probability measures defined on a Boolean algebra of subsets of X, and $>$ is a binary relation on P. Then axioms A1, A2, and A3 hold if and only if there is a linear functional u on P such that, for all $p, q \in P$, $p > q \Leftrightarrow u(p) > u(q)$. Moreover, such a u is unique up to positive linear transformations.*

This is the main representation and uniqueness theorem for linear (von Neumann–Morgenstern) utilities. The simple proof that the linear utility representation satisfying (1.3) and (1.4) implies A1, A2, and A3 is left to the reader. We also omit the proof of uniqueness, which, apart from notation, is essentially the same as the proof of Theorem 1.1.

For convenience, the proof that A1–A3 imply the existence of an order-preserving linear functional u on P is divided into three parts: part I establishes preliminary lemmas for $>$; part II constructs u on a closed preference interval; part III extends the results of part II to all of P. Axioms A1–A3 are presumed to hold throughout the rest of this section.

Part I. In this part we prove the following five lemmas, which apply to all $p, q, r, s \in P$ and all $\lambda, \mu \in [0, 1]$:

L1. $\{p \succ q, \lambda > \mu\} \Rightarrow \lambda p + (1 - \lambda)q \succ \mu p + (1 - \mu)q$.
L2. $\{p \succsim q \succsim r, p \succ r\} \Rightarrow q \sim \lambda p + (1 - \lambda)r$ for a unique λ.
L3. $\{p \succ q, r \succ s\} \Rightarrow \lambda p + (1 - \lambda)r \succ \lambda q + (1 - \lambda)s$.
L4. $p \sim q \Rightarrow p \sim \lambda p + (1 - \lambda)q$.
L5. $p \sim q \Rightarrow \lambda p + (1 - \lambda)r \sim \lambda q + (1 - \lambda)r$.

Lemmas L1 and L3 are monotonicity conditions for $\succ$, L4 is an antimonotonicity condition for the preservation of indifference, L2 is an intermediate-value property, and L5 is the independence axiom for indifference. Their proofs follow.

L1. Assume $p \succ q$ and $\lambda > \mu$. Then $p \succ \mu p + (1 - \mu)q$—by assumption if $\mu = 0$, by A2 otherwise. If $\lambda = 1$, this completes the proof of L1. If $\lambda < 1$, then A2 gives

$$\lambda p + (1 - \lambda)q = \left(\frac{\lambda - \mu}{1 - \mu}\right) p + \left(\frac{1 - \lambda}{1 - \mu}\right) (\mu p + (1 - \mu)q)$$

$$\succ \left(\frac{\lambda - \mu}{1 - \mu}\right) (\mu p + (1 - \mu)q)$$

$$+ \left(\frac{1 - \lambda}{1 - \mu}\right) (\mu p + (1 - \mu)q)$$

$$= \mu p + (1 - \mu)q.$$

L2. Assume $p \succsim q \succsim r$ and $p \succ r$. If $p \sim q$, then $q \sim 1p + 0r$, and $q \succ \mu p + (1 - \mu)r$ by L1 for any $\mu < 1$, so $\lambda = 1$ is the unique λ for the conclusion of L2. If $r \sim q$, the unique λ is 0. Suppose henceforth that $p \succ q \succ r$. It follows from A1, A3, and L1 that there is a unique λ in $(0, 1)$ such that

(1.8) $\alpha p + (1 - \alpha)r \succ q \succ \beta p + (1 - \beta)r$ for all $\alpha > \lambda > \beta$.

We claim that $q \sim \lambda p + (1 - \lambda)r$. To the contrary, if, say, $\lambda p + (1 - \lambda)r \succ q$, with $q \succ r$, then A3 implies that $\mu(\lambda p + (1 - \lambda)r) + (1 - \mu)r = (\lambda\mu)p + (1 - \lambda\mu)r \succ q$ for some $0 < \mu < 1$, which contradicts (1.8), since $\lambda > \lambda\mu$. A similar contradiction follows from $q \succ \lambda p + (1 - \lambda)r$.

L3. If $p \succ q, r \succ s$ and $0 < \lambda < 1$, two applications of A2 give $\lambda p + (1 - \lambda)r \succ \lambda q + (1 - \lambda)r \succ \lambda q + (1 - \lambda)s$. Hence $\lambda p + (1 - \lambda)r \succ \lambda q + (1 - \lambda)s$ by transitivity.

L4. Given $p \sim q$, if $p \succ \lambda p + (1 - \lambda)q$ then L3 and A1 yield

$$\lambda p + (1 - \lambda)q \succ \lambda[\lambda p + (1 - \lambda)q]$$

$$+ (1 - \lambda)[\lambda p + (1 - \lambda)q] = \lambda p + (1 - \lambda)q,$$

which contradicts asymmetry. A similar contradiction obtains if $\lambda p + (1 - \lambda)q \succ p$. Hence $p \sim \lambda p + (1 - \lambda)q$ by definition.

L5. Since this is obvious if $\lambda \in \{0, 1\}$, we assume $0 < \lambda < 1$ along with $p \sim q$. If $r \sim p$, the conclusion of L5 follows from L4, so we assume that $p \succ r$. (The proof for $r \succ p$ is similar.) Suppose $\lambda q + (1 - \lambda)r \succ \lambda p + (1 - \lambda)r$. Then, by L2,

$$\lambda p + (1 - \lambda)r \sim \alpha[\lambda q + (1 - \lambda)r]$$

$$+ (1 - \alpha)r = (\alpha\lambda)q + (1 - \alpha\lambda)r$$

for a unique $0 < \alpha < 1$. Since $q \succ r$, A2 implies $q \succ \alpha q + (1 - \alpha)r$. Hence $p \succ \alpha q + (1 - \alpha)r$ by transitivity. But then A2 implies

$$\lambda p + (1 - \lambda)r \succ \lambda[\alpha q + (1 - \alpha)r]$$

$$+ (1 - \lambda)r = (\alpha\lambda)q + (1 - \alpha\lambda)r,$$

which contradicts $\lambda p + (1 - \lambda)r \sim (\alpha\lambda)q + (1 - \alpha\lambda)r$. Hence not $[\lambda q + (1 - \lambda)r \succ \lambda p + (1 - \lambda)r]$, and similarly when p and q are interchanged. Hence $\lambda p + (1 - \lambda)r \sim \lambda q + (1 - \lambda)r$.

Part II. Assume $p \succ q$ for some $p, q \in P$; otherwise any constant functional on P satisfies (1.3) and (1.4). Fix $p \succ q$ and let $[pq] = \{r : p \succsim r \succsim q\}$, the closed and convex (by A2 and L5) preference interval between p and q. L2 implies that there is a unique $f(r)$ in $[0, 1]$ for each r in $[pq]$ such that

(1.9) $$r \sim f(r)p + [1 - f(r)]q$$

with $f(p) = 1$ and $f(q) = 0$.

Suppose $r, s \in [pq]$ and $f(r) > f(s)$. Then $f(r)p + [1 - f(r)]q \succ f(s)p + [1 - f(s)]q$ by L1, so (1.9) and transitivity give $r \succ s$. If $f(r) = f(s)$, then

$$r \sim f(r)p + [1 - f(r)]q = f(s)p + [1 - f(s)]q \sim s,$$

so $r \sim s$. Therefore f preserves $\succ$ on $[pq]$ since $r \succ s \Leftrightarrow f(r) > f(s)$.

To verify linearity for f on $[pq]$, take $r, s \in [pq]$ and $0 \leqslant \lambda \leqslant 1$. By convexity $\lambda r + (1 - \lambda)s$ is in $[pq]$, and by (1.9),

$$\lambda r + (1 - \lambda)s \sim f(\lambda r + (1 - \lambda)s)p + [1 - f(\lambda r + (1 - \lambda)s)]q.$$

Moreover, two applications of L5 give

$$\lambda r + (1 - \lambda)s \sim \lambda[f(r)p + (1 - f(r))q]$$
$$+ [1 - \lambda][f(s)p + (1 - f(s))q];$$

that is,

$$\lambda r + (1 - \lambda)s \sim [\lambda f(r) + (1 - \lambda)f(s)]p$$
$$+ \{1 - [\lambda f(r) + (1 - \lambda)f(s)]\}q.$$

By transitivity for $\sim$, the right sides of the preceding $\sim$ statements are indifferent, and it then follows from L1 that $f(\lambda r + (1 - \lambda)s) = \lambda f(r) + (1 - \lambda)f(s)$.

Thus, whenever $p > q$, there is an order-preserving linear functional on $[pq]$.

Part III. To show that one such functional serves for all of P, fix $p > q$ and let $[p_1 q_1]$ and $[p_2 q_2]$ be any closed preference intervals that include $[pq]$. Using the result of part II, let f_i be an order-preserving linear functional on $[p_i q_i]$, scaled by a positive linear transformation so that $f_1(p) = f_2(p) = 1$ and $f_1(q) = f_2(q) = 0$.

We show next that $r \in [p_1 q_1] \cap [p_2 q_2] \Rightarrow f_1(r) = f_2(r)$. Given r in the intersection, one of the following obtains:

$$p > q > r \quad \text{with } q \sim \alpha p + (1 - \alpha)r \text{ by L2,}$$
$$0 < \alpha < 1;$$

$$p \gtrsim r \gtrsim q \quad \text{with } r \sim \beta p + (1 - \beta)q \text{ by L2,}$$
$$0 \leqslant \beta \leqslant 1;$$

$$r > p > q \quad \text{with } p \sim \gamma r + (1 - \gamma)q \text{ by L2,}$$
$$0 < \gamma < 1.$$

Under order preservation and linearity for each f_i, these correspond respectively to

$$0 = \alpha + (1 - \alpha)f_i(r),$$
$$f_i(r) = \beta,$$
$$1 = \gamma f_i(r),$$

and therefore $f_1(r) = f_2(r)$ in each case. Hence $f_1 = f_2$ on $[p_1 q_1] \cap [p_2 q_2]$.

Finally, let $u(r)$ be the common value of $f_i(r)$ thus scaled for every $[p_i q_i]$ that contains p, q, and r. Since every pair of measures in P is in at least one $[p_i q_i]$ that includes $[pq]$, it follows that u is an order-preserving linear functional on P.

1.5 ALTERNATIVE AXIOMS FOR LINEAR UTILITY

The following axioms of Herstein and Milnor (1953) provide an interesting comparison to Jensen's axioms:

B1. Order: $\succ$ *on P is a weak order.*
B2. Independence: $p \sim q \Rightarrow \frac{1}{2}p + \frac{1}{2}r \sim \frac{1}{2}q + \frac{1}{2}r.$
B3. Continuity: $\{\alpha: 0 \leqslant \alpha \leqslant 1 \text{ } and \text{ } \alpha p + (1 - \alpha)r \succsim q\} \text{ } and \text{ } \{\beta:0 \leqslant \beta \leqslant 1 \text{ } and \text{ } q \succsim \beta p + (1 - \beta)r\}$ *are closed subsets of* $[0, 1].$

Although A1 and B1 are identical, neither A2 nor B2 implies the other; it can be shown (Fishburn, 1982a, p. 16) that B3 implies A3, but not conversely. The Herstein–Milnor independence axiom B2 is especially attractive in its simple statement of indifference preservation under 50-50 convex combinations. Their continuity axiom B3 brings the preference-or-indifference relation into the picture and implies, for example, that if $\alpha_i p + (1 - \alpha_i)r$ is as good as q for all i while the α_i converge to α, then $\alpha p + (1 - \alpha)r$ is also as good as q. The strengthening of A3 to B3 is compensated for by the weakening of A2 to B2.

Herstein and Milnor prove that their axioms are necessary and sufficient for the existence of an order-preserving linear functional u on P. An alternative proof in Fishburn (1982a) shows that $\{B1, B2, B3\} \Rightarrow \{A1, A2, A3\}$. Then Theorem 1.3 can be invoked to complete the sufficiency proof for their axioms.

Our next set of axioms that is equivalent to $\{A1, A2, A3\}$ has a very different flavor than those of von Neumann–Morgenstern, Jensen, and Herstein–Milnor in that it makes no mention of the ordering properties of asymmetry, negative transitivity, and transitivity. This set uses the Herstein–Milnor independence axiom B2 along with an ''intermediate-value'' continuity condition related to L2 in the preceding section and a convexity axiom. The new axioms, applied to all $p, q, r \in P$ and all $0 < \lambda < 1$, are the following:

C1. Continuity: $\{p \succ q, q \succ r\} \Rightarrow q \sim \alpha p + (1 - \alpha)r \text{ } for \text{ } some \text{ } 0 < \alpha < 1.$
C2. Convexity: $\{p \succ q, p \succsim r\} \Rightarrow p \succ \lambda q + (1 - \lambda)r;$
$\{p \sim q, p \sim r\} \Rightarrow p \sim \lambda q + (1 - \lambda)r;$
$\{q \succ p, r \succsim p\} \Rightarrow \lambda q + (1 - \lambda)r \succ p.$

We shall have more than a passing interest in C1 and C2, since they are cornerstones of the nonlinear utility theories introduced in Chapter 3 and examined in detail in Chapters 4 through 6.

Axiom C1 is an unremarkable condition that is clearly motivated by A3 and L2. As noted shortly, it implies that $>$ is asymmetric and, in conjunction with C2, that α in the statement of C1 is unique.

The convexity axiom C2 implies that, for every $p \in P$, each set $\{q:p > q\}$, $\{q:p \sim q\}$, and $\{q:q > p\}$ is convex. Hence, in the presence of C1's implication of asymmetry, these three sets partition P into convex components (the first or last of which might be empty). In addition, each nontrivial combination of a measure from $\{q: p > q\}$ and $\{q: p \sim q\}$ lies in $\{q: p > q\}$, and similarly with $>$ replaced by its dual.

A few basic implications of the new axioms are noted in the following theorem; others will be derived in Chapters 4 and 5.

THEOREM 1.4. *Suppose P is as specified in Theorem 1.3 and $>$ is a binary relation on P. Then*

    (a) *C1 $\Rightarrow$ $>$ is asymmetric.*
    (b) *$\{C1, C2\} \Rightarrow \alpha$ in the statement of C1 is unique.*
    (c) *$\{C1, C2, \sim$ is transitive$\} \Rightarrow >$ is transitive.*
    (d) *$\{C1, C2, B2\} \Rightarrow \{B1, B2, B3\}$.*

Proof. (a) If $p > q$ and $q > p$, C1 implies $q \sim p$, contrary to the definition of $\sim$.

(b) Suppose $p > q$, $q > r$, and $q \sim \alpha p + (1 - \alpha)r$, $0 < \alpha < 1$, as guaranteed by C1. Then C2 implies $q > \beta p + (1 - \beta)r$ if $\beta < \alpha$, and $\beta p + (1 - \beta)r > q$ if $\beta > \alpha$, so α is unique.

(c) Suppose first, contrary to the transitivity of $>$, that $\{p > q, q > r, p \sim r\}$. Then $q \sim \alpha p + (1 - \alpha)r$ for some α by C1, and $\alpha p + (1 - \alpha)r \sim r$ by C2. Hence $q \sim r$ by the transitivity of $\sim$, in contradiction to $q > r$. If $\{p > q, q > r, r > p\}$, the hypotheses of (c) give $\{q > r, r > \alpha p + (1 - \alpha)r, q \sim \alpha p + (1 - \alpha)r\}$ for some α, which is impossible by the result just proved. Hence $\{p > q, q > r\} \Rightarrow p > r$.

(d) Assume C1, C2, and B2. Suppose $\sim$ is not transitive, say with $\{p \sim q, q \sim r, p > r\}$. By B2, $r \sim \frac{1}{2}q + \frac{1}{2}r$; by C2, $p > \frac{1}{2}q + \frac{1}{2}r$; so by C2 again, $\frac{1}{2}p + \frac{1}{2}r > \frac{1}{2}q + \frac{1}{2}r$. But this contradicts B2. Therefore $\sim$ is transitive, and this in combination with (a) and (c) implies that $>$ is a weak order. Since B3 follows easily from C1 and C2, we conclude that the Herstein–Milnor axioms are implied by C1, C2, and B2. ■

We conclude our discussion of axioms equivalent to those of von Neumann–Morgenstern or Jensen by considering an approach based on *two* primitive binary relations on P, denoted by $>$ and $\approx$, that provides several generalizations of the basic linear utility theorem. This approach uses five axioms:

    1. $>$ is asymmetric; $\approx$ is reflexive and symmetric.

2. $\{p \succ q, r \succ s\} \Rightarrow \lambda p + (1 - \lambda)r \succ \lambda q + (1 - \lambda)s.$
3. $\{p \approx q, r \approx s\} \Rightarrow \lambda p + (1 - \lambda)r \approx \lambda q + (1 - \lambda)s.$
4. $\{p \succ q, r \approx s\} \Rightarrow \lambda p + (1 - \lambda)r \neq \lambda q + (1 - \lambda)s.$
5. $\{p \succ q, r \succ s\} \Rightarrow \alpha p + (1 - \alpha)s \succ \alpha q + (1 - \alpha)r$
   for some $0 < \alpha < 1.$

The second and third axioms are monotonicity–convexity conditions (cf. L3), the fourth prevents certain mixtures from being identical, and the fifth is another version of the continuity axiom. We usually think of $\approx$ as some portion of the indifference relation $\sim$ for $\succ$.

Drawing on a result for linearly ordered vector spaces in Hausner and Wendel (1952), Fishburn (1982b) proved that the preceding five axioms imply that there is a linear functional u on P such that, for all $p, q \in P$,

$$p \succ q \Rightarrow u(p) > u(q),$$

$$p \approx q \Rightarrow u(p) = u(q).$$

The maximal $\approx$ that can satisfy the axioms is the indifference relation $\sim$ defined from $\succ$, and in this case we obtain another equivalent to Jensen's set of axioms. The minimal $\approx$ for the axioms is $=$, in which case axioms 3 and 4 are redundant and the representation reduces just to the one-way implication $p \succ q \Rightarrow u(p) > u(q)$. Other possibilities for $\approx$ are discussed in Fishburn (1982b).

1.6 RISK ATTITUDES

This section and the next two comment briefly on special topics in linear utility theory that we return to later in our discussions of nonlinear utility. The present section considers risk attitudes and stochastic dominance with monetary outcomes; the next two consider more general types of outcomes.

The theory of risk attitudes developed by Pratt (1964) and Arrow (1974) is concerned with curvature properties of u on X as defined by (1.6) when X is an interval of monetary amounts interpreted either as wealth levels or gains and losses around a given present wealth. Its purpose is to interpret various types of economic behavior in risky situations in terms of curvature and perhaps other properties of u on X within the von Neumann–Morgenstern framework of maximizing expected utility. A classic example is the effort by Friedman and Savage (1948) to explain the simultaneous acts of insurance buying and gambling in actuarially unfair lotteries by a doubly inflected utility function.

Assume that u on X is twice differentiable and increasing in x, so $u^{(1)}(x) > 0$. Following Pratt and Arrow, we say that u is *risk averse* in an interval of X if $u^{(2)}(x) < 0$ on that interval; u is *risk seeking* if $u^{(2)}(x) > 0$; and u is *risk neutral* if $u^{(2)}(x) = 0$. Let p denote a nondegenerate simple measure in P.

The *certainty equivalent* of p, denoted by $c(p)$, is the sure amount in X at which the individual is indifferent between this amount and p. Its existence, with $c(p) \sim p$ and $u(c(p)) = \Sigma u(x)p(x)$, is ensured by our assumptions on u and p. With $E(x, p)$ the actuarial expectation of p, risk aversion, risk seeking, and risk neutrality imply $c(p) < E(x, p)$, $c(p) > E(x, p)$ and $c(p) = E(x, p)$, respectively. Risk-averse utility functions, which increase in x at a decreasing rate, are further characterized by their indices of *absolute risk aversion* $-u^{(2)}(x)/u^{(1)}(x)$ and *relative risk aversion* $-xu^{(2)}(x)/u^{(1)}(x)$. These indices, which can also be used when $u^{(2)}$ is not negative, are invariant to positive linear transformations of u.

The terminology of the preceding paragraph makes no reference to the riskless utility function v of the Bernoullian approach, since v plays no role in the theory of von Neumann and Morgenstern. Some writers, including Bernard (1986), would reserve the term *risk neutrality* only for the case in which $u = v$ (up to a linear transformation), regardless of curvature, and use *risk aversion* only when u is obtained as an increasing concave function of v. The papers by Camacho, Krzysztofowicz, and McCord and de Neufville in Stigum and Wenstøp (1983) provide extensive discussion of the u-versus-v comparison.

The basic Pratt–Arrow theory of risk has been generalized by Ross (1981) and Machina and Neilson (1987) to address questions of economic concern and risk attitudes not easily dealt with by the original approach. They are especially interested in the nonavailability of risk-free alternatives and the impact of this on comparative economic analysis. See their papers for details.

With respect to the Pratt–Arrow theory applied to *changes* in present wealth, it has been observed that some people tend to be risk averse in gains but risk seeking in losses (Fishburn and Kochenberger, 1979; Kahneman and Tversky, 1979; Schoemaker, 1980), although the generality of this finding is open to question (Hershey and Schoemaker, 1980; Cohen et al., 1985). If you prefer a sure gain of $4,000 to a lottery p with a 70% chance at $6,000 (nothing otherwise), then

$$c(p) < \$4,000 < \$4,200 = E(x, p).$$

If you also prefer a lottery q with a 70% chance of losing $6,000 (no loss otherwise) to a sure loss of $4,000, then

$$E(x, q) = -\$4,200 < -\$4,000 < c(q).$$

Although the ubiquity of attitude reversal between gains and losses is doubtful, there is little doubt that people's utility for money depends mainly on changes from present wealth rather than absolute level, at least locally.

To state an important result of the Pratt–Arrow theory when u is presumed to be defined on absolute wealth levels, let $u[x] = -u^{(2)}(x)/u^{(1)}(x)$, the absolute risk aversion of u at x. Also let $\pi(u, p) = E(x, p) -$

$c(p)$ be the *risk premium* for p, so

$$u(c(p)) = u(E(x, p) - \pi(u, p)) = \sum u(x)p(x).$$

Then the following are mutually equivalent for any two utility functions u and u^*:

1. $u^*(x) = f(u(x))$ for all x and some increasing concave f.
2. $u^*[x] \geqslant u[x]$ for all x.
3. $\pi(u^*, p) \geqslant \pi(u, p)$ for all simple p.

In addition, if both u and u^* are concave, and if one's initial wealth w_0 is divided between a riskless asset and a risky asset whose expected return per dollar invested exceeds that of the riskless asset, then each of 1, 2, and 3 is equivalent to the assertion that for all such w_0 and asset returns an expected utility maximizer with u^* would put at least as much into the riskless asset as would an expected utility maximizer with u.

Stochastic dominance also involves the shape of u on X. It is concerned with comparative aspects of measures p and q and with classes of utility functions whose members have the same preference implication between p and q. We consider only the standard forms of first ($>_1$)- and second ($>_2$)-degree stochastic dominance. An array of theory and applications of the subject is available in Whitmore and Findlay (1978), and Bawa (1982) gives an extensive bibliography.

Let p^1 and p^2 denote the first two cumulatives of the simple measure p on X:

$$p^1(x) = \sum_{y \leqslant x} p(y),$$

$$p^2(x) = \int_{-\infty}^{x} p^1(y)\, dy.$$

Then $>_1$ and $>_2$ are defined on P_X by

$$p >_1 q \text{ if } p \neq q \text{ and } p^1(x) \leqslant q^1(x) \text{ for all } x,$$

$$p >_2 q \text{ if } p \neq q \text{ and } p^2(x) \leqslant q^2(x) \text{ for all } x.$$

Thus $p >_1 q$ if the cumulative distribution of p lies at or below the cumulative distribution of q, and $p \neq q$. When $p >_1 q$, p generally has a better chance for better outcomes than does q. The second-degree relation $>_2$ has a similar effect with respect to concave (risk-averse) utility functions, as shown by the following well-known results.

Let U_1 be the class of all strictly increasing u on X, and let U_2 be the subclass of U_1 whose members are strictly concave ($u^{(2)} < 0$). Then, with

$u(p) = \Sigma\, u(x)p(x)$, it is not hard to show that

$$p >_1 q \Leftrightarrow u(p) > u(q) \qquad \text{for all } u \in U_1,$$

$$p >_2 q \Leftrightarrow u(p) > u(q) \qquad \text{for all } u \in U_2.$$

Thus, for $>_2$, all risk-averse utility functions correspond to $p \succ q$ when $p >_2 q$. We shall see in Section 6.8 that very similar results hold for nonlinear utilities.

1.7 MULTIATTRIBUTE LINEAR UTILITY

We turn now to decisions under risk that involve multiattribute outcomes of the form $x = (x_1, x_2, \ldots, x_n)$ with $X = X_1 \times X_2 \times \cdots \times X_n$. It is customary in economic theory to interpret x_i as a quantity of a good or commodity indexed by i, but X_i could refer to any number of things, such as levels of a qualitative variable or whatever happens in year i.

Multiattribute linear utility deals with problems of formulating and assessing von Neumann–Morgenstern utility functions on X. It has focused on special assumptions that simplify assessment by decomposing $u(x_1, \ldots, x_n)$ into algebraic combinations of functions of the individual variables and on interactive techniques that allow decision makers to maximize expected utility without having to assess all of u. A broad introduction is given by Keeney and Raiffa (1976), and useful surveys include Farquhar (1977, 1978) and Fishburn (1977a, 1978a).

The two simplest decomposed forms for u are the additive form

$$(1.10) \qquad u(x_1, x_2, \ldots, x_n) = u_1(x_1) + u_2(x_2) + \cdots + u_n(x_n)$$

and the multiplicative form

$$(1.11) \qquad ku(x_1, \ldots, x_n) + 1 = [ku_1(x_1) + 1] \cdots [ku_n(x_n) + 1]$$

where u_i is a functional on X_i and k is a nonzero constant. We say that the X_i are *value independent* if, for all $p, q \in P_X$,

$$(1.12) \qquad (p_i = q_i \text{ for } i = 1, \ldots, n) \Rightarrow p \sim q,$$

where p_i is the marginal distribution of p on X_i. It can then be proved (Fishburn, 1965; Pollak, 1967) that u can be decomposed additively as in (1.10) if and only if the X_i are value independent.

Multiplicative decompositions of u arise from utility independence conditions. We say that a nonempty proper subset I (or its corresponding attributes) of $\{1, 2, \ldots, n\}$ is *utility independent* of its complement $I^c = \{1, 2, \ldots, n\} \setminus I$ if the preference order over probability distributions on the product of the X_i for $i \in I$, conditioned on fixed levels of the X_j for $j \in I^c$, is independent of those fixed levels. If all such I are utility independent of their complements and the X_i are *not* value independent, then (Keeney, 1968; Pollak, 1967) u has a multiplicative decomposition like (1.11) with restrictions on signs of the terms in brackets over X_i on the right side of (1.11). We also say that I is *generalized utility independent* of I^c if any two conditional orders for the $i \in I$ (conditioned on fixed levels of the other attributes) are identical, duals of one another, or one is empty. Then (Fishburn and Keeney, 1975) if $\{1, \ldots, n\} \setminus \{i\}$ is generalized utility independent of $\{i\}$ for $i = 1, \ldots, n$, and if the X_i are not value independent, u can be decomposed multiplicatively as in (1.11). Since (1.11) is not generally preserved under positive linear transformations, it is necessary to scale u in a suitable manner so that (1.11) can be used.

A variety of other decomposed forms for u are discussed in the preceding references.

1.8 EXTENSIONS FOR PROBABILITY MEASURES

Theorem 1.2 shows that the linearity property for u on P and definition (1.6) imply that $u(p) = \Sigma\, u(x)p(x)$ for every simple probability measure in P, given convexity and one-point distributions in P. However, the same hypotheses do not imply the expected utility form

$$(1.13) \qquad u(p) = \int_X u(x)dp(x),$$

when p is a nonsimple measure on X. For example, if u on X is unbounded above and p is a discrete measure that assigns probability 2^{-n} to an outcome with utility at least 2^n for $n = 1, 2, \ldots$, then $\int u(x)\, dp(x)$ is infinite but $u(p)$ is finite by Theorem 1.3 under the axioms for linear utility.

A failure of (1.13) for bounded u is obtained by letting $\mathcal{Q}$ be the Borel field of subsets of $X = [0, 1]$, taking P as the set of countably additive measures on $\mathcal{Q}$, and setting

$$u(x) = -1 \quad \text{if } x < \tfrac{1}{2},$$

$$u(x) = 1 \quad \text{if } x \geq \tfrac{1}{2},$$

$$u(p) = \sum u(x)p(x) \quad \text{for all } p \in P.$$

Then $u(p)$ is well defined since $p(x) > 0$ for no more than a countable number of $x \in [0, 1]$. *Define* $>$ by $p > q \Leftrightarrow u(p) > u(q)$. It is easily checked that u is linear, so it satisfies the representation of Theorem 1.3. However, with p the uniform measure on $[\tfrac{1}{2}, 1]$, $u(p) = 0$ since $p(x) = 0$ for all x, but $\int u(x)\, dp(x) = 1$ since $u(x) = 1$ for all $x \geq \tfrac{1}{2}$.

These examples and others (Fishburn, 1970a, Chapter 10) show that axioms that go beyond A1, A2, and A3 are needed to obtain (1.13) when P

contains nonsimple measures. An early example is the axiom of Blackwell and Girshick (1954) that extends A2 to a denumerable form to yield (1.13) for all discrete measures. Other examples are given in Arrow (1958), Fishburn (1967, 1970a, 1975a, 1982a), DeGroot (1970), and Ledyard (1971). We consider two main cases here: one for bounded u, and the other for u not necessarily bounded. The proofs are given in Fishburn (1982a).

Some preliminary definitions are needed. Recall that $\mathcal{Q}$ is a *Boolean algebra* of subsets of X if $X \in \mathcal{Q}$ and $\mathcal{Q}$ is closed under complementation and finite unions. If, in addition, $\mathcal{Q}$ is closed under countable unions ($A_i \in \mathcal{Q}$ for $i = 1, 2, \ldots \Rightarrow \cup_i A_i \in \mathcal{Q}$), then $\mathcal{Q}$ is a *Borel algebra*. A probability measure p on $\mathcal{Q}$ is *countably additive* if

$$p\left(\bigcup_i A_i\right) = \sum_i p(A_i)$$

whenever the A_i are pairwise disjoint members of $\mathcal{Q}$ whose union is in $\mathcal{Q}$. When p is a probability measure on $\mathcal{Q}$ and $p(A) > 0$ for $A \in \mathcal{Q}$, the *conditional measure of p given A* is the measure p_A on $\mathcal{Q}$ defined by

$$p_A(B) = p(B \cap A)/p(A) \qquad \text{for all } B \in \mathcal{Q}.$$

P is said to be *closed under conditional measures* if $p_A \in P$ whenever $p \in P$, $A \in \mathcal{Q}$, and $p(A) > 0$.

A subset A of X is a *preference interval* if $z \in A$ whenever $x, y \in A$, $x \succsim z$ and $z \succsim y$. Here $\succsim$ on X is defined from one-point measures in the natural way from $\succsim$ on P. We say that P is *closed under conditional measures on preference intervals* if $p_A \in P$ whenever $p \in P$, A is a preference interval in $\mathcal{Q}$, and $p(A) > 0$.

Let f be an $\mathcal{Q}$-*measurable* functional on X; that is, $\{x : f(x) \in I\} \in \mathcal{Q}$ for every real interval I. The *expected value* of f with respect to $p \in P$, written $E(f, p)$ or $\int f(x)\,dp(x)$, is defined as follows. First, if f is constant on each set in a finite partition $\{A_1, \ldots, A_n\}$ of X, with $f = a_i$ on A_i, then $E(f, p) = \Sigma_i a_i p(A_i)$. Second, if f is bounded above and below, then

$$E(f, p) = \sup\{E(f_n, p) : n = 1, 2, \ldots\},$$

where $f_1, f_2, \ldots$ is any sequence of *simple* $\mathcal{Q}$-measurable functionals (constant on each set in a finite partition) that converges uniformly from below to f; that is, $f_1(x) \leqslant f_2(x) \leqslant \cdots$, $f(x) = \sup\{f_n(x)\}$, and for every $\delta > 0$ there is an n such that, for all x, $f(x) \leqslant f_n(x) + \delta$. Next, if f is bounded below,

$$E(f, p) = \sup\{E(f_{[a]}, p) : a \text{ real}\},$$

where $f_{[a]}(x) = f(x)$ if $f(x) \leqslant a$ and $f_{[a]}(x) = f(a)$ otherwise. If f is bounded above, $E(f, p) = -E(-f, p)$. Finally, for arbitrary f, define f^+ and f^- by

$$f^+(x) = \begin{cases} f(x) & \text{if } f(x) \geq 0, \\ 0 & \text{otherwise}; \end{cases} \quad f^-(x) = \begin{cases} f(x) & \text{if } f(x) < 0, \\ 0 & \text{otherwise.} \end{cases}$$

Then $E(f, p) = E(f^+, p) + E(f^-, p)$ unless $E(f^+, p) = \infty$ and $E(f^-, p) = -\infty$, in which case $E(f, p)$ is undefined.

Our bounded utility extension for $u(p) = \int u(x) \, dp(x) = E(u, p)$ uses the following appealing dominance principles, applied to all $p, q \in P$, all $A \in \mathcal{Q}$, and all $y \in X$:

A4. Dominance: *Suppose* $p(A) = 1$. *Then* $(x > q \text{ for all } x \in A) \Rightarrow p \gtrsim q$, *and* $(q > x \text{ for all } x \in A) \Rightarrow q \gtrsim p$.

A4*. Dominance: *Suppose* $p(A) = 1$. *Then* $(x \gtrsim y \text{ for all } x \in A) \Rightarrow p \gtrsim y$, *and* $(y \gtrsim x \text{ for all } x \in A) \Rightarrow y \gtrsim p$.

The weaker axiom A4* can be used under countable additivity.

THEOREM 1.5. *Suppose* $\mathcal{Q}$ *is a Boolean algebra of subsets of* X *that contains every singleton subset,* P *is a set of probability measures on* $\mathcal{Q}$ *that contains every one-point measure and is closed under countable convex combinations and under conditional measures,* $>$ *is a binary relation on* P *that satisfies* A1, A2, *and* A3, *and* $\mathcal{Q}$ *contains every preference interval. Then there is a bounded order-preserving linear functional* u *on* P *that satisfies* (1.13) *for all* $p \in P$ *if either* A4 *holds or all measures in* P *are countably additive and* A4* *holds.*

If we drop the assumption that P is closed under *countable* convex combinations ($p_i \in P$, $\lambda_i \geq 0$ for $i = 1, 2, \ldots$ and $\Sigma \lambda_i = 1$ imply $\Sigma \lambda_i p_i \in P$), then u can be unbounded. However, to ensure (1.13) in this case, it is necessary to add another axiom. To specify this axiom, we first define preference intervals $(-\infty, x) = \{y : x > y\}$, $(-\infty, x] = \{y : x \gtrsim y\}$, $(x, \infty) = \{y : y > x\}$, and $[x, \infty) = \{y : y \gtrsim x\}$, along with special classes of measures in P:

$$P^+ = \{p \in P : p([x, \infty)) = 1 \text{ for some}$$
$$x, p((x, \infty)) > 0 \text{ for all } x\},$$
$$P^- = \{p \in P : p((-\infty, x]) = 1 \text{ for some}$$
$$x, p((-\infty, x)) > 0 \text{ for all } x\}.$$

The measures in P^+ are bounded below with upper preference tails; those in P^- are bounded above with lower preference tails. As before, P_X is the set of simple measures. In addition, let x^* denote the one-point measure in P that assigns probability 1 to x. The following applies to all $p_0, p_1 \in P_X$ and all $x \in X$:

A5. Truncation: *If $p \in P^+$, $p\,((-\infty, x]) > 0$ and $p_1 > p_0$, then there is a $y \in X$ such that*

$$p((-\infty, y])p_1 + p((y, \infty))y^* \gtrsim p((-\infty, y])p_0 + p((y, \infty))p_{(y,\infty)};$$

if $p \in P^-$, $p\,([x, \infty)) > 0$, and $p_1 > p_0$, then there is a $y \in X$ such that

$$p((-\infty, y))p_{(-\infty,y)} + p([y, \infty))p_1 \gtrsim p((-\infty, y))y^* + p([y, \infty))p_0.$$

This basically says that the tails of measures in P^+ and P^- do not force infinite expectations. The notations $p_{(y,\infty)}$ and $p_{(-\infty,y)}$ refer to conditionals p_A of p with $A = (y, \infty)$ and $A = (-\infty, y)$, respectively. Axiom A5 can be simplified significantly under countable additivity to the following, for all $p \in P$ and all $p_0 \in P_X$:

A5*. Truncation: *$p > p_0 \Rightarrow p_{(-\infty,y]} \gtrsim p_0$ for some $y \in X$; $p_0 > p \Rightarrow p_0 \gtrsim p_{[y,\infty)}$ for some $y \in X$.*

THEOREM 1.6. *Suppose the hypotheses of Theorem 1.5 hold with the following changes: P is only assumed to be closed under finite convex combinations and under conditional measures on preference intervals. Then there is an order-preserving linear functional u on P that satisfies (1.13) for all $p \in P$ if either A4 and A5 hold or $\mathfrak{A}$ is a Borel algebra, all measures in P are countably additive, and A4* and A5* hold.*

1.9 SUMMARY

The version of expected utility developed by Daniel Bernoulli was based on a riskless notion of the utility of wealth coupled with maximization of expected utility as a guiding principle for decision making under risk. More than 200 years later, von Neumann and Morgenstern axiomatized another version of expected utility in terms of a preference relation on a mixture set or on a convex set of probability measures. Their utility measure for outcomes is inextricably intertwined with probability, and their expected utility representation is derived from the preference axioms.

The linear utility representation of von Neumann and Morgenstern follows from axioms for simple preference comparisons that refer to ordering, independence, and continuity properties. Several equivalent sets of axioms exist for their representation. Additional axioms are needed to extend the expected utility form from simple measures to nonsimple measures.

Special topics that have been extensively developed in the linear utility context of von Neumann and Morgenstern include the theory of risk attitudes, stochastic dominance, and multiattribute utility theory.

2 Critique of Expected Utility

Violations of the axioms and underlying principles of expected utility theory have been generated by certain experimental conditions and framing procedures. It is no longer regarded as an accurate descriptive theory, and many other models have been proposed to explain or describe risky choice behavior. An important task for normative theory is to decide which violations of the von Neumann–Morgenstern axioms are experimental artifacts and which violations constitute fundamental rejections of the axioms by intelligent and well-informed people. This chapter reviews the experimental evidence and philosophical arguments in preparation for the discussion of normative theories in the next chapter.

2.1 NORMATIVE VERSUS DESCRIPTIVE THEORY

In reviewing evidence against linear utility presented in this chapter and in interpreting alternative nonlinear theories in ensuing chapters, we shall differentiate between the normative status and the descriptive status of these theories. This is desirable for two reasons. First, most of the empirical evidence for avowed preferences or actual choices involves the descriptive, behavioral side of decision theory, and it is not always clear whether it should also affect the normative status of a theory. Second, our later chapters are primarily concerned with the normative side of decision theory. Hence, some care must be taken in deciding which arguments against linear utility or other theories also deserve consideration as arguments against their normative viability. This ultimately rests of course on personal opinion as well as collective wisdom, and I shall try to be clear about my own position as well as the positions of others.

The terms *normative* and *descriptive* are but two of a number of modifiers that signal particular interpretations and intended uses of decision theory. Each is a neighbor to other terms that have many of the same connotations, and I shall use them simply as representatives of their larger families.

Neighbors of *descriptive* include *behavioral, psychological, predictive, positive,* and *explanatory.* The descriptive approach seeks to identify patterns in an individual's preferences or actual choices and, subsequently, to develop a model that characterizes these patterns and which can be used to predict preferences or choices not yet revealed. Models with few parameters and high explanatory–predictive power are most desirable. A model may have a processing or algorithmic flavor, such as Tversky's elimination-by-aspects model (1972a, b), or be based on a simple parametric equation, such as some moment models for choices between monetary lotteries (Payne, 1973; Libby and Fishburn, 1977). Descriptive theory is interested in actual choice behavior rather than in guidelines or criteria for "right" decisions.

Neighbors of *normative* include *rational, prescriptive,* and *recommendatory.* The normative approach is concerned with criteria of coherence, consistency, and rationality in preference patterns that, as in linear utility theory, are often set forth as axioms. It does not necessarily assume that intended or actual choice behavior adheres to the axioms, but it does presume that reasonable people who understand the axioms would want their preferences or implied choices to agree with the axiomatic guidelines. Applications of normative theory should entail careful reasoning and evaluations so that its imperative for a "right" decision can be carried out properly. Desirable attributes of a normative model, in addition to its appeal as a transparently rational model, are clear specifications for the measurement of its components and a simple rule for combining these components for the evaluation of more complex alternatives. Proponents of expected utility in either the Bernoullian version or the von Neumann–Morgenstern version claim that their model epitomizes these attributes for decisions under risk.

The normative–descriptive distinction has an interesting history bounded by Bernoulli's views at one end and the research of Daniel Kahneman and Amos Tversky at the other end. Bernoulli appears not to distinguish between the two, saying in one place that his approach for evaluating risky ventures "renders the entire procedure universally acceptable without reservation" (1954, p. 24), and in another place that "all our propositions harmonize perfectly with experience" (p. 31). On the other hand, Tversky and Kahneman (1986) argue persuasively that "no theory of choice can be both normatively adequate and descriptively accurate" since some principles widely viewed as normatively essential are descriptively invalid. We consider this further in the next section.

2.2   FRAMING EFFECTS

Psychologists and sociologists have long known that the way a question is asked can affect its answer. This has been dramatically illustrated by Kahneman and Tversky in experiments on choice behavior conducted over many years and summarized, for example, in Kahneman and Tversky (1979, 1984) and Tversky and Kahneman (1981, 1986). They refer to ways in which questions are posed as *frames* for decisions, and to responses induced by different frames as *framing effects*. Roughly stated, a main conclusion of their research is that virtually any principal of choice, no matter how intuitively appealing, can be violated in certain frames.

A case in point is the axiom of asymmetry: if $p \succ q$, then not $(q \succ p)$. By placing the p/q comparison in different frames, it may be possible to induce a preference for p over q in one, and a preference for q over p in another. Well-known examples of this involve comparisons of situations involving life and death (McNeil et al., 1982; Tversky and Kahneman, 1981), where preferences can depend on whether the comparison is stated in terms of lives saved or of lives lost. Tversky and Kahneman (1981, p. 453) consider a situation paraphrased as follows. Six hundred people have contracted a potentially fatal disease. Two treatment programs are possible. If program 1 is adopted, 400 people will die and 200 will live. If program 2 is adopted, either all 600 will die, with probability $\frac{2}{3}$, or all will live, with probability $\frac{1}{3}$. One group of respondents preferred program 1 over program 2 by a ratio of 2.6 to 1 when the two were stated in terms of lives saved: 200 saved versus 600 saved with probability $\frac{1}{3}$, and nobody saved with probability $\frac{2}{3}$. Another group preferred program 2 over program 1 by a ratio of 3.5 to 1 in the lives-lost frame: 400 die versus nobody dies with probability $\frac{1}{3}$, and 600 die with probability $\frac{2}{3}$.

Tversky and Kahneman (1986) refer to the ability to elicit either $p \succ q$ or $q \succ p$, depending on frame, as a violation of invariance. We consider this along with a closely related reduction principle:

> *Reduction Principle:* For comparative purposes of preference and choice in risky decisions, it suffices to characterize each alternative in terms of its probability distribution over potential outcomes;

> *Invariance Principle:* "Different representations of the same choice problem should yield the same preference. That is, the preference between options should be independent of their description" (Tversky and Kahneman, 1986).

The reduction principle is invoked in the basic formulation of preference theory for risky alternatives by Bernoulli and by von Neumann and Morgenstern, and is widely regarded as a key normative principle. It presumes that the outcome probabilities are given, or known, or easily computable, and although this is seldom true in realistic situations we shall defer its consideration until Chapter 7. More to the point of our present discussion, the reduction principle asserts that the degrees of causal or stochastic dependence among the events that give rise to the probabilities across different alternatives should not affect preferences. In the original game-theoretic context of von Neumann and Morgenstern (1944), this was of little concern since probabilities are used there to form mixed strategies and we may imagine that each mixed strategy refers to its own random device that generates its probabilities. In other words, it is appropriate for mixed strategies in game theory to assume complete stochastic independence among their corresponding probability distributions. Under stochastic independence, the reduction principle seems essential for normative decision theory.

I believe that the case for the reduction principle is less compelling when the probability distributions are interdependent through their underlying events. For example, consider two different frames that have identical probability distributions for alternatives a_1 and a_2:

> SI: A fair coin is to be flipped. Under a_1 you win \$1,000 if a head appears and get \$0 if a tail appears; under a_2 you win \$1,200 if a head appears and lose \$80 if a tail appears.

> SII: Two fair coins are to be flipped. Under a_1 you win \$1,000 if the first coin lands heads and get \$0 otherwise; under a_2 you win \$1,200 if the second coin lands tails and lose \$80 otherwise.

Under the reduction principle, your choice should be the same in SI and SII. However, it is not obvious, to this writer at least, that one's reasoned choice in the interdependent SI ought to be the same as in the independent SII.

Many readers will recognize the preceding example as a situation that is better suited for analysis in the states-of-the-world formulation of Savage (1954) than for the reduced formulation of Chapter 1. Figure 2.1 shows the usual outcome matrix when the first coin in SII is the coin for SI. There are three different acts and four states, where H_i and T_i denote heads and tails, respectively, for coin i. Although we shall not consider Savage's formulation for decisions under uncertainty in any detail until Chapter 7, it is introduced here because it plays a role in subsequent examples.

Tversky and Kahneman (1986) regard the invariance principle as an essential condition for normative choice theory and note that it is tacitly assumed rather than explicitly stated by many writers. It has at least two variants. In the first, which is illustrated by the lives-saved-versus-lives-lost example given earlier in this section, only the wording of the frames is different. There is no difference between the probability distributions in the two frames or in the way the probabilities arise, insofar as this is specified. The second variant uses differences between the ways in which the probabilities arise, or are generated, to induce violations of asymmetry under the reduction principle that characterizes each alternative only by its probabilities for the outcomes. Violations of invariance in this case can also be viewed as violations of reduction.

The difference between the ways the probabilities arise in the two frames may be implicit or explicit. We illustrate the implicit mode first with a

FIGURE 2.1   Payoff matrix

	H_1 H_2	H_1 T_2	T_1 H_2	T_1 T_2
a_1(SI OR SII)	1,000	1,000	0	0
SI a_2	1,200	1,200	-80	-80
SII a_2	-80	1,200	-80	1,200

violation of first-degree stochastic dominance, and then we consider an explicit violation of invariance or reduction that illustrates a so-called isolation or pseudocertainty effect.

Tversky and Kahneman (1981, 1986) report that 150 subjects were asked to choose between (A) a sure gain of $240 and (B) a 25% chance to gain $1,000 but nothing otherwise, and between (C) a sure loss of $750 and (D) a 75% chance to lose $1,000 but nothing otherwise, with the understanding that the two selected options would be played out independently and simultaneously. About 84% chose (A) over (B) and 87% chose (D) over (C), 73% chose the (AD) combination, and 3% the (BC) combination.

Also consider a choice between (E) a 25% chance to win $240 and a 75% chance to lose $760, and (F) a 25% chance to win $250 and a 75% chance to lose $750. It is "natural" to think of the outcome of (E) or (F) as being determined by a "coin" with probability $\frac{1}{4}$ for heads and $\frac{3}{4}$ for tails. In this comparison subjects invariably prefer (F) to (E), which adheres to the first-degree stochastic dominance principle. However, the (AD) combination is identical to (E) in its aggregate outcome probabilities, and (BC) is identical to (F) in its aggregate outcome probabilities. Thus the prevalent choice of (AD) in the preceding paragraph violates first-degree stochastic dominance through the separated-choice framing effect.

Three further remarks on this example are in order. First, the implicit difference between the two frames is probably not the main reason for (AD) $\succ$ (BC) and (F) $\succ$ (E). It is more likely due to the psychological difference between attitudes to gains and losses in the first frame, perhaps coupled with an inability in that frame to mentally or manually aggregate pairs before making the two choices. Second, the authors note that preferences agree with first-degree stochastic dominance when dominance is transparent, as in (E) versus (F). Finally, although the probability aggregated comparison between (AD) and (BC) seems straightforward in the pure outcomes form, the actual comparison between the two in Savage's states formulation is not so obvious. See Figure 2.2, where coin 1 refers to (B), coin 2 to (D), and the probabilities of H_i and T_i are $\frac{1}{4}$ and $\frac{3}{4}$, respectively. Although (BC) stochastically

FIGURE 2.2   Another payoff matrix

	H_1 H_2 (1/16)	H_1 T_2 (3/16)	T_1 H_2 (3/16)	T_1 T_2 (9/16)
AD	240	−760	240	−760
BC	250	250	−750	−750

dominates (AD) in the reduced form, (BC) does not dominate (AD) in state-by-state comparisons since (AD) is better in the third state.

The final example of this section, based on Tversky and Kahneman (1981, p. 455), assumes that probabilities are generated by drawing a marble at random from a bag of 100 marbles, numbered 1 through 100. The first comparison is between (A) win \$30 if number drawn is $\leqslant 25$, and nothing otherwise, and (B) win \$45 if number drawn is $\leqslant 20$, and nothing otherwise. This is reframed as a two-stage game for the second comparison. In stage 1 the game ends with no payoff if the number drawn is $\leqslant 75$, and goes to stage 2 otherwise. If you get to stage 2, your choice is between (A*) win \$30 and (B*) win \$45 if number drawn in a second draw is $\leqslant 80$, and nothing otherwise. You must choose (A*) or (B*) before the draw in stage 1. Despite the fact that the overall outcome probabilities for (A) and (A*) are identical, and similarly for (B) and (B*), most subjects chose (B) in the first case and (A*) in the second. The reversal in this example is referred to as an *isolation effect* in Kahneman and Tversky (1979, p. 271), because subjects tend to pay attention only to the dissimilar parts in the two-stage frame, and as a *pseudocertainty effect* in Tversky and Kahneman (1986), because of its relationship to the certainty effect of Allais (1953, 1979a, 1979b) that we shall consider later in our discussion of the independence axiom.

2.3   MONEY

Because monetary outcomes have been so important in expected utility theories, a few comments on money and wealth are in order before we turn to other aspects.

As seen in Section 1.1, monetary outcomes were central to Bernoulli's expected utility theory. He believed that utility or subjective value should be defined on wealth without intervention of probability or risk, and he proposed a logarithmic function $v(w) = \log w$ for the psychological value of wealth, unique up to positive linear transformations. This is pictured in Figure 2.3.

The preeminent proponent in modern times of Bernoulli's position on the utility of monetary outcomes is Allais (1979a, b), whose experimental measurements (1979b) lend support to Bernoulli's logarithm function. Let w_0

FIGURE 2.3 $v(w) = \log w$

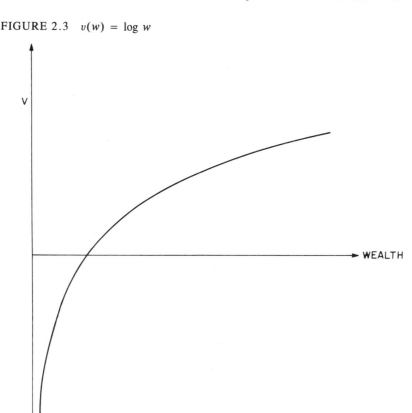

denote an individual's estimate of the present value of his or her stream of future income, and let x be a gain or loss presently considered. Then Allais believes (1979b, pp. 480–81, 614–20, 627–33; footnote 34, p. 639) that his experimental results justify the proposition that, with very little error, the psychological value of $w_0 + x$ for *all* subjects is given by $\log(1 + x/w_0)$, or, more precisely, that $v(w_0 + x) = f(x/w_0)$, where f is the same for all subjects but is not given explicitly (p. 633).

   Unlike Bernoulli, Allais does not assume that individuals act to maximize the expected value of their riskless utility. Moreover, he presume that an individual's preferences on a set P of probability distributions (granting the reduction principle, which he adopts as a basic axiom) are weakly ordered and that they satisfy first-degree stochastic dominance, referred to as the "axiom of absolute preference" (1979b, p. 457). It follows (p. 465) that preferences on P depend not only on expected subjective values $\Sigma v(w_0 + x)p(x)$ but on the distributions of the v values about their expected values. His theory, which he interprets normatively but believes to be in good accord with people's behavior, will be discussed further in the next chapter.

Allais believes (1979b, pp. 591-93) that von Neumann and Morgenstern, whose formulation he refers to as neo-Bernoullian, intended their cardinal utility function u on monetary outcomes to measure psychological or subjective value, in the manner of Bernoulli or Allais. Although there are hints of this in their writing, other commentators, including Strotz (1953), Luce and Raiffa (1957), and Baumol (1958), make it quite clear that such an identification is unjustified, and they themselves (1953 edition, pp. 16, 20) deny it.

One of the great attractions of the von Neumann-Morgenstern theory is its complete generality on the nature of outcomes. However, *monetary* outcomes have played a prominent role in later work based on their theory (Section 1.6) largely because of its fascination for economists, its convenience in experiments on risky choice, and its use as a measurement surrogate for other outcomes. These aspects explain the prevalence of the monetary factor in our critique of linear utility theory.

Numerous studies, beginning with Mosteller and Nogee (1951), report assessments of people's von Neumann-Morgenstern utility functions u for monetary outcomes. Some studies are normatively oriented, and others are purely descriptive. Most focus on the measurement of utility for modest gains and losses, but a few, including Grayson (1960), consider large changes. Regardless of scope, and in sharp contrast to the everywhere concave v of Bernoulli and Allais, a prevalent, but by no means universal, finding is that u is concave in gains and convex in losses except for losses in the vicinity of ruin, where concavity reappears.

The prevalence of risk aversion in gains and risk seeking in losses has led Kahneman and Tversky to refer to its increasing S-shaped pattern as the *reflection effect*. They also observe that their u tends to be steeper for losses than for gains (see Figure 2.4). I say "their u" because their assessment of value is made according to their descriptive theory of choice between risky monetary prospects, referred to as "prospect theory," and not according to the von Neumann-Morgenstern paradigm. However, like von Neumann and Morgenstern, they assess values by comparisons between simple lotteries, and the qualitative aspects of the two are similar.

As noted in Section 1.6, several studies take exception to the prevalence of the reflection effect, and others confirm it. A recent confirmation is given by Budescu and Weiss (1985). On the other hand, Cohen et al. (1985) conclude that, while subjects exhibit consistent risk attitudes in gains, and also in losses, there is *no* correlation between a subject's attitudes toward gains and losses. They also note that probabilities are accounted for rather precisely in the gains region but not in the loss region, where they are treated coarsely, if at all. Related work on the relative importance of four risk

FIGURE 2.4   *u* convex in losses, concave in gains

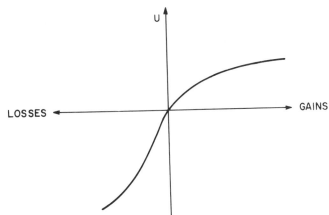

dimensions, namely win probability, loss probability, amount to win, and amount to lose, was reported by Slovic and Lichtenstein (1968) and Payne and Braunstein (1971). An overview of this and similar descriptive research is presented by Schoemaker (1980).

The importance of changes from one's "present position" is highlighted by the following example from Tversky and Kahneman (1986):

Situation 1. Assume yourself richer by $300 than you are today. You have to choose between (A) a sure gain of $100 and (B) a 50% chance to gain $200 but nothing otherwise.

Situation 2. Assume yourself richer by $500 than you are today. You have to choose between (A') a sure loss of $100 and (B') a 50% chance to lose $200, but nothing otherwise.

Although the final positions of (A) and (A') are the same, and probabilistically so for (B) and (B'), 72% of 126 respondents chose (A) in Situation 1, and 64% of 128 respondents chose (B') in Situation 2. The majority choices thus agree with risk aversion for gains and risk seeking for losses.

On the basis of available evidence, Kahneman and Tversky conclude that the effective carriers of values in decisions between risky prospects are gains and losses, or changes in wealth, rather than levels of wealth. I concur. Moreover, so long as one's wealth level is not drastically changed, the utility function on gains and losses will not be significantly sensitive to current wealth.

Although these conclusions apply first and foremost to descriptive theory, I believe they have important implications for normative theory. In particular, in accord with the considered choices of reasonable people, normative decision theory for risky decisions with monetary outcomes ought to be primarily concerned with changes from present positions. For the linear utility theory of von Neumann and Morgenstern, this suggests that the outcomes in X should be such changes (i.e., gains and losses). Insofar as present position is considered explicitly, it could be included in u as a parameter, giving the bivariate functional $u(x, w_0)$. In fact, this is often assumed implicitly with w_0 suppressed in writing $u(x)$.

Since it might be imagined that this position is inconsistent with the reduction principle when applied to a series of potential payoffs over time, we note that outcomes in the series context are much more involved than the simple monetary outcomes we have considered. Normative theory does not seek to collapse such a series into a single number, such as present monetary value, but regards it for what it is—a vector of payoffs with timing clearly noted. The probabilities for outcomes in such a case refer to the holistic payoff vectors.

2.4 PROBABILITY TRANSFORMATIONS, PROBABILITY PREFERENCES

The experimental work of Preston and Baratta (1948), perhaps the earliest reported test of the von Neumann–Morgenstern theory, explored whether subjects accounted for chance events at their true (mathematical) probabilities or whether they systematically distorted probabilities in their presumed expectation-maximizing choices. Unlike Mosteller and Nogee (1951), Preston and Baratta assumed $u(x) = ax + b$ for small changes in wealth. Since the logarithmic function is approximately linear locally, their results also pertain to the descriptive accuracy of Bernoulli's theory. However, they do not pertain to Allais's theory because he does not adopt an expectation maximization principle.

Preston and Baratta found that subjects tend to overvalue small probabilities and undervalue large ones, with accurate valuation at about 0.2. Thus, if $\tau(\lambda)$ denotes a person's valuation of probability λ, with $\tau(\lambda)x$ the holistic value for a random prospect with probability λ for x and $1 - \lambda$ for 0, then $\tau(\lambda) > \lambda$ for small λ, $\tau(\lambda) < \lambda$ for large λ, and $\tau(0.2) \cong 0.2$ (see Figure 2.5). Edwards (1954a, p. 397) cites other studies with similar results, except perhaps for the points, if any, where $\tau(\lambda) = \lambda$.

In other early work on the psychology of probability, Edwards (1953) observed that subjects' bets revealed preferences among probabilities. For example, for lotteries with equal expected values, subjects consistently liked bets with win probability $\frac{1}{2}$ to others with different win probabilities, and avoided bets with win probability $\frac{3}{4}$. Moreover, these probability preferences were reversed in the loss domain, were insensitive to the amounts of money

FIGURE 2.5   Distortion of probabilities

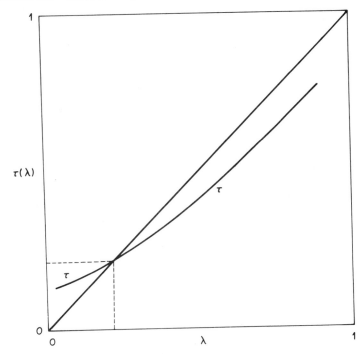

involved (Edwards, 1954b), and could not be explained by curved utility functions (Edwards, 1954b, c).

There is now a huge literature on the psychology of probabilistic information processing and its biases, distortions, and illusions. Interested readers will find discussions and further references in Edwards (1954a, 1961, 1968), Karmarkar (1978), Schoemaker (1980), Kahneman et al. (1982), Machina (1983a), Kahneman and Tversky (1972), Tversky and Kahneman (1973), and papers of Kahneman and Tversky cited earlier.

Various descriptive models that incorporate transformed or subjectively weighted probabilities $\tau(\lambda)$ have been proposed. Handa (1977) discusses the natural extension of the Preston–Baratta model with $p \rightarrow \Sigma\tau(p(x))x$, Karmarkar (1978) proposes $p \rightarrow \Sigma\tau(p(x))u(x)/\Sigma\tau(p(x))$ with $\tau(\lambda) = \lambda^{\alpha}/[\lambda^{\alpha} + (1 - \lambda)^{\alpha}]$ for a positive parameter α, and Kahneman and Tversky (1979) use a τ function in their prospect theory. The properties for τ suggested by Kahneman and Tversky include $\tau(0) = 0$, $\tau(1) = 1$, $\tau(\mu\lambda) > \mu\tau(\lambda)$ for small $\lambda > 0$ and $0 < \mu < 1$, subadditivity for complementary events (i.e., $\tau(\lambda) + \tau(1 - \lambda) < 1$ for $0 < \lambda < 1$), and $\tau(\mu\lambda)\tau(\mu\rho) < \tau(\mu)\tau(\mu\lambda\rho)$ for $0 < \mu, \lambda, \rho < 1$.

The large body of evidence already alluded to supports the claim that a normative theory that does not include a transformation of probabilities cannot be an accurate descriptive theory. However, even if a normative theory includes τ in some form, it would still not be an acceptable descriptive theory according to Tversky and Kahneman (1986) because of violations of reduction and invariance that lead to contradictions of the asymmetry of strict preference and first-degree stochastic dominance.

In fact, most normatively interpreted theories of preference and choice among risky prospects do not include a probability transformation feature. They take probabilities as given and, without alteration, combine them in some way with values or utilities of outcomes under the reduction principle. Moreover, framing effects that lead to violations of asymmetry are felt to have no place in normative theory even if they are acknowledged as psychologically valid. It follows that tests of the axioms of a normative theory ought to avoid framing effects insofar as possible by, for example, simply listing the holistic outcomes and their probabilities when comparisons between prospects are considered. However, since even the way that outcomes are listed (e.g., worst to best, best to worst, randomly) might induce framing effects, it seems difficult to avoid such effects altogether. Despite this difficulty, it is my understanding that most normative theorists would be disturbed by a purported empirical violation of an axiom or principle of choice viewed normatively only if they were convinced that the violation was not induced by framing. At the same time, an axiom proposed as a normative principle should not be taken too seriously if its general satisfaction is induced only by special framing. A case in point is considered in the next section.

2.5 INDEPENDENCE AND THE CERTAINTY EFFECT

Of the three numbered axioms in Section 1.4, the one most often denied, relaxed or abandoned as both a descriptive and normative principle of choice is A2, the independence axiom. It is also the most extensively investigated axiom from an empirical perspective. Several investigators, beginning with Allais (1953, 1979a) and including Morrison (1967), MacCrimmon (1968), MacCrimmon and Larsson (1979), Hagen (1979), Kahneman and Tversky (1979), and Tversky and Kahneman (1981), have shown persistent and systematic violations of independence. An extensive review is provided by Machina (1983a, pp. 62–76).

To paraphrase an early example of Allais (1979a, p. 91), consider first your preference between p and q:

p: \$1 million with probability 1,

q: \$3 million with probability 0.98, nothing otherwise.

Consider also your preference between

r: $1 million with probability 0.050, nothing otherwise,

s: $3 million with probability 0.049, nothing otherwise.

Many people have $p > q$ because of p's certainty of giving $1 million, yet also have $s > r$ because the difference between their payoff probabilities of 1 chance in 1000 is outweighed by the significantly larger payoff for s. This pair of preferences violates A2 since

$$r = (1/20)p + (19/20)t, \qquad s = (1/20)q + (19/20)t,$$

where $t(\$0) = 1$. According to A2, if $p > q$, then $r > s$.

A similar example in Kahneman and Tversky (1979) uses more modest payoffs:

p: $3,000 with probability 1,

q: $4,000 with probability 0.8, nothing otherwise;

r: $3,000 with probability 0.25, nothing otherwise,

s: $4,000 with probability 0.20, nothing otherwise.

Of 95 respondents, 80% had $p > q$, 65% had $s > r$, and more than half had the independence-violating pair $\{p > q, s > r\}$.

In such examples it is instructive to consider the effect of λ on preferences when $p > q$:

$$r = \lambda p + (1 - \lambda)t, \qquad s = \lambda q + (1 - \lambda)t.$$

Assuming that t's payoff, if any, is less attractive than those for p and q, as λ decreases from 1 the attraction to certainty in the p/q comparison fades and the difference between their payoffs assumes more significance in the overall comparison between r and s. When independence is violated, we expect $r > s$ for large λ and $s > r$ for small λ. The change point as λ decreases from 1 will depend of course on the person as well as on the parameters of p, q, and t.

Allais refers in various places to the effect, advantage, or security of certainty as the driving force behind violations of independence of the type just illustrated. This is commonly known today as the *certainty effect*, although it is well to bear in mind that this does not mean that the violation is due to a framing effect, as discussed earlier, since, in adherence to the reduction principle, the prospects are presented in a straightforward manner without special framing devices, such as decompositions or multiple stages. When certainty as such is not involved, but the ratio of positive-payoff probabilities is the same in two comparisons (such as 0.9/0.6 and 0.3/0.2), failures of independence are sometimes described as the *common ratio effect*.

Another descriptor is the *common consequence effect*, which has been used in connection with Allais's most famous example (1979a, p. 89), which was designed, in part, to challenge Savage's independence principle. You are asked to compare

p: $1 million with probability 1,

q: $5 million with probability 0.10, $1 million with probability 0.89, nothing otherwise;

and to compare

p': $1 million with probability 0.11, nothing otherwise,

q': $5 million with probability 0.10, nothing otherwise.

Many people have $p > q$ and $q' > p'$, and it is clear that certainty plays a role in this. Now with $t(\$0) = 1$ and with s the prospect with probability $\frac{10}{11}$ for $5 million and nothing otherwise, we have

$$p = (0.11)p + (0.89)p, \qquad q = (0.11)s + (0.89)p,$$

and

$$p' = (0.11)p + (0.89)t, \qquad q' = (0.11)s + (0.89)t.$$

The "common consequence" in p versus q is $1 million, and in p' versus q' it is $0 (i.e., t). According to A2 and its indifference companion L5 in Section 1.4, the preference between p and q, and between p' and q', should depend on the p-versus-s preference, independent of the common consequence in each case. Thus A2 requires $p > q$ and $p' > q'$ if $p > s$, or $q > p$ and $q' > p'$ if $s > p$; also, L5 requires $p \sim q$ and $p' \sim q'$ if $p \sim s$.

The most common defense of independence as a postulate of rationality involves the two-stage argument of Section 1.4. Consider the first example of this section, where $r = \frac{1}{20}p + \frac{19}{20}t$ and $s = \frac{1}{20}q + \frac{19}{20}t$. The two-stage argument imagines that either s or t would be played out in two stages. In the first stage you get t (i.e., $0) with probability $\frac{19}{20}$ and p (if r) or q (if s) with probability $\frac{1}{20}$. Your final payoff is then determined in the second stage according to whatever results from the first stage. Since you shouldn't care which of r and s is chosen if t comes up in the first stage, your preference between r and s ought to depend solely on your preference between p and q.

This argument once persuaded many theorists to accept A2 as a valid normative principle, and it may still appeal to some. However, as Allais originally argued and has insistently maintained, it is inadmissible as a guide to rationality since it destroys the holistic natures of the prospects under consideration and is based on a specialized framing effect illustrated in the final example of Section 2.2. When distributions are viewed holistically, important comparative aspects may be evident that could be disguised by the two-stage argument. Moreover, there is a potentially unlimited number of ways that two distributions could be decomposed for multiple-stage presentation that, because of psychological suggestions induced by decompositional framing that should have no part of our conception of rationality, could lead to opposite preferences between the two. Examples of this have already been given in Section 2.2.

Since Allais defends first-degree stochastic dominance as a normative principle but denies independence the same status, it is interesting to compare his position with that of Tversky and Kahneman (1986). These authors believe that the two principles are on a similar footing. They say that both rules are intuitively compelling as abstract principles of choice, and note that they are consistently obeyed in situations where their structure is transparent and frequently violated otherwise.

My own view differs slightly from both Allais and Kahneman–Tversky and requires qualification of the degree of interdependence among events that generate probabilities for alternative prospects. We hold a common view on the normative status of first-degree stochastic dominance, and I am convinced by Tversky and Kahneman that descriptive failures of this principle can arise when dominance is not transparent or is disguised by framing.

If the reduction principle is accepted as a normative criterion, which I feel comfortable about, but only when the underlying events for different prospects are causally independent, then I must agree with Allais on the normative inadmissibility of the independence axiom. In the independent-prospects case, the independence axiom seems intuitively compelling only by way of an illusion created by two-stage interdependent framing. When the prospects are presented in holistic form, which suggests that their underlying events are more or less independent, the judgments of reasonable people speak strongly against the independence axiom as a normative principle.

On the other hand, both the reduction principle and the independence axiom appear in a different light if the underlying events are interdependent, as I have suggested in Section 2.2. In particular, if the framing of independence by the two-stage argument discussed earlier adheres to the actual process by which final payoffs are determined, then independence *is* normatively attractive, and I tend to side with Tversky and Kahneman in this case.

There is also, I believe, a substantive difference between the dominance and independence principles. With monetary outcomes, first-degree stochastic dominance is the natural probabilistic extension of the greater-than relation between sure outcomes. On the other hand, independence is merely one of a large number of rules of combination for preferences between convex combinations of distributions. Its simplicity is appealing, and it is enormously useful mathematically via the linear utility representation, but it does not have the same intuitive standing as dominance.

Violations of A2 and related independence conditions can be accommodated by probability–utility models by the use of subjectively weighted probabilities (see τ in Section 2.4) or by a conception of how probabilities and utilities combine to form values or utilities of risky alternatives that differs in some way from the expected utility form. The descriptive models of Handa (1977) and Kahneman and Tversky (1979) use both means since their quasi-expectational forms are not true expectations. However, Karmarkar (1978) uses only the τ device, since his weighted probabilities are normalized. Theories interpreted normatively that do not transform probabilities rely on the combination aspect to accommodate independence violations. The rules of combination are not specified explicitly in the theories of Allais (1953, 1979a, b) and Machina (1982a), but are given concrete form in the weighted expected utility theory of Chew (1982, 1983) and in Fishburn's (1982c) SSB utility theory. We consider these further in the next chapter.

We note also that plausible violations of independence can occur outside the narrow realm of monetary outcomes. Kahneman and Tversky (1979, p. 267) give an example with tours of European countries as outcomes, and Sen (1985) presents three examples with various kinds of outcomes. Sen's first example illustrates the potential of psychological dependence among outcomes in the common consequence format. In abstract form consider (A) a 10% chance for a, 90% chance for b and (B) a 10% chance for a, 90% chance for c as one comparison, and (A*) a 10% chance for $a*$, 90% chance for b and (B*) a 10% chance for $a*$, 90% chance for c as a second comparison. Although independence requires a similar preference between (A*) and (B*) as between (A) and (B), the individual may view the b versus c comparison differently in the two cases because of different psychological dispositions caused by association with common consequence a in one case and with $a*$ in the other. Even though the outcomes are mutually exclusive, psychological associations and interdependence could lead to (A) > (B) and (B*) > (A*).

Sen's paper also contains an interesting analysis of notions of rational choice that emphasizes the correspondence of actual choice with the use of reason. He distinguishes irrationality due to hasty or unthinking action (something else would have been done on careful reflection) from failures of rational action due to limited reasoning ability. Those of us who are sometimes perplexed by the notion of rationality may find some solace in Sen's claim (1985, p. 113) that it involves inherent ambiguities.

2.6 VAGUENESS AND NONTRANSITIVE INDIFFERENCE

The asymmetry part of the weak ordering axiom A1 was considered in Section 2.2 as part of our discussion of reduction and invariance. We now consider transitivity implications of A1, beginning with the most innocuous failure of transitivity—nontransitive indifference. Failures of the transitivity of strict preference will be discussed in the next two sections.

We say that the indifference relation $\sim$ is *nontransitive, or intransitive*, if $a \sim b$, $b \sim c$, and $a > c$ for some a, b, and c. In the risky-prospects setting, a, b, and c could be outcomes in X or probability measures in P or a mixture of the two. When outcomes are involved, we identify x with the one-point measure that yields x with certainty.

Early discussants of nontransitive indifference in economics include Georgescu–Roegen (1936, 1958) and Armstrong (1939, 1948, 1950). Armstrong speaks in one place (1950, p. 122) about nontransitive indifference as arising from "the imperfect powers of discrimination of the human mind whereby inequalities become recognizable only when of sufficient magnitude" and asserts elsewhere (1948, p. 3) "that indifference is not transitive is indisputable, and a world in which it were transitive is indeed unthinkable." A more recent examination of nontransitive indifference in consumer demand theory is provided by Chipman (1971).

Armstrong's first quote is reminiscent of the notion of a just noticeable difference in psychophysical measurement as it arose from the work of E. H. Weber and Gustav Fechner in the mid-1800s. An example suggested by Luce (1956) makes the point in the preference domain. A person who likes sugarless coffee will be indifferent between x and $x + 1$ grains of sugar in his coffee, between $x + 1$ and $x + 2$ grains, . . . , but for each x there will come a smallest $y = f(x)$ at which $x > y$ (granting imprecision in y's determination) so that $\sim$ is not transitive. One might also expect $f(x)$ to increase as x increases, so the threshold of discriminability shifts upward as the base stimulus x increases.

When $>$ is assumed to be asymmetric and transitive (but $\sim$ is not assumed transitive), we refer to $>$ as a *partial order* instead of a weak order. The partial order of the preceding paragraph is likely to have the additional properties

$$(x > a, y > b) \Rightarrow (x > b \text{ or } y > a),$$

$$(x > y, y > z) \Rightarrow (x > c \text{ or } c > z),$$

in which case it is called a *semiorder* (Luce, 1956). If it has only the first of these properties then it is an *interval order* (Fishburn, 1970a). These and related concepts are discussed at length in Fishburn (1985a).

A single-peaked example (Fishburn, 1970b) illustrates a partial order that is not an interval order. A planning board member feels that \$200,000 is the right sum for a community to budget for a new playground. The member's preference decreases in both directions from \$200,000, but some comparisons on opposite sides of the peak are problematic. Although

$191,000 > $190,000 and $205,000 > $206,000, the member finds that $191,000 \sim $206,000 and $190,000 \sim $205,000.

The difficulty of specifying certainty equivalents precisely leads to simple examples of nontransitive indifference with risky prospects. Let p be a 50-50 gamble for $0 or $1000. Then the combination of $367 \sim p$ and $p \sim $366 seems reasonable, but surely $367 > $366.

Failures of transitivity, both for $\sim$ and $>$, are usually dealt with in descriptive preference theory either by stochastic or random utility models (Luce and Suppes, 1965; Manski, 1977) or, in multiattribute cases, by deterministic models whose algebraic rules of evaluation allow intransitivities (Tversky, 1969; Luce, 1978; Fishburn, 1980a).

In normative utility theory, Aumann (1962) and Fishburn (1970a, 1982a) axiomatized linear utility models for $>$ on P that reflect $>$ (i.e., $p > q \Rightarrow u(p) > u(q)$), but not $\sim$, since they do not assume that indifference is transitive. The axioms at the end of Section 1.5 are indicative of this approach. The SSB model discussed in ensuing chapters accommodates certain forms of nontransitive indifference and preference. However, it is *not* designed to deal with the certainty-equivalent vagueness illustrated in the preceding example.

2.7 PREFERENCE CYCLES AND MONEY PUMPS

A *preference cycle,* usually written as $a_1 > a_2 > \cdots > a_n > a_1$, is a set $\{a_i > a_{i+1}: i = 1, \cdots, n, n \geq 3, a_{n+1} = a_1\}$. There are two types of nontransitive preference patterns for asymmetric $>$, those with cycles and those without cycles (but $a > b, b > c, a \sim c$). In the noncyclic case the transitive closure $>^t$ of $>$, defined by

$$a >^t b \qquad \text{if } a = a_1 > a_2 > \cdots > a_n = b$$

$$\text{for some } n \geq 2 \text{ and some } a_i,$$

is a partial order. This case can be grouped with partial orders in the preceding section, so we focus here on patterns with cycles.

Several writers, including Flood (1951–2), May (1954), and MacCrimmon and Larsson (1979), suggest that preference cycles have the best chance to arise in multiattribute situations. For example, May asked 62 college students to make binary comparisons between hypothetical marriage partners x, y, and z who were characterized by three attributes:

	Intelligence	Looks	Wealth
x:	Very intelligent	Plain	Well off
y:	Intelligent	Very good looking	Poor
z:	Fairly intelligent	Good looking	Rich

Seventeen of the 62 students had cyclic choices. Since there are two cyclic patterns ($x > y > z > x$ and $x > z > y > x$) among the eight possible patterns ($\sim$ was not permitted), about eight cycles of each type would occur if the students chose randomly on each comparison. However, all 17 of the transitivity violators had cycle $x > y > z > x$, and May (1954, p. 7) notes that "the intransitivity pattern is easily explained as the result of choosing the alternative that is superior in two out of three criteria."

Some people, including Davis (1958), have argued that preference cycles can be explained purely on the basis of random choice and do not represent systematic patterns, but May's example shows that this is not always true.

An example from Tversky (1969) gives another case of systematic intransitivity. Let $[x, \lambda]$ denote the lottery that pays x with probability λ and nothing otherwise. Tversky observed that a number of people have the cyclic pattern

$$[\$5.00, 7/24] > [\$4.75, 8/24] > [\$4.50, 9/24] > [\$4.25, 10/24]$$

$$> [\$4.00, 11/24] > [\$5.00, 7/24].$$

He notes that this and other intransitive patterns can be explained by Morrison's (1962) nonlinear additive difference model, which is one of the deterministic models alluded to in the penultimate paragraph of Section 2.6.

The following example (Fishburn, 1984a) reverses the relative importance of changes in payoff and probability from Tversky's example. Let $[x, \lambda]$ be the lottery that gives you an $x\%$ raise in salary with probability λ and no raise with probability $1 - \lambda$. Although your preferences might not be cyclic, the cyclic pattern $[6, 0.90] > [7, 0.80] > [8, 0.72] > [9, 0.66] > [10, 0.61] > [6, 0.90]$ does not seem unreasonable. Here the amount of the raise is less important than the chance of getting some raise until the difference in raises (10% versus 6%) becomes large enough to incur the added risk. In Tversky's example, payoff probabilities were relatively unimportant until they showed a sizable difference.

Normative decision theorists are often averse to the notion that cyclic preferences may be quite reasonable or rational, in part because there is no basis for choice from a set on which preferences cycle so long as choice is to be governed by the existence of an alternative that is preferred or indifferent to all others. To show how foolish or irrational cyclic preferences are, they have invented the *money pump*. Suppose you have the cycle $p > q > r > p$ and presently have title to p. Then, since you prefer r to p, you would surely be willing to pay something to exchange p for r; then, given r, you will surely pay something to exchange it for the preferred q; finally, given q, you will again pay something to exchange it for the preferred p. Thus, you begin and end at p but are poorer in the process. In short, you are a money pump.

There are, however, a few things about this invention that can be criticized. First, it envisions a dynamic situation with aspects of strategy and deception that transcend the basic choice problem. It is indeed irrational to be a money pump, but it is also hard to imagine a sensible person engaged in the money-pump game if he or she understands what is involved, cyclic preferences notwithstanding.

The money-pump concept also reveals a narrow perspective on how choice might be based on preferences, and perhaps a lack of imagination in dealing with cyclic patterns. Although there is no transparent way to make a sensible choice from $\{p, q, r\}$ when $p > q > r > p$, nothing prevents a person from considering preferences over the set of convex combinations of p, q, and r. And if there is a combination in this set that is preferred or indifferent to everything else in the set, then that person has an ex ante maximally preferred alternative. As first shown by Kreweras (1961), this can indeed be the case, and we shall consider it later as a part of the SSB theory.

2.8   THE PREFERENCE REVERSAL PHENOMENON

Section 2.2 illustrated reversals in preferences that violate asymmetry through framing. We now consider a systematic form of intransitivity known as the preference reversal phenomenon that does not appear to rely on special framing and which must therefore be addressed by normative as well as descriptive theories. This phenomenon is second only to violations of independence in the extent to which it has been investigated empirically.

Let p and q be risky prospects for monetary outcomes with certainty equivalents $c(p)$ and $c(q)$. Thus $c(p)$ is the (assumed unique) minimum amount the individual would accept in exchange for title to p, and similarly for $c(q)$. Then the preference reversal phenomenon occurs if $p > q$ and $c(p) < c(q)$, i.e., if the individual prefers p to q but would sell title to p for *less* than he or she would sell title to q.

Given that more money is preferred to less, $>$ cannot be a weak order when $p > q$ and $c(p) < c(q)$, since otherwise

$$c(p) \sim p > q \sim c(q) \Rightarrow c(p) > c(q) \Leftrightarrow c(p) > c(q).$$

Moreover, preference reversals generate cyclic preferences since for small positive δ for which $c(p) + 2\delta < c(q)$,

$$p > q > c(q) - \delta > c(p) + \delta > p.$$

To illustrate, consider

p: $30 with probability 0.9, nothing otherwise,

q: $100 with probability 0.3, nothing otherwise.

I have used this example informally with several groups and note a majority response of $p > q$, $c(p)$ about \$25, and $c(q)$ about \$27. It reflects a predominant theme of experiments on preference reversals that use a "probability lottery" or "p-bet" with a high chance for modest winnings (p) and a "money lottery" or "\$-bet" with a lower chance for large winnings (q). Comparatively small losses are often included as parts of p and q. When reversals occur, they usually follow the pattern given earlier: $p > q$ and $c(p) < c(q)$. When the lotteries are turned around and stated primarily in terms of losses, the reversal goes the other way, as might be expected from our previous comments on different attitudes toward gains and losses in Sections 1.6 and 2.3. Although preference reversals can be seen as violations of transitivity, an alternative explanation of the phenomenon is suggested by Karni and Safra (1987); see Section 3.5.

Initial experiments on the preference reversal phenomenon were made by Lichtenstein and Slovic (1971, 1973) and Lindman (1971). More recent experiments, motivated in part by skepticism with previous findings, are discussed by Grether and Plott (1979), Pommerehne et al. (1982), Reilly (1982), and Goldstein and Einhorn (1985). Slovic and Lichtenstein (1983) provide extensive commentary on prior research and other matters related to the phenomenon. They emphasize information processing aspects that are involved with people's preference judgments and that could play a significant role in the elicitation of choices that lead to preference reversals. They note, as did Grether and Plott (1979), that modifications in extant theories might yield reasonable models that could accommodate preference reversals. The recent work by Goldstein and Einhorn (1985), which emphasizes psychological dispositions toward judgments, choices, and evaluations of worth, suggests one such descriptive model that they refer to as "expression theory."

Despite a succession of attempts to tighten experimental controls and give subjects greater motivation to reflect carefully on their choices, partly in the hope that these measures might banish preference reversals, the phenomenon has persisted. In reviewing the recent experiments of Grether and Plott (1979) and others, Slovic and Lichtenstein (1983, p. 599) say that, in their opinion, "the most striking result of these studies is the persistence of preference reversals in the face of determined efforts to minimize or eliminate them."

It thus seems reasonable to submit that preference reversals are no mere artifact of casual experiments, framing effects, or unmotivated subjects. The task this poses for normative theory is either to provide defensible normative models that allow preference reversals or to explain convincingly why they are irrational.

To consider the normative side a bit further at this time, we distinguish between weak and strong preference reversals. Assume as before for the probability lottery p and the money lottery q that q has positive probability for an outcome that is larger than anything that can be won under p *and* that the total probability assigned by q to outcomes that are greater than the largest amount m that can be won under p is less than $p(m)$. Formally,

$$m = \max\{x : p(x) > 0\},$$

$$p(m) > \sum \{q(x) : x > m\} > 0.$$

Then, given a preference reversal $p \succ q$ and $c(p) < c(q)$, we refer to it as a *weak reversal* if $c(q) < m$, and as a *strong reversal* if $c(q) \geq m$. Thus a strong reversal occurs if the certainty equivalent of the money lottery q is as large as the most that can be won with the probability lottery p.

Although I see nothing unreasonable about weak reversals, strong reversals are another matter. Assume

$$q \sim c(q) \geq m \geq c(p) \quad \text{and} \quad c(q) > c(p),$$

so a strong reversal occurs if $p \succ q$. Suppose first that $c(q) > m$. Then, by the definition of $c(q)$, the individual would refuse to exchange title to q for m. Moreover, since m is as large as anything that might result from p, it is reasonable to suppose that an individual would not exchange q for p either. But then $q \succ p$, contrary to strong reversal. Similarly, if $c(q) = m$ and $p(m) < 1$, then $q \succ p$ is the only reasonable conclusion. Finally, if $c(q) = m$ and $p(m) = 1$, then p is tantamount to $c(q)$, so $q \sim p$.

The argument against strong reversals can be stated the other way around, as follows. Suppose that $p(m) < 1$, you prefer p to q, and z is any amount as great as the most you can win under p. It then seems reasonable that you will prefer z to q. But then, by the definition of certainty equivalence, $z > c(q)$ for all $z \geq m$; hence $m > c(q)$. This allows a weak reversal but not a strong reversal.

The data presented in the experimental studies cited earlier do not reveal the proportions of reversals in the predominant direction $[p \succ q, c(p) < c(q)]$ that were weak and strong, but it seems likely that at least some were strong.

2.9 NON-ARCHIMEDEAN PREFERENCES

The Archimedean or continuity axiom A3 says that if you prefer p to q and q to r, then you will prefer some nontrivial convex combination of p and r to q, and prefer q to some nontrivial combination of p and r. Plausible examples of its failure are suggested by Georgescu-Roegen (1954), Thrall (1954), and Chipman (1960) among others, but there is almost no experimental evidence for such failures. It would be violated when (p, q, r) = (win \$2, win \$1, be executed), and there is no probability $\alpha < 1$ at which $\alpha p + (1 - \alpha)r \succ q$. Less dramatically, suppose you are faced with a choice between (A) receive $10,000,020 if the first head in a series of flips of a fair coin comes before the nth toss, receive $0 otherwise; and (B) receive $10,000,000 with certainty. If you prefer (B) regardless of how big n is, then you violate A3. The certainty of a large prize could overwhelm a risky prospect with an even larger prize no matter how absurdly small its probability of no payoff becomes.

Three aspects of A3 and its comparison to A1 and A2 deserve comment. First, many normative theorists regard it more as a technical convenience than a rationality postulate, and some have suggested that its standard defense (Section 1.4) using extremely small probabilities removes it from the class of easily intuited principles. Second, as emphasized by Narens (1974, 1985), A3 has a different formal standing in logic than the other axioms. In a manner of speaking, it lies in a more complex class of axioms than do A1 and A2. Third, unlike cyclic preference violations of A1 or failures of the independence axiom A2, denial of A3 leaves the underlying notion of expected utility intact.

The third aspect has been discussed by various people, including Hausner (1954), Chipman (1960), Richter (1971), Narens (1974), Skala (1975), and Fishburn (1982a), and I shall say more about it in the next chapter. The basic idea is that if A3 is not assumed to hold, but the other axioms of von Neumann and Morgenstern are adopted, then there is a mapping U from P into a linear space ordered by a relation $>'$ such that U on P is a linear function and $p > q \Leftrightarrow U(p) >' U(q)$.

Apart from the discussion in Section 3.2, we shall generally assume that utilities are real valued. Thus the failure of A3 and other Archimedean-continuity axioms will not be at issue in the main part of the book.

2.10 SUMMARY

Virtually any axiom of preference or principle of choice can be violated by suitable framing in experiments on preference judgments and choice behavior. Moreover, even when special effects due to framing are minimized, systematic and persistent violations of some traditional axioms are observed. This has been the case most notably for violations of the independence axiom and for the preference reversal phenomenon.

The empirical evidence amassed in support of violations of traditional axioms poses a twofold challenge for normative decision theory. First, the experimental and philosophical evidence must be weighed to decide which principles and axioms remain acceptable as characteristics of reasonable or "rational" decision making and which do not. Acceptable relaxations may emerge in the latter case. Second, it is necessary, or at least desirable, to specify a mathematical model that incorporates the acceptable principles and axioms in an efficient representation of underlying preference structures. The next chapter discusses several models of this type along with some of their principles.

Although the evidence weighing process involves personal judgment, there is some agreement as well as disagreement about normative acceptability. At the present time, most theorists regard the reduction principle (perhaps qualified), asymmetry of strict preference, and first-degree stochastic dominance as normatively essential, and there is little concern about possible failures of the Archimedean axiom. Some people stand by the independence axiom, but many theorists no longer accept its normative inviolability and have replaced it with weaker conditions. Of the von Neumann–Morgenstern axioms, this leaves transitivity, the bulwark of economic rationality. My own view that transitivity can no longer be regarded as a tenet of the normative creed is presently a minority position.

3 Generalizations of Expected Utility

Many generalizations of the Bernoullian and von Neumann–Morgenstern expected utility theories have been proposed to accommodate violations of those theories. Systematic failures of the independence axiom or expectation principle have received special attention, but continuity failures and intransitivities have not been ignored. This chapter reviews a number of more general theories that appear to be of some normative interest, then discusses how they accommodate independence violations and, in one instance, nontransitive preferences and preference cycles.

3.1 ALTERNATIVES TO EXPECTED UTILITY

The following generalizations of the expected utility theories of Bernoulli and von Neumann and Morgenstern will be considered in this chapter:

  I. Linear, arbitrary outcomes
    A. Non-Archimedean weak order (Hausner, 1954; Chipman, 1960)
    B. Archimedean partial order (Aumann, 1962)
    C. Non-Archimedean partial order (Kannai, 1963)
  II. Nonlinear Archimedean weak order, monetary outcomes
    A. Intensity (Allais, 1953, 1979a; Hagen, 1972)
    B. Smooth (Machina, 1982a)
    C. Decumulative (Quiggin, 1982; Yaari, 1987)
  III. Nonlinear Archimedean weak order, arbitrary outcomes
    A. Weighted (Chew and MacCrimmon, 1979; Chew, 1982, 1983; Fishburn, 1981a, 1983a)
    B. Transitive convex (Fishburn, 1983a; Dekel, 1986; Chew, 1985)
  IV. Nonlinear nontransitive Archimedean, arbitrary outcomes
    A. Nontransitive convex (Fishburn, 1982c)
    B. SSB (Kreweras, 1961; Fishburn, 1981a, 1982c).

The generalizations of von Neumann and Morgenstern (1944) in category **I** that preserve linearity and at least the transitivity of strict preference had run their course by about 1970. The reason is that these generalizations exhaust the obvious linearity-preserving weakenings of the von Neumann–Morgenstern theory.

During the 1970s, while Hagen (1972) and others promoted and refined Allais's approach, there was a small explosion of interest from other quarters in violations of the independence axiom, due in part to new experiments that supported Allais's (1953, 1979b) findings. The first wave of new nonlinear theories were plainly descriptive (Handa, 1977; Karmarkar, 1978; Kahneman and Tversky, 1979) and normatively inadequate for reasons noted shortly. These were soon followed by other theories (Chew and MacCrimmon, 1979; Machina, 1982a; Quiggin, 1982; Fishburn, 1982c) that were often interpreted descriptively but could, I believe, be seen also as normatively interesting. The third and most recent wave, including Chew (1984, 1985), Nakamura (1984), Yaari (1987), Dekel (1986), and others mentioned in this chapter represents refinements and extensions of the second wave.

The preceding list makes no pretense of being exhaustive, and I shall mention a few omissions as we proceed. One of these, which is axiomatized by Gilboa (1986), is a tradeoff model between expected utility and the utility of a worst consequence. It was designed to account for Allais-type violations of independence in a very simple way.

The only theories in the list that are overtly Bernoullian in their use of a riskless "cardinal" value function v on outcomes are those in category **IIA** (Allais and Hagen) although it is possible to interpret Kreweras (1961) and perhaps the theories in **IIB** and **IIC** in this way. Other theories that involve the use of a riskless intensity-measured v on monetary outcomes, including Bell (1982) and Loomes and Sugden (1982), will be discussed in Chapter 8 since they follow Savage's (1954) states formulation. The theories in categories **I**, **III**, and **IV** (and **IIB-C** if so interpreted) adhere to the von Neumann–Morgenstern approach in which outcomes' utilities follow from simple preference comparisons between risky prospects that do not involve riskless comparable preference differences.

All theories in categories **I** through **IV** have three things in common. First, they subscribe to the reduction principle of Section 2.2. To the extent that this creates problems for normative interpretation because of interdependent events, one might suppose that prospects are stochastically independent and refer to Chapter 8 for other cases.

Second, the theories assume that $>$ on a set P of probability measures is asymmetric. Third, each theory in categories **I**, **III**, and **IV** satisfies one or more monotonicity or dominance principles involving convex combinations of measures, such as independence or $(p > q, r > s) \Rightarrow (\lambda p + (1 - \lambda)r > \lambda q + (1 - \lambda)s)$ or $(p > q, \lambda > \mu) \Rightarrow (\lambda p + (1 - \lambda)q > \mu p + (1 - \mu)q)$

or $(p \succ q, p \succ r) \Rightarrow (p \succ \lambda q + (1 - \lambda)r)$. Moreover, the monetary theories in category **II** assume a version of first-degree stochastic dominance. The theories in **IA** and **II** through **IV**, like those of Bernoulli and von Neumann and Morgenstern, assume that preferences are "precise" (if not always transitive) in the sense of excluding fuzzy indifference zones that are better handled by partial orders or stochastic utility.

In view of the discussion in Chapter 2 and the foregoing properties, I feel that each of the theories in the list is normatively interesting. Since some of them have been proposed only in a descriptive spirit, I apologize to authors who might feel misrepresented by this judgment.

At the same time, not all theories on the list have equal claims to normative adequacy. My own position is that the category **I** theories are not normatively suitable because of their linearity implications, and that those in **II** are normatively questionable to the extent that they are insensitive to differential local attitudes towards gains and losses. The normative adequacy of the theories in **IIC** can be challenged because of effects involved with transformed probabilities that are mentioned later. Moreover, unless they are restricted, the theories in **II** often violate monotonicity conditions such as $(p \succ q, \lambda > \mu) \Rightarrow \lambda p + (1 - \lambda)q \succ \mu p + (1 - \mu)q$. People who still regard transitivity as an essential part of rationality and normative theory must find **IVA** and **IVB** normatively inadmissible; others, myself included, who believe that a general normative theory must accommodate some intransitivities, regard the weak order theories in **II** and **IIIA-B** as too narrow.

Only subcategory **IIC** uses direct transformations of probabilities, but does so in a different way than the descriptive theories mentioned in Section 2.4. Recall that Handa (1977) uses $\Sigma \, \tau(p(x))x$ and Karmarkar (1978) uses $\Sigma \, \tau(p(x))u(x)/\Sigma \, \tau(p(x))$ with a power form for $\tau(\lambda)$. The presentation of prospect theory in Kahneman and Tversky (1979) views outcomes as increments to present wealth and considers prospects with at most two nonzero outcomes. Let $(x, \lambda; y, \mu)$ denote a prospect with probability λ for x, μ for y and $1 - \lambda - \mu \geqslant 0$ for 0. Their form for u on prospects varies in different regions. If either $\lambda + \mu < 1$, or $x \geqslant 0 \geqslant y$, or $x \leqslant 0 \leqslant y$, then

$$u(x, \lambda; y, \mu) = \tau(\lambda)u(x) + \tau(\mu)u(y),$$

where $u(0) = \tau(0) = 0$, $\tau(1) = 1$, and both u and τ are increasing. On the other hand, if $\lambda + \mu = 1$ and either $x > y > 0$ (sure minimum gain of y) or $x < y < 0$ (sure minimum loss of y) then

$$u(x, \lambda; y, 1 - \lambda) = u(y) + \tau(\lambda)[u(x) - u(y)].$$

Kahneman and Tversky (1979) axiomatize the first form in their appendix but do not axiomatize the second form.

The problem with theories that transform probabilities unconditionally is that, under modest structural assumptions for P, they either force τ to be the identity function or violate simple forms of first-degree stochastic dominance. Fishburn (1978b) shows that Handa's assumptions lead to $\tau(\lambda) = \lambda$, so his model reduces to maximization of expected return. Quiggin (1982) shows the same thing for models like Karmarkar's, which therefore reduce to the von Neumann–Morgenstern form. Kahneman and Tversky (1979, pp. 283–84) note that their representation yields violations of first-degree stochastic dominance if τ is not the identity. However, they also assume that dominated alternatives are eliminated prior to the evaluation of prospects in a preliminary editing phase. But this can lead to further difficulties as discussed, for example, by Kahneman and Tversky (1979, p. 284) and Machina (1983a, pp. 96–98), which detract from its normative interest. Readers interested in the proponents' recent thoughts on the descriptive accuracy of prospect theory should consult Tversky and Kahneman (1986).

The theories in subcategory **IIC** avoid the preceding problems by transformations of probabilities that depend on the entire structure of each risky prospect. They are designed to honor first-degree stochastic dominance, but in the process introduce second-order problems for normative theory. We say more about this in Section 3.5.

The theories in our list are described in modest detail in the next eight sections. Section 3.2 discusses category **I**. Sections 3.3 through 3.9 consider **IIA** through **IVB** in sequence. Section 3.10 explains how violations of independence are accommodated by the theories of **II** through **IV**, and 3.11 shows how **IVB** accommodates some violations of transitivity.

3.2 RELAXATIONS THAT PRESERVE LINEARITY

We assume throughout the rest of this chapter that the reduction principle of Section 2.2 holds and that $>$ is a binary relation on a convex set P of probability measures or distributions with $\sim$ and $\succeq$ defined from $>$ as in Section 1.4.

The category **I** theories are mainly of historical interest from this book's perspective since they do not accommodate common violations of independence (A2). Since they will not be used later, their descriptions will be brief.

The generalization of the von Neumann–Morgenstern linear utility theory that may be most faithful to their conception arises when the Archimedean axiom A3 is dropped, but the others are retained in their entirety. This was mentioned by von Neumann and Morgenstern (1953 edition, p. 631) and worked out in detail by Hausner (1954) with axioms A1, A2 and its indifference companion L5 ($p \sim q \Rightarrow \lambda p + (1 - \lambda)r \sim \lambda q + (1 - \lambda)r$). With A3 absent, the linear utility representation of Theorem 1.3 holds for vector-valued utilities $U(p)$ ordered lexicographically.

Lexicographic orders ($>_L$) are widely discussed and used (Fishburn,

1974). For points in $\mathbf{R}^n$,

$$(x_1, \ldots, x_n) >_L (y_1, \ldots, y_n) \text{ if } (x_1, \ldots, x_n) \neq (y_1, \ldots, y_n)$$

and $x_i > y_i$ for $\min\{i : x_i \neq y_i\}$.

More generally, suppose $(T, <_0)$ is a linearly ordered set ($<_0$ is a weak order with $\sim_0$ the identity relation) and F is the set of all $f: T \to \mathbf{R}$ that are nonzero on at most a well-ordered subset of $(T, <_0)$, with addition and scalar multiplication defined pointwise: $(\lambda f + \mu g)(t) = \lambda f(t) + \mu g(t)$. Then with $>_L$ defined on F by

$$f >_L g \text{ if } f \neq g \text{ and } f(t) > g(t) \text{ for the first } t \text{ in } (T, <_0)$$

$$\text{at which } f(t) \neq g(t),$$

$(F, >_L)$ is a linearly ordered vector (linear) space. Hausner proves that A1, A2, and L5 hold for $(P, \succ)$ if and only if there is such an $(F, >_L)$ and a linear mapping $U: P \to F$ such that for all $p, q \in P$,

$$p \succ q \Leftrightarrow U(p) >_L U(q),$$

with $U(\lambda p + (1 - \lambda)q) = \lambda U(p) + (1 - \lambda)U(q)$. Additional discussions of this lexicographic representation appear in Chipman (1960) and Fishburn (1971a, 1974, 1982a).

The first axiomatization for Archimedean partially ordered or acyclic preferences in **IB** is due to Aumann (1962) with later versions in Fishburn (1971b, 1972, 1982a). One set of sufficient conditions for the one-way linear utility representation $p \succ q \Rightarrow u(p) > u(q)$ is L3 from Section 1.4 ($p \succ q$ and $r \succ s \Rightarrow \lambda p + (1 - \lambda)r \succ \lambda q + (1 - \lambda)s$) and the following Archimedean condition mentioned near the end of Section 1.5: $(p \succ q, r \succ s) \Rightarrow \lambda p + (1 - \lambda)s \succ \lambda q + (1 - \lambda)r$ for some $0 < \lambda < 1$. The original Archimedean axiom, A3, is not sufficient along with L3 for the one-way representation (Fishburn, 1982a, p. 58).

The main axiomatization for non-Archimedean partially ordered preference in **IC**, due to Kannai (1963), was inspired by Aumann's contribution. As Kannai shows, this case is rather delicate mathematically. Under suitably strong conditions he obtains the one-way lexicographic linear utility representation $p \succ q \Rightarrow U(p) >_L U(q)$.

Fishburn (1971b, 1979) sought to reduce the linearity idea of von Neumann and Morgenstern to its lowest common denominator by assuming only asymmetry and L3. He notes that if the set X of outcomes is finite, say $|X| = m > 1$, then the one-way linear lexicographic representation holds in some dimension $n < m$. Thus, if P contains each one-point distribution and $u_i(x)$ is defined as $u_i(p)$ when $p(x) = 1$, then for some $n < m$ there are $u_i: X$

$\rightarrow$ **R** for $i = 1, \ldots, n$ such that

$$p > q \Rightarrow \left(\sum u_1(x)p(x), \ldots, \sum u_n(x)p(x) \right)$$
$$>_L \left(\sum u_1(x)q(x), \ldots, \sum u_n(x)q(x) \right).$$

When Hausner's axioms hold in this context, this one-way lexicographic expected utility representation become a two-way ($\Leftrightarrow$) representation. Uniqueness properties for the u_i in the latter case are specified in Fishburn (1982a, p. 40).

3.3 ALLAIS'S NONLINEAR INTENSITY THEORY

We shall summarize Allais's nonlinear preference theory for risky prospects on monetary outcomes before considering the other theories in category **II**. As already noted in Section 2.3, the basic carriers of value for Allais are levels of wealth, suitably interpreted, combined with potential changes in wealth. When w_0 denotes present wealth and x is a potential increment to wealth, the psychological value of the final position $w_0 + x$, conditioned on w_0, is a function of x/w_0 that is essentially the same for all people. Moreover, this function, which is assessed in a riskless comparison-of-preference-differences manner, is approximated very well by $\log(1 + x/w_0)$.

Apart from an addition noted shortly, the core of Allais's position as set forth in his early writings (1953, 1979a) and refined in (1979b), consists of the reduction principle, his viewpoint on psychological value, and the following:

1. A1: $>$ on P is a weak order.
2. Weak first-degree stochastic dominance: if $p >_1 q$ or $p = q$, then $p \gtrsim q$.
3. An Archimedean axiom sufficient to ensure the existence of $V: P \rightarrow$ **R** such that, for all $p, q \in P$, $p > q \Leftrightarrow V(p) > V(q)$.

Axioms 1 and 3 are combined in Allais's axiom for the "existence of an ordered field of choice" (1979b, p. 457), and he does not specify a separate Archimedean axiom. The existence of a countable order dense subset (Fishburn, 1970a, p. 27; Krantz et al., 1971, p. 40) would suffice for axiom 3. Axiom 2 is regarded as an acceptable weakening of the von Neumann–Morgenstern independence axiom A2. As already mentioned, Allais strongly rejects A2, believes that V cannot be decomposed into an expectational form, and does not promote an alternative algebraic decomposition for V.

Hagen (1972, 1979) elaborates on Allais's theme with some additional axioms and a focus on the first three moments (in terms of psychological value) of risky prospects as determinants of V. One of his new axioms was subsequently adopted by Allais (1979b, pp. 481, 549). This axiom says that if p' is obtained from p by replacing each x by x' such that $v(x') - v(x) = \Delta$, then $V(p') - V(p) = \Delta$. In Hagen's words (1979, p. 272), "a uniform addition to all utilities in the probability distribution of a game adds the same amount to the utility of the game." When this restriction is placed on V, it can be written as

$$V(p) = \sum v(x)p(x) + f(p^*),$$

where f is a functional and p^* denotes the probability distribution induced by p on the differences $v(x) - \Sigma v(x)p(x)$ of psychological values from their mean (Allais, 1979b, pp. 481–82, 607–9). A further refinement on this form is described in Allais (1986).

3.4 SMOOTH PREFERENCES

Machina (1982a) considers the set of cumulative distribution functions defined on a bounded interval $[0, M]$ whose elements are interpreted as levels of wealth. Thus, in his case it is appropriate to view P as the set of countably additive probability measures on the Borel field of subsets of $[0, M]$. The distribution function for $p \in P$ is p^1, where $p^1(x) = \int_0^x dp(y) = p([0, x])$.

Three of Machina's assumptions are essentially the same as axioms 1–3 for Allais in the preceding section, with axiom 2 replaced by regular first-degree stochastic dominance; that is, $(p^1(x) \leqslant q^1(x)$ for all $x \in [0, M]$ and $p^1 \neq q^1) \Rightarrow p > q$. Machina does not, however, overtly adopt the Bernoulli–Allais viewpoint on psychological value, and his formulation is phrased as a nonlinear alternative to the von Neumann–Morgenstern theory. Although we write Machina's representation as

$$p > q \Leftrightarrow V(p) > V(q)$$

with $V{:}P \to \mathbf{R}$, his V should not be confused with V of the preceding section.

The distinctive feature of Machina's approach is his assumption that V is "smooth" over P. In crude terms, this means that V changes continuously as p changes continuously and that $V(p)$ is nearly a linear functional in a neighborhood around p. More precisely, it is assumed that V is Fréchet differentiable on P with respect to the norm $\|\lambda(p - q)\| = |\lambda| \int_0^M |p^1(x) - q^1(x)| \, dx$, which defines p and q as "close together" if the integral of the absolute difference of their cumulative distributions is small.

An alternative characterization of Fréchet differentiability is obtained by writing

$$V(p) - V(q) = \int_0^M u(x; q) (dp(x) - dq(x)) + o(\|p - q\|),$$

where $u(\cdot\ ; q)$ is absolutely continuous on $[0, M]$ for each $q \in P$ and o denotes a function that equals 0 at 0 and that approaches 0 at a faster rate than the decrease in its argument as the argument goes to 0. The function $u(\cdot\ ; q)$ is Machina's *local utility function*, that is, local with respect to q. He assumes (1982a, p. 296) that $u(x; q)$ strictly increases in x, from which it follows that $>$ satisfies first-degree stochastic dominance.

If the higher-order terms summarized by o in the preceding characterization are ignored, then it reduces to essentially the von Neumann–Morgenstern expected utility form. Thus, when p and q are "close together," $>$ behaves very much like the von Neumann–Morgenstern $>$. Machina (1982a, b, 1983b, 1984) uses this to good advantage to show that many economically interesting results obtained by expected utility analysis also follow from his "generalized expected utility analysis."

In a similar vein, if $f(p^*) - f(q^*)$ in the preceding section is $o(\|p - q\|)$, then the Allais–Hagen V will emulate Bernoullian expected utility locally.

Recently, others have commented on Machina's use of Fréchet differentiability and have proposed alternative versions of "smooth" preferences over P. Allen (1987) adapts Debreu's (1972) notion of smooth preferences to the risky prospects setting, and Chew, Karni and Safra (1985) argue that Gateaux differentiability, which is weaker than Fréchet differentiability, is still strong enough to give Machina's (1982a) main results.

3.5   DECUMULATIVE REPRESENTATIONS

I refer to the final nonlinear Archimedean weak-order theories for monetary outcomes in our list (**IIC**) as "decumulative" since their representations transform decumulative probabilities defined by

$$^1p(x) = p((x, \infty)) = 1 - p^1(x).$$

The representations can also be stated in terms of transformations of cumulative probabilities, but the decumulative form seems more natural. First-degree stochastic dominance with decumulative probabilities is characterized by

$$p >_1 q \text{ if } {}^1p \neq {}^1q \text{ and } {}^1p(x) \geqslant {}^1q(x) \text{ for all } x.$$

This is equivalent to the closed-interval characterization

$$p >_1 q \text{ if } {}^1p \neq {}^1q \text{ and } p([x, \infty)) \geqslant q([x, \infty)) \text{ for all } x,$$

so that $p >_1 q$ if, for any x, p yields at least x with probability greater than or equal to q yielding at least x, with strict inequality for some x.

For convenience we assume that $X = [0, M]$ with P as defined in the preceding section. As in the two preceding sections, the decumulative representations for $(P, >)$ postulate or derive a functional V on P such that, for all $p, q \in P$,

$$p > q \Leftrightarrow V(p) > V(q).$$

What distinguishes decumulative representations is the form of V. When p is a simple measure with support $\{x_1 < x_2 < \cdots < x_n\}$ and $p_i = p(x_i)$, $\Sigma\, p_i = 1$,

$$V(p) = \sum_{j=1}^{n-1} u(x_j) \left[\tau\left(\sum_{i=j}^{n} p_i \right) - \tau\left(\sum_{i=j+1}^{n} p_i \right) \right] + u(x_n)\tau(p_n)$$

$$= u(x_1) + \sum_{j=2}^{n} [u(x_j) - u(x_{j-1})]\tau\left(\sum_{i=j}^{n} p_i \right)$$

where u, the utility function on the outcomes, is continuous and usually assumed to be strictly increasing on $[0, M]$, and τ, the probability transformation function, is a continuous nondecreasing function from $[0, 1]$ onto $[0, 1]$ with $\tau(0) = 0$ and $\tau(1) = 1$. When $\tau(\lambda) = \lambda$ for all λ, $V(p) = \Sigma\, u(x)p(x)$, the von Neumann–Morgenstern form for expected utility. Note also that $V(p) = u(x)$ when $p(x) = 1$.

Although the form of $V(p)$ for simple measures is written in the decumulative closed-interval form, with $\Sigma_j^n\, p_i = p([x_j, M])$, representations for arbitrary measures in P are usually written in the open form of ^1p as

$$V(p) = \int_0^M u(x)\, d[\tau \circ {}^1p](x) = \int_0^M \tau({}^1p(x))\, du(x),$$

where the integrals here correspond to the two lines for the simple case in the preceding paragraph. The properties of u and τ in the preceding paragraph apply also to the general case. Given these properties, including strictly increasing u, we easily see that $>$ satisfies weak first-degree stochastic dominance as expressed by axiom 2 in Section 3.3. If, in addition, τ is strictly increasing, then $>$ satisfies first-degree stochastic dominance: $p >_1 q \Rightarrow p > q$. For example, if $^1p(x) \geq {}^1q(x)$ for all x, then $\tau({}^1p(x)) \geq \tau({}^1q(x))$ for all x and, since $du > 0$, $V(p) - V(q) \geq 0$.

Thus, even though transformed probabilities are used directly in decumulative representations, their structure is designed to satisfy first-degree stochastic dominance. Hence the decumulative representations share basic ordering, Archimedean, and stochastic dominance properties with the representations of Allais and Machina.

The first axiomatization for the decumulative model is due to Quiggin (1982) although problems have been noted with his axioms (Yaari, 1987, p. 113). His representation has the special feature $\tau(\frac{1}{2}) = \frac{1}{2}$, which implies that preferences adhere to the von Neumann–Morgenstern model for simple 50-50 gambles. This restriction was subsequently removed in the axiomatizations of Chew (1984) and Segal (1984). In the general case, the axioms include weak-order, first-degree stochastic dominance, and Archimedean axioms sufficient to ensure the existence of certainty equivalents in X for each $p \in P$ and extension from simple to nonsimple measures. The key axiom for the specific form of the decumulative representation can be expressed in several ways. The following version is similar to Chew's third axiom.

Suppose n is any positive integer, $x_1 < \cdots < x_n, y_1 < \cdots < y_n, x_i \leqslant y_i$ for all i, $x_i < y_i$ for some i, $\alpha_i > 0$ for $i = 1, \ldots, n$ and $\Sigma \, \alpha_i = 1$. Define simple distributions p and q by $p(x_i) = q(y_i) = \alpha_i$ for $i = 1, \ldots, n$ (so $q >_1 p$, hence $q \succ p$). Let x^* denote the distribution with probability 1 for x, and let $c(r)$ be the certainty equivalent of measure r so that $c(r) \sim r$. Then, for all $0 < \lambda < 1$,

$$\lambda c(p)^* + (1 - \lambda)c(q)^* \sim \sum \alpha_i c(\lambda x_i^* + (1 - \lambda)y_i^*)^*.$$

This is an independence axiom for indifference applied to distributions defined on monetary equivalents of other distributions rather than on those distributions themselves. Its necessity for the decumulative representation is demonstrated as follows. Suppose the representation holds. Then, given the special structures defined earlier,

$$V(\lambda c(p)^* + (1 - \lambda)c(q)^*)$$

$$= u(c(p)) + [u(c(q)) - u(c(p))]\tau(1 - \lambda)$$

$$= V(p) + [V(q) - V(p)]\tau(1 - \lambda)$$

$$= \sum_{j=1}^{n-1} u(x_j) \left[\tau\left(\sum_{i \geqslant j} \alpha_i \right) - \tau\left(\sum_{i \geqslant j+1} \alpha_i \right) \right] + u(x_n)\tau(\alpha_n)$$

$$+ \left\{ \sum_{j=1}^{n-1} [u(y_j) - u(x_j)] \left[\tau\left(\sum_{i \geqslant j} \alpha_i \right) - \tau\left(\sum_{i \geqslant j+1} \alpha_i \right) \right] \right.$$

$$\left. + [u(y_n) - u(x_n)]\tau(\alpha_n) \right\} \tau(1 - \lambda)$$

$$= \sum_{j=1}^{n-1} \{u(x_j) + [u(y_j) - u(x_j)]\tau(1 - \lambda)\} \left[\tau\left(\sum_{i \geqslant j} \alpha_i\right)\right.$$

$$\left. - \tau\left(\sum_{i \geqslant j+1} \alpha_i\right)\right] + \{u(x_n) + [u(y_n) - u(x_n)]\tau(1 - \lambda)\}\tau(\alpha_n)$$

$$= \sum_{j=1}^{n-1} V(\lambda x_j^* + (1 - \lambda)y_j^*) \left[\tau\left(\sum_{i \geqslant j} \alpha_i\right) - \tau\left(\sum_{i \geqslant j+1} \alpha_i\right)\right]$$

$$+ V(\lambda x_n^* + (1 - \lambda)y_n^*)\tau(\alpha_n)$$

$$= V\left(\sum \alpha_i c(\lambda x_i^* + (1 - \lambda)y_i^*)^*\right).$$

The utility function u on X in the general decumulative representation is unique up to positive linear transformations, and τ is unique when $\tau(0) = 0$ and $\tau(1) = 1$.

Yaari (1987), independently of Quiggin (1982), axiomatized the decumulative representation for the special case of $u(x) = x$, so that

$$V(p) = \int_0^M \tau(^1p(x)) \, dx.$$

Part of Yaari's aim was to show that even if the underlying utility or value function on money is linear in the amount, one can characterize nonneutral risk attitudes by special properties of τ in the decumulative representation. His theory is technically interesting because it turns the von Neumann–Morgenstern theory on its side, yielding a representation that is "linear in money" rather than "linear in the probabilities." This feature allows him to use the linear utility theorem to obtain a very short proof of his own theorem.

An analysis of risk aversion in the general decumulative context is provided by Chew et al. (1987), and Karni and Safra (1987) use the decumulative model in an attempt to reconcile transitivity and the preference reversal phenomenon. Yaari (1986) explores the notion of risk aversion in an extension of his "dual theory" to the multidimensional context.

As suggested in Section 3.1, decumulative theories may have descriptive and normative problems of their own even if they avoid violations of first-degree stochastic dominance. Yaari (1987) observes that violations of linear utility that rely on linearity in the probabilities have dual violations in his theory that rely on linearity in money. One example is suggested by the common ratio effect of Section 2.5. Let $p^{(\alpha)}$ denote the risky prospect obtained from p by multiplying each of p's outcomes by $\alpha > 0$. Then Yaari's theory requires $p^{(\alpha)} \sim q^{(\alpha)}$ for all $\alpha > 0$ (within limits) when $p \sim q$, and this is unattractive descriptively and normatively.

Apart from intransitivities, reasonable violations of the general decumulative theory are less apparent. One natural thing to examine is the axiom that delineates the decumulative form. In the foregoing, this is the axiom with conclusion $\lambda c(p)^* + (1 - \lambda)c(q)^* \sim \Sigma \alpha_i c(\lambda x_i^* + (1 - \lambda)y_i^*)^*$. For the special case of $n = 2$, this axiom says that if $x_1 < x_2$, $y_1 < y_2$, $x_1 \leqslant y_1$, $x_2 \leqslant y_2$, $x_i < y_i$ for some i, $0 < \alpha < 1$, and $0 < \lambda < 1$, then

$$\lambda[c(\alpha x_1^* + (1 - \alpha)x_2^*)]^* + (1 - \lambda)[c(\alpha y_1^* + (1 - \alpha)y_2^*)]^*$$

$$\sim \alpha[c(\lambda x_1^* + (1 - \lambda)y_1^*)]^* + (1 - \alpha)[c(\lambda x_2^* + (1 - \lambda)y_2^*)]^*.$$

Even more specially, and omitting * for convenience, we require

$$\tfrac{1}{2}[c(\tfrac{1}{2}x_1 + \tfrac{1}{2}x_2)] + \tfrac{1}{2}[c(\tfrac{1}{2}y_1 + \tfrac{1}{2}y_2)]$$

$$\sim \tfrac{1}{2}[c(\tfrac{1}{2}x_1 + \tfrac{1}{2}y_1)] + \tfrac{1}{2}[c(\tfrac{1}{2}x_2 + \tfrac{1}{2}y_2)].$$

There are two problems even with this very simple case. First, it is almost surely inaccurate descriptively and is likely to be violated in some situations by careful people. Second, since it posits a second-order indifference effect, it has little direct appeal to rational intuition. A plausible example of its failure in the gains and losses setting with $(x_1, x_2, y_1, y_2) = (-\$1000, \$0, \$2000, \$2002)$ is

$$\left. \begin{array}{l} c(\tfrac{1}{2}(- \$1{,}000) + \tfrac{1}{2}(\$0)) = -\$300 \\ c(\tfrac{1}{2}(\$2{,}000) + \tfrac{1}{2}(\$2{,}002)) = \$2{,}001 \end{array} \right\}$$

$$\& \ c(\tfrac{1}{2}(- \$300) + \tfrac{1}{2}(\$2{,}001)) = \$600,$$

$$\left. \begin{array}{l} c(\tfrac{1}{2}(- \$1{,}000) + \tfrac{1}{2}(\$2{,}000)) = \$200 \\ c(\tfrac{1}{2}(\$0) + \tfrac{1}{2}(\$2{,}002)) = \$900 \end{array} \right\}$$

$$\& \ c(\tfrac{1}{2}(\$200) + \tfrac{1}{2}(\$900)) = \$450.$$

Since $[0, M]$ is often presumed to represent a rescaling of monetary outcomes that include gains and losses, the theory accommodates the setting of this example.

A somewhat different violation of the general decumulative model is suggested by Chew (1984). As a consequence of his method of assessing τ he shows that either $\tau(\lambda) = \lambda$ for all λ, in which case the representation reduces to that of von Neumann and Morgenstern, or there must be an indifference between probability distributions defined by similar mixtures of certainty equivalents such that the underlying distribution for one of the mixtures first-degree stochastically dominates the underlying distribution for the other mixture. This does not occur in the preceding example, since the underlying distributions are identical—that is, probability $\frac{1}{4}$ for each of $-\$1,000$, $\$0$, $\$2,000$, and $\$2,002$.

3.6 WEIGHTED UTILITY THEORY

This section and the next three begin our examination of nonlinear Archimedean theories with arbitrary outcomes. Each theory has been axiomatized with assumptions for $>$ on P as in the von Neumann–Morgenstern approach. The axioms will be introduced in this chapter after the functional representations are specified. Theories that assume weak order are presented in this section and the next; theories that accommodate intransitivities are discussed in Sections 3.8 and 3.9. Proofs and further discussion for the nontransitive theories are in Chapter 4, and those for the transitive theories are in Chapter 5.

It is worth reemphasizing that the theories in categories **III** and **IV**, unlike those in **II**, apply to arbitrary outcomes so that they lay claim to a degree of generality and applicability not shared by the monetary-oriented theories. In fact, as was done by von Neumann–Morgenstern and others (Section 1.3) for linear utility, outcomes need never enter our discussion when P is assumed to be a "mixture set." However, we forego this modest technical generalization and maintain the assumption that P is a convex set of probability measures defined on an algebra of subsets of X.

The following definitions for subsets of P will be used here and in ensuing chapters:

$$P^* = \{q \in P : p > q > r \text{ for some } p, r \in P\},$$

$$P_{\max} = \{p \in P : p \gtrsim q \text{ for all } q \in P\},$$

$$P_{\min} = \{p \in P : q \gtrsim p \text{ for all } q \in P\}.$$

P^* is the *preference interior* of P, and $P_{\max}$ and $P_{\min}$ are the preference-maximal and preference-minimal subsets of P, respectively. We define $(P, >)$, or just $>$, as *closed* if $P_{\max}$ and $P_{\min}$ are nonempty, *open* if $P_{\max} = P_{\min} = \varnothing$, and *half-open* otherwise. When $>$ is closed, some authors refer to it as bounded, especially when $\gtrsim$ is assumed to be a weak order. Finally, we say that $>$ is *countably bounded* if there is a countable subset Q of P such that, for all $p \in P$,

$$p \in P \Rightarrow \text{ there are } q, q' \in Q \text{ such that } q \gtrsim p \gtrsim q'.$$

If $>$ is closed, it is clearly countably bounded; otherwise, it need not be. Countable boundedness is comparable to and has much the same effect as confinal and coinitial sequences in Chew and MacCrimmon (1979).

The first nonlinear Archimedean weak-order theory for arbitrary outcomes that we consider is Chew's weighted utility theory. This was introduced in Chew and MacCrimmon (1979) and refined by Chew (1982, 1983), Fishburn (1981a, 1983a), and Nakamura (1984, 1985). Its functional representation can be specified in two basic ways. Exercising author's prerogative, I shall begin with my own characterization.

We say that $(P, >)$ has a *weighted linear representation* if there are *linear* functionals u and w on P with w nonnegative, and w strictly positive if $>$ is closed or open, such that, for all $p, q \in P$,

$$p > q \Leftrightarrow u(p)w(q) > u(q)w(p).$$

If $>$ is half-open, w might be strictly positive, but some half-open situations force w to vanish on the one of P_{min} and P_{max} that is not empty. In all cases, w must be positive throughout P^*, else with $w(q) = 0$ and $p > q > r$ we get $u(q)w(r) > 0 > u(q)w(p)$, hence $u(q) > 0 > u(q)$.

The w functional is called the *weighting function*. If it is constant, then the weighted linear representation reduces to the von Neumann–Morgenstern form with utility functional u. Otherwise, if w cannot be made constant, the weighted linear representation is not equivalent to any linear representation and, by Theorem 1.3, the independence axiom A2 must fail since A1 and A3 are easily seen to hold.

Suppose w is positive everywhere. Then, for all $p, q \in P$,

$$p > q \Leftrightarrow u(p)/w(p) > u(q)/w(q),$$

so $>$ is represented by a quotient of linear functionals with positive denominator. This form is attractive because it arranges the same argument on the same side of the inequality and gives the sense of $u(p)$ being weighted by $1/w(p)$. A related representation by quotients of probability measures for another type of utility theory is axiomatized by Bolker (1966, 1967) and Jeffrey (1978). Fishburn (1983a, pp. 301–2) provides a summary; see also Section 5.3.

Continuing with $w > 0$, define v as u/w. Then the weighted linear representation can be expressed by

$$p > q \Leftrightarrow v(p) > v(q),$$

$$v(\lambda p + (1 - \lambda)q) = \frac{\lambda w(p)v(p) + (1 - \lambda)w(q)v(q)}{\lambda w(p) + (1 - \lambda)w(q)},$$

without mention of u. This is Chew's form: v is the main utility functional, w and vw $(= u)$ are linear, and the expression for $v(\lambda p + (1 - \lambda)q)$ is the *weighted linearity property*. If w is constant, it cancels and we are left with von Neumann–Morgenstern linearity. When $>$ is closed or open, Chew's form can be used as an alternative definition of the weighted linear representation. Chew (1983) also argues that his form can be used in the general case, but this necessitates the possibility of letting $v(p) = +\infty$ or $v(p) = -\infty$ and is somewhat awkward. I refer interested readers to his paper for details.

As the original axiomatization for the weighted linear representation of Chew and MacCrimmon (1979) was refined by Chew and others, several equivalent systems of axioms emerged. I note three of these here. For convenience, we first recall some axioms from Chapter 1 and introduce a few new ones.

Ordering Axioms

A1. $\succ$ *on P is a weak order.*

A1($\sim$). $\sim$ *on P is transitive.*

Archimedean Axioms

A3. $\{p \succ q, q \succ r\} \Rightarrow \alpha p + (1 - \alpha)r \succ q \text{ and } q \succ \beta p$
$+ (1 - \beta)r \text{ for some } \alpha \text{ and } \beta \text{ in } (0, 1).$

C1. $\{p \succ q, q \succ r\} \Rightarrow q \sim \alpha p + (1 - \alpha)r$
for some $0 < \alpha < 1.$

Convexity Axioms $(0 < \lambda < 1)$

C2. $\{p \succ q, p \succsim r\} \Rightarrow p \succ \lambda q + (1 - \lambda)r,$
$\{p \sim q, p \sim r\} \Rightarrow p \sim \lambda q + (1 - \lambda)r,$
$\{q \succ p, r \succsim p\} \Rightarrow \lambda q + (1 - \lambda)r \succ p.$

C2($\succ$). $\{p \succ q, p \succsim r\} \Rightarrow p \succ \lambda q + (1 - \lambda)r,$
$\{q \succ p, r \succsim p\} \Rightarrow \lambda q + (1 - \lambda)r \succ p.$

Symmetry Axiom $(0 < \lambda < 1)$

C3. $\{p \succ q, q \succ r, p \succ r, q \sim \frac{1}{2}p + \frac{1}{2}r\}$
$\Rightarrow [\lambda p + (1 - \lambda)r \sim \frac{1}{2}p + \frac{1}{2}q$
$\Leftrightarrow \lambda r + (1 - \lambda)p \sim \frac{1}{2}r + \frac{1}{2}q].$

Weak Independence Axioms

D2. $p \sim q \Rightarrow$ *for every* $0 < \alpha < 1$ *there is a*
$0 < \beta < 1$ *such that, for every* $r \in P$, $\alpha p + (1 - \alpha)r$
$\sim \beta q + (1 - \beta)r.$

E2. $p \sim q \Rightarrow$ *there is a* $0 < \beta < 1$ *such that,*

for every $r \in P$, $\frac{1}{2}p + \frac{1}{2}r \sim \beta q + (1 - \beta)r$.

Axiom A1($\sim$) retains only the transitive indifference part of A1, and C2($\succ$) retains only the strict preference parts of convexity axiom C2. As noted in Theorem 1.4, {A1($\sim$), C1, C2} $\Rightarrow$ A1.

The symmetry axiom C3 is a way of extending the notion that q is midway in preference between p and r to other comparisons of convex combinations of p, q and r. Call q a $\succ$-*midpoint* between p and r if $p \succ r$, $p \succ q \succ r$ and $q \sim \frac{1}{2}p + \frac{1}{2}r$. Note that this is based solely on $\succ$ and does *not* entail any notion of (riskless) intensity comparisons (Section 1.2). The general principle behind C3 is that if q is a $\succ$-midpoint between p and r then every $\sim$ comparison between two measures in the convex hull of {p, q, r} will remain an $\sim$ comparison when p and r are interchanged throughout.

The form of C3 written above is a simple example of this interchange principle: If q is a $\succ$-midpoint between p and r, then $\lambda p + (1 - \lambda)r$ is a $\succ$-midpoint between p and q if and only if (interchanging p and r throughout) $\lambda r + (1 - \lambda)p$ is a $\succ$-midpoint between q and r. This is illustrated in Figure 3.1, where the arrows denote directions of decreasing preferences.

The weak independence axiom D2 was introduced in Chew and MacCrimmon (1979), and its specialization to $\alpha = \frac{1}{2}$ is used by Nakamura (1984, 1985). The intuition behind Nakamura's E2 is that, given $p \sim q$, the asymmetry reflected by the difference between the coefficients $\frac{1}{2}$ and β in the indifference statement $\frac{1}{2}p + \frac{1}{2}r \sim \beta q + (1 - \beta)r$ when r is not indifferent to p or q will be invariant to changes in r. The Herstein–Milnor independence axiom B2 of Section 1.5 is precisely E2 when $\beta = \frac{1}{2}$. Chew's D2 has a similar interpretation to E2 when α values other than $1/2$ are used for $\alpha p + (1 - \alpha)r$.

The three systems of axioms alluded to earlier that are necessary and sufficient for the weighted linear representation and are therefore mutually equivalent are

Chew: A1, A3, C2($\succ$), D2
Fishburn: A1($\sim$), C1, C2, C3
Nakamura: C1, C2, E2.

Chew's axioms are most like the von Neumann–Morgenstern axioms since they use A1 and A3, replacing A2 by the jointly weaker C2($\succ$) and D2. Fishburn uses the symmetry axiom C3 in conjunction with C1 and full convexity C2, then requires transitive indifference A1($\sim$) since C1, C2, and C3 jointly do not imply A1($\sim$). Nakamura also uses C1 and C2, but replaces A1($\sim$) and C3 by E2 to obtain an axiomatization devoid of explicit transitivity assumptions. This is similar to the set {C1, C2, B2} of Theorem 1.4, which is necessary and sufficient for linear utility. When B2 is weakened

FIGURE 3.1   Illustration of C3

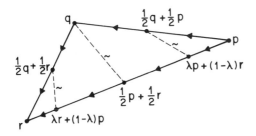

to E2, we see that $\{C1, C2, E2\}$ is necessary and sufficient for weighted linear utility. (Proofs are in Chapter 5.)

One can challenge axioms like C3, D2, and E2 in much the same way that independence was challenged in Section 2.5. Consider the following three pairs of monetary prospects:

a_1. $0 (status quo) with certainty,
b_1. 50% chance to win $2,000, 50% chance to lose $1,000;

a_2. 50% chance to win $2,000, nothing otherwise,
b_2. 80% chance to win $2,000, 20% chance to lose $1,000;

a_3. 50% chance to lose $1,000, nothing otherwise,
b_3. 70% chance to lose $1,000, 30% chance to win $2,000.

Suppose a person has $a_i \sim b_i$ for each i, which does not seem unreasonable. Then, under usual monotonicity assumptions such as first-degree stochastic dominance, C3 and E2 are violated. For C3 let p, q, and r have probability 1 for $2,000, $0, and $-$1,000, respectively. Then the hypotheses of C3 hold, but $\lambda = 0.8$ for $\lambda p + (1 - \lambda)r \sim \frac{1}{2}p + \frac{1}{2}q$ and $\lambda = 0.7$ for $\lambda r + (1 - \lambda)p \sim \frac{1}{2}r + \frac{1}{2}q$. For E2 let $p(\$0) = 1$ and $q(\$2,000) = q(-\$1,000) = \frac{1}{2}$. Then $\beta = 0.4$ for the conclusion of E2 when $r(\$2,000) = 1$, and $\beta = 0.6$ when $r(-\$1,000) = 1$.

Generalizations of weighted linear utility are discussed by Nakamura (1984) and Chew (1985). Nakamura axiomatizes weighted linear utility for the multilinear context (Fishburn, 1982a, Chapter 7) in which $>$ is defined on the Cartesian product $P_1 \times P_2 \times \cdots \times P_n$ of convex sets of probability measures and linearity is to apply to each P_i when $p_j = q_j$ for all $j \neq i$. This is especially relevant to the n-person game situation in which P_i denotes the set of mixed strategies for player i. Chew (1985) axiomatizes a semiweighted form that uses two weighting functions on X, say w^- and w^+. In the semiweighted expression for $v(p)$ with p simple, w^- applies if x is less preferred than p, and w^+ applies otherwise:

$$v(p) = \frac{\Sigma_{x<p}p(x)w^-(x)v(x) + \Sigma_{x\geq p}p(x)w^+(x)v(x)}{\Sigma_{x<p}p(x)w^-(x) + \Sigma_{x\geq p}p(x)w^+(x)}.$$

This reduces to Chew's original weighted form if $w^- = w^+$.

3.7 TRANSITIVE CONVEXITY

This section and the next two consider weakenings of weighted utility theory. In terms of the set $\{A1(\sim), C1, C2, C3\}$ for the weighted linear representation, the present section drops symmetry (C3), the next section drops $A1(\sim)$ as well, then Section 3.9 restores C3 but not $A1(\sim)$.

We say that $(P, >)$ has a *transitive convex representation* if there is an order-preserving functional u on P such that, for all $p, q \in P$,

$$p > q \Rightarrow u(\lambda p + (1 - \lambda)q) \text{ is continuous and increasing in } \lambda.$$

This entails

$$p \sim q \Rightarrow u(\lambda p + (1 - \lambda)q) \text{ is constant in } \lambda,$$

for if, say, $\lambda p + (1 - \lambda)q > q \sim p$, then

$$\lambda p + (1 - \lambda)q > (\lambda/2)p + (1 - \lambda/2)q > p \sim q,$$

but the second $>$ gives

$$(\lambda/2)p + (1 - \lambda/2)q > \lambda p + (1 - \lambda)q > p$$

for a contradiction of asymmetry.

This is the weakest *weak-order* representation that we shall consider in ensuing chapters. It is not, however, weaker than some theories discussed earlier. In particular, the monetary theories in category **II** do not generally assume monotonicity conditions such as L1 and L4 of Section 1.4, and these conditions are implied by the transitive convex representation.

The following observations are from Fishburn (1983a, b). If $>$ is closed, or bounded ($P_{max} \neq \varnothing, P_{min} \neq \varnothing$), then $(P, >)$ has a transitive convex representation if and only if axioms $A1(\sim)$, C1, and C2 hold. If $>$ is not closed, we also require $>$ to be countably bounded (Section 3.6) since this is necessary for the representation but is not implied by $A1(\sim)$, C1, and C2.

Chew (1985) and Dekel (1986) obtain the transitive convex representation from other axioms under the assumption that $>$ is closed. Chew uses A1, the Herstein–Milnor continuity axiom B3 of Section 1.5 (in its open-set form), and the following weakening of D2:

D2W. $p \sim q \Rightarrow$ *for every* $0 < \alpha < 1$ *and every* $r \in P$ *there is a* $0 < \beta < 1$ *such that* $\alpha p + (1 - \alpha)r \sim \beta q + (1 - \beta)r$.

Dekel assumes that X is a compact metric space and uses A1, C1, and the monotonicity axioms L1 and L4. He characterizes transitive convex utilities $u(p)$ implicitly as the unique solutions of

$$\int_X \psi(x, u(p))\, dp(x) = u(p),$$

where ψ increases in the induced preference order over its first argument and is continuous in its second argument. In this simplified form, Dekel notes that $\psi(x_{min}, \cdot) \equiv 0$ and $\psi(x_{max}, \cdot) \equiv 1$, where $x_{max} \succeq p \succeq x_{min}$ for all p. The expected utility form is the special case of his representation in which $\psi(x, u(p)) = u(x)$.

Dekel first obtains the preceding representation when P is the set of simple probability measures on X. He then extends it to all countably additive measures on the Borel field of X by strengthening C1 to B3.

3.8 NONTRANSITIVE CONVEXITY

When transitivity is dropped, it is no longer possible to represent preferences in the familiar $p \succ q \Leftrightarrow u(p) > u(q)$ form. There is, however, a simple way to represent $\succ$ numerically in the presence of intransitivities and preference cycles, namely to adopt a two-argument functional ϕ on $P \times P$ with $p \succ q \Leftrightarrow \phi(p, q) > 0$. With no other restrictions on ϕ this representation is uninteresting since it holds universally with $\phi(p, q) = 1$ when $p \succ q$ and $\phi(p, q) = 0$ otherwise. On the other hand, it can be very demanding when restrictions are imposed on ϕ. For example, if we require ϕ to be decomposable as $\phi(p, q) = u(p) - u(q)$ with u linear, then it represents von Neumann–Morgenstern preferences.

We consider two nontransitive versions of the ϕ representation. A nontransitive convex form is outlined here; the SSB form is discussed in the next section.

We say that $(P, \succ)$ has a *nontransitive convex representation* if there is a functional ϕ on $P \times P$ such that, for all $p, q, r \in P$ and all $0 < \lambda < 1$,

$$p \succ q \Leftrightarrow \phi(p, q) > 0,$$

$$\phi(p, q) > 0 \Leftrightarrow \phi(q, p) < 0,$$

$$\phi(\lambda p + (1 - \lambda)q, r) = \lambda \phi(p, r) + (1 - \lambda)\phi(q, r).$$

The second expression is an asymmetry property for ϕ. By the definition of $\sim$, $p \sim q \Leftrightarrow \phi(p, q) = \phi(q, p) = 0$. The final expression says that ϕ is *linear in its first argument.*

This representation can also be thought of as a conditional linear representation. Let v_q be defined by

$$v_q(p) = \phi(p, q).$$

Then the nontransitive convex representation says that each v_q is a linear functional on P with $p \succ q \Leftrightarrow v_q(p) > 0 \Leftrightarrow v_p(q) < 0$.

When $\succ$ is open, so that $P^* = P$, $(P, \succ)$ has a nontransitive convex representation if and only if C1 and C2 hold. Moreover, each v_q or $\phi(\cdot\, , q)$ is *unique up to similarity transformations*; that is, given $\{v_q\}$ that satisfy the representation, $\{v_q'\}$ also satisfy the representation if and only if for each q there is positive a_q such that

$$v_q'(p) = a_q v_q(p) \qquad \text{for all } p \in P.$$

Similarity transformations are also referred to as multiplicative transformations or proportionality transformations.

Comments on the nontransitive convex representation for cases in which P is closed or half-open will be deferred to Section 4.3.

3.9   SSB UTILITY THEORY

The functional ϕ on $P \times P$ is *skew-symmetric* if

$$\phi(q, p) = -\phi(p, q)$$

for all $p, q \in P$. If this property is added to those for the nontransitive convex representation of the preceding section, then ϕ is linear also in its second argument:

$$\phi(r, \lambda p + (1 - \lambda)q) = \lambda \phi(r, p) + (1 - \lambda)\phi(r, q).$$

When ϕ is linear separately in each argument, it is said to be *bilinear*, and it is called an *SSB functional* if it is skew-symmetric and bilinear.

We say that $(P, \succ)$ has an *SSB representation* if there is an SSB functional ϕ on $P \times P$ such that, for all $p, q, \in P$,

$$p \succ q \Leftrightarrow \phi(p, q) > 0.$$

Thus, $(P, \succ)$ has an SSB representation precisely when it has a nontransitive convex representation in which ϕ is skew-symmetric.

It is known (Fishburn, 1982c) that $(P, \succ)$ has an SSB representation if and only if C1, C2, and the symmetry axiom C3 hold. This will be proved in the next chapter along with the uniqueness property for the SSB utility function ϕ, which says that ϕ is unique up to similarity transformations.

The SSB representation was previously discussed by Kreweras (1961), who proved two important theorems for SSB utilities concerning the existence of maximally preferred prospects and the existence of Nash equilibria in noncooperative n-person games whose players have SSB instead of von Neumann–Morgenstern utilities. We consider these in Chapter 6.

Suppose $\phi(p, q) = \phi(q, r) > 0$. Then by skew-symmetry,

$$\tfrac{1}{2}\phi(p, q) + \tfrac{1}{2}\phi(r, q) = 0,$$

and by linearity in the first argument,

$$\phi(\tfrac{1}{2}p + \tfrac{1}{2}r, q) = 0,$$

which by the SSB representation says that $\tfrac{1}{2}p + \tfrac{1}{2}r \sim q$. One might therefore think of $\phi(p, q)$ and $\phi(q, r)$ as representing equal increments of preference for p over q and for q over r. However, as in the case of von Neumann–Morgenstern utilities, this must be qualified by the fact that the equality is obtained within the probabilistic setting, and it does not mean that the preference intensity for p over q equals that for q over r in the sense of Bernoulli or Allais. Moreover, when $\phi(p, q)$ and $\phi(q, r)$ are both positive in the SSB representation, this does not imply $\phi(p, r) > 0$ since it is quite possible to have $\phi(r, p) > 0$ for the preference cycle $p \succ q \succ r \succ p$. Thus, in the language used to describe C3 in Section 3.6, $\phi(p, q) = \phi(q, r) > 0$ and therefore $q \sim \tfrac{1}{2}p + \tfrac{1}{2}r$ characterize q as a $\succ$-midpoint between p and r only if $p \succ r$.

On the other hand, one can use the SSB representation with a riskless intensity interpretation for $\phi(x, y)$, as done by Bell (1982) and Loomes and Sugden (1982) in the states setting of Chapter 7. Suppose in the present context that preference intensities or strength-of-preference differences for outcome pairs are measured by a functional ϕ on $X \times X$ with

$$(x, y) \succ^* (z, w) \Leftrightarrow \phi(x, y) > \phi(z, w)$$

and with ϕ skew-symmetric on $X \times X$, which is perfectly natural in the intensity mode. Even though $\succ^*$ is a weak order on $X \times X$, there is nothing inherent in this approach that requires $\succ$ to be transitive on X, so there can be basic preference cycles (Fishburn, 1986a). Given ϕ on $X \times X$, we extend it bilinearly to pairs of simple measures in $P \times P$, *defining* $\phi(p, q)$ by

$$\phi(p, q) = \sum_x \sum_y p(x)q(y)\phi(x, y).$$

Then, in the manner of Bernoulli, we can postulate that p is more desirable than q precisely when $\phi(p, q) > 0$. In fact, this is precisely the approach taken by Bernoulli when ϕ happens to have the separable form $\phi(x, y) = v(x) - v(y)$, since then $\phi(p, q) = \Sigma\, p(x)v(x) - \Sigma\, q(x)v(x)$ by the bilinear extension.

The extension process can be reversed when $\phi(p, q)$ is obtained for the SSB representation through axioms C1, C2, and C3. Given the SSB functional ϕ on $P \times P$, define ϕ on $X \times X$ by

$$\phi(x, y) = \phi(p, q) \qquad \text{when } p(x) = q(y) = 1.$$

Then, by Theorem 1.2 we have

$$\phi(p, q) = \phi \left(\sum_x p(x)x^*, q \right) = \sum_x p(x)\phi(x^*, q)$$

$$= \sum_x p(x)\phi \left(x^*, \sum_y q(y)y^* \right)$$

$$= \sum_x p(x) \sum_y q(y)\phi(x^*, y^*)$$

$$= \sum_x \sum_y p(x)q(y)\phi(x, y)$$

for simple measures p and q. In other words, for SSB utilities and simple measures, $\phi(p, q)$ is the expected value of $\phi(x, y)$ with respect to the product measure $p \times q$. The extension of this expectation to the integral form

$$\phi(p, q) = \int\int \phi(x, y) \, dp(x) \, dq(y)$$

will be considered at the end of the next chapter.

3.10   ACCOMMODATION OF INDEPENDENCE VIOLATIONS

Figure 3.2 illustrates differences among linear utility and the theories in categories **II** through **IV** with indifference lines through the convex hull

$$H(\{p, q, r\}) = \left\{ \lambda_1 p + \lambda_2 q + \lambda_3 r : \lambda_i \geq 0, \sum \lambda_i = 1 \right\}$$

of measures p, q, and r represented barycentrically. Each point in H corresponds to a point in an equilateral triangle with vertices p, q, and r. When the perpendicular distance from each side to its opposite vertex is 1, $\lambda_1 p + \lambda_2 q + \lambda_3 r$ is the point with perpendicular distances λ_1, λ_2, and λ_3 from sides qr, pr, and pq, respectively. Selected points are described in the top triangle.

A common orientation for the lower six diagrams is provided by assuming in each case that $p \succ q$, $q \succ r$, and $q \sim \frac{2}{3}p + \frac{1}{3}r$. All points on a line within a triangle are mutually indifferent. The arrows show directions of decreasing preference. The lower right triangle has $r \succ p$ for the preference cycle $p \succ q \succ r \succ p$. The other five have $p \succ r$ for cases in which $\succ$ is a weak order on H.

The key differences between the indifference maps in H for our theories are as follows. The indifference lines for von Neumann–Morgenstern linear

FIGURE 3.2   Indifference lines

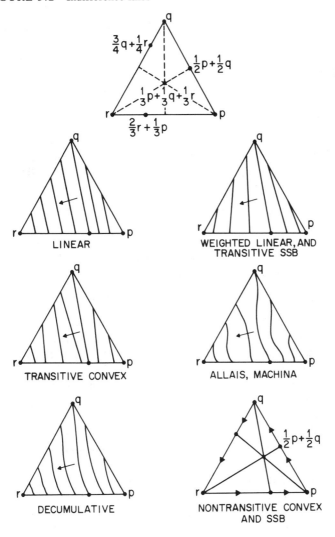

utility are parallel straight lines. Those for weighted linear utility (**IIIA**, Section 3.6) and, equivalently, SSB when $p > r$, are also straight lines; when w is not constant, these lines intersect at a common point outside the triangle. For the right-hand diagram in the second row of the figure, the common point lies above q and slightly to the left of the vertical through q. Transitive convex utility (**IIIB**, Section 3.7) also has straight indifference lines that do not touch or intersect within the triangle, but since it does not presume the symmetry axiom there is no other restriction on the slopes of its indifference lines.

Theories in category **II** allow curvilinear indifference lines. The theories of Allais and Machina (**IIA-B**, Sections 3.3 and 3.4) are shown with wavy indifference lines in the middle right diagram. Since decumulative theories (**IIC**, Section 3.5) use a separable algebraic form for $V(p)$, there must be more regularity in their indifference lines as suggested in the lower left diagram of Figure 3.2.

The cyclic preference case for SSB utilities is shown in the lower right of the figure. Given $p > q > r > p$ with $q \sim \frac{2}{3}p + \frac{1}{3}r$, suppose also that $r \sim \frac{1}{2}p + \frac{1}{2}q$. Then the third indifference line from a vertex, namely p, to the opposite side *must* pass through the intersection point of the other two indifference lines through vertices. For the particular case of the figure,

$$q \sim \tfrac{2}{3}p + \tfrac{1}{3}r \Leftrightarrow 2\phi(p, q) = \phi(q, r),$$

$$r \sim \tfrac{1}{2}p + \tfrac{1}{2}q \Leftrightarrow \phi(r, p) = \phi(q, r).$$

Therefore $2\phi(p, q) = \phi(r, p)$; hence $p \sim \frac{2}{3}q + \frac{1}{3}r$. The common intersection point $\lambda_1^* p + \lambda_2^* q + \lambda_3^* r$ has

$$\lambda_1^* = \phi(q, r)/d, \qquad \lambda_2^* = \phi(r, p)/d, \qquad \lambda_3^* = \phi(p, q)/d,$$

with $d = \phi(p, q) + \phi(q, r) + \phi(r, p)$. This point is indifferent to all other points in $H(\{p, q, r\})$ by the indifference part of C2, so it is both a maximal preference point and a minimal preference point in H that is contained in every indifference line through H. When preferences cycle on $\{p, q, r\}$, the nontransitive convex representation of Section 3.8 is equivalent to the SSB representation on H because C3 is implied by C1 and C2 for this case; otherwise, when $p > r$, the transitive and nontransitive representations are equivalent on H.

All nonlinear theories illustrated in Figure 3.2 accommodate violations of standard independence axioms such as A2 and B2 (Section 1.5). Since these theories were partly designed to accommodate Allais-type violations of independence associated with the certainty, common ratio, and common consequences effects of Section 2.5, their authors usually mention this, but only briefly in most cases. The most eloquent spokesman of independence violations is Machina (1982a, pp. 302–306; 1983a, b, 1985). Machina observes that the most common independence violations are described by indifference lines that fan out from a "central vertex line" such as the one from q to $\frac{1}{3}r + \frac{2}{3}p$ on Figure 3.2. When the indifference lines for $\{p > q > r, p > r\}$ are straight, we get the picture for weighted linear utility shown in the figure. The predominance of this form of weighted utility is corroborated by experiments reported in Chew and Waller (1986). When the lines are curved, as allowed by category **II** theories, a similar picture obtains with bowed lines that tend to spread out as we come down toward the rp boundary. Machina (1985, p. 579) also cites experimental evidence that suggests that the straight-line indifference hypothesis is often violated.

For a simple example, suppose weighted linear utility theory applies with

$$x = \$5000 \qquad p(x) = 1 \qquad u(x) = 1 \qquad w(x) = 4$$

$$y = \$3000 \qquad q(y) = 1 \qquad u(y) = 3/5 \qquad w(y) = 3$$

$$z = \$0 \qquad r(z) = 1 \qquad u(z) = 0 \qquad w(z) = 2.$$

Then $y \sim \frac{2}{3}x^* + \frac{1}{3}z^*$, since

$$u(y)[2w(x) + w(z)] = 6 = [2u(x) + u(z)]w(y).$$

In addition,

$$\tfrac{1}{2}x^* + \tfrac{1}{2}y^* \sim \tfrac{16}{19}x^* + \tfrac{3}{19}z^*, \qquad \tfrac{16}{19} = 0.842. . . ,$$

$$\tfrac{1}{2}y^* + \tfrac{1}{2}z^* \sim \tfrac{6}{19}x^* + \tfrac{13}{19}z^*, \qquad \tfrac{6}{19} = 0.316. . . ,$$

so that this case approximates the weighted linear picture in Figure 3.2. If utilities were linear with $y \sim \frac{2}{3}x^* + \frac{1}{3}z^*$, then the leading coefficients on the right sides of the preceding indifferences would be $\frac{5}{6}$ instead of $0.842 . . .$ and $\frac{1}{3}$ instead of $0.316 . . . .$ With the weighted linear model,

$$\tfrac{1}{2}y^* + \tfrac{1}{2}x^* > \tfrac{1}{2}(\tfrac{2}{3}x^* + \tfrac{1}{3}z^*) + \tfrac{1}{2}x^*,$$

$$\tfrac{1}{2}(\tfrac{2}{3}x^* + \tfrac{1}{3}z^*) + \tfrac{1}{2}z^* > \tfrac{1}{2}y^* + \tfrac{1}{2}z^*$$

for a violation of B2.

To illustrate independence accommodation in the general SSB context of the preceding section with nonnegative monetary outcomes, suppose $X = [0, \infty)$ and

$$\phi(x, y) = (x - y)f(y) \qquad \text{for } x \geqslant y \geqslant 0$$

with f positive, continuous and decreasing. Thus the "preference differential" for x over y is a weighted difference of the outcomes, the weight $f(y)$ depending only on the smaller outcome. Suppose $\lim f(x) < f(0)/2$, and let y be the unique outcome with $f(y) = f(0)/2$. Consider gambles

$$p(\lambda) : y \text{ with probability } \lambda, \ 0 \text{ otherwise,}$$

$$q_\alpha(\lambda) : 2y \text{ with probability } \alpha\lambda, \ 0 \text{ otherwise,}$$

with $0 < \alpha < 1$. Under bilinear extension and skew-symmetry,

$$\phi(p(\lambda), q_\alpha(\lambda)) = \alpha\lambda^2\phi(y, 2y) + \lambda(1 - \alpha\lambda)\phi(y, 0)$$
$$+ (1 - \lambda)\alpha\lambda\phi(0, 2y) + (1 - \lambda)(1 - \alpha\lambda)\phi(0, 0)$$
$$= (\alpha\lambda - 4\alpha + 2)\lambda y f(0)/2.$$

If $\lambda = 1$, then $p(1) \succ q_\alpha(1)$ for each $\alpha < 2/3$, so y as a sure thing is preferred to a gamble with probability α for $2y$ so long as $\alpha < \frac{2}{3}$. Moreover, with α fixed and $\frac{1}{2} < \alpha < \frac{2}{3}$,

$$p(\lambda) \succ q_\alpha(\lambda) \qquad \text{for } \lambda > 4 - 2/\alpha,$$

$$p(\lambda) \sim q_\alpha(\lambda) \qquad \text{for } \lambda = 4 - 2/\alpha,$$

$$q_\alpha(\lambda) \succ p(\lambda) \qquad \text{for } \lambda < 4 - 2/\alpha.$$

This is an example of the common ratio effect since the ratio of the positive payoff probabilities, $\lambda/(\alpha\lambda) = 1/\alpha$, does not change as λ varies over $(0, 1]$.

3.11 INTRANSITIVITY ACCOMMODATION

Since the SSB theory makes no demands on ϕ on $X \times X$ other than skew-symmetry, it accommodates cyclic preferences over outcomes in a straightforward manner. For example, May's (1954) preference cycle $x \succ y \succ z \succ x$ of Section 2.7 is reflected by $\phi(x, y) > 0$, $\phi(y, z) > 0$, and $\phi(z, x) > 0$. But, as noted in the preceding section, there will still be a distribution p^* in the convex hull $H(\{x^*, y^*, z^*\})$ of the one-point measures for x, y, and z such that $p^* \succeq p$ for every $p \in H$.

It is also entirely possible for $\succ$ to be a weak order on X while $\succ$ on P has intransitivities. In other words, with

$$\phi(p, q) = \sum_x \sum_y p(x)q(y)\phi(x, y)$$

for simple measures p and q, skew-symmetry for ϕ on $X \times X$ induces skew-symmetry for ϕ on $P \times P$, but negative transitivity for $\succ$ on $X \times X$—that is, $\phi(x, y) > 0 \Rightarrow (\phi(x, z) > 0 \text{ or } \phi(z, y) > 0)$—does not induce negative transitivity for $\succ$ on $P \times P$. Fishburn (1984a) shows how the preference cycles of Section 2.7 that use monetary outcomes and percentage raises in salary can be accounted for by the SSB representation even when $\phi(x, y)$ depends only on the difference between x and y. Consider, for example, the short cycle $[6, 0.90] \succ [8, 0.72] \succ [10, 0.61] \succ [6, 0.90]$ for the salary situation, where $[x, \lambda]$ is the gamble that gives you an $x\%$ raise with probability λ, and no raise otherwise. Suppose $\phi(x, y) = v(x - y)$, $x \geq y$, with $(v(2), v(4), v(6), v(8), v(10)) = (1.2, 3, 6, 8, 9.8)$; see Figure 3.3. Then $\phi([6, 0.90], [8, 0.72]) = 0.1584$, $\phi([8, 0.72], [10, 0.61]) = 0.04552$, $\phi([10,$

FIGURE 3.3

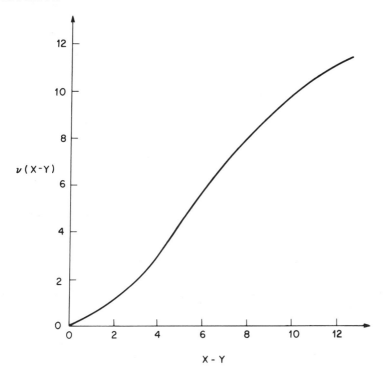

0.61], [6, 0.90)] $= 0.1388$, so ϕ is positive for each successive pair in the cycle.

Weak order for $>$ on monetary X without entailing transitivity of $>$ on P also accounts for the preference reversal phenomenon of Section 2.8 as shown by Bell (1982), Loomes and Sugden (1983), and Fishburn (1984a, 1985b). In the monetary context we assume that $x > y \Rightarrow \phi(x, y) > 0$, so $>$ on X is the natural linear order. It is also natural to assume that ϕ is nondecreasing in its first argument so that

$$x > y \Rightarrow \phi(x, z) \geqslant \phi(y, z) \qquad \text{for all } x, y, z \in X.$$

This additional condition allows weak reversals but prohibits strong reversals. To consider the strong reversal prohibition, recall that the typical form of preference reversal is $p > q$ and $c(p) < c(q)$ with p the probability lottery, q the money lottery, and $m = \max\{x : p(x) > 0\}$, $p(m) > \Sigma \{q(x) : x > m\} > 0$. The reversal is *strong* if $c(q) \geqslant m$. Given a strong reversal, the SSB representation and the assumption that ϕ is nondecreasing in its first argument on $X \times X$ imply

$$0 < \sum_x \sum_y \phi(x, y)p(x)q(y) \qquad \text{by } p > q$$

$$\leqslant \sum_x \sum_y \phi(m, y)p(x)q(y) \qquad \text{by } \phi(m, y) \geqslant \phi(x, y)$$

$$= \sum_y \phi(m, y)q(y)$$

$$\leqslant \sum_y \phi(c(q), y)q(y) \qquad \text{by } c(q) \geqslant m$$

$$= 0 \qquad \text{by } c(q) \sim q.$$

Hence $0 < 0$, which is absurd.

To simplify our examination of weak reversals, suppose p and q are two-outcome prospects with

$$\begin{array}{ll} p(m) = \alpha, \quad p(0) = 1 - \alpha, \\ q(M) = \beta, \quad q(0) = 1 - \beta, \end{array} \qquad 0 < m < M, \ \alpha > \beta > 0.$$

Suppose $p > q$ and $c(p) < c(q)$. Then, by decreasing M or β or both continuously, we can reach a point where q thus modified satisfies $p > q$ and $c(p) = c(q)$. We refer to this as the *boundary case* for preference reversal and will proceed with this case because of its analytical tractability. Thus, suppose $p > q$ and $c(p) = c(q) = x$. Then, by the SSB representation,

$$\phi(p, q) = \alpha\beta\phi(m, M) + \alpha(1 - \beta)\phi(m, 0)$$
$$+ (1 - \alpha)\beta\phi(0, M) > 0,$$

$$\phi(p, x) = \alpha\phi(m, x) + (1 - \alpha)\phi(0, x) = 0,$$

$$\phi(q, x) = \beta\phi(M, x) + (1 - \beta)\phi(0, x) = 0.$$

When the inequality for $\phi(p, q)$ is divided by $\alpha\beta$ and substitutions are made therein from the equations for $p \sim x$ and $q \sim x$, the inequality $\phi(p, q) > 0$ can be rewritten as

$$(*) \qquad \phi(M, x)\phi(m, 0) > \phi(M, 0)\phi(m, x) + \phi(M, m)\phi(x, 0).$$

When this inequality holds, we can reverse the process to recover p and q by way of $(1 - \alpha)/\alpha = \phi(m, x)/\phi(x, 0)$ and $(1 - \beta)/\beta = \phi(M, x)/\phi(x, 0)$. In other words, each instance of the boundary case $p > q$ and $c(p) = c(q) = x$ is precisely captured by an inequality like $(*)$. Consequently, weak reversals will arise for the simple two-outcome prospects p and q if and only if $(*)$ holds for values of x, m, and M that satisfy $0 < x < m < M$.

We illustrate $(*)$ with ϕ functions similar to those discussed in the preceding section. Suppose first that

$$\phi(a, b) = [g(a) - g(b)]f(b) \qquad \text{for } a \geqslant b \geqslant 0$$

with g strictly increasing and f positive, continuous, and decreasing. When this form is used in (*), that inequality reduces to $1 > f(m)/f(x)$, which is true since f is assumed to be decreasing. Hence our first form for $\phi(a, b)$ guarantees weak reversals in abundance.

Suppose next that $\phi(a, b)$ is a simple power function of the difference between a and b:

$$\phi(a, b) = (a - b)^\gamma \qquad \text{for } a \geqslant b \geqslant 0$$

with $\gamma > 0$. Then (*) always holds when $\gamma > 1$, but it cannot hold when $\gamma \leqslant 1$.

Also note that (*) can never hold when $>$ on P is a weak order, which is as it should be since weak order on P prohibits the preference reversal phenomenon. As will be shown in Chapter 5, if ϕ is an SSB functional on $P \times P$ with $p > q \Leftrightarrow \phi(p, q) > 0$, and if $>$ on P is a weak order, then there are linear functionals u and $w \geqslant 0$ on P such that

$$\phi(p, q) = u(p)w(q) - u(q)w(p),$$

thus giving the weighted linear representation of Section 3.6. When $\phi(a, b) = u(a)w(b) - u(b)w(a)$, substitution in (*) and cancellation leaves $0 > 0$.

3.12   SUMMARY

Generalizations of the expected utility theories of Bernoulli and von Neumann–Morgenstern are conveniently partitioned into four main categories:

I. Theories that preserve linearity
II. Nonlinear Archimedean weak-order theories designed for monetary outcomes
III. Nonlinear Archimedean weak-order theories designed for arbitrary outcomes
IV. Nonlinear nontransitive Archimedean theories

The theories in category **I** do not accommodate common violations of independence and are included mainly for historical continuity. They are not discussed later. The theories in categories **II–IV** were all designed to account for independence violations. Those in category **II** will receive scant attention later, due in part to their concentration on particular types of outcomes and in part to their broad generality and attendant lack of clear axiomatization. This should not be interpreted negatively since these theories, especially as set forth by Allais and Machina, hold significant promise for the monetary context. However, the emphases of ensuing chapters lie elsewhere, and I encourage readers to consult the primary sources for category **II**.

All category **III** and **IV** theories were developed for arbitrary outcomes and share the axioms of continuity and convexity, C1 and C2, introduced in Section 1.5. The four main theories of **III** and **IV** are distinguished by whether they presume A1($\sim$) or C3:

A1($\sim$)?	C3?	Theory
No	No	Nontransitive convex
No	Yes	SSB
Yes	No	Transitive convex
Yes	Yes	Weighted linear

The two cases that do not assume A1($\sim$), which are the only theories described in this chapter that avoid transitivity and hence accommodate preference reversals, are examined in detail in the next chapter; the other two are analyzed in Chapter 5.

4 Nontransitive Nonlinear Utility Theory

The preference axioms for the SSB utility representation are easily stated, but it is no easy matter to show that they imply the representation. The principal aim of this chapter is to develop a series of lemmas from the SSB axioms and to construct the representation on the basis of the lemmas. The nontransitive convex representation will be considered along the way, and the final section shows what is needed to extend the SSB expectational form to pairs of nonsimple measures.

4.1 THE SSB THEOREM

The main purpose of this chapter is to prove the fundamental SSB representation and uniqueness theorem. For convenience we recall the SSB properties,

skew-symmetry: $\phi(q, p) = -\phi(p, q)$
bilinearity: ϕ is linear in each argument

and restate the SSB axioms: for all p, q, $r \in P$ and all $0 < \lambda < 1$,

C1. Continuity: $p > q > r \Rightarrow q \sim \alpha p + (1 - \alpha)r$ *for some* $0 < \alpha < 1$;

C2. Convexity: $\{p > q, p \gtrsim r\} \Rightarrow p > \lambda q + (1 - \lambda)r$,
$\{p \sim q, p \sim r\} \Rightarrow p \sim \lambda q + (1 - \lambda)r$,
$\{q > p, r \gtrsim p\} \Rightarrow \lambda q + (1 - \lambda)r > p$;

C3. Symmetry:

$$\{p > q > r, p > r, q \sim \tfrac{1}{2}p + \tfrac{1}{2}r\}$$
$$\Rightarrow [\lambda p + (1 - \lambda)r \sim \tfrac{1}{2}p + \tfrac{1}{2}q$$
$$\Leftrightarrow \lambda r + (1 - \lambda)p \sim \tfrac{1}{2}r + \tfrac{1}{2}q].$$

See Sections 1.5 and 3.6 for discussion of C1–C3.

THEOREM 4.1. *Suppose P is a nonempty convex set of probability measures defined on a Boolean algebra of subsets of X, and* $>$ *is a binary relation on P. Then axioms* C1, C2, *and* C3 *hold if and only if there is an SSB functional* ϕ *on* $P \times P$ *such that, for all* $p, q \in P, p > q$ $\leftrightarrow \phi(p, q) > 0$. *Moreover, such a* ϕ *is unique up to multiplication by a positive constant.*

The uniqueness conclusion says that ϕ is unique up to similarity transformations or proportionality transformations, or, to use Stevens's (1946) term, that ϕ is measured on a ratio scale. That is, if ϕ is one SSB functional on $P \times P$ for which $> = \{(p, q):\phi(p, q) > 0\}$, then ϕ' is another such functional if and only if there is a $c > 0$ such that $\phi'(p, q) = c\phi(p, q)$ for all $p, q \in P$.

The necessity of the SSB axioms for the representation of Theorem 4.1 is easily verified. For C3, suppose the representation holds with $p > q > r, p > r$, and $q \sim \frac{1}{2}p + \frac{1}{2}r$ as in the hypotheses of C3. If $\lambda p + (1 - \lambda)r \sim \frac{1}{2}p + \frac{1}{2}q$ also, then

$$0 = \phi(\lambda p + (1 - \lambda)r, \tfrac{1}{2}p + \tfrac{1}{2}q)$$

$$= \tfrac{1}{2}[\lambda\phi(p, q) + (1 - \lambda)\phi(r, p) + (1 - \lambda)\phi(r, q)]$$

$$= [-(1 - \lambda)\phi(p, q) + \phi(p, q) - (1 - \lambda)\phi(p, r)$$

$$\quad - \lambda\phi(r, q) + \phi(r, q)]/2$$

$$= -\tfrac{1}{2}[\lambda\phi(r, q) + (1 - \lambda)\phi(p, r) + (1 - \lambda)\phi(p, q)]$$

$$= -\phi(\lambda r + (1 - \lambda)p, \tfrac{1}{2}r + \tfrac{1}{2}q),$$

so $\lambda r + (1 - \lambda)p \sim \frac{1}{2}r + \frac{1}{2}q$. Necessity proofs of C1 and C2 are included in Section 4.3.

Henceforth in this chapter we focus on the sufficiency proof for the SSB representation and on the uniqueness of ϕ in that representation. The next three sections deal solely with implications of C1 and C2, including comments on the nontransitive convex representation in Section 4.3. Implications that follow from the addition of the symmetry axiom C3 are noted in Sections 4.5 and 4.6, and the sufficiency proof is completed in Section 4.7. The final section considers the extension of the SSB expectational form from simple measures to all measures in P.

4.2 PRELIMINARY LEMMAS

Axioms C1 *and* C2 *are assumed to hold throughout this section along with the initial hypotheses of Theorem* 4.1. As in Section 3.6, P^*, P_{max}, and P_{min} denote the preference interior of P, the preference-maximal subset of P, and the preference-minimal subset of P, respectively. Thus $P^* = \{p{:}q \succ p \succ r \text{ for some } q, r\}$, $P_{\max} = \{p{:}q \succ p \text{ for no } q\}$, and $P_{\min} = \{p{:}p \succ q \text{ for no } q\}$. In addition, let

$$\lambda^* = (1 - \lambda)/\lambda \qquad \text{for all } 0 < \lambda < 1.$$

The following three lemmas lead to a characterization of preferences between a fixed $r \in P^*$ and all $p \in P$ by a linear functional v_r on P. This characterization is central to our construction of the SSB functional in later sections. After proving Lemmas 4.1 through 4.3 we consider the nontransitive convex representation in the next section. The sufficiency proof of Theorem 4.1 then resumes in Section 4.4.

LEMMA 4.1. *If $p \succ r \succ s$, $q \succ r \succ t$, and*

$$\alpha p + (1 - \alpha)s \sim r,$$

$$\beta q + (1 - \beta)t \sim r,$$

$$\lambda p + (1 - \lambda)t \sim r,$$

$$\mu q + (1 - \mu)s \sim r,$$

then $\alpha^*\beta^* = \lambda^*\mu^*$.

LEMMA 4.2. *If $0 < \lambda < 1$, either $\{p \succ r \succ s, q \succ r\}$ or $\{s \succ r \succ p, r \succ q\}$, and*

$$\alpha p + (1 - \alpha)s \sim r,$$

$$\beta q + (1 - \beta)s \sim r,$$

$$\mu(\lambda p + (1 - \lambda)q) + (1 - \mu)s \sim r,$$

then $\mu^* = \lambda\alpha^* + (1 - \lambda)\beta^*$. If the same hypotheses hold except that $q \sim r$, then $\mu^* = \lambda\alpha^*$.

Remark. Theorem 1.4(a), (b) says that α, β, λ and μ in Lemmas 4.1 and 4.2 are unique numbers strictly between 0 and 1. We use this fact henceforth without special mention.

LEMMA 4.3. *Suppose $r \in P^*$. Then there is a linear functional v_r on P such that, for all $p \in P$,*

$$p \succ r \Leftrightarrow v_r(p) > 0,$$

$$r \succ p \Leftrightarrow v_r(p) < 0,$$

and such a v_r is unique up to similarity transformations.

Proof of Lemma 4.1. Given the hypotheses of the lemma, the $\sim$ part of C2 yields

$$\left(\frac{1 - \lambda}{2 - \alpha - \lambda}\right)(\alpha p + (1 - \alpha)s) + \left(\frac{1 - \alpha}{2 - \alpha - \lambda}\right)$$
$$\cdot (\lambda p + (1 - \lambda)t) \sim r,$$

$$\left(\frac{1 - \mu}{2 - \beta - \mu}\right)(\beta q + (1 - \beta)t) + \left(\frac{1 - \beta}{2 - \beta - \mu}\right)$$
$$\cdot (\mu q + (1 - \mu)s) \sim r,$$

$$\left(\frac{\mu}{\alpha + \mu}\right)(\alpha p + (1 - \alpha)s) + \left(\frac{\alpha}{\alpha + \mu}\right)$$
$$\cdot (\mu q + (1 - \mu)s) \sim r,$$

$$\left(\frac{\lambda}{\beta + \lambda}\right)(\beta q + (1 - \beta)t) + \left(\frac{\beta}{\beta + \lambda}\right)$$
$$\cdot (\lambda p + (1 - \lambda)t) \sim r.$$

Rearrangements give

$$ap + (1 - a)(\tfrac{1}{2}s + \tfrac{1}{2}t) \sim r,$$
$$bq + (1 - b)(\tfrac{1}{2}s + \tfrac{1}{2}t) \sim r,$$
$$c(\tfrac{1}{2}p + \tfrac{1}{2}q) + (1 - c)s \sim r,$$
$$d(\tfrac{1}{2}p + \tfrac{1}{2}q) + (1 - d)t \sim r,$$

where $a = [\alpha(1 - \lambda) + \lambda(1 - \alpha)]/(2 - \alpha - \lambda)$, $b = [\beta(1 - \mu) + \mu(1 - \beta)]/(2 - \beta - \mu)$, $c = 2\alpha\mu/(\alpha + \mu)$, and $d = 2\beta\lambda/(\beta + \lambda)$.

The first two of the preceding $\sim r$ expressions combine under C2 to give

$$\frac{2ab}{a + b}\left(\frac{1}{2}p + \frac{1}{2}q\right) + \left[1 - \frac{2ab}{a + b}\right]\left(\frac{1}{2}s + \frac{1}{2}t\right) \sim r$$

when the first is multiplied by $b/(a + b)$ and the second by $a/(a + b)$. Similarly, when the third and forth $\sim r$ expressions (in c and d) are multiplied by $(1 - d)/(2 - c - d)$ and $(1 - c)/(2 - c - d)$, respectively, and then added, we get

$$\left[\frac{c(1 - d) + d(1 - c)}{2 - c - d}\right]\left(\frac{1}{2}p + \frac{1}{2}q\right)$$
$$+ \left[\frac{2(1 - c)(1 - d)}{2 - c - d}\right]\left(\frac{1}{2}s + \frac{1}{2}t\right) \sim r.$$

Since $\frac{1}{2}p + \frac{1}{2}q > r > \frac{1}{2}s + \frac{1}{2}t$ by C2, it follows from the two preceding $\sim r$ expressions and uniqueness from Theorem 1.4(b) that

$$\frac{2ab}{a + b} = \frac{c(1 - d) + d(1 - c)}{2 - c - d}.$$

The conclusion of Lemma 4.1 follows from this equation by algebraic reduction and rearrangement. Let $x' = 1 - x$, replace a through d in the equation by their definitions in α through μ and clear fractions to get

$$(\alpha\lambda' + \lambda\alpha')(\beta\mu' + \mu\beta')[(\alpha + \mu)(\beta\lambda' + \lambda\beta')$$

$$+ (\beta + \lambda)(\alpha\lambda' + \lambda\alpha')]$$

$$= [(\alpha\lambda' + \lambda\alpha')(\beta' + \mu') + (\beta\mu' + \mu\beta')(\alpha' + \lambda')]$$

$$\times [\alpha\mu(\beta\lambda' + \lambda\beta') + \beta\lambda(\alpha\mu' + \mu\alpha')].$$

Multiplication and cancellations yield

$$\alpha\mu^2\alpha'\lambda'\beta' + \alpha^2\mu\beta\lambda'\mu'\beta' + \alpha^2\beta^2(\lambda')^2\mu' + \alpha^2\beta^2\lambda'(\mu')^2$$

$$+ \lambda^2\mu^2\alpha'(\beta')^2 + \lambda^2\mu^2(\alpha')^2\beta' + \alpha\lambda\beta^2\alpha'\lambda'\mu' + \lambda^2\mu\beta\alpha'\mu'\beta'$$

$$= \alpha^2\mu\beta(\lambda')^2\mu' + \alpha\lambda\mu\beta\alpha'\lambda'\mu' + \alpha\lambda\mu\beta\alpha'\lambda'\beta' + \lambda^2\mu\beta(\alpha')^2\beta'$$

$$+ \alpha\lambda\mu^2\alpha'(\beta')^2 + \alpha\lambda\mu\beta\alpha'\mu'\beta' + \alpha\lambda\mu\beta\lambda'\mu'\beta' + \alpha\lambda\beta^2\lambda'(\mu')^2,$$

which rearranges to

$$0 = (\alpha\beta\lambda'\mu' - \lambda\mu\alpha'\beta')(\alpha\mu\beta' + \alpha\beta\lambda' + \alpha\beta\mu'$$

$$+ \lambda\beta\alpha' - \alpha\mu\lambda' - \lambda\mu\alpha' - \lambda\mu\beta' - \lambda\beta\mu')$$

$$= 2(\alpha\beta\lambda'\mu' - \lambda\mu\alpha'\beta')^2.$$

Therefore $\alpha\beta\lambda'\mu' = \lambda\mu\alpha'\beta'$; that is, $\lambda^*\mu^* = \alpha^*\beta^*$. ∎

Proof of Lemma 4.2. Suppose first that $0 < \lambda < 1$, $\{p > r > s, q > r\}$, with $\alpha p + (1 - \alpha)s \sim r \sim \beta q + (1 - \beta)s$ and $\mu(\lambda p + (1 - \lambda)q) + (1 - \mu)s \sim r$. By C2,

$$\left[\frac{\lambda\beta}{\lambda\beta + \alpha(1 - \lambda)}\right](\alpha p + (1 - \alpha)s)$$

$$+ \left[\frac{\alpha(1 - \lambda)}{\lambda\beta + \alpha(1 - \lambda)}\right](\beta q + (1 - \beta)s) \sim r.$$

Rearranging the left side, we have

$$\left[\frac{\alpha\beta}{\lambda\beta + \alpha(1 - \lambda)}\right](\lambda p + (1 - \lambda)q)$$

$$+ \left[1 - \frac{\alpha\beta}{\lambda\beta + \alpha(1 - \lambda)}\right]s \sim r.$$

Since $\lambda p + (1 - \lambda)q > r > s$ by C2, we conclude that $\mu = \alpha\beta/[\lambda\beta + \alpha(1 - \lambda)]$, which is tantamount to $\mu^* = \lambda\alpha^* + (1 - \lambda)\beta^*$. The same conclusion clearly holds if we begin with $\{s > r > p, r > q\}$. Finally, if $q \sim r$, then $\beta = 1$, so $\beta^* = 0$ and $\mu^* = \lambda\alpha^*$. ∎

Proof of Lemma 4.3. Take $r \in P^*$. Fix p and s in P with $p > r > s$ and $\alpha p + (1 - \alpha)s \sim r$. The representation of the lemma requires $v(p) > 0 > v(s)$ and $0 = v(\alpha p + (1 - \alpha)s) = \alpha v(p) + (1 - \alpha)v(s)$, where for convenience we omit r from v_r. Assign any positive number to $v(p)$ and define $v(s)$ by linearity: $v(s) = -[\alpha/(1 - \alpha)]v(p)$. The same thing is done for any t for which $r > t$: If $\beta p + (1 - \beta)t \sim r$, set $v(t) = -v(p)/\beta^*$. In addition, for any $q \neq p$ such that $q > r$, define $v(q)$ linearly as $v(q) = -\mu^*v(s) = v(p)\mu^*/\alpha^*$ when $\mu q + (1 - \mu)s \sim r$. Finally, set $v(r') = 0$ whenever $r' \sim r$.

Thus v is defined on P, it satisfies $v(q) > 0 \Leftrightarrow q > r$, and $v(q) < 0 \Leftrightarrow r > q$, and if it is linear then it is essentially unique, for if the value assigned to $v(p)$ is changed then all other v values change by the same proportion.

It remains to show that v is linear—that $v(\gamma q + (1 - \gamma)t) = \gamma v(q) + (1 - \gamma)v(t)$ for all $q, t \in P$ and all $0 < \lambda < 1$. The ensuing four cases cover the possibilities for q and t in relation to r.

Case 1. $q \sim r \sim t$. By C2, $\gamma q + (1 - \gamma)t \sim r$, so the definition of v gives $v(\gamma q + (1 - \gamma)t) = 0 = \gamma v(q) + (1 - \gamma)v(t)$.

Case 2. $\{q > r, t > r\}$ or $\{r > q, r > t\}$. Assume for definiteness that $q > r$ and $t > r$. Then $\gamma q + (1 - \gamma)t > r$ by C2. With $r > s$ for fixed s, let α, β, and μ satisfy $\alpha q + (1 - \alpha)s \sim r$, $\beta t + (1 - \beta)s \sim r$, and $\mu(\gamma q + (1 - \gamma)t) + (1 - \mu)s \sim r$. Then, by the definition of v,

$$\alpha v(q) + (1 - \alpha)v(s) = 0,$$

$$\beta v(t) + (1 - \beta)v(s) = 0,$$

$$\mu v(\gamma q + (1 - \gamma)t) + (1 - \mu)v(s) = 0,$$

with $\mu^* = \gamma\alpha^* + (1 - \gamma)\beta^*$ by Lemma 4.2. Therefore

$$v(\gamma q + (1 - \gamma)t) = -\mu^*v(s) = -(\gamma\alpha^* + (1 - \gamma)\beta^*)v(s)$$

$$= \gamma v(q) + (1 - \gamma)v(t).$$

Case 3. $q > r \sim t$ or $t \sim r > q$. The proof of linearity is similar to the preceding case. Use the final part of Lemma 4.2.

Case 4: $q > r > t$. Suppose first that $\gamma = \beta$, where $\beta q + (1 - \beta)t \sim r$. Then, by the construction of v along with the notation and conclusion of Lemma 4.1,

$$\alpha v(p) + (1 - \alpha)v(s) = 0,$$

$$\lambda v(p) + (1 - \lambda)v(t) = 0,$$

$$\mu v(q) + (1 - \mu)v(s) = 0$$

and $\alpha^*\beta^* = \lambda^*\mu^*$. Therefore

$$\beta v(q) + (1 - \beta)v(t) = \beta[v(q) + \beta^*v(t)]$$
$$= \beta[- \mu^*v(s) - v(p)\beta^*/\lambda^*]$$
$$= \beta v(p)[\mu^*/\alpha^* - \beta^*/\lambda^*] = 0.$$

Moreover, $v(\beta q + (1 - \beta)t) = 0$ by definition. Hence linearity holds when $\beta = \gamma$.

Suppose next for Case 4 that $\gamma q + (1 - \gamma)t > r$. Let β and σ satisfy $\beta q + (1 - \beta)t \sim r \sim \sigma(\gamma q + (1 - \gamma)t) + (1 - \sigma)t$. Then, using the result just proved, we have

$$v(\beta q + (1 - \beta)t) = 0 = \beta v(q) + (1 - \beta)v(t)$$

and

$$v(\sigma(\gamma q + (1 - \gamma)t) + (1 - \sigma)t) = 0$$
$$= \sigma v(\gamma q + (1 - \gamma)t) + (1 - \sigma)v(t).$$

Therefore $v(\gamma q + (1 - \gamma)t) = -\sigma^*v(t)$ and, since $\beta = \sigma\gamma$ by uniqueness (Theorem 1.4),

$$\gamma v(q) + (1 - \gamma)v(t) = -\gamma\beta^*v(t) + (1 - \gamma)v(t)$$
$$= -v(t)(\gamma - \beta)/\beta = -\sigma^*v(t).$$

Hence $v(\gamma q + (1 - \gamma)t) = \gamma v(q) + (1 - \gamma)v(t)$. A similar proof applies if $r > \gamma q + (1 - \gamma)t$. ∎

4.3 NONTRANSITIVE CONVEX UTILITY

Lemma 4.3 puts us in position to consider the nontransitive convex representation of Section 3.8. We recall that $(P, >)$ has a *nontransitive convex representation* if there is a functional ϕ on $P \times P$ such that, for all $p, q, r \in P$ and all $0 < \lambda < 1$,

$$p > q \Leftrightarrow \phi(p, q) > 0,$$

$$\phi(p, q) > 0 \Leftrightarrow \phi(q, p) < 0,$$

$$\phi(\lambda p + (1 - \lambda)q, r) = \lambda\phi(p, r) + (1 - \lambda)\phi(q, r).$$

In addition, $(P, >)$ is *open* if $P_{max} \cup P_{min} = \varnothing$, *closed* if $P_{max} \neq \varnothing \neq P_{min}$, and *half-open* otherwise.

Comments on uniqueness and cases of $(P, >)$ not covered by the following theorem will be made after it is proved.

THEOREM 4.2. *Suppose the initial hypotheses of Theorem* 4.1 *hold. If* $(P, \succ)$ *has a nontransitive convex representation then* C1 *and* C2 *hold. Conversely, if* C1 *and* C2 *hold, and either* $(P, \succ)$ *is open or P is the convex hull of a finite number of measures, then* $(P, \succ)$ *has a nontransitive convex representation.*

Necessity Proof. Assume that ϕ provides a nontransitive convex representation. If $p \succ q \succ r$, then, since ϕ is linear in its first argument, $\phi(\alpha p + (1 - \alpha)r, q) = \alpha\phi(p, q) + (1 - \alpha)\phi(r, q)$. By the representation, $\phi(p, q) > 0$ and $\phi(r, q) < 0$. Hence $\alpha\phi(p, q) + (1 - \alpha)\phi(r, q) = 0$ for some $0 < \alpha < 1$, and this verifies C1 since $\phi(s, t) = 0 \Leftrightarrow s \sim t$. For the first part of C2 suppose $p \succ q, p \succsim r$, and $0 < \lambda < 1$, so $\phi(q, p) < 0$ and $\phi(r, p) \leqslant 0$. Linearity then gives $\phi(\lambda q + (1 - \lambda)r, p) < 0$; hence $\phi(p, \lambda q + (1 - \lambda)r) > 0$, so $p \succ \lambda q + (1 - \lambda)r$. The other parts of C2 are proved similarly. ∎

The preceding proof establishes the necessity of C1 and C2 for the SSB representation, since the SSB representation obviously implies that $(P, \succ)$ has a nontransitive convex representation.

Sufficiency Proof When $(P, \succ)$ *is Open.* Assume that C1 and C2 hold with $(P, \succ)$ open. Given v_r on P for each $r \in P = P^*$ as in Lemma 4.3, define ϕ on $P \times P$ by $\phi(p, q) = v_q(p)$. The nontransitive convex representation then follows directly from Lemma 4.3. ∎

To prepare for the proof when P is the convex hull of a finite number of measures, we state a standard theorem for the existence of a solution to a finite set of linear inequalities (Kuhn, 1956; Goldman, 1956; Fishburn, 1970a, Theorem 4.2; 1985a, Theorem 7.1) that is often referred to as a theorem of the alternative or a linear separation theorem. In the theorem, K, N, and n denote positive integers.

THEOREM 4.3. *Suppose* $1 \leqslant K \leqslant N$ *and* $x_i = (x_{i1}, \ldots, x_{in})$ *is in* $\mathbf{R}^n$ *for* $i = 1, \ldots, N$. *Then exactly one of* (a) *and* (b) *is true:*
(a) *There is a* $w = (w_1, \ldots, w_n)$ *in* $\mathbf{R}^n$ *such that*

$$\sum_{j=1}^{n} w_j x_{ij} > 0 \quad \text{for } i = 1, \ldots, K,$$

$$\sum_{j=1}^{n} w_j x_{ij} \geqslant 0 \quad \text{for } i = K + 1, \ldots, N.$$

(b) *There are* $r_i \geqslant 0$ *for* $i = 1, \ldots, N$ *with* $r_i > 0$ *for some* $i \leqslant K$ *such that*

$$\sum_{i=1}^{N} r_i x_{ij} = 0 \quad \text{for } j = 1, \ldots, n.$$

Thus, if the linear system in (a) has no w solution then its dual system in (b) vanishes for some nonnegative r_i for which $r_1 + \cdots + r_K > 0$.

Sufficiency Proof of Theorem 4.2 When P is Finitely Generated. Assume that C1 and C2 hold with $P = H(\{p_1, \ldots, p_m\})$, where $H(A)$ is the convex hull of A. It suffices to prove that if $r \in P_{\max} \cup P_{\min}$ then there is a linear v_r on P for which $v_r(p) > 0 \leftrightarrow p \succ r$ and $v_r(p) < 0 \leftrightarrow r \succ p$. We then use Lemma 4.3 for $r \in P^*$ and proceed as in the previous sufficiency proof.

Assume for definiteness that $r \in P_{\min}$, and let

$$I(r) = \{p \in P : p \sim r\}, \qquad P(r) = \{p \in P : p \succ r\}.$$

It follows from C2 that $I(r)$ and $P(r)$ are convex. We wish to define linear v on P so that $v(p) = 0$ for all $p \in I(r)$ and $v(p) > 0$ for all $p \in P(r)$. To do this, observe first that $I(r) \cap \{p_1, \ldots, p_m\} \neq \varnothing$, since otherwise $p_i \succ r$ for all i and, by applications of C2, $r \succ r$ since $r \in H(\{p_1, \ldots, p_m\})$. For definiteness let $p_1, \ldots, p_k$ be in $I(r)$ and let $p_{k+1}, \ldots, p_m$ be in $P(r)$, with $1 \leqslant k < m$, since if $k = m$ then the desired result follows from C2 and $v \equiv 0$. Also, by C2, $I(r) = H(\{p_1, \ldots, p_k\})$.

Because $P = H(\{p_1, \ldots, p_m\})$, it suffices to define v on $\{p_1, \ldots, p_m\}$ with $v(p_i) = 0$ for $i \leqslant k$ and $v(p_i) > 0$ for $i > k$ since linear extension to P then gives the desired result. However, since nothing has been assumed about linear independence among the p_i, some care must be used in defining v on $\{p_1, \ldots, p_m\}$ so that the entire v is linear.

To deal with the possibility of linear dependence among the p_i, first let L_1 be a maximal linearly independent subset of $\{p_1, \ldots, p_k\}$. Then each $q \in I(r)$ is uniquely representable in the form $q = \Sigma_{L_1} \lambda_i p_i$ with $\lambda_i \in \mathbf{R}$ and $\Sigma \lambda_i = 1$. Also let L_2 be a subset of $\{p_{k+1}, \ldots, p_m\}$ for which $L_1 \cup L_2$ is a maximal linearly independent subset of $\{p_1, \ldots, p_m\}$, and let $L = \{p_{k+1}, \ldots, p_m\} \setminus L_2$. If L is empty, we obtain the desired result simply by taking $v = 0$ on L_1 and $v = 1$ on L_2, and then using linear extension to obtain v on all of P.

Suppose henceforth that $L \neq \varnothing$. Then each $p_j \in L$ has a unique representation of the form

$$p_j = \sum_{L_1} \lambda_{ij} p_i + \sum_{L_2} \mu_{ij} p_i$$

with the λ_{ij} and μ_{ij} real numbers (some of which can be negative) that sum to 1. Moreover, at least one μ_{ij} for $p_i \in L_2$ must be positive, since otherwise transpositions, normalization, and the use of C2 yield a contradiction of the form $\{p \succ r, p \sim r\}$. Since we require $v(p_i) = 0$ for all $p_i \in L_1$, our method of linear extension requires

$$v(p_j) = \sum_{L_2} \mu_{ij} v(p_i) \qquad \text{for each } p_j \in L_2.$$

It follows that we obtain $v > 0$ throughout $P(r)$ if and only if there is a v solution to the following system of linear inequalities:

$$v(p_i) > 0 \qquad \text{for each } p_i \in L_2,$$

$$\sum_{L_2} \mu_{ij} v(p_i) > 0 \qquad \text{for each } p_j \in L.$$

This system corresponds to $\{\Sigma w_j x_{ij} > 0\}$ in (a) of Theorem 4.3 with the $v(p_i)$ playing the role of the w_j. If it has a v solution, we are done. Suppose there is no v solution. Then (b) of Theorem 4.3 applies. With $I = \{i : p_i \in L_2\}$ and $J = \{j : p_j \in L\}$, (b) says that there are $s_i \geqslant 0$ for each $i \in I$ and $r_j \geqslant 0$ for each $j \in J$ such that $\Sigma s_i + \Sigma r_j > 0$ and

$$s_i + \sum_J r_j \mu_{ij} = 0 \qquad \text{for each } i \in I.$$

Consider the system of characterizations of p_{k+1} through p_m that we began with in the preceding paragraph:

$$p_i = p_i \qquad \text{for each } i \in I,$$

$$p_j = \sum_{L_1} \lambda_{ij} p_i + \sum_I \mu_{ij} p_i \qquad \text{for each } j \in J.$$

Multiply each equation here by its corresponding s_i or r_j, add the resulting weighted equations, and use the final set of equations in the preceding paragraph to conclude that

$$\sum_I s_i p_i + \sum_J r_j p_j = \sum_{L_1} \left(\sum_J r_j \lambda_{ij} \right) p_i,$$

where all s_i and r_j are nonnegative, $\Sigma s_i + \Sigma r_j > 0$, each p on the left side has $p > r$, and each p on the right side has $p \sim r$. When the negative terms from the right side (for $\Sigma_j r_j \lambda_{ij} < 0$) are transposed and we normalize and use C2 for convex combinations, we obtain an expression of the form $\alpha p + (1 - \alpha)q = q'$ where $0 < \alpha \leqslant 1, p > r$, and $q \sim r \sim q'$. But then C2 applied to $p > r$ and $q \sim r$ yields $\alpha p + (1 - \alpha)q > r$, a contradiction to $q' \sim r$.

It follows that (b) of Theorem 4.3 cannot hold; hence (a) holds. ■

I do not presently know whether C1 and C2 are sufficient for the nontransitive convex representation in cases not covered by Theorem 4.2. In view of Lemma 4.3, the only problem is whether v_r can be defined linearly on P with the correct signs when r is in $P_{\max}$ or $P_{\min}$. As just proved, this can be done when P is finitely generated, but it might not be possible in other cases.

There is, however, some question about the desirability of having v_r or $\phi(\cdot, r)$ linear when $r \in P_{\max} \cup P_{\min}$ owing to uniqueness considerations. When r is in the preference interior of P and $\phi(\cdot, r)$ is linear over P, we know from Lemma 4.3 that this r-conditional part of ϕ is unique up to similarity transformations. However, this is not generally true when r is preference-extreme. For example, if $P = H(\{p_1, \ldots, p_m\})$ and the p_i are linearly independent, then *every* $\phi(\cdot, r)$ based on linear extension from $v_r(p_i) = 0$ for $p_i \sim r$ and $v_r(p_i) > 0$ for $p_i \succ r$ when $r \in P_{\min}$ will suffice for the nontransitive convex representation.

An alternative to linearity of $\phi(\cdot, r)$ when $r \in P_{\max} \cup P_{\min}$ is simply to require that this piece of ϕ satisfy the sign properties of the representation without being linear. Then C1 and C2 are sufficient for the nontransitive convex representation thus modified.

4.4 FURTHER IMPLICATIONS OF C1 AND C2

Axioms C1 *and* C2 *are assumed to hold throughout the rest of this chapter along with the initial hypotheses of Theorem* 4.1.

The present section first proves lemmas involving cyclic triples in P and transitivity, and then establishes four limit lemmas that will be needed in Sections 4.6 and 4.7 to complete the sufficiency proof of Theorem 4.1.

LEMMA 4.4. *If* $p \succ q \succ r \succ p$ *and*

$$\alpha p + (1 - \alpha)r \sim q,$$

$$\beta q + (1 - \beta)p \sim r,$$

$$\gamma r + (1 - \gamma)q \sim p,$$

then $\alpha^* \beta^* \gamma^* = 1$.

Proof. Given the hypotheses, apply C2 to the first two indifference statements to get

$$\alpha p + (1 - \alpha)r \sim (\alpha\beta/a)q + ((1 - \beta)/a)(\alpha p + (1 - \alpha)r) \sim q,$$

$$\beta q + (1 - \beta)p \sim (\alpha/a)(\beta q + (1 - \beta)p)$$
$$+ ((1 - \alpha)(1 - \beta)/a)r \sim r,$$

where $a = \alpha\beta + 1 - \beta$. The middle parts of these two $\sim$ chains are identical and can be written as

$$t = \left(\frac{\alpha(1 - \beta)}{a}\right) p + \left[\frac{\alpha\beta + (1 - \alpha)(1 - \beta)}{a}\right]$$

$$\cdot \left\{\frac{1}{1 + \alpha^*\beta^*} q + \frac{\alpha^*\beta^*}{1 + \alpha^*\beta^*} r\right\}.$$

According to C2 and the final $\sim$ statements in the preceding $\sim$ chains, $p \sim$

$\gamma r + (1 - \gamma)q \sim t$. Since $\gamma r + (1 - \gamma)q \sim p$ and $\gamma r + (1 - \gamma)q \sim t$, C2 and the definition of t imply $\gamma r + (1 - \gamma)q \sim (q + \alpha^*\beta^* r)/(1 + \alpha^*\beta^*)$. Since $q > r$, we conclude that $\gamma = \alpha^*\beta^*/(1 + \alpha^*\beta^*)$, or $\alpha^*\beta^*\gamma^* = 1$. ∎

It can also be shown that if $p > q > r > p$, then the SSB representation holds on the convex hull $H(\{p, q, r\})$ of $\{p, q, r\}$. That is, axioms C1 and C2 imply C3 on $H(\{p, q, r\})$ in the cyclic case. This is not true, however, if $>$ is transitive on $\{p, q, r\}$.

LEMMA 4.5. *If $p > q > r$ and $p > r$, then $\sim$ is transitive on $H(\{p, q, r\})$. Moreover, if $Q \subseteq P$ and $\sim$ is transitive on $H(Q)$, then $>$ is transitive on $H(Q)$.*

Proof. The second part of the lemma follows immediately from Theorem 1.4(c). For the first part, given $p > q > r$ and $p > r$, let α satisfy $q \sim \alpha p + (1 - \alpha)r$. Then, by C2, $p > \lambda p + (1 - \lambda)r > q$ for $\alpha < \lambda < 1$, and $q > \lambda p + (1 - \lambda)r > r$ for $0 < \lambda < \alpha$. The use of C1 then generates a family of $\sim$ lines in $H(\{p, q, r\})$ based on $f_\lambda p + (1 - f_\lambda)q \sim \lambda p + (1 - \lambda)r$ for $\alpha < \lambda < 1$, and on $g_\lambda q + (1 - g_\lambda)r \sim \lambda p + (1 - \lambda)r$ for $0 < \lambda < \alpha$ (see the "weighted linear" diagram in Figure 3.2). It is easily seen that this family in conjunction with the line for $q \sim \alpha p + (1 - \alpha)r$ and the corner points p and r covers $H(\{p, q, r\})$.

Suppose $x, y \in H(\{p, q, r\})$, $x \neq y$, and $x \sim y$. Then, by C2, the two points x' and y' on the boundary of H determined by the straight line through x and y must be indifferent. It follows that x' and y' must be the end points of one of the $\sim$ lines in the generated family (or q and $\alpha p + (1 - \alpha)r$). Therefore x and y are themselves on an $\sim$ line in the family (or the q line). Since $\sim$ is transitive on each such line, it is transitive throughout H. ∎

In the following limit lemmas, which do not depend on C3, "$\mu_\lambda \downarrow \mu$ as $\lambda \uparrow 1$" means that μ_λ decreases to μ as λ increases to 1. Similarly, "$\mu_\lambda \uparrow \mu$ as $\lambda \uparrow 1$" says that μ_λ increases to μ as λ increases to 1, and "$f_\mu \uparrow a(f_\mu \downarrow a)$ as $\mu \downarrow 0$" says that f_μ increases (decreases) to a as μ approaches 0 from above. In the lemmas x, p, q, r, and s are elements in P.

LEMMA 4.6. *If $p > q > r$, $p > \lambda q + (1 - \lambda)s > r$ for all λ near 1 ($\lambda < 1$), $\mu p + (1 - \mu)r \sim q$, and $\mu_\lambda p + (1 - \mu_\lambda)r \sim \lambda q + (1 - \lambda)s$, then*

$$\mu_\lambda \downarrow \mu \text{ as } \lambda \uparrow 1 \quad if \quad s > \mu p + (1 - \mu)r,$$

$$\mu_\lambda \uparrow \mu \text{ as } \lambda \uparrow 1 \quad if \quad \mu p + (1 - \mu)r > s,$$

$$\mu_\lambda = \mu \text{ as } \lambda \uparrow 1 \quad if \quad s \sim \mu p + (1 - \mu)r.$$

LEMMA 4.7. *Suppose $x \sim q$ and $x > \mu p + (1 - \mu)q > r$ for all $\mu \in (0, 1]$, and that $f_\mu x + (1 - f_\mu)r \sim \mu p + (1 - \mu)q$ for all $\mu \in (0, 1]$. Then f_μ remains constant in $(0, 1)$ as $\mu \downarrow 0$ if $q \sim r$, and $f_\mu \uparrow 1$ as $\mu \downarrow 0$ if $q > r$.*

LEMMA 4.8. *If* $x \sim q \sim p$, $x \succ p$, *and* $f_\mu x + (1 - f_\mu)(\mu p + (1 - \mu)q)$ $\sim \frac{1}{2}x + \frac{1}{2}p$ *for all* μ *near* 0 $(\mu > 0)$, *then* $f_\mu \downarrow 0$ *as* $\mu \downarrow 0$.

LEMMA 4.9. *If* $x \succ p$, $x \succ q$, *and* $f_\mu x + (1 - f_\mu)(\mu p + (1 - \mu)q) \sim$ $\frac{1}{2}x + \frac{1}{2}q$ *for all* μ *near* 0 $(\mu > 0)$, *then* $f_\mu \uparrow \frac{1}{2}$ *as* $\mu \downarrow 0$.

Proof of Lemma 4.6. Given the lemma's hypotheses, suppose first that $s \sim \mu p + (1 - \mu)r$. Then, by C2, $\lambda q + (1 - \lambda)s \sim \mu p + (1 - \mu)r$ for all λ; hence $\mu_\lambda = \mu$ for all λ near 1.

Suppose next that $s \succ \mu p + (1 - \mu)r$. By C2, $\lambda q + (1 - \lambda)s \succ \mu p +$ $(1 - \mu)r$ for $0 < \lambda < 1$. Since $p \succ q$, $p \succ \lambda q + (1 - \lambda)s$ for all λ near 1, so by Theorem 1.4(a), (b) we get $\rho p + (1 - \rho)[\mu p + (1 - \mu)r] \sim \lambda q + (1 - \lambda)s$, and therefore $\mu_\lambda = \rho + (1 - \rho)\mu > \mu$ for all λ near 1. By C2 and $\mu_\lambda > \mu$, $\mu_\lambda p + (1 - \mu_\lambda)r \succ q$, so C2 requires $s \succ \mu_\lambda p + (1 - \mu_\lambda)r$ in view of $\lambda q + (1 - \lambda)s \sim \mu_\lambda p + (1 - \mu_\lambda)r$. Consequently, if $\gamma < \lambda$, then $p \succ \gamma q + (1 - \gamma)s \succ \mu_\lambda p + (1 - \mu_\lambda)r$ (the latter $\succ$ by C2), and therefore $\mu_\gamma > \mu_\lambda$. It follows that μ_λ decreases as $\lambda \uparrow 1$. Finally, for some small positive δ we have $s \succ (\mu + \delta)p + (1 - \mu - \delta)r \succ q$, so $\mu_\lambda = \mu + \delta$ for some λ, and therefore $\mu_\lambda \downarrow \mu$ as $\lambda \uparrow 1$.

The proof for $\mu p + (1 - \mu)r \succ s$ is similar to the proof in the preceding paragraph. ∎

Proof of Lemma 4.7. Assume $x \sim q$, $x \succ \mu p + (1 - \mu)q \succ r$, and $f_\mu x + (1 - f_\mu)r \sim \mu p + (1 - \mu)q$ for all $0 < \mu \leqslant 1$. If $q \sim r$ also, then $q \sim f_\mu x + (1 - f_\mu)r$ by C2 for all μ so, again by C2, $p \sim f_\mu x + (1 - f_\mu)r$. Since $\mu = 1$ in the hypotheses gives $x \succ p \succ r$, it follows that f_μ is constant in $(0, 1)$ for all $0 < \mu \leqslant 1$.

Suppose now that $q \succ r$ for the final conclusion of the lemma. By C2, $q \succ f_\mu x + (1 - f_\mu)r$. Then $x \succ \rho q + (1 - \rho)[\mu p + (1 - \mu)q] \succ f_\mu x + (1 - f_\mu)r$. This requires $f_{(1-\rho)\mu} > f_\mu$, so f_μ increases as μ decreases. Since $q \succ fx + (1 - f)r \succ p$ for f near 1, it follows that $f = f_\mu$ for some μ in $(0, 1)$. Therefore $f_\mu \uparrow 1$ as $\mu \downarrow 0$. ∎

Proof of Lemma 4.8. Assume $x \sim q \sim p$, $x \succ p$, and $f_\mu x + (1 - f_\mu)(\mu p + (1 - \mu)q) \sim \frac{1}{2}x + \frac{1}{2}p$ for μ near 0. Take $0 < \sigma < \mu$, define β by $\sigma = \beta\mu$, and note that

$$f_\mu x + (1 - f_\mu)(\sigma p + (1 - \sigma)q) = \beta[f_\mu x + (1 - f_\mu)(\mu p + (1 - \mu)q)]$$
$$+ (1 - \beta)[f_\mu x + (1 - f_\mu)q].$$

By C2, $q \sim \frac{1}{2}x + \frac{1}{2}p$ and $x \succ \frac{1}{2}x + \frac{1}{2}p$, so $f_\mu x + (1 - f_\mu)q \succ \frac{1}{2}x + \frac{1}{2}p$. Therefore C2 implies

$$f_\mu x + (1 - f_\mu)(\sigma p + (1 - \sigma)q) \succ \frac{1}{2}x + \frac{1}{2}p \succ \sigma p + (1 - \sigma)q.$$

Let ρ satisfy

$$\rho[f_\mu x + (1 - f_\mu)(\sigma p + (1 - \sigma)q)]$$

$$+ (1 - \rho)[\sigma p + (1 - \sigma)q] \sim \tfrac{1}{2}x + \tfrac{1}{2}p,$$

so $f_\sigma = \rho f_\mu$. Therefore f_μ decreases as μ decreases. Since $fx + (1 - f)q > \tfrac{1}{2}x + \tfrac{1}{2}p > p$ for small $f > 0$, there is a τ in $(0, 1)$ such that $\tau(fx + (1 - f)q) + (1 - \tau)p \sim \tfrac{1}{2}x + \tfrac{1}{2}p$. Hence with $\alpha = (1 - \tau)/(1 - \tau f)$,

$$(\tau f)x + (1 - \tau f)(\alpha p + (1 - \alpha)q) \sim \tfrac{1}{2}x + \tfrac{1}{2}p.$$

That is, $f_\alpha = \tau f$. It follows that $f_\mu \downarrow 0$ as $\mu \downarrow 0$. ∎

Proof of Lemma 4.9. Assume $x > p$, $x > q$, and $f_\mu x + (1 - f_\mu)(\mu p + (1 - \mu)q) \sim \tfrac{1}{2}x + \tfrac{1}{2}q$ for μ near 0. Take $0 < \sigma < \mu$, Let $\sigma = \beta\mu$, and obtain the first displayed equation in the preceding proof. Since β's coefficient on its right side is $\sim \tfrac{1}{2}x + \tfrac{1}{2}q$ by present hypotheses, and the multiplier $f_\mu x + (1 - f_\mu)q$ of $1 - \beta$ is $>$, $\sim$, or $<$ (dual of $>$) $\tfrac{1}{2}x + \tfrac{1}{2}q$ according to whether $f_\mu > \tfrac{1}{2}$, $f_\mu = \tfrac{1}{2}$, or $f_\mu < \tfrac{1}{2}$, respectively, it follows readily from C1 and C2 that

$$f_\mu > 1/2 \Rightarrow f_\sigma < f_\mu \qquad \text{for } 0 < \sigma < \mu,$$

$$f_\mu = 1/2 \Rightarrow f_\sigma = 1/2 \qquad \text{for } 0 < \sigma < \mu,$$

$$f_\mu < 1/2 \Rightarrow f_\sigma > f_\mu \qquad \text{for } 0 < \sigma < \mu.$$

For example, if $f_\mu > \tfrac{1}{2}$, then $f_\mu x + (1 - f_\mu)(\sigma p + (1 - \sigma)q) > \tfrac{1}{2}x + \tfrac{1}{2}q > \sigma p + (1 - \sigma)q$, so by Theorem 1.4, $f_\sigma < f_\mu$.

Suppose $f_\mu \geq \tfrac{1}{2}$. Then $f_\mu > (1 - f_\mu)(1 - \mu)$. Let $\tau_\mu = [1 - (2 - \mu)(1 - f_\mu)]/[1 - 2(1 - f_\mu)(1 - \mu)]$. Then

$$f_\mu x + (1 - f_\mu)(\mu p + (1 - \mu)q) = 2(1 - f_\mu)(1 - \mu)(\tfrac{1}{2}x + \tfrac{1}{2}q)$$

$$+ [1 - 2(1 - f_\mu)(1 - \mu)](\tau_\mu x + (1 - \tau_\mu)p),$$

so C2 requires $\tfrac{1}{2}x + \tfrac{1}{2}q \sim \tau_\mu x + (1 - \tau_\mu)p$. Since $x > \tfrac{1}{2}x + \tfrac{1}{2}q$, C2 also requires $\tfrac{1}{2}x + \tfrac{1}{2}q > p$ and therefore $\alpha x + (1 - \alpha)p \sim \tfrac{1}{2}x + \tfrac{1}{2}q$ for a unique α in $(0, 1)$. Since $x > p$, it follows that $\tau_\mu = \alpha$ whenever $f_\mu \geq \tfrac{1}{2}$.

If $f_\mu \geq \tfrac{1}{2}$ for a sequence of μ values that approach 0, then α is forced to 1, which contradicts its uniqueness in $(0, 1)$. We conclude that $f_\mu < \tfrac{1}{2}$ for all μ near 0; as already noted, f_μ increases as μ decreases.

Finally, suppose $0 < f < \tfrac{1}{2}$. Then $\tfrac{1}{2}x + \tfrac{1}{2}q > fx + (1 - f)q$. If $\gamma > 0$ satisfies $fx + (1 - f)(\gamma p + (1 - \gamma)q) > \tfrac{1}{2}x + \tfrac{1}{2}q$, we get a δ in $(0, 1)$ for which

$$\delta[fx + (1 - f)(\gamma p + (1 - \gamma)q)] + (1 - \delta)[fx + (1 - f)q]$$

$$= fx + (1 - f)[\delta\gamma p + (1 - \delta\gamma)q] \sim \tfrac{1}{2}x + \tfrac{1}{2}q$$

so that, by C2, $\tfrac{1}{2}x + \tfrac{1}{2}q > fx + (1 - f)(\tau p + (1 - \tau)q)$ for $0 < \tau < \delta\gamma$. A similar conclusion follows from C2 if $\tfrac{1}{2}x + \tfrac{1}{2}q \gtrsim fx + (1 - f)(\gamma p + (1$

$- \gamma)q)$. That is, given $f < 1/2$,

$$\tfrac{1}{2}x + \tfrac{1}{2}q > fx + (1 - f)(\mu p + (1 - \mu)q)$$

for all small $\mu > 0$. For such μ we get ρ in $(0, 1)$ for which $\rho x + (1 - \rho)[fx + (1 - f)(\mu p + (1 - \mu)q)] \sim \tfrac{1}{2}x + \tfrac{1}{2}q$, or

$$[\rho + (1 - \rho)f]x + (1 - \rho)(1 - f)(\mu p + (1 - \mu)q) \sim \tfrac{1}{2}x + \tfrac{1}{2}q.$$

By the preceding paragraph, $\rho + (1 - \rho)f < \tfrac{1}{2}$. Clearly, $\rho + (1 - \rho)f > f$. Hence there are $f < \tfrac{1}{2}$ arbitrarily close to $\tfrac{1}{2}$ that are f_μ values for small μ, and therefore $f_\mu \uparrow \tfrac{1}{2}$ as $\mu \downarrow 0$. ∎

4.5 IMPLICATIONS OF SYMMETRY

Axiom C3 *is assumed to hold throughout the rest of this chapter* along with C1 and C2. Our purpose in this section is to derive a key result, Lemma 4.12, that is needed in the next section where we begin our construction of the SSB functional ϕ. We approach Lemma 4.12 through two intermediaries.

LEMMA 4.10. *If $p > q > r, p > r$, and $q \sim \tfrac{1}{2}p + \tfrac{1}{2}r$, then $\alpha p + (1 - \alpha)r \sim \beta p + (1 - \beta)q \Leftrightarrow \alpha r + (1 - \alpha)p \sim \beta r + (1 - \beta)q.$*

LEMMA 4.11. *If $p > q > r, p > r$, and*

$$\beta p + (1 - \beta)q \sim \alpha_1 p + (1 - \alpha_1)r,$$

$$q \sim \alpha_2 p + (1 - \alpha_2)r,$$

$$\gamma q + (1 - \gamma)r \sim \alpha_3 p + (1 - \alpha_3)r,$$

then $(\alpha_1 - \alpha_2)\alpha_3(1 - \beta)(1 - \gamma) = (1 - \alpha_1)(\alpha_2 - \alpha_3)\beta\gamma.$

LEMMA 4.12. *If $\sim$ and $>$ are transitive on $H(\{p, q, r, s, t\})$, if $p > q > r > s > t$, and if*

$$\alpha p + (1 - \alpha)r \sim q,$$

$$\beta q + (1 - \beta)s \sim r,$$

$$\gamma r + (1 - \gamma)t \sim s,$$

and

$$\delta p + (1 - \delta)s \sim q,$$

$$\theta q + (1 - \theta)t \sim s,$$

then $\alpha^*\beta^*\gamma^* = \delta^*\theta^*.$

Proof of Lemma 4.10. Given $p > q > r, p > r$, and $q \sim \tfrac{1}{2}p + \tfrac{1}{2}r$ as in the hypotheses of C3, and given $\alpha p + (1 - \alpha)r \sim \beta p + (1 - \beta)q$, we are

FIGURE 4.1

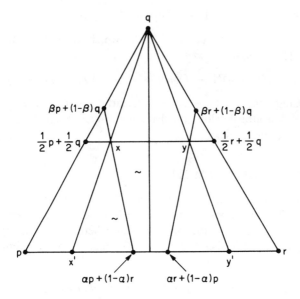

to prove that $\alpha r + (1 - \alpha)p \sim \beta r + (1 - \beta)q$. This is true by C3 if $\beta = \frac{1}{2}$. Other values of β are now considered.

Suppose first that $0 < \beta < \frac{1}{2}$ as illustrated barycentrically in Figure 4.1. Let x be the point at which the line from $\beta p + (1 - \beta)q$ to $\alpha p + (1 - \alpha)r$ intersects the horizontal between $\frac{1}{2}p + \frac{1}{2}q$ and $\frac{1}{2}r + \frac{1}{2}q$. Let y be the mirror image of x about the vertical between q and $\frac{1}{2}p + \frac{1}{2}r$. Extend lines through q and x and through q and y to determine x' and y' as shown. By C2, $x \sim \alpha p + (1 - \alpha)r$. Since $q \sim \frac{1}{2}x' + \frac{1}{2}y' = \frac{1}{2}p + \frac{1}{2}r$, C3 (with $x = \frac{1}{2}q + \frac{1}{2}x'$ and $y = \frac{1}{2}q + \frac{1}{2}y'$) implies $y \sim \alpha r + (1 - \alpha)p$, and this implies by C2 that $\alpha r + (1 - \alpha)p \sim \beta r + (1 - \beta)q$.

We now suppose that $\frac{1}{2} < \beta < 1$ as illustrated in Figure 4.2. Our construction proceeds as follows. First, draw the $\sim$ lines between $\beta p + (1 - \beta)q$ and $\alpha p + (1 - \alpha)r$, and between $(2\beta - 1)p + 2(1 - \beta)q$ and point **1**. Position **7, 5, 3, 2**, and **6** along the base so that **1** and **7** are equidistant from $q' = \frac{1}{2}p + \frac{1}{2}r$ and on opposite sides of q'; that is, $d(\mathbf{1}, q') = d(q', \mathbf{7})$, along with $d(p, \mathbf{1}) = d(\mathbf{1}, \mathbf{5})$, $d(\mathbf{3}, \mathbf{7}) = d(\mathbf{7}, r)$, $d(p, \alpha p + (1 - \alpha)r) = d(\mathbf{2}, \mathbf{5})$, and $d(\alpha r + (1 - \alpha)p, r) = d(\mathbf{3}, \mathbf{6})$. Finally, locate **8** and **9** on the horizontal between $\beta p + (1 - \beta)q$ and $\beta r + (1 - \beta)q$, where the indicated slanted lines from **5** and **3** intersect the horizontal β line, then extend lines through **2** and **8** to x and through **6** and **9** to y. When C3 is applied to the triangles $\{p, (2\beta - 1)p + 2(1 - \beta)q, \mathbf{5}\}$ and $\{\mathbf{3}, (2\beta - 1)r + 2(1 - \beta)q,$

FIGURE 4.2

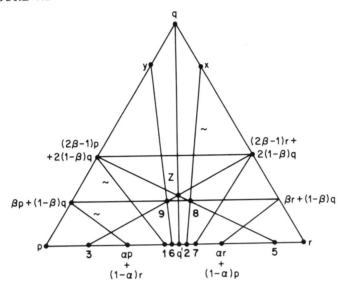

$r\}$, we get **2** $\sim$ **8** along with

$$9 \sim 6 \Leftrightarrow \beta r + (1 - \beta)q \sim \alpha r + (1 - \alpha)p$$

$$\text{if } 7 \sim (2\beta - 1)r + 2(1 - \beta)q.$$

If $\frac{1}{2} < \beta \leqslant \frac{3}{4}$, so that $0 < (2\beta - 1) \leqslant \frac{1}{2}$, then **7** $\sim (2\beta - 1)r + 2(1 - \beta)q$ by the result of the preceding paragraph, given $(2\beta - 1)p + 2(1 - \beta)q \sim \mathbf{1}$. If **8** equals or lies to the right of **9**, then **9** $\sim$ **6** by the preceding paragraph since **2** $\sim$ **8** (using triangle $\{3, z, 5\}$). If **8** is to the left of **9**, then x must be between $(2\beta - 1)p + 2(1 - \beta)q$ and q, and y must be between $(2\beta - 1)r + 2(1 - \beta)q$ and q. In this case the preceding paragraph gives $y \sim \mathbf{6}$ since $x \sim$ **2** (by C2 applied to **2** $\sim$**8**), provided that $0 < (2\beta - 1) \leqslant \frac{1}{2}$. Hence if $\frac{1}{2} < \beta \leqslant \frac{3}{4}$, then $y \sim$ **6**, so **9** $\sim$ **6** by C2; then $\beta r + (1 - \beta)q \sim \alpha r + (1 - \alpha)p$ since $7 \sim (2\beta - 1)r + 2(1 - \beta)q$.

Thus the desired conclusion holds if $\beta \leqslant \frac{3}{4}$. More generally, if the desired conclusion holds for $\beta \leqslant (2^{n-1} - 1)/2^{n-1}$, then the type of analysis in the preceding paragraph shows that it holds when $2\beta - 1 \leqslant (2^{n-1} - 1)/2^{n-1}$, that is, when $\beta \leqslant (2^n - 1)/2^n$. It follows by induction that $\beta r + (1 - \beta)q \sim \alpha r + (1 - \alpha)p$ for all $\beta < 1$. ∎

Proof of Lemma 4.11. Given the lemma's hypotheses we are to show that $(\alpha_1 - \alpha_2)\alpha_3(1 - \beta)(1 - \gamma) = (1 - \alpha_1)(\alpha_2 - \alpha_3)\beta\gamma$. Since the conclusion follows easily from C1 and C2 if either β or γ is in $\{0, 1\}$, assume $\beta, \gamma \in (0, 1)$. By Lemma 4.10, if $\beta p + (1 - \beta)q \sim \alpha p + (1 - \alpha)r$, $q \sim$

$\frac{1}{2}p + \frac{1}{2}r$, and $\gamma q + (1 - \gamma)r \sim (1 - \alpha)p + \alpha r$, then $\gamma = 1 - \beta$. This is the special case of the present lemma for $\alpha_2 = \frac{1}{2}$ and $\alpha_1 - \alpha_2 = \alpha_2 - \alpha_3$, so $\alpha_1 = \alpha$ and $\alpha_3 = 1 - \alpha$ are equidistant from $\alpha_2 = \frac{1}{2}$ and on opposite sides of $\frac{1}{2}$. (Whether or not $\alpha_2 = \frac{1}{2}$, the assumptions for the general case with $\beta, \gamma \in (0, 1)$ require $\alpha_1 > \alpha_2 > \alpha_3$; see Lemma 4.5.)

As just noted, Lemma 4.10 implies the conclusion of Lemma 4.11 when $(\alpha_1, \alpha_2, \alpha_3) = (\frac{1}{2} + \tau, \frac{1}{2}, \frac{1}{2} - \tau)$ for $0 < \tau < \frac{1}{2}$. Our next step is to prove that if $\beta p + (1 - \beta)q \sim (\alpha + \tau)p + (1 - \alpha - \tau)r$, $q \sim \alpha p + (1 - \alpha)r$, and $\gamma q + (1 - \gamma)r \sim (\alpha - \tau)p + (1 - \alpha + \tau)r$, then $(\alpha - \tau)(1 - \beta)(1 - \gamma) = (1 - \alpha - \tau)\beta\gamma$ when $0 < \tau < \min\{\alpha, 1 - \alpha\}$, which gives the desired conclusion of Lemma 4.11 whenever $\alpha_1 - \alpha_2 = \alpha_2 - \alpha_3$. Suppose for definiteness that $\alpha > \frac{1}{2}$, since the proof for $\alpha < \frac{1}{2}$ is similar and Lemma 4.10 covers $\alpha = \frac{1}{2}$. Given $\alpha > \frac{1}{2}$,

$$q \sim \tfrac{1}{2}p + \tfrac{1}{2}[(2\alpha - 1)p + 2(1 - \alpha)r] = \alpha p + (1 - \alpha)r.$$

Then, with $(2\alpha - 1)p + 2(1 - \alpha)r$ playing the role of r in Lemma 4.10,

$$\beta p + (1 - \beta)q \sim \left[\frac{1 - \alpha + \tau}{2(1 - \alpha)}\right]p + \left[\frac{1 - \alpha - \tau}{2(1 - \alpha)}\right]$$
$$\cdot \{(2\alpha - 1)p + 2(1 - \alpha)r\} = (\alpha + \tau)p + (1 - \alpha - \tau)r$$

by hypothesis, so, by Lemma 4.10,

$$(1 - \beta)q + \beta[(2\alpha - 1)p + 2(1 - \alpha)r]$$
$$\sim \left[\frac{1 - \alpha - \tau}{2(1 - \alpha)}\right]p + \left[\frac{1 - \alpha + \tau}{2(1 - \alpha)}\right]\{(2\alpha - 1)p + 2(1 - \alpha)r\}$$
$$= (\alpha - \tau)p + (1 - \alpha + \tau)r.$$

The β mixture in the preceding expression can be rewritten as

$$\left[\frac{\beta(2\alpha - 1)}{\alpha - \tau}\right]\{(\alpha - \tau)p + (1 - \alpha + \tau)r\}$$
$$+ \left[\frac{\alpha - \tau - \beta(2\alpha - 1)}{\alpha - \tau}\right]$$
$$\cdot \left\{\frac{(1 - \beta)(\alpha - \tau)}{\alpha - \tau - \beta(2\alpha - 1)}q + \left[1 - \frac{(1 - \beta)(\alpha - \tau)}{\alpha - \tau - \beta(2\alpha - 1)}\right]r\right\}$$

where the multiplying coefficients are positive. For example, $\alpha - \tau - \beta(2\alpha - 1) > \alpha - (1 - \alpha) - \beta(2\alpha - 1) = (2\alpha - 1)(1 - \beta) > 0$. Since the preceding expression as rewritten is indifferent to $(\alpha - \tau)p + (1 - \alpha + \tau)r$, C2 requires its second term in braces to be indifferent to $(\alpha - \tau)p + (1 - \alpha + \tau)r$. Moreover, $\gamma q + (1 - \gamma)r \sim (\alpha - \tau)p + (1 - \alpha + \tau)r$ by hypothesis, and therefore C2 implies

$$\gamma = \frac{(1 - \beta)(\alpha - \tau)}{\alpha - \tau - \beta(2\alpha - 1)},$$

which is equivalent to $(\alpha - \tau)(1 - \beta)(1 - \gamma) = (1 - \alpha - \tau)\beta\gamma$. Therefore Lemma 4.11 is valid whenever $\alpha_1 - \alpha_2 = \alpha_2 - \alpha_3$.

We next extend the result to cases in which $(\alpha_1 - \alpha_2)/(\alpha_2 - \alpha_3)$ is rational. Let $\alpha = \alpha_2$ for convenience. With all (α, τ) coefficients in $(0, 1)$, a first step is made with the hypotheses

$$(\alpha + \tau)p + (1 - \alpha - \tau)r \sim \beta p + (1 - \beta)q,$$

$$\alpha p + (1 - \alpha)r \sim q \sim [\alpha(1 - \gamma)/(1 - \alpha\gamma)]p$$
$$+ [(1 - \alpha)/(1 - \alpha\gamma)]s,$$

$$(\alpha - \tau)p + (1 - \alpha + \tau)r \sim \gamma q + (1 - \gamma)r = s,$$

$$(\alpha - 2\tau)p + (1 - \alpha + 2\tau)r \sim \delta q + (1 - \delta)r$$
$$= (\delta/\gamma)s + [(\gamma - \delta)/\gamma]r,$$

where s is defined as $\gamma q + (1 - \gamma)r$. Since $q \sim \alpha p + (1 - \alpha)r$,

$$q \sim \left(\frac{1 - \gamma}{1 - \alpha\gamma}\right)(\alpha p + (1 - \alpha)r) + \left(\frac{\gamma - \alpha\gamma}{1 - \alpha\gamma}\right)q$$

$$= \left(\frac{\alpha(1 - \gamma)}{1 - \alpha\gamma}\right)p + \left(\frac{1 - \alpha}{1 - \alpha\gamma}\right)s.$$

When the result established for $\alpha_1 - \alpha_2 = \alpha_2 - \alpha_3$ is applied to the left parts of the first three displayed lines in the preceding paragraph, and is applied again to the last three lines for s, we get

$$(\alpha - \tau)(1 - \beta)(1 - \gamma) = (1 - \alpha - \tau)\beta\gamma$$

and

$$(\alpha - 2\tau)\left(\frac{1 - \alpha}{1 - \alpha\gamma}\right)\left(\frac{\gamma - \delta}{\gamma}\right) = (1 - \alpha)\left(\frac{\alpha(1 - \gamma)}{1 - \alpha\gamma}\right)\left(\frac{\delta}{\gamma}\right).$$

We solve the first of these for γ, substitute this solution for γ into the second equation, then solve the second for δ to get

$$\delta = \frac{(\alpha - 2\tau)(1 - \beta)}{2(1 - \alpha - \tau)\beta + (\alpha - 2\tau)(1 - \beta)},$$

or $(\alpha - 2\tau)(1 - \beta)(1 - \gamma) = (1 - \alpha - \tau)2\beta\delta$, which is the desired conclusion of Lemma 4.11 when $\alpha_1 = \alpha_2 + \tau$ and $\alpha_3 = \alpha_2 - 2\tau$.

A similar proof applies when $\alpha_1 = \alpha_2 + 2\tau$ and $\alpha_3 = \alpha_2 - \tau$. The general case for rational $(\alpha_1 - \alpha_2)/(\alpha_2 - \alpha_3)$ follows by induction. For example, suppose that

$$(\alpha + n\tau)p + (1 - \alpha - n\tau)r \sim \beta p + (1 - \beta)q,$$

$$\alpha p + (1 - \alpha)r \sim q \sim [\alpha(1 - \gamma)/(1 - \alpha\gamma)]p$$
$$+ [(1 - \alpha)/(1 - \alpha\gamma)]s,$$

$$(\alpha - n\tau)p + (1 - \alpha + n\tau)r \sim \gamma q + (1 - \gamma)r = s,$$

$$(\alpha - (n + m)\tau)p + (1 - \alpha + (n + m)\tau)r \sim \delta q + (1 - \delta)r$$
$$= (\delta/\gamma)s + (1 - \delta/\gamma)r,$$

and that the conclusion of the lemma has been verified when $(\alpha_1 - \alpha_2)/(\alpha_2 - \alpha_3) = n/m$. Then the procedure of the preceding paragraph yields the desired conclusion for $(\alpha_1 - \alpha_2)/(\alpha_2 - \alpha_3) = n/(n + m)$ (i.e., for lines 1, 2, and 4 in the preceding display). The desired result for rational ratios follows easily.

Finally, let $a = \alpha_1 - \alpha_2$ and $b = \alpha_2 - \alpha_3$ and suppose a/b is irrational. Let the lemma's hypotheses hold as stated. Keep b fixed and let a' be near a with a'/b rational. Also let $\alpha_1' = \alpha_2 + a'$ with β' satisfying $\beta'p + (1 - \beta')q \sim \alpha_1'p + (1 - \alpha_1')r$. Then the result for rationals gives

$$a'(\alpha_2 - b)(1 - \beta')(1 - \gamma) = (1 - \alpha_2 - a')b\beta'\gamma.$$

When $a' > a$, we require $\beta' > \beta$, and $a > a' \Rightarrow \beta > \beta'$, as is easily checked. Let $\beta^+ = \inf\{\beta':a' > a\}$, $\beta^- = \sup\{\beta':a > a'\}$ so that $\beta^+ \geq \beta \geq \beta^-$. Note also that

$$a(\alpha_2 - b)(1 - \beta^+)(1 - \gamma) = (1 - \alpha_2 - a)b\beta^+\gamma,$$

$$a(\alpha_2 - b)(1 - \beta^-)(1 - \gamma) = (1 - \alpha_2 - a)b\beta^-\gamma.$$

Therefore $\beta^+ = \beta = \beta^-$; hence $a(\alpha_2 - b)(1 - \beta)(1 - \gamma) = (1 - \alpha_2 - a)b\beta\gamma$. ■

Proof of Lemma 4.12. As in the hypotheses, assume $p > q > r > s > t$ with $\sim$ and $>$ transitive on the convex hull $H(\{p, q, r, s, t\})$. Let the α_i, β_i, and γ_i satisfy

$$\alpha_1 p + (1 - \alpha_1)t \sim r, \qquad \beta_1 p + (1 - \beta_1)r \sim q,$$

$$\alpha_2 p + (1 - \alpha_2)s \sim r, \qquad \beta_2 p + (1 - \beta_2)s \sim q,$$

$$\alpha_3 q + (1 - \alpha_3)t \sim r, \qquad \beta_3 p + (1 - \beta_3)t \sim q,$$

$$\alpha_4 q + (1 - \alpha_4)s \sim r,$$

$$\gamma_1 p + (1 - \gamma_1)t \sim s,$$

$$\gamma_2 q + (1 - \gamma_2)t \sim s,$$

$$\gamma_3 r + (1 - \gamma_3)t \sim s.$$

The conclusion of Lemma 4.12 in these terms is $\beta_1^* \alpha_4^* \gamma_3^* = \beta_2^* \gamma_2^*$. To verify this, note first from the transitivity of $\sim$ with θ and δ defined in context that

$$\beta_1 p + (1 - \beta_1)r \sim \beta_3 p + (1 - \beta_3)t,$$

$$r \sim \alpha_1 p + (1 - \alpha_1)t,$$

$$\gamma_3 r + (1 - \gamma_3)t \sim \gamma_1 p + (1 - \gamma_1)t;$$

$$\beta_2 p + (1 - \beta_2)s \sim \beta_3 p + (1 - \beta_3)t,$$

$$s \sim \gamma_1 p + (1 - \gamma_1)t,$$

$$\tfrac{1}{2}s + \tfrac{1}{2}r \sim \theta p + (1 - \theta)t;$$

$$\alpha_2 p + (1 - \alpha_2)s \sim \alpha_1 p + (1 - \alpha_1)t,$$

$$s \sim \gamma_1 p + (1 - \gamma_1)t,$$

$$\tfrac{1}{2}s + \tfrac{1}{2}t \sim \theta p + (1 - \theta)t;$$

$$\tfrac{1}{2}p + \tfrac{1}{2}q \sim \delta p + (1 - \delta)t,$$

$$q \sim \beta_3 p + (1 - \beta_3)t,$$

$$\gamma_2 q + (1 - \gamma_2)t \sim \gamma_1 p + (1 - \gamma_1)t;$$

$$\tfrac{1}{2}p + \tfrac{1}{2}q \sim \delta p + (1 - \delta)t,$$

$$q \sim \beta_3 p + (1 - \beta_3)t,$$

$$\alpha_3 q + (1 - \alpha_3)t \sim \alpha_1 p + (1 - \alpha_1)t.$$

Apply Lemma 4.11 to each of the five three $\sim$ sets to get

$$(\beta_3 - \alpha_1)\gamma_1(1 - \beta_1)(1 - \gamma_3) = (1 - \beta_3)(\alpha_1 - \gamma_1)\beta_1\gamma_3,$$

$$(\beta_3 - \gamma_1)\theta(1 - \beta_2)(1/2) = (1 - \beta_3)(\gamma_1 - \theta)\beta_2(1/2),$$

$$(\alpha_1 - \gamma_1)\theta(1 - \alpha_2)(1/2) = (1 - \alpha_1)(\gamma_1 - \theta)\alpha_2(1/2),$$

$$(\delta - \beta_3)\gamma_1(1/2)(1 - \gamma_2) = (1 - \delta)(\beta_3 - \gamma_1)(1/2)\gamma_2,$$

$$(\delta - \beta_3)\alpha_1(1/2)(1 - \alpha_3) = (1 - \delta)(\beta_3 - \alpha_1)(1/2)\alpha_3,$$

respectively, with each difference, $\beta_3 - \alpha_1, 1 - \beta_1, \ldots$ positive. We now multiply these five equations alternately [(left of first)(right of second)(left of third) $\cdots$ = (right of first)(left of second) $\cdots$] and cancel identical terms to conclude that

$$\beta_1^* \gamma_3^* \alpha_2^* \alpha_3^* = \beta_2^* \gamma_2^* \alpha_1^*.$$

By Lemma 4.1, $\alpha_1^* \alpha_4^* = \alpha_2^* \alpha_3^*$. Therefore $\beta_1^* \alpha_4^* \gamma_3^* = \beta_2^* \gamma_2^*$. ∎

4.6 PARTIAL CONSTRUCTION OF ϕ

The preceding lemmas will now be used to construct an SSB functional ϕ on $P \times P$ for which $> = \{(p, q):\phi(p, q) > 0\}$ with ϕ unique up to similarity transformations. The sufficiency proof of Theorem 4.1 from this point on has four parts:

1. Define ϕ on $P \times P^*$ so that it is linear in its first argument and has $p > q \Leftrightarrow \phi(p, q) > 0$ and $p \sim q \Leftrightarrow \phi(p, q) = 0$ for all $(p, q) \in P \times P^*$.
2. Verify that ϕ is skew-symmetric on $P^* \times P^*$.
3. Extend ϕ to all of $P \times P$ in the only way possible for it to be skew-symmetric everywhere.
4. Verify that ϕ extended is linear in its first argument.

We deal with parts **1** and **2** in this section and with **3** and **4** in the next section. The uniqueness property of ϕ will be verified as we proceed. It is assumed that P^* is not empty since otherwise $\sim = P \times P$ and ϕ must be identically 0 for Theorem 4.1, in which case it is trivially unique up to similarity transformations.

    1. For each $p \in P^*$ let v_p satisfy the representation of Lemma 4.3 and define

$$P^*(p) = \{q \in P^* : q > p \text{ or } p > q\}$$

so that v_p never vanishes on $P^*(p)$ and $v_p \equiv 0$ on $P^* \setminus P^*(p)$. If ϕ is to satisfy the SSB representation then the linearity and order-preserving properties of v_p and ϕ require

$$\phi(\cdot, p) = a_p v_p(\cdot) \qquad \text{for some } a_p > 0.$$

We adhere to this correspondence in defining ϕ on $P \times P^*$.

    Henceforth, fix $r \in P^*$ and define $\phi(p, r) = v_r(p)$ for all $p \in P$. For every $t \in P^*(r)$, scale v_t (by means of a_t) so that $v_t(r) = -v_r(t)$ and define $\phi(\cdot, t)$ by

$$\phi(p, t) = v_t(p) \qquad \text{for all } p \in P.$$

The $\phi(\cdot, t)$ for $t \in P^*(r)$ must be defined in this way, for only then will we have $\phi(r, t) = -\phi(t, r)$ as required for skew-symmetry. With v_r fixed, ϕ as defined thus far is unique.

To complete the definition of ϕ on $P \times P^*$ we need to specify $\phi(\cdot, w)$ when $w \in P^*$ and $w \notin P^*(r) \cup \{r\}$, but we cannot use v_r to do this since $v_r(w) = 0$ by $w \sim r$. For any such w it is easily seen that $P^*(r) \cap P^*(w) \neq \varnothing$. Accordingly, choose $s \in P^*(r) \cap P^*(w)$, scale v_w so that $v_w(s) = -v_s(w)$, and define $\phi(\cdot, w)$ by

$$\phi(p, w) = v_w(p) \qquad \text{for all } p \in P.$$

A different s can be used for different w's. Since $-v_s(w) = -\phi(w, s)$ by the preceding paragraph [since $s \in P^*(r)$], $\phi(\cdot, w)$ must be defined in this way if the SSB presentation is to hold. Only then do we get $\phi(s, w) = -\phi(w, s)$.

We have defined ϕ on $P \times P^*$ and it is unique, given $\phi(\cdot, r) = v_r(\cdot)$ and the s choices of the preceding paragraph. If the SSB representation holds then, given $\phi(\cdot, r) = v_r(\cdot)$, the rest of ϕ on $P \times P^*$ is uniquely determined. If v_r is replaced by av_r with $a > 0$, then ϕ is replaced by $a\phi$.

By construction, ϕ on $P \times P^*$ is linear in its first argument and has $\phi(p, q) > 0 \Leftrightarrow p \succ q$ and $\phi(p, q) < 0 \Leftrightarrow q \succ p$.

2. To prove that ϕ is skew-symmetric on $P^* \times P^*$, we assume throughout this part that $p, q \in P^*$ with $p \not\sim q$ (p not indifferent to q) and $r \notin \{p, q\}$, since otherwise skew-symmetry for (p, q) follows from the definitions. Several cases need to be considered to prove that $\phi(p, q) = -\phi(q, p)$,

Case 1. $p, q \in P^*(r)$. Then, by the definitions,

$$\phi(p, q) = v_q(p) \qquad \text{where } v_q(r) = -v_r(q),$$

$$\phi(q, p) = v_p(q) \qquad \text{where } v_p(r) = -v_r(p).$$

Then no two of p, q, and r are indifferent in Case 1; the three form either a preference cycle or a transitive triple. We examine these subcases in turn.

Case 1A. *Cycle.* Assume for definiteness that $p \succ q \succ r \succ p$. Let α, β, and γ satisfy the hypotheses of Lemma 4.4. Then, by linearity and $v_x(y) = 0$ when $x \sim y$,

$$\alpha v_q(p) + (1 - \alpha)v_q(r) = 0 \qquad [\alpha p + (1 - \alpha)r \sim q],$$

$$\beta v_r(q) + (1 - \beta)v_r(p) = 0 \qquad [\beta q + (1 - \beta)p \sim r],$$

$$\gamma v_p(r) + (1 - \gamma)v_p(q) = 0 \qquad [\gamma r + (1 - \gamma)q \sim p].$$

By Lemma 4.4, $\alpha^*\beta^*\gamma^* = 1$. Therefore

$$\left[-\frac{v_q(p)}{v_q(r)} \right]\left[-\frac{v_r(q)}{v_r(p)} \right]\left[-\frac{v_p(r)}{v_p(q)} \right] = 1,$$

and cancellation leaves $v_q(p) = -v_p(q)$; that is, $\phi(p, q) = -\phi(q, p)$.

Case 1B. *Transitive Triple.* Two further subcases arise depending on whether r is between p and q. We consider betweenness first, assuming that p

$\succ r \succ q$ and $p \succ q$. Let $\lambda < 1$ be near 1 so that, by C2, $p \succ \lambda p + (1 - \lambda)r$
$\succ r \succ \lambda q + (1 - \lambda)r \succ q$. Let $p' = \lambda p + (1 - \lambda)r$ and $q' = \lambda q + (1 - \lambda)r$. Then $p \succ p' \succ r \succ q' \succ q$ with $p', q' \in P*(r)$. By Lemma 4.5, $\sim$ and $\succ$ are transitive on $H(\{p, q, r\})$, and we therefore have $\alpha, \beta, \gamma, \delta$ and θ in $(0, 1)$ such that

$$\alpha p + (1 - \alpha)r \sim p', \qquad \beta p' + (1 - \beta)q' \sim r,$$

$$\gamma r + (1 - \gamma)q \sim q', \qquad \delta p + (1 - \delta)q' \sim p',$$

$$\theta p' + (1 - \theta)q \sim q'.$$

According to Lemma 4.12, $\alpha*\beta*\gamma* = \delta*\theta*$. This result and linearity for each v imply

$$\left[-\frac{v_{p'}(p)}{v_{p'}(r)} \right] \left[-\frac{v_r(p')}{v_r(q')} \right] \left[-\frac{v_{q'}(r)}{v_{q'}(q)} \right]$$

$$= \left[-\frac{v_{p'}(p)}{v_{p'}(q')} \right] \left[-\frac{v_{q'}(p')}{v_{q'}(q)} \right].$$

Since $p', q' \in P*(r)$, $v_{p'}(r) = -v_r(p')$, and $v_{q'}(r) = -v_r(q')$, so cancellations in the preceding equation leave

$$v_{p'}(q') = -v_{q'}(p').$$

Fix q' for the time being, but let $\lambda \uparrow 1$ for $p' = \lambda p + (1 - \lambda)r$. Since $p, r \in P*$, we can choose $x \in P$ such that $x \succ p$ and $x \succ r$. Given such an x we have $x \succ p \succ r$, $x \succ \lambda p + (1 - \lambda)r \succ r$, so, by Theorem 1.4, let τ and τ_λ satisfy

$$\tau x + (1 - \tau)r \sim p, \qquad \tau_\lambda x + (1 - \tau_\lambda)r \sim \lambda p + (1 - \lambda)r.$$

Since $\tau x + (1 - \tau)r \succ r$ by C2, Lemma 4.6 implies that $\tau_\lambda \uparrow \tau$ as $\lambda \uparrow 1$. By the preceding $\sim$ statements and the definitions and properties of the v's, we have

$$\tau v_p(x) = -(1 - \tau)v_p(r) = (1 - \tau)v_r(p), \text{ and}$$

$$\tau_\lambda v_{\lambda p + (1 - \lambda)r}(x) = -(1 - \tau_\lambda)v_{\lambda p + (1 - \lambda)r}(r)$$

$$= (1 - \tau_\lambda)v_r(\lambda p + (1 - \lambda)r) = \lambda(1 - \tau_\lambda)v_r(p).$$

Letting $\lambda \uparrow 1$ in the latter equation, we get

$$\tau \lim_{\lambda \uparrow 1} v_{\lambda p + (1 - \lambda)r}(x) = (1 - \tau)v_r(p).$$

So, by the former equation,

$$\lim_{\lambda \uparrow 1} v_{\lambda p + (1-\lambda)r}(x) = v_p(x).$$

We also have $x \succ p \succ q'$ and $x \succ \lambda p + (1 - \lambda)r \succ q'$, so let $\mu x + (1 - \mu)q' \sim p$ and $\mu_\lambda x + (1 - \mu_\lambda)q' \sim \lambda p + (1 - \lambda)r$ to obtain

$$\mu v_p(x) = -(1 - \mu)v_p(q'),$$

$$\mu_\lambda v_{\lambda p + (1-\lambda)r}(x) = -(1 - \mu_\lambda)v_{\lambda p + (1-\lambda)r}(q').$$

By Lemma 4.6, $\mu_\lambda \to \mu$ as $\lambda \uparrow 1$. Thus, using the preceding limit result for x, we get

$$-(1 - \mu)v_p(q') = \mu v_p(x) = \mu \lim_{\lambda \uparrow 1} v_{\lambda p + (1-\lambda)r}(x)$$

$$= -(1 - \mu) \lim_{\lambda \uparrow 1} v_{\lambda p + (1-\lambda)r}(q'),$$

and therefore $v_p(q') = \lim_{\lambda \uparrow 1} v_{\lambda p + (1-\lambda)r}(q')$. Since $v_{q'}(p') = v_{q'}(\lambda p + (1 - \lambda)r) = \lambda v_{q'}(p) + (1 - \lambda)v_{q'}(r)$, which approaches $v_{q'}(p)$ as $\lambda \uparrow 1$, we have

$$v_p(q') = -v_{q'}(p).$$

We now fix p and vary λ for $q' = \lambda q + (1 - \lambda)r$, using y for which $r \succ y$ and $q \succ y$ in a manner symmetric to the foregoing analysis to obtain

$$v_p(q) = \lim_{\lambda \uparrow 1} v_p(\lambda q + (1 - \lambda)r) = \lim v_p(q')$$

$$= \lim (-v_{q'}(p)) = -\lim_{\lambda \uparrow 1} v_{\lambda p + (1-\lambda)r}(p) = -v_q(p).$$

Hence skew-symmetry holds for Case 1B when $p \succ r \succ q$.

Assume henceforth for Case 1B that $p \succ q \succ r$ and $p \succ r$. (The proof with $r \succ q \succ p$ is similar.) Let $p' = \lambda p + (1 - \lambda)q$ and $r' = \lambda r + (1 - \lambda)q$ for $0 < \lambda < 1$, so $p \succ p' \succ q \succ r' \succ r$. As in the preceding paragraph, we use Lemmas 4.5 and 4.12 to conclude that

$$v_q(p')v_{r'}(q)v_{p'}(r') = -v_{p'}(q)v_q(r')v_{r'}(p').$$

Since r' is used here instead of r, cancellation based on r does not apply. Based on $x \succ p$, $x \succ q$ with $\{x \succ p \succ r, x \succ \lambda p + (1 - \lambda)q \succ r\}$ and $\{x \succ p \succ q, x \succ \lambda p + (1 - \lambda)q \succ q\}$, an analysis that is almost identical to that for x in the preceding paragraph gives

$$v_p(q) = \lim_{\lambda \uparrow 1} v_{\lambda p + (1-\lambda)q}(q) = \lim v_{p'}(q).$$

We observe next that, with $r' \in P^*(r)$,

$$
\begin{aligned}
0 &= v_{\lambda r + (1-\lambda)q}(\lambda r + (1-\lambda)q) \\
&= \lambda v_{\lambda r + (1-\lambda)q}(r) + (1-\lambda)v_{\lambda r + (1-\lambda)q}(q) \\
&= -\lambda v_r(\lambda r + (1-\lambda)q) + (1-\lambda)v_{\lambda r + (1-\lambda)q}(q) \\
&= -\lambda(1-\lambda)v_r(q) + (1-\lambda)v_{\lambda r + (1-\lambda)q}(q),
\end{aligned}
$$

so that $\lambda v_r(q) = v_{\lambda r + (1-\lambda)q}(q)$. Therefore

$$
v_r(q) = \lim_{\lambda \uparrow 1} v_{\lambda p + (1-\lambda)q}(q).
$$

This result is used along with $q \succ y$, $r \succ y$, $\{q \succ r \succ y, q \succ \lambda r + (1 - \lambda)q \succ y\}$, and $\{p' \succ r \succ y, p' \succ \lambda r + (1 - \lambda)q \succ y\}$ in a limit analysis like that done earlier to obtain

$$
v_r(p') = \lim_{\lambda \uparrow 1} v_{\lambda r + (1-\lambda)q}(p').
$$

Finally, note that

$$
\begin{aligned}
v_{p'}(r) &= -v_r(p') = -v_r(\lambda p + (1-\lambda)q) \\
&= -\lambda v_r(p) - (1-\lambda)v_r(q) = \lambda v_p(r) - (1-\lambda)v_r(q),
\end{aligned}
$$

so

$$
v_p(r) = \lim_{\lambda \uparrow 1} v_{\lambda p + (1-\lambda)q}(r).
$$

Given $v_q(p')v_{r'}(q)v_{p'}(r') = -v_{p'}(q)v_q(r')v_{r'}(p)$, as earlier in this paragraph, first let $\lambda \uparrow 1$ in $r' = \lambda r + (1 - \lambda)q$ to get $v_q(p')v_{r'}(q)v_{p'}(r) = -v_{p'}(q)v_q(r)v_r(p)$. Since $v_q(r) = -v_r(q)$, cancel to obtain $v_q(p')v_{p'}(r) = v_{p'}(q)v_r(p)$. Then let $\lambda \uparrow 1$ in $p' = \lambda p + (1 - \lambda)q$ to get $v_q(p)v_p(r) = v_p(q)v_r(p)$, and cancel $v_p(r) = -v_r(p)$ to conclude that $v_q(p) = -v_p(q)$.

Case 2. $p \in P^*(r)$, $q \in P^* \setminus P^*(r)$. Let s be the measure in $P^*(r) \cap P^*(q)$ used to define $\phi(\cdot, q)$ in part **1**: then

$$
\phi(p, q) = v_q(p) \quad \text{where } v_q(s) = -v_s(q),
$$

$$
\phi(q, p) = v_p(q) \quad \text{where } v_p(r) = -v_r(p).
$$

Since $p, s \in P^*(r)$, the Case 1 proof gives $v_p(s) = -v_s(p)$. Since $p \not\sim q$ by earlier assumption, assume with no loss in generality that $p \succ q$. We consider subcases for p versus s.

Case 2A. $s \not\sim p$. Then, since $q \not\sim s$ because $s \in P^*(q)$, $\{p, q, s\}$ form either a preference cycle or a transitive triple. If a preference cycle obtains ($p \succ q \succ s \succ p$), an analysis with Lemma 4.4 as in Case 1A gives $v_q(p) = -v_p(q)$ since $v_p(s) = -v_s(p) \neq 0$ and $v_q(s) = -v_s(q) \neq 0$.

Assume henceforth for Case 2A that $\{p, q, s\}$ forms a transitive triple. Suppose first that $p > s > q$. Take y such that $p > y$ and $q > y$, let $\{\alpha s + (1 - \alpha)y \sim q, \alpha_\lambda s + (1 - \alpha_\lambda)y \sim \lambda q + (1 - \lambda)p\}$ correspond by C1 to $\{s > q > y, s > \lambda q + (1 - \lambda)p > y\}$ for λ near 1, and use the properties of the v's and the fact that $\alpha_\lambda \to \alpha$ as $\lambda \uparrow 1$ by Lemma 4.6 to get

$(1 - \alpha)v_q(y)$

$\qquad = -\alpha v_q(s)$

$\qquad = \lim_{\lambda \uparrow 1} [-\alpha_\lambda \lambda v_q(s) + \alpha_\lambda(1 - \lambda)v_s(p)]$

$\qquad = \lim [\alpha_\lambda \lambda v_s(q) + \alpha_\lambda(1 - \lambda)v_s(p)] \qquad$ (Definition of v_q)

$\qquad = \lim [\alpha_\lambda v_s(\lambda q + (1 - \lambda)p)]$

$\qquad = \lim [-\alpha_\lambda v_{\lambda q + (1 - \lambda)p}(s)] \qquad$ (Case 1)

$\qquad = \lim [(1 - \alpha_\lambda)v_{\lambda q + (1 - \lambda)p}(y)]$

$\qquad = (1 - \alpha) \lim v_{\lambda q + (1 - \lambda)p}(y)$

so that

$$v_q(y) = \lim_{\lambda \uparrow 1} v_{\lambda q + (1 - \lambda)p}(y).$$

Also let $\{\beta p + (1 - \beta)y \sim q, \beta_\lambda p + (1 - \beta_\lambda)y \sim \lambda q + (1 - \lambda)p\}$ correspond to $\{p > q > y, p > \lambda q + (1 - \lambda)p > y\}$, and use Lemma 4.6 $(\beta_\lambda \to \beta$ as $\lambda \uparrow 1)$ and the result just proved to obtain

$\beta v_q(p) = -(1 - \beta)v_q(y) = -(1 - \beta)\lim_{\lambda q + (1 - \lambda)p}(y)$

$\qquad = \lim [-(1 - \beta_\lambda)v_{\lambda q + (1 - \lambda)p}(y)] = \lim [\beta_\lambda v_{\lambda q + (1 - \lambda)p}(p)]$

$\qquad = \lim [-\beta_\lambda v_p(\lambda q + (1 - \lambda)p)] \qquad$ (Case 1)

$\qquad = \lim [-\lambda \beta_\lambda v_p(q)] = -\beta v_p(q)$

so that $v_q(p) = -v_p(q)$ as desired.

The next subcase of Case 2A has $p > q > s$ and $p > s$. With $q' = \lambda q + (1 - \lambda)p$, preceding methods applied to $p > q > s, p > \lambda q + (1 - \lambda)p > s\}$ give $v_q(p) = \lim v_{q'}(p)$, and Case 1 gives $v_p(q') = -v_{q'}(p)$. Since $\lim v_p(q') = v_p(q)$, it follows that $v_q(p) = -v_p(q)$. The proof for $s > p > q$ and $s > q$ is similar.

Case 2B. $s \sim p$. We get

$0 = v_{p/2 + q/2}(\tfrac{1}{2}p + \tfrac{1}{2}q) = \tfrac{1}{2}v_{p/2 + q/2}(p) + \tfrac{1}{2}v_{p/2 + q/2}(q)$

$\qquad = -\tfrac{1}{2}[v_p(\tfrac{1}{2}p + \tfrac{1}{2}q) + v_q(\tfrac{1}{2}p + \tfrac{1}{2}q)]$

$\qquad = -\tfrac{1}{4}[v_p(q) + v_q(p)],$

and therefore $v_q(p) = -v_p(q)$. Here Case 1 is used to go from $v_{p/2+q/2}(p)$ to $-v_p(\frac{1}{2}p + \frac{1}{2}q)$, and, since $\frac{1}{2}p + \frac{1}{2}q \not\sim s$, Case 2A is used to go from $v_{p/2+q/2}(q)$ to $-v_q(\frac{1}{2}p + \frac{1}{2}q)$.

Case 3. $p, q \in P^* \setminus P^*(r)$. Then $p \sim r \sim q$ with $p \succ q$. Let s be any element in $P^*(r)$ so that $\frac{1}{2}p + \frac{1}{2}s$ and $\frac{1}{2}q + \frac{1}{2}s$ are in $P^*(r)$. Then, by Cases 1 and 2,

$$
\begin{aligned}
0 &= v_{p/2+s/2}(\tfrac{1}{2}q + \tfrac{1}{2}s) + v_{q/2+s/2}(\tfrac{1}{2}p + \tfrac{1}{2}s) \\
&= \tfrac{1}{2}[v_{p/2+s/2}(q) + v_{p/2+s/2}(s) + v_{q/2+s/2}(p) + v_{q/2+s/2}(s)] \\
&= -\tfrac{1}{2}[v_q(\tfrac{1}{2}p + \tfrac{1}{2}s) + v_s(\tfrac{1}{2}p + \tfrac{1}{2}s) + v_p(\tfrac{1}{2}q + \tfrac{1}{2}s) \\
&\qquad + v_s(\tfrac{1}{2}q + \tfrac{1}{2}s)] \\
&= -\tfrac{1}{4}[v_q(p) + v_q(s) + v_s(p) + v_p(q) + v_p(s) + v_s(q)] \\
&= -\tfrac{1}{4}[v_q(p) + v_p(q)],
\end{aligned}
$$

so $v_q(p) = -v_p(q)$.

Cases 1, 2, and 3 exhaust the possibilities and therefore ϕ is skew-symmetric on $P^* \times P^*$.

4.7 PROOF COMPLETION

Since there is nothing more to prove if $P = P^*$, assume in this section that $P_{max} \cup P_{min}$ is not empty. We complete the sufficiency proof of Theorem 4.1 with parts **3** and **4** outlined at the start of the preceding section. *Throughout this section x and y always denote elements in $P_{max} \cup P_{min}$.*

3. To complete the definition of ϕ, define v_x on P and ϕ on $P \times (P \setminus P^*)$ as follows. First, if $p \in P^*$ let

$$
v_x(p) = \phi(p, x) = -\phi(x, p).
$$

Given $\phi(x, p)$ for $p \in P^*$ as defined earlier, $\phi(p, x)$ must be defined in this way to satisfy skew-symmetry. Second, for all $p \sim x$ take

$$
v_x(p) = \phi(p, x) = 0
$$

as required for the SSB representation. If $p \sim x$ and $p \in P^*$, then $v_x(p) = \phi(p, x) = 0$ by both definitions. Moreover, if x and y are in the same one of P_{max} and P_{min}, then $x \sim y$ and $v_x(y) = v_y(x) = 0$.

The only cases not covered in the preceding paragraph occur when $x \in P_{max}, y \in P_{min}$, and $x \succ y$. Suppose this is so. Let $t = \frac{1}{2}x + \frac{1}{2}y$, so $x \succ t \succ y$ and $t \in P^*$. To have v_x and v_y linear, we require

$$
v_x(t) = \tfrac{1}{2}v_x(x) + \tfrac{1}{2}v_x(y) = \tfrac{1}{2}v_x(y),
$$
$$
v_y(t) = \tfrac{1}{2}v_y(x) + \tfrac{1}{2}v_y(y) = \tfrac{1}{2}v_y(x).
$$

Since $v_x(t) = -v_t(x)$ and $v_y(t) = -v_t(y)$ by the preceding paragraph, define

$$v_x(y) = \phi(y, x) = -2v_t(x),$$
$$v_y(x) = \phi(x, y) = -2v_t(y).$$

Skew-symmetry holds here for x and y since

$$\phi(x, y) + \phi(y, x) = -2[v_t(x) + v_t(y)]$$
$$= -4[v_t(x)/2 + v_t(y)/2] = -4v_t(t) = 0,$$

where v_t is linear since $t \in P^*$.

Thus ϕ is now defined on $P \times P^*$ in a manner that is unique, given the original $\phi(\cdot, r) = v_r(\cdot)$ in part **1**, if it is to satisfy the SSB representation. Hence if the defined ϕ does satisfy skew-symmetry and bilinearity everywhere, then it is unique up to similarity transformations.

The constructions in this part of the proof along with the conclusion of part **2** show that ϕ is skew-symmetric on $P \times P$. Moreover, it should be clear that, for all $p, q \in P$, $p \succ q \Leftrightarrow \phi(p, q) > 0$.

4. It remains only to verify that v_x, or $\phi(\cdot, x)$, is linear for each $x \in P_{max} \cup P_{min}$. We prove this for $x \in P_{max}$. A symmetric proof applies for $x \in P_{min}$.

Given $x \in P_{max}$ we are to show that

$$(p, q \in P, 0 < \lambda < 1) \Rightarrow v_x(\lambda p + (1 - \lambda)q)$$
$$= \lambda v_x(p) + (1 - \lambda)v_x(q).$$

If $p \sim x \sim q$, then $x \sim \lambda p + (1 - \lambda)q$ by C2, and all v_x terms in the preceding equation vanish. Assume henceforth that $x \succ p$. We examine specific cases as follows:

1. $p \in P^*, q \in P^*$.
2. $p \in P^*, q \in P_{max}$.
3. $p \in P^*, q \in P_{min}$.
4. $p \in P_{min}, q \in P^*$.
5. $p \in P_{min}, q \in P_{max}$.
6. $p \in P_{min}, q \in P_{min}$.

These exhaust the possibilities. Separate proofs are needed for the first three cases; the last three can be handled together. Because ϕ satisfies skew-symmetry, the desired linear form for v_x converts to

$$v_{\lambda p + (1-\lambda)q}(x) = \lambda v_p(x) + (1 - \lambda)v_q(x).$$

We work with this expression in the ensuing analysis.

Case 1. $p, q \in P^*$. Let $t = \frac{1}{2}x + \frac{1}{2}p$ so $t \in P^*$ along with $\lambda p + (1 - \lambda)q \in P^*$. By linearity for fixed elements in P^*, $v_t(\lambda p + (1 - \lambda)q) = \lambda v_t(p) + (1 - \lambda)v_t(q)$, so by skew-symmetry $v_{\lambda p + (1 - \lambda)q}(t) = \lambda v_p(t) + (1 - \lambda)v_q(t)$. Then linearity and $v_p(p) = 0$ give

$$v_{\lambda p + (1 - \lambda)q}(x) + v_{\lambda p + (1 - \lambda)q}(p)$$
$$= [\lambda v_p(x) + (1 - \lambda)v_q(x)] + (1 - \lambda)v_q(p).$$

Since

$$v_{\lambda p + (1 - \lambda)q}(p) - (1 - \lambda)v_q(p)$$
$$= -v_p(\lambda p + (1 - \lambda)q) + (1 - \lambda)v_p(q)$$
$$= -(1 - \lambda)v_p(q) + (1 - \lambda)v_p(q) = 0,$$

the desired result follows.

Case 2. $p \in P^*$, $q \in P_{\max}$. Then $q \sim x$, so $v_x(q) = v_q(x) = 0$ and we are to prove that

$$v_{\lambda p + (1 - \lambda)q}(x) = \lambda v_p(x).$$

Let $\mu = (\lambda - \tau)/(1 - \tau)$ for $0 < \tau < \lambda$ with $\mu p + (1 - \mu)q \in P^*$ for all $0 < \mu \leqslant 1$ by C1 and C2. Since $\lambda p + (1 - \lambda)q = \tau p + (1 - \tau)(\mu p + (1 - \mu)q)$, Case 1 implies

$$v_{\lambda p + (1 - \lambda)q}(x) = \tau v_p(x) + (1 - \tau)v_{\mu p + (1 - \mu)q}(x).$$

Hence, with $\tau \uparrow \lambda \Leftrightarrow \mu \downarrow 0$, the desired result holds if and only if

$$\lim_{\mu \downarrow 0} v_{\mu p + (1 - \mu)q}(x) = 0.$$

To prove this, choose $t \in P^*$ with $p \succ t$. Since $\{x \succ p \succ t, x \sim q \succsim t\}$, C2 gives $x \succ \mu p + (1 - \mu)q \succ t$ for all $0 < \mu \leqslant 1$, so there is a unique f_μ in $(0, 1)$ such that

$$f_\mu x + (1 - f_\mu)t \sim \mu p + (1 - \mu)q,$$

with

$$f_\mu v_{\mu p + (1 - \mu)q}(x) + (1 - f_\mu)v_{\mu p + (1 - \mu)q}(t) = 0$$

for all $0 < \mu \leqslant 1$. Since $t \in P^*$, $v_{\mu p + (1 - \mu)q}(t) = -v_t(\mu p + (1 - \mu)q) = -\mu v_t(p) - (1 - \mu)v_t(q)$. Therefore

$$\lim_{\mu \downarrow 0} v_{\mu p + (1 - \mu)q}(t) = -v_t(q).$$

If $q \sim t$, then $v_t(q) = 0$ and, since f_μ remains constant as $\mu \downarrow 0$ by the first part of Lemma 4.7, $\lim v_{\mu p + (1 - \mu)q}(x) = 0$. If $q \succ t$, then $f_\mu \uparrow 1$ as $\mu \downarrow 0$ by the latter part of Lemma 4.7, so again $\lim v_{\mu p + (1 - \mu)q}(x) = 0$.

Case 3. $p \in P^*$, $q \in P_{\min}$. As in Case 2 let $\mu = (\lambda - \tau)/(1 - \tau)$ for $0 < \tau < \lambda$ to get

$$v_{\lambda p + (1 - \lambda)q}(x) = \tau v_p(x) + (1 - \tau)v_{\mu p + (1 - \mu)q}(x).$$

We examine x versus q in subcases.

Case 3A. $x \sim q$. Then $v_q(x) = 0$, so the desired result $v_{\lambda p + (1 - \lambda)q}(x) = \lambda v_p(x)$ holds if and only if $v_{\mu p + (1 - \mu)q}(x)$ goes to 0 as $\mu \downarrow 0$. Suppose first that $p > q$. Then $x > p > q$, so $p \sim \alpha x + (1 - \alpha)q$ for a unique α in $(0, 1)$. Therefore, since $x \sim q$, $\mu p + (1 - \mu)q \sim \alpha x + (1 - \alpha)q$ for all μ by C2. Hence

$$0 = v_{\mu p + (1 - \mu)q}(\alpha x + (1 - \alpha)q)$$

$$= \alpha v_{\mu p + (1 - \mu)q}(x) + (1 - \alpha)v_{\mu p + (1 - \mu)q}(q)$$

$$= \alpha v_{\mu p + (1 - \mu)q}(x) - (1 - \alpha)\mu v_q(p)$$

since

$$v_{\mu p + (1 - \mu)q}(q) = -v_q(\mu p + (1 - \mu)q)$$

$$= -[\mu v_q(p) + (1 - \mu)v_q(q)] = -\mu v_q(p),$$

where the linearity for $v_q(\mu p + (1 - \mu)q)$ follows from the dual of Case 2 [$q \in P_{\min}$, $p \in P^*$]. Hence $\lim v_{\mu p + (1 - \mu)q}(x) = 0$.

Suppose henceforth in Case 3A that $p \sim q$ as well as $x \sim q$. Since $x > \frac{1}{2}x + \frac{1}{2}p > \mu p + (1 - \mu)q$, let f_μ satisfy

$$f_\mu x + (1 - f_\mu)(\mu p + (1 - \mu)q) \sim \frac{1}{2}x + \frac{1}{2}p.$$

By Lemma 4.8, $f_\mu \downarrow 0$ as $\mu \downarrow 0$. Since $\frac{1}{2}x + \frac{1}{2}p \in P^*$,

$$0 = v_{x/2 + p/2}(f_\mu x + (1 - f_\mu)(\mu p + (1 - \mu)q))$$

$$= f_\mu v_{x/2 + p/2}(x) + (1 - f_\mu)v_{x/2 + p/2}(\mu p + (1 - \mu)q)$$

$$= \frac{1}{2}f_\mu v_p(x) - (1 - f_\mu)v_{\mu p + (1 - \mu)q}(\tfrac{1}{2}x + \tfrac{1}{2}p) \qquad \text{(Case 2)}$$

$$= \frac{1}{2}f_\mu v_p(x) - \frac{1}{2}(1 - f_\mu)v_{\mu p + (1 - \mu)q}(x) \qquad (p \sim \mu p + (1 - \mu)q).$$

Therefore $v_{\mu p + (1 - \mu)q}(x)$ goes to 0 as $\mu \downarrow 0$.

Case 3B. $x > q$. Let $t = \frac{1}{2}x + \frac{1}{2}q$. By the definitions in part 3, $v_q(x) = -2v_t(q) = 2v_q(t)$, so the desired linearity conclusion in the present case is

$$v_{\lambda p + (1 - \lambda)q}(x) = \lambda v_p(x) + (1 - \lambda)2v_q(t).$$

According to the initial paragraph for Case 3, this will be true if $v_{\mu p + (1 - \mu)q}(x) \to 2v_q(t)$ as $\mu \downarrow 0$. Since $x > t > \mu p + (1 - \mu)q$ for small μ, let f_μ in $(0, 1)$ satisfy

$$f_\mu x + (1 - f_\mu)(\mu p + (1 - \mu)q) \sim t = \frac{1}{2}x + \frac{1}{2}q.$$

Then $f_\mu \uparrow \frac{1}{2}$ as $\mu \downarrow 0$ by Lemma 4.9. Now

$$f_\mu v_t(x) + (1 - f_\mu)v_t(\mu p + (1 - \mu)q) = 0,$$

$v_t(x) = -v_x(q)/2 = v_q(x)/2 = -v_t(q) = v_q(t)$ by definition and skew-symmetry, and, since $\mu p + (1 - \mu)q \in P^*$,

$$v_t(\mu p + (1 - \mu)q) = -v_{\mu p + (1 - \mu)q}(\tfrac{1}{2}x + \tfrac{1}{2}q)$$
$$= -\tfrac{1}{2}[v_{\mu p + (1 - \mu)q}(x) + v_{\mu p + (1 - \mu)q}(q)]$$
$$= -\tfrac{1}{2}[v_{\mu p + (1 - \mu)q}(x) + \mu v_p(q)],$$

where the dual of Case 2 is used in the final step if $p > q$. Therefore

$$f_\mu v_q(t) = (1 - f_\mu)[v_{\mu p + (1 - \mu)q}(x) + \mu v_p(q)]/2,$$

and it follows that $v_{\mu p + (1 - \mu)q}(x) \to 2v_q(t)$ as $\mu \downarrow 0$.

Cases 4, 5, and 6. $x \in P_{\max}$, $p \in P_{\min}$, $x > p$. Let

$$t = \tfrac{1}{2}x + \tfrac{1}{2}(\lambda p + (1 - \lambda)q).$$

Then $x > t > p$ by C2. Moreover, $t > \lambda p + (1 - \lambda)q$ since $x > \lambda p + (1 - \lambda)q$. Because $\tfrac{1}{2}x + \tfrac{1}{2}t \in P^*$,

$$v_{x/2 + t/2}(\lambda p + (1 - \lambda)q) = \lambda v_{x/2 + t/2}(p) + (1 - \lambda)v_{x/2 + t/2}(q),$$

which skew-symmetry converts to

$$v_{\lambda p + (1 - \lambda)q}(\tfrac{1}{2}x + \tfrac{1}{2}t) = \lambda v_p(\tfrac{1}{2}x + \tfrac{1}{2}t) + (1 - \lambda)v_q(\tfrac{1}{2}x + \tfrac{1}{2}t).$$

We claim that each v term here decomposes linearly. For the first term, $\lambda p + (1 - \lambda)q \in P^* \cup P_{\min}$ since $x > \lambda p + (1 - \lambda)q$. Hence, by either linearity of v_s for $s \in P^*$ or by the dual of Case 3 when $\lambda p + (1 - \lambda)q \in P_{\min}$ [noting that $t > \lambda p + (1 - \lambda)q$, which corresponds to $x > p$ in Case 3], we have

$$v_{\lambda p + (1 - \lambda)q}(\tfrac{1}{2}x + \tfrac{1}{2}t) = \tfrac{1}{2}v_{\lambda p + (1 - \lambda)q}(x) + \tfrac{1}{2}v_{\lambda p + (1 - \lambda)q}(t).$$

Since $t > p$ and $p \in P_{\min}$, the dual of Case 3 gives

$$v_p(\tfrac{1}{2}x + \tfrac{1}{2}t) = \tfrac{1}{2}v_p(x) + \tfrac{1}{2}v_p(t).$$

Finally, we also have

$$v_q(\tfrac{1}{2}x + \tfrac{1}{2}t) = \tfrac{1}{2}v_q(x) + \tfrac{1}{2}v_q(t)$$

for the following reasons: Case 4 has $q \in P^*$. Case 5 has $q \in P_{\max}$, so apply Case 2 if $q > t$ [corresponds to $x > p$ in the original], and otherwise note that $t \sim q \sim x$ with $v_q(\tfrac{1}{2}x + \tfrac{1}{2}t) = v_q(x) = v_q(t) = 0$. Case 6 has $q \in P_{\min}$, so apply the dual of Case 3 if $t > q$ and note that if not ($t > q$) then all three v_q terms vanish. When the three decomposed terms are applied to their predecessor earlier in this paragraph, we get

$$v_{\lambda p + (1-\lambda)q}(x) + v_{\lambda p + (1-\lambda)q}(t)$$
$$= [\lambda v_p(x) + (1 - \lambda)v_q(x)] + [\lambda v_p(t) + (1 - \lambda)v_q(t)].$$

Since $t \in P^*$, linearity and skew-symmetry give $v_{\lambda p + (1-\lambda)q}(t) = \lambda v_p(t) + (1 - \lambda)v_q(t)$, and cancellation in the preceding equations leaves $v_{\lambda p + (1-\lambda)q}(x) = \lambda v_p(x) + (1 - \lambda)v_q(x)$. This completes the sufficiency proof of Theorem 4.1.

4.8 EXTENSION FOR PROBABILITY MEASURES

We have seen in Section 3.9 that the SSB representation implies

$$\phi(p, q) = \sum_x \sum_y p(x)q(y)\phi(x, y)$$

whenever p and q are simple measures in P, P includes the set of one-point measures on X, and ϕ on $X \times X$ is defined from ϕ on $P \times P$ by

$$\phi(x, y) = \phi(p, q) \quad \text{when } p(x) = q(y) = 1.$$

The extension of the SSB expectational form to

$$\phi(p, q) = \int_{x \in X} \int_{y \in X} \phi(x, y) \, dp(x) \, dq(y)$$

for more general measures $p, q \in P$ will conclude the present chapter.

As in Section 1.8 for the extension of the expected utility form, further assumptions are needed for the SSB extension. Instead of considering two sets of structural conditions as in Theorems 1.5 and 1.6, we consider only the following set of conditions:

S0. *$\mathcal{Q}$ is a Borel algebra of subsets of X that contains $\{x\}$ for every $x \in X$ and contains $\{x : \phi(p, x) < c\}$ and $\{x : \phi(p, x) > c\}$ for every $p \in P$ and every real number c. Moreover, P is a convex set of countably additive probability measures on $\mathcal{Q}$ that contains every one-point measure and is closed under conditional measures.*

The direct appearance of ϕ in our structural axiom S0 might be objected to since it is preferable to avoid mention of derived functions in the axioms. It is possible to replace ϕ in S0 by assumptions about $\mathcal{Q}$'s containment of conditional preference intervals, but it is awkward to do so, and we therefore proceed with S0 as stated (Fishburn, 1984c, p. 135).

Two other axioms patterned after A4 and A5 are used in the extension. We let x^* denote the measure in P that assigns probability 1 to $x \in X$. The axioms apply to all $p, r, s \in P$, all $A \in \mathcal{Q}$, and all $0 < \beta \leq 1$:

C4. Dominance: *Suppose $p(A) = 1$. Then $(\beta x^* + (1 - \beta)s) \succsim r$ for* *all $x \in A) \Rightarrow \beta p + (1 - \beta)s \succsim r$, and $(r \succsim \beta x^* + (1 - \beta)s$ for all $x \in A) \Rightarrow r \succsim \beta p + (1 - \beta)s$;*

C5. Truncation: *Let $A(c) = \{x:\phi(x, r) \geq c\}$ and $B(c) = \{x:\phi(x, r) \leq c\}$ for each real number c. Then*

$$\beta p + (1 - \beta)s \succ r \Rightarrow \beta p_{B(c)} + (1 - \beta)s \succsim r \quad \text{for some } c,$$

$$r \succ \beta p + (1 - \beta)s \Rightarrow r \succsim \beta p_{A(c)} + (1 - \beta)s \quad \text{for some } c.$$

The special case of C4 for $\beta = 1$ is almost the same as A4. The generalization for $0 < \beta < 1$ allows for "separation" by the $(1 - \beta)s$ term that is needed for the SSB case. A similar remark holds for $(1 - \beta)s$ in C5.

The idea behind the truncation axiom C5 is that whenever $p \succ r$ and p has positive probability for consequences x for which $\phi(x, r)$ is arbitrarily large, then p can be truncated at its upper end to the conditional measure $p_{B(c)}$ without reversing the preference between $\beta p + (1 - \beta)s$ and r. A dual interpretation applies to the second half of C5. If ϕ is bounded, then C5 holds trivially by taking $A(c) = B(c) = X$.

THEOREM 4.4. *Suppose* S0 *holds along with* C1, C2, *and* C3. *Let* ϕ *satisfy the SSB representation of Theorem* 4.1, *and define* $\phi(x, y) = \phi(p, q)$ *when* $p(x) = q(y) = 1$. *Then* $\phi(p, q) = \iint \phi(x, y)\, dp(x)\, dq(y)$ *for all* $p, q \in P$ *if and only if* C4 *and* C5 *hold.*

Our proof is based partly on the final part of Theorem 1.6 that uses A4* and A5* in Section 1.8, and partly on elementary properties of integrals, the monotone convergence theorem and the iterated integrals (Fubini's) theorem. We refer to readers to Loève (1960, pp. 118–24, 136) for statements and proofs of the latter results.

Necessity Proof. Assume the integral form holds. As in the first part of C4, assume that $p(A) = 1$ and $\beta x^* + (1 - \beta)s \succsim r$ for all $x \in A$. Then $\phi(\beta x^* + (1 - \beta)s, r) \geq 0$ for all $x \in A$, and therefore

$$\phi(\beta p + (1 - \beta)s, r) = \beta\phi(p, r) + (1 - \beta)\phi(s, r)$$

$$= \beta \int_A \phi(x, r)\, dp(x) + (1 - \beta)\phi(s, r)$$

$$= \int_A [\beta\phi(x, r) + (1 - \beta)\phi(s, r)]\, dp(x)$$

$$= \int_A \phi(\beta x^* + (1 - \beta)s, r)\, dp(x) \geq 0,$$

so that $\beta p + (1 - \beta)s \succsim r$, the conclusion of the first part of C4. The second part of C4 follows similarly. The necessity of C5 follows from the monotone convergence theorem. ■

Sufficiency Proof. Assume the hypotheses of Theorem 4.4 along with

C4 and C5. We prove that

$$(*) \qquad \phi(p, q) = \int \phi(x, q) \, dp(x) \qquad \text{for all } p, q \in P.$$

Since this holds when either measure is a one-point measure, iteration and skew-symmetry yield

$$\phi(p, q) = \int \phi(p, y) \, dq(y) = \int \left[\int \phi(x, y) \, dp(x) \right] dq(y)$$

$$= \int\int \phi(x, y) \, dp(x) \, dq(y),$$

the desired conclusion.

To verify $(*)$, suppose first that $>$ is empty. Then $p \sim q$ throughout P, so $\phi(p, q) = \phi(x, y) = 0$ for all $p, q \in P$ and all $x, y \in X$. Thus $(*)$ holds trivially.

Suppose henceforth that $>$ is not empty, so P^* is not empty. Fix $q \in P^*$, and let $>_q$ denote the weak order on P established by v_q or $\phi(\cdot, q)$; that is, $p >_q r \Leftrightarrow \phi(p, q) > \phi(r, q)$, with $p \geqslant_q r$ if $\phi(p, q) \geqslant \phi(r, q)$. We prove that $>_q$ satisfies two conditions that mimic A4* and A5* and allow us to conclude that $(*)$ holds for all $p \in P$ at the fixed $q \in P^*$. The final paragraph of the proof notes that $(*)$ also holds when q is in $P_{\max}$ or $P_{\min}$.

The conditions desired for $>_q$ are

a4 (cf. A4*). Suppose $p(A) = 1$. Then $(x \geqslant_q r$ for all $x \in A) \Rightarrow p \geqslant_q r$, and $(r \geqslant_q x$ for all $x \in A) \Rightarrow r \geqslant_q p$;

a5 (cf. A5*). $p >_q r \Rightarrow p_B \geqslant_q r$ for some B of the form $\{x:\phi(x, q) \leqslant c\}$; $r >_q p \Rightarrow r \geqslant_q p_A$ for some A of the form $\{x:\phi(x, q) \geqslant c\}$.

It will suffice to prove the first parts of a4 and a5.

We begin with a4, assuming that $p(A) = 1$ and $x \geqslant_q r$ for all $x \in A$. Three cases are considered depending on how q and r are related.

Case 1. $q \sim r$. Then $x \geqslant_q r \Leftrightarrow \phi(x, q) \geqslant 0 \Leftrightarrow x \succsim q$, and if $x \succsim q$ for all $x \in A$, then the first part of C4 with $\beta = 1$ implies $p \succsim q$; hence $p \geqslant_q r$.

Case 2. $r > q$. Since $q \in P^*$, let $s \in P$ satisfy $q > s$. Since $x \geqslant_q r$ for $x \in A$ (i.e., $\phi(x, q) \geqslant \phi(r, q) > 0$), we have $x > q$. Let $\alpha(x)$ and β satisfy

$$\alpha(x)x^* + (1 - \alpha(x))s \sim q,$$

$$\beta r + (1 - \beta)s \sim q$$

with $\alpha(x) \leqslant \beta$ for all $x \in A$ since $\phi(x, q) \geqslant \phi(r, q) > 0$. Because $\beta \geqslant \alpha(x)$ and $x > q$, it follows that

$$\beta x^* + (1 - \beta)s \succsim q \qquad \text{for all } x \in A,$$

so we conclude from the first part of C4 that $\beta p + (1 - \beta)s \succsim q$. This gives

$\beta\phi(p, q) \geqslant (1 - \beta)\phi(q, s)$ and, since $\beta r + (1 - \beta)s \sim q \Rightarrow (1 - \beta)\phi(q, s) = \beta\phi(r, q)$, we get $\phi(p, q) \geqslant \phi(r, q)$; hence $p \geqslant_q r$ as desired for a4.

Case 3. $q > r$. The proof for this case is similar to the proof for Case 2. Choose $s > q$ and get $\beta x^* + (1 - \beta)s \gtrsim q$ for all $x \in A$.

Consider a5 next with $p >_q r$. Again specific cases are examined as follows.

Case 1. $p > q \gtrsim r$. Since $p > q$, the first part of C5 with $\beta = 1$ implies $p_B \gtrsim q$ for some $B = \{x : \phi(x, q) \leqslant c\}$. Hence $p_B \gtrsim q \gtrsim r$, so $\phi(p_B, q) \geqslant \phi(r, q)$ and $p_B \geqslant_q r$, the desired conclusion of a5.

Case 2. $p \sim q > r$. Let $s \in P$ satisfy $s > q$, and let β in $(0, 1)$ satisfy $q \sim \beta r + (1 - \beta)s$. Then $\beta\phi(q, r) = (1 - \beta)\phi(s, q)$. Since $p \sim q$ and $s > q$, we have $\beta p + (1 - \beta)s > q$, and the first part of C5 gives $B = \{x : \phi(x, q) \leqslant c\}$ such that $\beta p_B + (1 - \beta)s \gtrsim q$, or $(1 - \beta)\phi(s, q) \geqslant \beta\phi(q, p_B)$. Hence $\phi(q, r) \geqslant \phi(q, p_B)$, or by skew-symmetry $\phi(p_B, q) \geqslant \phi(r, q)$. Therefore $p_B \geqslant_q r$.

Case 3. $p > q, r > q$. Let s satisfy $q > s$ with $\alpha p + (1 - \alpha)s \sim q$ and $\beta r + (1 - \beta)s \sim q$. By hypothesis $(p >_q r)$, $\alpha < \beta$, and it follows that $\beta p + (1 - \beta)s > q$. By C5, $\beta p_B + (1 - \beta)s \gtrsim q$ for some $B = \{x : \phi(x, q) \leqslant c\}$, and this plus $\beta r + (1 - \beta)s \sim q$ gives $\phi(p_B, q) \geqslant \phi(r, q)$, or $p_B \geqslant_q r$.

Case 4: $q > p$ and $q > r$. (This is the final case possible when $p >_q r$.) With $s > q$, an analysis like that in the preceding paragraph gives $p_B \geqslant_q r$.

This verifies a4 and a5 for $q \in P^*$. Because these axioms subsume A4* and A5* when $>$ in those axioms is replaced by $>_q$, it follows from the final part of Theorem 1.6 that (*) holds for all $p \in P$ at the fixed q. Hence (*) holds for all $(p, q) \in P \times P^*$.

To show that (*) holds also when $q \in P_{\max} \cup P_{\min}$, suppose for definiteness that $q \in P_{\min}$. If $q \in P_{\max}$ also, then $0 = \phi(p, q) = \phi(x, q)$ for all $p \in P$ and all $x \in X$, so (*) holds. Assume henceforth that $q \notin P_{\max}$ and take $s > q$ for $s \in P^*$. Since $s > \frac{1}{2}s + \frac{1}{2}q > q$, $\frac{1}{2}s + \frac{1}{2}q$ is in P^*, and therefore

$$
\begin{aligned}
\phi(p, \tfrac{1}{2}s + \tfrac{1}{2}q) &= \int \phi(x, \tfrac{1}{2}s + \tfrac{1}{2}q) \, dp(x) \\
&= \int [\tfrac{1}{2}\phi(x, s) + \tfrac{1}{2}\phi(x, q)] \, dp(x) \\
&= \frac{1}{2} \int \phi(x, s) \, dp(x) + \frac{1}{2} \int \phi(x, q) \, dp(x) \\
&= \frac{1}{2} \phi(p, s) + \frac{1}{2} \int \phi(x, q) \, dp(x).
\end{aligned}
$$

Moreover, $\phi(p, \tfrac{1}{2}s + \tfrac{1}{2}q) = \tfrac{1}{2}\phi(p, s) + \tfrac{1}{2}\phi(p, q)$, and therefore $\phi(p, q) = \int \phi(x, q) \, dp(x)$. ∎

5 Transitive Nonlinear Utility Theory

When transitivity is added to the axioms of the preceding chapter, the SSB representation reduces to the weighted linear representation, and the nontransitive convex representation, with a further technical assumption, reduces to the transitive convex representation. This chapter begins with the latter representation, including its reliance on the assumption of countable boundedness. It then looks at the weighted linear representation in detail, concluding with uniqueness features, equivalent axiom sets, and extension to an expectational form.

5.1 TRANSITIVE CONVEX UTILITY

This chapter considers the effects of transitivity on the nontransitive convex representation and the SSB representation of the preceding chapter. The transitive convex representation is examined in this section and the next. The weighted linear representation that results when transitivity is imposed on the SSB structure is discussed in Sections 5.3 through 5.7. Both representations accommodate violations of independence.

We recall from Section 3.7 that $(P, \succ)$ has a *transitive convex representation* if there is a functional u on P such that, for all $p, q \in P$,

$$p \succ q \Leftrightarrow u(p) > u(q),$$

$p \succ q \Rightarrow u(\lambda p + (1 - \lambda)q)$ is continuous and increasing in λ.

As noted there, these properties imply that $u(\lambda p + (1 - \lambda)q)$ is constant in λ when $p \sim q$.

Our axioms for the transitive convex representation consist of A1($\sim$) [$\sim$ is transitive on P], C1, C2, and countable boundedness, where $\succ$ is *countably bounded* if there is a countable subset Q of P such that for every $p \in P$ there are $q, q' \in Q$ for which $q \succsim p \succsim q'$. Recall also from Theorem 1.4 that A1($\sim$), C1, and C2 imply that $\succ$ on P is a weak order.

THEOREM 5.1. *Suppose P is a nonempty convex set of probability measures defined on a Boolean algebra of subsets of X, and $\succ$ is a binary relation on P. Then $(P, \succ)$ has a transitive convex representation if and only if* A1($\sim$), C1, *and* C2 *hold and* $\succ$ *is countably bounded.*

Remark. Countable boundedness is automatic if P is closed; that is, P_{max} and P_{min} are not empty. The need for countable boundedness in other cases is discussed in the next section.

Proof. We consider necessity first, assuming that $(P, \succ)$ has a transitive convex representation. Axioms A1($\sim$) and C1 are then obvious. For C2, assume first that $p \succ q$ and $p \succsim r$ with $0 < \lambda < 1$. Then $u(p) \geqslant \max\{u(q), u(r)\} > u(\lambda q + (1 - \lambda)r)$, so $p \succ \lambda q + (1 - \lambda)r$. The other parts of C2 follow similarly. Since u is real valued, there must be a countable $Q \subseteq P$ with sup $u(Q) =$ sup $u(P)$, inf $u(Q) =$ inf $u(P)$, and with Q containing an element of maximum (minimum) utility if such exists. Any such Q verifies countable boundedness.

For sufficiency, assume A1($\sim$), C1, C2, and countable boundedness. Assume also that $\succ$ is not empty since otherwise the desired conclusion is transparent. Let Q be a countable subset of P that verifies countable boundedness, and enumerate Q as $\{q_1, q_2, \ldots\}$. Fix $p_1 \succ p_0$ in Q and construct $p_2, p_3, \ldots$ and $p_{-1}, p_{-2}, \ldots$ as long as possible in the following ways:

p_2 is the first q_i (smallest i) for which $q_i \succ p_1$.
p_{n+1} for $n \geqslant 2$ is the first q_i for which $q_i \succ p_n$.
p_{-1} is the first q_i for which $p_0 \succ q_i$.
p_{-n-1} for $n \geqslant 1$ is the first q_i for which $p_{-n} \succ q_i$.

We refer to $\cdots p_2 \succ p_1 \succ p_0 \succ p_{-1} \cdots$ as the *dual standard sequence*. Clearly, for every $p \in P$ either $p \sim p_i$ for a unique i or $p_{i+1} \succ p \succ p_i$ for a unique i.

Let

$$P_0 = \{\lambda p_{i+1} + (1 - \lambda)p_i : 0 \leqslant \lambda \leqslant 1, p_{i+1}$$

and p_i are in the dual standard sequence$\}$

and define u on P_0 by (for each i and λ)

$$u(\lambda p_{i+1} + (1 - \lambda)p_i) = \lambda(i + 1) + (1 - \lambda)i = i + \lambda.$$

Then, by C2 and weak order, $p \succ q \Leftrightarrow u(p) > u(q)$ for all $p, q \in P_0$. In view of Theorem 1.4 and the remark at the end of the preceding paragraph, we extend u from P_0 to P by taking $u(p) = u(p')$ when $p \sim p'$ and $p' \in P_0$. It follows that, for all $p, q \in P, p \succ q \Leftrightarrow u(p) > u(q)$.

To verify the final part of the representation, assume $p \succ q$ and let

$$f(\lambda) = u(\lambda p + (1 - \lambda)q) \qquad \text{for } 0 \leqslant \lambda \leqslant 1.$$

By C2, $\lambda > \mu \Rightarrow \lambda p + (1 - \lambda)q \succ \mu p + (1 - \mu)q$, so f increases in λ. Contrary to continuity, suppose f is not continuous. For definiteness assume that $f(\alpha) < f(\alpha)^+ = \inf\{f(\lambda):\lambda > \alpha\}$ with $\alpha < 1$. Choose β so that $\alpha < \beta < 1$. By construction, $f(\alpha) < u(r) < f(\alpha)^+$ for some $r \in P$, so $\beta p + (1 - \beta)q \succ r \succ \alpha p + (1 - \alpha)q$. But then $r \sim \gamma p + (1 - \gamma)q$ for a unique γ in (α, β), so $u(r) = u(\gamma p + (1 - \gamma)q) = f(\gamma)$. But this is impossible since there is no γ with $f(\alpha) < f(\gamma) < f(\alpha)^+$. We conclude that f must be continuous. ∎

It should be clear from the sufficiency proof that u for the transitive convex representation does not have simple uniqueness properties. Any transformation of u that preserves order and increasing continuity in λ for mixtures $\lambda p + (1 - \lambda)q$ when $p \succ q$ is an acceptable transformation.

5.2 THE NEED FOR COUNTABLE BOUNDEDNESS

The following theorem asserts that countable boundedness cannot be deleted from the axioms of Theorem 5.1 without affecting its conclusion.

THEOREM 5.2. *Suppose the initial hypotheses of Theorem 5.1 hold. Then there are (P, $\succ$) that satisfy A1($\sim$), C1, and C2 but do not have transitive convex representations.*

We prove this in the rest of this section by constructing a $(P, \succ)$ that satisfies the initial hypothesis along with weak order, C1 and C2 but for which $\succ$ is not countably bounded so that, by Theorem 5.1, $(P, \succ)$ does not have a transitive convex representation. Familiarity with ordinal and cardinal numbers is presumed (Rubin, 1967; Pinter, 1971). Connections between our construction and other interests in representation theory are discussed in Fishburn (1983b). We begin with a few preliminaries.

Ordinals will often be denoted by $\alpha, \beta, \ldots$, and $<$ is their natural well ordering: $0 < 1 < 2 < \cdots < \omega_0 < \omega_0 + 1 < \cdots$. The first uncountable ordinal is denoted by ω_1 and we take

$$X = \{\alpha : \alpha \text{ is an ordinal and } \alpha < \omega_1\},$$

the uncountable set of countable ordinals. Also, $P = P_X$, the set of simple distributions on X. The distribution in P that assigns probability 1 to α is also denoted by α. For convenience in correspondence to the well ordering we shall work with the dual $\prec$ of $\succ$, where $p \prec q$ means that $q \succ p$.

Our definition of $\prec$ on P begins with $\alpha \prec \beta$ if $\alpha < \beta$ for the one-point distributions. We extend $\prec$ to P with the use of functions v_q like those in

Lemma 4.3, with v_q linear on P, $q \prec p \Leftrightarrow v_q(p) > 0$, and $p \prec q \Leftrightarrow v_q(p)$ < 0. This extension will be shown to satisfy the axioms of Theorem 5.2 when $\prec$ is defined in the natural way, with either $p \sim \alpha$ or $\alpha \prec p \prec \alpha + 1$ for each $p \in P$ and some $\alpha \in X$. It then follows that *if* $\prec$ were countably bounded then there would be a countable $Y \subseteq X$ such that every $\alpha \in X$ has a $\beta \in Y$ with $\alpha \leqslant \beta$. But this is impossible since $\{\alpha : \alpha \leqslant \beta, \beta \in Y\}$ is countable when Y is countable by the fact that $\{\alpha : \alpha \leqslant \beta\}$ is countable for each $\beta \in Y$, whereas X is uncountable. We now consider the construction of the v_q.

First, define $v_\alpha(\beta)$ for all α, $\beta \in X$ by

$$v_\alpha(\alpha) = 0,$$

$$v_\alpha(\beta) = -1 \quad \text{if } \beta < \alpha,$$

and, if $\alpha < \beta$, proceed as follows. Given any $\beta > 0$, let $\gamma_1, \gamma_2, \ldots$ be a countable enumeration of $\{\alpha : \alpha < \beta\}$, take

$$v_{\gamma_1}(\beta) = 1,$$

$$v_{\gamma_2}(\beta) = 1/2 \quad \text{if } \gamma_1 < \gamma_2,$$

$$= 2 \quad \text{if } \gamma_2 < \gamma_1,$$

and for $n > 2$ define $v_{\gamma_n}(\beta)$ recursively by

$$v_{\gamma_n}(\beta) = 1/n \quad \text{if } \gamma_i < \gamma_n \text{ for all } i < n,$$

$$= n \quad \text{if } \gamma_n < \gamma_i \text{ for all } i < n,$$

$$= \tfrac{1}{2}[v_{\gamma_a}(\beta) + v_{\gamma_b}(\beta)] \quad \text{when } \gamma_a < \gamma_n < \gamma_b \text{ for } a, b < n$$

$$\text{and } \gamma_i < \gamma_a \text{ or } \gamma_b < \gamma_i \text{ for}$$

$$\text{all other } i < n.$$

Thus $v_\alpha(\beta)$ is defined for all α, $\beta \in X$. If $\alpha_1, \ldots, \alpha_n$ are the first n γ_i in the preceding construction with $\alpha_1 < \alpha_2 < \cdots < \alpha_n < \beta$, then $v_{\alpha_1}(\beta) > v_{\alpha_2}(\beta)$ $> \cdots > v_{\alpha_n}(\beta) > 0$. Hence $v_0(\beta) > v_1(\beta) > \cdots > v_\alpha(\beta) > \cdots$ for all α $< \beta$, with all such $v_\alpha(\beta)$ positive. Since $v_\alpha(\alpha) = 0$, v_α will play the role of v_r in the stated representation of Lemma 4.3 when $r = \alpha$.

The definition of v_α is completed by linear extension to all of P:

$$v_\alpha(p) = \sum_{\beta \in X} v_\alpha(\beta)p(\beta).$$

The sum is well defined since $p(\beta) > 0$ for only a finite number of β. By the preceding paragraph,

$$v_\alpha(p) = -\sum_{\beta < \alpha} p(\beta) + \sum_{\beta > \alpha} v_\alpha(\beta)p(\beta)$$

with $v_\alpha(\beta) > 0$ when $\beta > \alpha$. To adhere to $\prec$ for the representation of Lemma 4.3 for α versus $p \in P$, we define

$$\alpha \prec p \quad \text{if } v_\alpha(p) > 0,$$

$$\alpha \sim p \quad \text{if } v_\alpha(p) = 0,$$

$$p \prec \alpha \quad \text{if } v_\alpha(p) < 0.$$

Our definition of v_p for nondegenerate $p \in P$ will be based on Lemma 5.1, which we prove before continuing with the construction. The lemma shows that for each $p \in P$ there is an $\alpha \in X$ such that either $p \sim \alpha$ or $\alpha \prec p \prec \alpha + 1$.

LEMMA 5.1. *For every $p \in P \setminus X$ either $v_\alpha(p) = 0$ for exactly one $\alpha > 0$, or $v_\alpha(p) > 0 > v_{\alpha+1}(p)$ for exactly one $\alpha > 0$.*

Proof. Let p denote a distribution in $P \setminus X$. By definition, $v_0(p) > 0$ and $v_\alpha(p) = -1$ for every $\alpha > \max\{\beta : p(\beta) > 0\}$. For each $\alpha < \omega_1$,

$$v_\alpha(p) - v_{\alpha+1}(p) = p(\alpha) + p(\alpha + 1)v_\alpha(\alpha + 1)$$
$$+ \sum_{\beta > \alpha+1} p(\beta)[v_\alpha(\beta) - v_{\alpha+1}(\beta)],$$

where $v_\alpha(\alpha + 1) > 0$ and $v_\alpha(\beta) - v_{\alpha+1}(\beta) > 0$ for $\beta > \alpha + 1$. Hence

$$v_\alpha(p) \geqslant v_{\alpha+1}(p) \quad \text{for all } \alpha \in X,$$

$$v_\alpha(p) > v_{\alpha+1}(p) \Leftrightarrow \sum_{\beta \geqslant \alpha} p(\beta) > 0.$$

Moreover, it is easily seen that $v_\alpha(p) \geqslant v_\beta(p)$ whenever $\alpha < \beta$. Because $v_0(p) > 0$ and $v_\alpha(p) = -1$ for large α, there is a smallest α, say α^*, where $v_\alpha(p)$ is nonpositive,

$$v_\alpha(p) > 0 \quad \text{if } \alpha < \alpha^*,$$

$$v_\beta(p) \leqslant 0 \quad \text{if } \alpha^* \leqslant \beta.$$

If in fact $v_{\alpha^*}(p) = 0$ then $\Sigma \{p(\beta) : \beta \geqslant \alpha^*\} > 0$, and therefore $v_{\alpha^*+1}(p) < 0$, so $v_\beta(p) < 0$ for all $\beta > \alpha^*$. It follows that either

(i) $v_{\alpha^*}(p) = 0$ and $v_\alpha(p) \neq 0$ for all $\alpha \neq \alpha^*$, or
(ii) $v_{\alpha^*}(p) < 0$ and α^* is not a limit ordinal, or
(iii) $v_{\alpha^*}(p) < 0$ and α^* is a limit ordinal.

An ordinal is a *limit ordinal* if it is nonzero and has no immediate predecessor under $<$. Hence if (ii) holds then α^* has an immediate predecessor, say $\alpha^* - 1$, so that $v_{\alpha^*-1}(p) > 0 > v_{\alpha^*}(p)$. Consequently,

Lemma 5.1 is true if (iii) is impossible, for then (i) and (ii) constitute the conclusion of the lemma.

To prove that (iii) cannot occur, suppose to the contrary that α^* is a limit ordinal with $v_\alpha(p) > 0 > v_{\alpha^*}(p)$ for all $\alpha < \alpha^*$. Then $v_\alpha(p) - v_{\alpha^*}(p) > \delta$ for all $\alpha < \alpha^*$ and some $\delta > 0$. Clearly,

$$v_\alpha(p) - v_{\alpha^*}(p) = \sum_{\{\gamma : \alpha \leqslant \gamma < \alpha^*\}} p(\gamma) + \sum_{\{\gamma : \alpha < \gamma \leqslant \alpha^*\}} v_\alpha(\gamma) p(\gamma)$$

$$+ \sum_{\{\gamma : \alpha^* < \gamma < \omega_1\}} p(\gamma)[v_\alpha(\gamma) - v_{\alpha^*}(\gamma)].$$

Since p is simple, the first sum vanishes as $\alpha \to \alpha^*$, and the second converges to $v_\alpha(\alpha^*)p(\alpha^*)$. Therefore, for large $\alpha < \alpha^*$,

$$v_\alpha(p) - v_{\alpha^*}(p) = v_\alpha(\alpha^*)p(\alpha^*) + \sum_{\gamma > \alpha^*} [v_\alpha(\gamma) - v_{\alpha^*}(\gamma)]p(\gamma).$$

We claim that $v_\alpha(\alpha^*) \to 0$ and $v_\alpha(\gamma) - v_{\alpha^*}(\gamma) \to 0$ as $\alpha \to \alpha^*$ which, if true, implies that $v_\alpha(p) - v_{\alpha^*}(p) \to 0$ as $\alpha \to \alpha^*$, in contradiction to $v_\alpha(p) - v_{\alpha^*}(p) > \delta > 0$ for all $\alpha < \alpha^*$. So if the claim is true, then (iii) is impossible and Lemma 5.1 is proved.

To substantiate the claim, consider $v_\alpha(\alpha^*)$ first. By the definition of $v_\alpha(\alpha^*)$ for $\alpha < \alpha^*$ according to the enumeration $\gamma_1, \gamma_2, \ldots$ of $\{\alpha : \alpha < \alpha^*\}$, there must be an infinite number of n for which $\gamma_i < \gamma_n$ for all $i < n$ so that $v_\alpha(\alpha^*) = 1/n$ for an infinite number of n. Therefore $v_\alpha(\alpha^*) \to 0$.

Consider $v_\alpha(\gamma) - v_{\alpha^*}(\gamma)$ next for $\alpha < \alpha^* < \gamma$ with α^* and γ fixed. Let $\gamma_1, \gamma_2, \ldots$ be the enumeration of the countably many β that precede γ used in defining the $v_\beta(\gamma)$ for $\beta < \gamma$. Let N be such that $\gamma_N = \alpha^*$. Then all but a finite number of $\alpha < \alpha^*$ follow γ_N in the enumeration and, since α^* is a limit ordinal, there must be an infinite number of such α whose $v_\alpha(\gamma)$ are determined by the midpoint part of the definition, i.e., by $v_\alpha(\gamma) = \frac{1}{2}[v_{\alpha'}(\gamma) + v_{\alpha^*}(\gamma)]$ with $\alpha' < \alpha < \alpha^*$. Since the successive averages clearly approach $v_{\alpha^*}(\gamma)$, it follows that $v_\alpha(\gamma) - v_{\alpha^*}(\gamma) \to 0$ as $\alpha \to \alpha^*$. ∎

With Lemma 5.1 at hand, let p be a nondegenerate distribution in P. If the first alternative of Lemma 5.1 holds [$v_\alpha(p) = 0$, $\alpha \sim p$], define v_p by

$$v_p(q) = v_\alpha(q) \qquad \text{for all } q \in P,$$

i.e., $v_p = v_\alpha$. If the second alternative holds [$v_\alpha(p) > 0 > v_{\alpha+1}(p)$, $\alpha < p < \alpha + 1$], let

$$\lambda(p) = \frac{v_\alpha(p)}{v_\alpha(p) - v_{\alpha+1}(p)}$$

and define v_p by

$$v_p = \lambda(p)v_{\alpha+1} + [1 - \lambda(p)]v_\alpha.$$

Clearly, v_p is linear for each alternative. Moreover,

LEMMA 5.2. *For all p, $q \in P$, $v_p(q) > 0 \Leftrightarrow v_q(p) < 0$.*

Proof. By Lemma 5.1 and the preceding paragraph there are unique ordinals α and β with $v_\alpha(p) \geqslant 0 > v_{\alpha+1}(p)$, $v_\beta(q) \geqslant 0 > v_{\beta+1}(q)$, and unique numbers $\lambda(p)$, $\lambda(q) \in [0, 1)$ for which

$$\lambda(p)v_{\alpha+1}(p) + [1 - \lambda(p)]v_\alpha(p) = 0,$$

$$\lambda(q)v_{\beta+1}(q) + [1 - \lambda(q)]v_\beta(q) = 0$$

such that

$$v_p = \lambda(p)v_{\alpha+1} + [1 - \lambda(p)]v_\alpha,$$

$$v_q = \lambda(q)v_{\beta+1} + [1 - \lambda(q)]v_\beta.$$

We show first that $v_p(q) = 0 \Rightarrow v_q(p) = 0$. Suppose $v_p(q) = 0$. Then the definition of v_p gives

$$\lambda(p)v_{\alpha+1}(q) + [1 - \lambda(p)]v_\alpha(q) = 0,$$

so $v_\alpha(q) \geqslant 0 > v_{\alpha+1}(q)$. [If $\lambda(p) = 0$, then $v_\alpha(q) = 0$ and Lemma 5.1 and monotonicity give $0 > v_{\alpha+1}(q)$; if $\lambda(p) > 0$, then $v_\alpha(q) > 0 > v_{\alpha+1}(q)$ since Lemma 5.1 prohibits $v_\alpha(q) = 0 = v_{\alpha+1}(q)$. (This remains true if $q \in X$.)] Since $v_\alpha(q) \geqslant 0 > v_{\alpha+1}(q)$ and $v_\beta(q) \geqslant 0 > v_{\beta+1}(q)$, $\alpha = \beta$ and therefore, by the definition of $\lambda(q)$,

$$\lambda(q)v_{\alpha+1}(q) + [1 - \lambda(q)]v_\alpha(q) = 0.$$

Since the preceding two displayed equations imply $\lambda(q) = \lambda(p)$, we have $v_q = v_p$, so $v_q(p) = v_p(p) = 0$.

Thus $v_p(q) = 0 \Leftrightarrow v_q(p) = 0$. To complete the proof of Lemma 5.2, we show that $v_p(q)$ and $v_q(p)$ cannot both be negative or positive. We consider the negative case; the positive proof is similar.

Suppose $v_p(q) < 0$. Then $\lambda(p)v_{\alpha+1}(q) + [1 - \lambda(p)]v_\alpha(q) < 0$. Since $v_{\alpha+1}(q) \leqslant v_\alpha(q)$ and $0 \leqslant \lambda(p) < 1$, $v_{\alpha+1}(q) < 0$. But $v_{\beta+1}(q) < 0 \leqslant v_\beta(q)$ by initial specification for β, and therefore $\alpha + 1 \geqslant \beta + 1$, or $\alpha \geqslant \beta$. Similarly, if $v_q(p) < 0$, then $\beta \geqslant \alpha$. Hence if *both* $v_p(q) < 0$ and $v_q(p) < 0$, then $\alpha = \beta$ and

$$\lambda(p)v_{\alpha+1}(q) + [1 - \lambda(p)]v_\alpha(q) < 0 \qquad [v_p(q) < 0],$$

$$\lambda(q)v_{\alpha+1}(p) + [1 - \lambda(q)]v_\alpha(p) < 0 \qquad [v_q(p) < 0],$$

$$\lambda(p)v_{\alpha+1}(p) + [1 - \lambda(p)]v_\alpha(p) = 0 \qquad [\text{definition of } \lambda(p)],$$

$$\lambda(q)v_{\alpha+1}(q) + [1 - \lambda(q)]v_\alpha(q) = 0 \qquad [\text{definition of } \lambda(q)].$$

Since $v_\alpha(p) > v_{\alpha+1}(p)$ by initial specification for α, the second and third expressions require $\lambda(q) > \lambda(p)$. But since $v_\alpha(q) > v_{\alpha+1}(q)$, the first and fourth require $\lambda(p) > \lambda(q)$. Thus $v_p(q) < 0$ and $v_q(p) < 0$ are inconsistent. ∎

We are now ready to complete the proof of Theorem 5.2. Thus far we have defined linear v_p for every $p \in P$ with $v_p(q) > 0 \Leftrightarrow v_q(p) < 0$. In correspondence to Lemma 4.3 we now *define* $\prec$ completely on P by $q \prec p$ if $v_q(p) > 0$. It remains to show that C1, C2, and A1($\sim$) hold.

C1. Suppose $p \prec q \prec r$, so $v_q(p) < 0 < v_q(r)$, where $0 < v_q(r)$ by Lemma 5.2 applied to $v_r(q) < 0$. Hence, for some $0 < \lambda < 1$, $\lambda v_q(p) + (1 - \lambda)v_q(r) = 0 = v_q(\lambda p + (1 - \lambda)r)$, so $q \sim \lambda p + (1 - \lambda)r$.

C2. This follows immediately from the definition of $\prec$, linearity, and Lemma 5.2.

A1($\sim$). Suppose $p \sim q$ and $q \sim r$, so $v_p(q) = v_q(r) = 0$. By the second paragraph of the proof of Lemma 5.2, $v_p = v_q$ and $v_q = v_r$, so $v_p = v_r$ with $v_p(r) = v_r(r) = 0$ and $p \sim r$.

5.3   WEIGHTED LINEAR UTILITY

This section states our main representation theorem for weighted linear utility and shows by example that the weighting functional w may have to vanish at the closed extreme of P when $(P, \succ)$ is half-open. The sufficiency proof of the theorem appears in the next section. Section 5.5 then presents and proves the uniqueness theorem for the weighted linear representation, and Section 5.6 establishes equivalence among the weighted linear axiom sets of Section 3.6. The final section of the chapter discusses the extension of the weighted linear expectational form to general probability measures.

We say that $(P, \succ)$ has a *weighted linear representation* if there are linear functionals u and w on P with $w \geq 0$ such that, for all $p, q \in P$,

$$p \succ q \Leftrightarrow u(p)w(q) > u(q)w(p),$$
$$w(p) > 0 \text{ if } (P, \succ) \text{ is open or closed.}$$

If $(P, \succ)$ is half-open, the representation requires $w(p) > 0$ for every $p \in P^*$.

THEOREM 5.3. *Suppose the initial hypotheses of Theorem 5.1 hold. Then $(P, \succ)$ has a weighted linear representation if and only if* A1($\sim$), *C1, C2, and C3 hold.*

Necessity Proof. Assume that u and w satisfy the weighted linear representation as specified above. Let $\phi(p, q) = u(p)w(q) - u(q)w(p)$. Then ϕ is an SSB functional on $P \times P$ with $> = \{(p, q):\phi(p, q) > 0\}$, so C1, C2, and C3 hold by Theorem 4.1.

To verify A1($\sim$), suppose $p \sim q$ and $q \sim r$. Then

$$u(p)w(q) = u(q)w(p),$$

$$u(q)w(r) = u(r)w(q).$$

If all w terms are positive, then $u(p)/w(p) = u(q)/w(q) = u(r)/w(r)$, and therefore $u(p)w(r) = u(r)w(p)$ and $p \sim r$. Suppose henceforth that some w term vanishes, so $(P, >)$ is half-open. Assume first that $w(q) = 0$. If $u(q) = 0$ also, then $u(s)w(q) = u(q)w(s)$ and $s \sim q$ for all $s \in P$. But then $q \in P_{\max} \cap P_{\min}$, so $(P, >)$ is closed in contradiction to half-openness. Hence $w(q) = 0$ implies $u(q) \neq 0$, and, consequently, $w(p) = w(r) = 0$, so $u(p)w(r) = u(r)w(p)$ and $p \sim r$. Assume next that $w(q) \neq 0$ and $w(p) = 0$. Then $u(p) = 0$, so $s \sim p$ for all $s \in P$, for another contradiction. A similar contradiction obtains if $w(q) \neq 0$ and $w(r) = 0$. Hence either all w terms are positive or all vanish. ∎

Although there is no direct precedent to weighted linear utility in the literature prior to Chew and MacCrimmon (1979), one previous contribution deserves mention. Recall that if $w > 0$, then we can write the weighted linear representation using ratios of linear functionals:

$$p > q \Leftrightarrow u(p)/w(p) > u(q)/w(q).$$

Bolker (1966, 1967), in a modification of the von Neumann–Morgenstern theory that was motivated in part by Jeffrey (1965), applies $>$ to $\mathcal{Q} \setminus \{\varnothing\}$, where $\mathcal{Q}$ is a complete, atom-free Boolean algebra. He proves that axioms for $>$ on $\mathcal{Q} \setminus \{\varnothing\}$ that resemble those of Theorem 5.3 in some ways imply that there are countably additive measures σ and ρ on $\mathcal{Q}$ with $\rho > 0$ on $\mathcal{Q} \setminus \{\varnothing\}$ such that, for all $A, B \in \mathcal{Q} \setminus \{\varnothing\}$,

$$A > B \Leftrightarrow \sigma(A)/\rho(A) > \sigma(B)/\rho(B).$$

Bolker's representation involves quotients of measures rather than quotients of linear functionals, with additivity rather than linearity the key property. He avoids the vanishing-denominator problem by removing $\varnothing$ from the domain of $>$ and by investing $\mathcal{Q}$ with nice structural properties. Jeffrey's (1978) later axiomatization applies $>$ to $\mathcal{Q}$ and allows $\rho(A) = 0$.

By Theorem 5.3, the weighted linear axioms enable $w > 0$ when either $P_{\max} = P_{\min} = \varnothing$ or $P_{\max} \neq \varnothing \neq P_{\min}$. We conclude this section with a half-open $(P, >)$ in which $P_{\min} \neq \varnothing$ and w must vanish on $P_{\min}$ for the weighted linear representation. In the example $P_{\min} = \{0\}$.

Let $X = \{0, 1, 2, \ldots\}$ and $P = P_X$. Define ϕ on $X \times X$ by

$$\phi(0, 0) = 0,$$

$$\phi(n, 0) = -\phi(0, n) = 1, \quad n \geqslant 1,$$

$$\phi(n, m) = n - m, \quad n, m \geqslant 1.$$

Then define ϕ on $P \times P$ by bilinear extension,

$$\phi(p, q) = \sum_{n, m} \phi(n, m) p(n) q(m),$$

and take $p > q \Leftrightarrow \phi(p, q) > 0$. Since ϕ is an SSB functional, C1, C2, and C3 hold by Theorem 4.1.

Since no $p \in P$ is indifferent to all distributions in P, A1($\sim$) holds if, for all $p, q, r, s \in P$,

$$(*) \qquad \phi(p, q)\phi(r, s) + \phi(p, s)\phi(q, r) + \phi(p, r)\phi(s, q) = 0.$$

For, if $p \sim q$ and $q \sim r$, then $\phi(p, q) = \phi(q, r) = 0$, so $(*)$ reduces to $\phi(p, r)\phi(s, q) = 0$, and, since $\phi(s, q) \neq 0$ for some s, $\phi(p, r) = 0$ and $p \sim r$. To show that $(*)$ holds for our example, suppose first that p, q, r, and s are integers in X. If all are nonzero, then

$$(p - q)(r - s) + (p - s)(q - r) + (p - r)(s - q) = 0;$$

if one of p, q, r, and s is 0, say $s = 0$, then

$$(p - q)1 + 1(q - r) + (p - r)(-1) = 0;$$

and so forth. Next, if one of p, q, r, and s is nondegenerate and the others are integers, then linearity with the result just proved shows that $(*)$ holds. If exactly two of p, q, r, and s are nondegenerate, then linearity and the one nondegenerate result imply $(*)$, and so forth. Hence A1($\sim$) holds.

Now suppose that the weighted linear representation holds with w strictly positive. The uniqueness part of Theorem 4.1 allows us to presume that $\phi(p, q) = u(p)w(q) - u(q)w(p)$ since the right side is an SSB form. Since $w > 0$, $\phi(p, q)/[w(p)w(q)] = u(p)/w(p) - u(q)/w(q)$ and therefore

$$\frac{\phi(p, q)}{w(p)w(q)} + \frac{\phi(q, r)}{w(q)w(r)} + \frac{\phi(r, p)}{w(r)w(p)} = 0.$$

For definiteness set $w(q) = 1$ and $w(r) = a > 0$ and consider $(p, r, q) = (n, 1, 0)$. Then

$$\frac{\phi(n, 0)}{w(n)} + \frac{\phi(0, 1)}{a} + \frac{\phi(1, n)}{aw(n)} = 0$$

so that

$$a\phi(n, 0) + \phi(1, n) = w(n)\phi(1, 0).$$

Since $w(n)\phi(1, 0) > 0$, this implies that $a\phi(n, 0) > \phi(n, 1)$ for all n, or $a > 0$ for all n, which is impossible. Therefore w cannot be strictly positive.

It is easily checked that the weighted linear representation requires $w(0) = 0$ in the example. A (u, w) pair that satisfies $\phi(p, q) = u(p)w(q) - u(q)w(p)$ for all $p, q \in P$ is specified by

$$u(0) = -1, \quad u(n) = n, \quad w(0) = 0, \quad w(n) = 1, \qquad n \geqslant 1,$$

with u and w defined on nondegenerate distributions by linear extension.

5.4   SUFFICIENCY PROOF

We assume throughout this section that $A1(\sim)$, C1, C2, and C3 hold and that ϕ on $P \times P$ satisfies the SSB representation of Theorem 4.1. We wish to prove that there are linear u and w on P that satisfy the representation of Theorem 5.3. To do this, three lemmas will first be established. The last of these is then used to construct w and u for the weighted linear representation. The first lemma is essentially the same as axiom E2 in Section 3.6.

LEMMA 5.3. *If $r \sim q$, not $(p \sim r)$ and $\lambda p + (1 - \lambda)q \sim \frac{1}{2}p + \frac{1}{2}r$, then $\lambda s + (1 - \lambda)q \sim \frac{1}{2}s + \frac{1}{2}r$ for all $s \in P$.*

LEMMA 5.4. *For all $p, q, r, s \in P$,*

(*) $\phi(p, q)\phi(r, s) + \phi(p, r)\phi(s, q) + \phi(p, s)\phi(q, r) = 0.$

LEMMA 5.5. *If $(P, \succ)$ is open or closed, then there is a positive functional f on P whose reciprocal is linear such that, for all $p, q, r \in P$,*

$$f(p)f(q)\phi(p, q) + f(q)f(r)\phi(q, r) + f(r)f(p)\phi(r, p) = 0.$$

Proof of Lemma 5.3. Assume for definiteness that $p \succ r \sim q$ with $\lambda p + (1 - \lambda)q \sim \frac{1}{2}p + \frac{1}{2}r$. If $s \sim r$ then, by C2 and $A1(\sim)$, all measures in $H(\{r, s, q\})$ are indifferent to each other, so $\lambda s + (1 - \lambda)q \sim \frac{1}{2}s + \frac{1}{2}r$.

Assume henceforth that $s \nsim r$. Then $A1(\sim)$, C1, and C2 imply that there is a unique μ in $(0, 1)$ with $\mu s + (1 - \mu)q \sim \frac{1}{2}s + \frac{1}{2}r$. We prove that $\mu = \lambda$.

For convenience, denote by $\alpha = (\alpha_1, \alpha_2, \alpha_3, \alpha_4)$ the measure $\alpha_1 p + \alpha_2 q + \alpha_3 r + \alpha_4 s$ in $H(\{p, q, r, s\})$. For measures α and $\alpha' = (\alpha'_1, \cdots, \alpha'_4)$, $\alpha \sim \alpha' \Leftrightarrow \phi(\alpha, \alpha') = 0$ by the SSB representation. Using skew-symmetry and bilinearity,

$$\alpha \sim \alpha' \Leftrightarrow (\alpha_1\alpha_2' - \alpha_1'\alpha_2)\phi(p, q) + (\alpha_1\alpha_3' - \alpha_1'\alpha_3)\phi(p, r)$$
$$+ (\alpha_1\alpha_4' - \alpha_1'\alpha_4)\phi(p, s) + (\alpha_2\alpha_4' - \alpha_2'\alpha_4)\phi(q, s)$$
$$+ (\alpha_3\alpha_4' - \alpha_3'\alpha_4)\phi(r, s) = 0.$$

Assume first for $s \not\succ r$ that $r \succ s$ so $p \succ r \sim q \succ s$. Then all ϕ terms in the preceding expression are positive. By the definitions of λ and μ, $\lambda\phi(p, r) = (1 - \lambda)\phi(p, q)$ and $\mu\phi(r, s) = (1 - \mu)\phi(q, s)$, so with $\lambda^* = (1 - \lambda)/\lambda$ and so forth,

$$\phi(p, r) = \lambda^*\phi(p, q), \qquad \phi(r, s) = \mu^*\phi(q, s).$$

Consider $\alpha \sim (0, \frac{1}{2}, \frac{1}{2}, 0)$. By the preceding paragraph this is equivalent to

$$0 = \alpha_1\phi(p, q) + \alpha_1\phi(p, r) - \alpha_4\phi(q, s) - \alpha_4\phi(r, s)$$
$$= \alpha_1(1 + \lambda^*)\phi(p, q) - \alpha_4(1 + \mu^*)\phi(q, s).$$

Let $\alpha_1 > 0$ and $\alpha_4 > 0$ satisfy $\alpha_1 + \alpha_4 < 1$ and satisfy the preceding equation:

$$\frac{\alpha_4}{\alpha_1} = \frac{(1 + \lambda^*)\phi(p, q)}{(1 + \mu^*)\phi(q, s)}.$$

Also let $\rho = 1 - \alpha_1 - \alpha_4$ and consider $\alpha = (\alpha_1, \rho, 0, \alpha_4)$ and $\alpha' = (\alpha_1, 0, \rho, \alpha_4)$. Since $\alpha \sim (0, \frac{1}{2}, \frac{1}{2}, 0) \sim \alpha'$ by construction, A1($\sim$) gives $\alpha \sim \alpha'$, and therefore

$$0 = \phi(p, q)[(\alpha_1 \cdot 0 - \alpha_1\rho) + \lambda^*(\alpha_1\rho - \alpha_1 \quad 0)]$$
$$+ \phi(q, s)[(\rho\alpha_4 - 0 \cdot \alpha_4) + \mu^*(0 \cdot \alpha_4 - \rho\alpha_4)]$$
$$+ \phi(p, s)(\alpha_1\alpha_4 - \alpha_1\alpha_4)$$
$$= -\alpha_1\rho\phi(p, q)(1 - \lambda^*) + \alpha_4\rho\phi(q, s)(1 - \mu^*).$$

By the definition of α_4/α_1 we require

$$\alpha_1\rho[\alpha_4(1 + \mu^*)](1 - \lambda^*) = \alpha_4\rho[\alpha_1(1 + \lambda^*)](1 - \mu^*),$$

which after cancellation leaves $\mu^* = \lambda^*$. Hence $\mu = \lambda$.

Assume henceforth in the proof of Lemma 5.3 that $s \succ r$. We assume also that $s \succsim p$. (The proof for $p \succsim s$ is similar.) Then

$$\alpha \sim \alpha' \Leftrightarrow (\alpha_1\alpha_2' - \alpha_1'\alpha_2)\phi(p, q) + (\alpha_1'\alpha_3 - \alpha_1\alpha_3')\phi(p, r)$$
$$= (\alpha_1\alpha_4' - \alpha_1'\alpha_4)\phi(s, p) + (\alpha_2\alpha_4' - \alpha_2'\alpha_4)\phi(s, q)$$
$$+ (\alpha_3\alpha_4' - \alpha_3'\alpha_4)\phi(s, r)$$

with all $\phi > 0$ except perhaps for $\phi(s, p)$, which is 0 if $s \sim p$. Moreover, $\phi(p, r) = \lambda^*\phi(p, q)$ and $\phi(s, r) = \mu^*\phi(s, q)$. Then $\alpha \sim (\frac{1}{3}, \frac{1}{3}, \frac{1}{3}, 0)$ if and only if

$$\phi(p, q)[(\alpha_2 - \alpha_1) + \lambda^*(\alpha_3 - \alpha_1)] = \alpha_4[\phi(s, p) + (1 + \mu^*)\phi(s, q)].$$

Take $\alpha_1 = 0$ so that $\alpha_4 = 1 - \alpha_2 - \alpha_3$. The preceding equation becomes

$$(\alpha_2 + \lambda^*\alpha_3)\phi(p, q) + (\alpha_2 + \alpha_3)A = A,$$

where $A = \phi(s, p) + (1 + \mu^*)\phi(s, q)$. Particular solutions are obtained by setting α_2 or α_3 to 0:

$$\alpha_2 = 0: \quad \alpha_3 = A/(A + \lambda^*\phi(p, q)), \quad \alpha_4 = 1 - \alpha_3,$$

$$\alpha_3' = 0: \quad \alpha_2' = A/(A + \phi(p, q)), \quad \alpha_4' = 1 - \alpha_2'.$$

Let $\alpha = (0, 0, \alpha_3, \alpha_4)$ for the first particular solution, with $\alpha' = (0, \alpha_2', 0, \alpha_4')$ for the second. Since $\alpha \sim (\frac{1}{3}, \frac{1}{3}, \frac{1}{3}, 0) \sim \alpha'$, we have $\alpha \sim \alpha'$, and therefore

$$0 = -\alpha_2'\alpha_4\phi(s, q) + \alpha_3\alpha_4'\phi(s, r)$$

$$= \phi(s, q) \left\{ -\left[\frac{A}{A + \phi(p, q)}\right]\left[\frac{\lambda^*\phi(p, q)}{A + \lambda^*\phi(p, q)}\right] \right.$$

$$\left. + \mu^*\left[\frac{A}{A + \lambda^*\phi(p, q)}\right]\left[\frac{\phi(p, q)}{A + \phi(p, q)}\right]\right\}$$

which reduces to $\mu^* = \lambda^*$. ∎

Proof of Lemma 5.4. Assume that no more than two of p, q, r, and s are in the same $\sim$ class, since otherwise all three products in (*) are 0. For definiteness take $p \succ r$ and $p \succ q$. If $r \sim q$, then $\phi(q, r) = 0$, and we need to show that $\phi(p, q)\phi(r, s) + \phi(p, r)\phi(s, q) = 0$. Given $p \succ r \sim q$, let λ satisfy $\lambda p + (1 - \lambda)q \sim \frac{1}{2}p + \frac{1}{2}r$. Then, by Lemma 5.3, $\lambda s + (1 - \lambda)q \sim \frac{1}{2}s + \frac{1}{2}r$, so $\lambda\phi(p, r) = (1 - \lambda)\phi(p, q)$ and $\lambda\phi(s, r) = (1 - \lambda)\phi(s, q)$ with all $\phi \neq 0$, since $s \nsim r$ by our initial assumption and $r \sim q$. Therefore $\phi(p, q)\phi(s, r) = \phi(p, r)\phi(s, q) = \lambda(1 - \lambda)$; hence $\phi(p, q)\phi(r, s) + \phi(p, r)\phi(s, q) = 0$. Thus (*) holds when there is one $\sim$ pair.

Assume henceforth that no two of p, q, r and s are indifferent. Take $p \succ q \succ r \succ s$ with no loss in generality. Let λ satisfy $q \sim \lambda p + (1 - \lambda)s$. Then $\lambda\phi(p, q) = (1 - \lambda)\phi(q, s)$ and, by the result of the preceding paragraph,

$$\phi(p, q)\phi(\lambda p + (1 - \lambda)s, r) = \phi(p, \lambda p + (1 - \lambda)s)\phi(q, r),$$

$$\phi(p, q)\phi(\lambda p + (1 - \lambda)s, s) = \phi(p, \lambda p + (1 - \lambda)s)\phi(q, s)$$

with all $\phi > 0$. We divide the preceding equations and use linearity of ϕ in its first argument to get

$$[\lambda\phi(p, r) + (1 - \lambda)\phi(s, r)]\phi(q, s) = [\lambda\phi(p, s)]\phi(q, r),$$

which by $\lambda\phi(p, q) = (1 - \lambda)\phi(q, s)$ and skew-symmetry yields (∗). ∎

Proof of Lemma 5.5 for Closed $(P, \succ)$. Assume that $\succ$ is closed and nonempty (otherwise $\phi \equiv 0$ and $f \equiv 1$ satisfy the desired conclusion). Take $r \in P_{max}$ and $q \in P_{min}$. Then $r \succ q$ and $r \succsim p \succsim q$ for all p. Let a and b be any positive numbers and set $f(r) = a, f(q) = b$. The lemma's conclusion then requires

$$f(p)[a\phi(r, p) + b\phi(p, q)] = ab\phi(r, q),$$

so f must be defined on P by

$$f(p) = \frac{ab\phi(r, q)}{a\phi(r, p) + b\phi(p, q)},$$

which is positive for every p. Let $w = 1/f$. Then bilinearity of ϕ gives $w(\lambda p + (1 - \lambda)s) = \lambda w(p) + (1 - \lambda)w(s)$, so the reciprocal of f is linear.

To complete the proof, let p, s, and t be any three elements in P and use the definition of f and then Lemma 5.4 to get

$$f(p)f(s)\phi(p, s) + f(s)f(t)\phi(s, t) + f(t)f(p)\phi(t, p)$$

$$= \{[a\phi(r, p) + b\phi(p, q)][a\phi(r, s) + b\phi(s, q)][a\phi(r, t)$$

$$+ b\phi(t, q)]\}^{-1} \times [ab\phi(r, q)]^2\{[a\phi(r, t) + b\phi(t, q)]\phi(p, s)$$

$$+ [a\phi(r, p) + b\phi(p, q)]\phi(s, t) + [a\phi(r, s)$$

$$+ b\phi(s, q)]\phi(t, p)\}$$

$$= K\{a[\phi(r, t)\phi(p, s) + \phi(r, p)\phi(s, t) + \phi(r, s)\phi(t, p)]$$

$$+ b[\phi(t, q)\phi(p, s) + \phi(p, q)\phi(s, t) + \phi(s, q)\phi(t, p)]\}$$

$$= K\{a[0] + b[0]\} = 0. \quad ∎$$

Proof of Lemma 5.5 for Open $(P, \succ)$. With both P_{max} and P_{min} empty, choose $r, q \in P$ with $r \succ q$. We propose to set $f(r) = a > 0$ and $f(q) = b > 0$, in which case the lemma's conclusion requires $f(p)[a\phi(r, p) + b\phi(p, q)] = ab\phi(r, q)$ as before. If a and b can be chosen so that $f(p)$ as defined in the obvious way is positive for all $p \in P$, then the latter part of the preceding proof shows that Lemma 5.5 holds when $\succ$ is open.

Since $ab\phi(r, q) > 0$, we get $f > 0$ if and only if, for all $p \in P$, $a\phi(r, p) + b\phi(p, q) > 0$. This is clearly true if $r \succsim p \succsim q$. If $p \succ r \succ q$, then $a\phi(r, p) + b\phi(p, q) > 0$ if and only if $\phi(p, q)/\phi(p, r) > a/b$; and if $r \succ q \succ t$, then $a\phi(r, t) + b\phi(t, q) > 0$ if and only if $a/b > \phi(q, t)/\phi(r, t)$. Hence positive f can be defined to satisfy the lemma if and only if there is a number c such that

$$\phi(p, q)/\phi(p, r) > c > \phi(q, t)/\phi(r, t)$$

for all p and t for which $p \succ r \succ q \succ t$. Given $p \succ r \succ q \succ t$, (*) says that

$$\phi(p, r)\phi(q, t) + \phi(p, t)\phi(r, q) = \phi(p, q)\phi(r, t).$$

Since all ϕ terms here are positive, we have $\phi(p, q)\phi(r, t) > \phi(p, r)\phi(q, t)$, and therefore

$$\phi(p, q)/\phi(p, r) > \phi(q, t)/\phi(r, t).$$

If $p' \succ p \succ r \succ q$, then (*) yields $\phi(p, q)/\phi(p, r) > \phi(p', q)/\phi(p', r)$; and if $r \succ q \succ t \succ t'$, then $\phi(q, t')/\phi(r, t') > \phi(q, t)/\phi(r, t)$. Therefore

$$\inf_{p} \{ \phi(p, q)/\phi(p, r) : p \succ r \} \geq \sup_{t} \{ \phi(q, t)/\phi(r, t) : q \succ t \},$$

and, since $\succ$ is open, no p attains the inf value and no t attains the sup value. Hence a c exists as desired. Any c in the closed interval from sup to inf suffices; then, given such a c, any positive a and b for which $a/b = c$ serve to define a suitable f. ∎

Sufficiency Proof of Theorem 5.3. Assume first that $\succ$ is closed or open and let f be as specified in Lemma 5.5. Fix $x \in P$ and define w and u on P by

$$w(p) = 1/f(p), \qquad u(p) = f(x)\phi(p, x).$$

By Lemma 5.5 and Theorem 4.1, w and u are linear and $w > 0$. Also, by Lemma 5.5 and the definitions,

$$\phi(p, q) = w(p)w(q)[f(x)\phi(p, x)/w(p) - f(x)\phi(q, x)/w(q)]$$

$$= u(p)w(q) - u(q)w(p),$$

so $p \succ q \Leftrightarrow u(p)w(q) > u(q)w(p)$. This completes the proof if $\succ$ is open or closed.

Assume henceforth that $\succ$ is half-open, and for definiteness take $P_{\min} \neq \varnothing$ and $P_{\max} = \varnothing$. (A dual proof applies to the other case.) Given $r \succ q$ with $q \in P_{\min}$, the analysis in the open $(P, \succ)$ proof of Lemma 5.5 shows that the conclusion of Lemma 5.5 with $f > 0$ holds if $\inf_p \{ \phi(p, q)/\phi(p, r):p \succ r \} > 0$. When this is true, the preceding paragraph shows that Theorem 5.3 holds with $w > 0$. In the rest of this proof we allow for the possibility that the inf equals 0.

Continuing with $P_{\min} \neq \varnothing$ and $P_{\max} = \varnothing$, it is easily seen that the interior P^* is convex. Therefore, by the sufficiency proof of Theorem 5.3 for open $\succ$, there are linear u and w on P^* with $w > 0$ such that, for all $p, q \in P^*$, $p \succ q \Leftrightarrow u(p)w(q) > u(q)w(p)$. It remains only to extend u and w linearly to $P_{\min}$ and to note that $w \geq 0$ on $P_{\min}$ with $u(p)w(q) > (=)$ $u(q)w(p)$ whenever p is in $P^*(P_{\min})$ and $q \in P_{\min}$.

Given $q \in P_{\min}$ and $p \in P^*$ with $p \succ q$, $\lambda q + (1 - \lambda)p$ is in P^* for all $0 < \lambda < 1$, so linearity for w and u requires

$$w(q) = \frac{w(\lambda q + (1 - \lambda)p) - (1 - \lambda)w(p)}{\lambda},$$

$$u(q) = \frac{u(\lambda q + (1 - \lambda)p) - (1 - \lambda)u(p)}{\lambda}.$$

To show that $w(q)$ is invariant to the choice of $(\lambda, p) \in (0, 1) \times P^*$, suppose $\lambda, \mu \in (0, 1)$ and $p, t \in P^*$. Let $\tau = (\lambda + \mu - \lambda\mu)^{-1}$. Then

$$\mu\tau w(\lambda q + (1 - \lambda)p) + (\lambda - \lambda\mu)\tau w(t)$$
$$= w((\lambda\mu\tau)q + [(\mu - \lambda\mu)\tau]p + [(\lambda - \lambda\mu)\tau]t)$$
$$= w(\lambda\tau(\mu q + (1 - \mu)t) + [(\mu - \lambda\mu)\tau]p)$$
$$= \lambda\tau w(\mu q + (1 - \mu)t) + (\mu - \lambda\mu)\tau w(p),$$

so that

$$[w(\lambda q + (1 - \lambda)p) - (1 - \lambda)w(p)]/\lambda$$
$$= [w(\mu q + (1 - \mu)t) - (1 - \mu)w(t)]/\mu.$$

A similar computation shows that the value of $u(q)$ is invariant to the choice of (λ, p). Therefore w and u are uniquely defined on $P_{\min}$ by linear extension from w and u on P^* in the preceding paragraph. Moreover, the extended w and u are linear on all of P. For example, if $q, q' \in P_{\min}$ and $0 < \lambda < 1$, then with $0 < \mu < 1$ and $p \in P^*$ we have

$$w(\lambda q + (1 - \lambda)q')$$
$$= [w(\mu(\lambda q + (1 - \lambda)q') + (1 - \mu)p) - (1 - \mu)w(p)]/\mu$$
$$= [w(\lambda(\mu q + (1 - \mu)p) + (1 - \lambda)(\mu q'$$
$$+ (1 - \mu)p)) - (1 - \mu)w(p)]/\mu$$
$$= \lambda[w(\mu q + (1 - \mu)p) - (1 - \mu)w(p)]/\mu$$
$$+ (1 - \lambda)[w(\mu q' + (1 - \mu)p) - (1 - \mu)w(p)]/\mu$$
$$= \lambda w(q) + (1 - \lambda)w(q').$$

It is clear also that $w(q) \geqslant 0$: fix $p \in P^*$ and take $\lambda \uparrow 1$ in the initial equation of this paragraph. Note too that since the right side of that equation is the same for all $0 < \lambda < 1$, $w(q) = \lim\{w(\lambda q + (1 - \lambda)p):\lambda \uparrow 1\}$. Similarly $u(q) = \lim\{u(\lambda q + (1 - \lambda)p):\lambda \uparrow 1\}$.

Finally, since ϕ is bilinear and $\phi(p, p) = 0$, when $p \in P^*$ and $q \in P_{\min}$ we have

$$\lambda\phi(p, q) = \phi(p, \lambda q + (1 - \lambda)p)$$

$$= u(p)w(\lambda q + (1 - \lambda)p) - u(\lambda q + (1 - \lambda)p)w(p),$$

so $\lambda \uparrow 1$ gives $\phi(p, q) = u(p)w(q) - u(q)w(p)$. Therefore $u(p)w(q) > u(q)w(p)$ when $p \in P^*$ and $q \in P_{min}$. Moreover, if $p, q \in P_{min}$ then with $t \in P^*$ we have

$$\lambda\phi(p, q) + (1 - \lambda)\phi(t, q) = \phi(\lambda p + (1 - \lambda)t, q)$$

$$= u(\lambda p + (1 - \lambda)t)w(q) - u(q)w(\lambda p + (1 - \lambda)t)$$

by linearity and the result just proved, so $\lambda \uparrow 1$ gives $0 = \phi(p, q) = u(p)w(q) - u(q)w(p)$. Hence $u(p)w(q) = u(q)w(p)$ whenever $p, q \in P_{min}$. ∎

5.5 WEIGHTED LINEAR UNIQUENESS

Suppose (u, w) is a pair of linear functionals on P that satisfies $p \succ q \Leftrightarrow u(p)w(q) > u(q)w(p)$ for the weighted linear representation. Theorem 5.3 emphasizes the special role of one of these functionals as a weighting function by specifying $w \geq 0$ with $w > 0$ if $\succ$ is open or closed. However, since $(u', w') = (-u, -w)$ and $(u', w') = (w, -u)$ satisfy $p \succ q \Leftrightarrow u'(p)w'(q) > u'(q)w'(p)$, the basic representation without the sign constraint admits other possibilities that are not covered by the theorem.

In this section we prove two theorems that address the sign and uniqueness questions. The first shows precisely when a general linear pair (u, w) for which $p \succ q \Leftrightarrow u(p)w(q) > u(q)w(p)$ admits a weighted linear representation. We assume throughout that the initial hypotheses of Theorem 5.1 hold.

THEOREM 5.4. *Suppose* $\succ$ *is nonempty and* (u, w) *is a pair of linear functionals on* P *such that, for all* $p, q \in P$,

$$p \succ q \Leftrightarrow u(p)w(q) > u(q)w(p).$$

Then C1, C2, *and* C3 *hold, and* A1($\sim$) *holds if and only if* $(0, 0) \notin \{(u(p), w(p)):p \in P\}$.

Proof. Given the hypotheses, C1–C3 are immediate from Theorem 4.1 on defining $\phi(p, q) = u(p)w(q) - u(q)w(p)$. For the transitivity part, suppose first that $u(p) = w(p) = 0$ for some $p \in P$. Then $p \sim q$ for all $q \in P$, and, since $\succ$ is presumed to be nonempty, A1($\sim$) cannot hold. Hence A1($\sim$) $\Rightarrow (0, 0) \notin \{(u(p), w(p)):p \in P\}$. To prove the converse, assume $(u(s), w(s)) \neq (0, 0)$ for every $s \in P$, and suppose $p \sim q$ and $q \sim r$. Then $u(p)w(q) = u(q)w(p)$ and $u(q)w(r) = u(r)w(q)$. If $w(q) \neq 0$, then $u(p)w(r) = [u(q)/w(q)]w(p)w(r) = u(r)w(p)$, so $p \sim r$. If $w(q) = 0$, then $u(q) \neq 0$ and $u(p)w(r) = [w(q)/u(q)]u(p)u(r) = u(r)w(p)$, so again $p \sim r$ and A1($\sim$) holds. ∎

Theorem 5.4 raises the question of whether the generalized representation in its hypotheses forces at least one of u and w to have constant sign (nonpositive or nonnegative) throughout P when A1($\sim$) holds. The answer is no, as we show in Remark 1, which follows the uniqueness theorem.

THEOREM 5.5. *Suppose* $>$ *is a nonempty weak order on P and* (u, w) *is a pair of linear functionals on P that satisfies* $p > q \Leftrightarrow u(p)w(q) > u(q)w(p)$ *for all* $p, q \in P$. *Then a pair* (u', w') *of linear functionals on P satisfies* $p > q \Leftrightarrow u'(p)w'(q) > u'(q)w'(p)$ *for all* $p, q \in P$ *if, and only if, there are numbers a, b, c, and d such that* $u' = au + bw$, $w' = cu + dw$, *and* $ad > bc$.

Remark 1. Let $X = \mathbf{R}$ and $P = P_X$. Suppose u and w on X have codomains $u(X) = \mathbf{R}$ and $w(X) = (0, 1)$. Extend u and w linearly to P and define $>$ on P by $p > q \Leftrightarrow u(p)w(q) > u(q)w(p)$. Then, by definition, $(P, >)$ has a weighted linear representation. Let $a = 2$ and $b = c = d = 1$ in Theorem 5.5 so that $ad > bc$, $u' = 2u + w$, and $w' = u + w$. Then $p > q \Leftrightarrow u'(p)w'(q) > u'(q)w'(p)$ for all $p, q \in P$, and $u'(X)$ and $w'(X)$ both contain positive and negative numbers.

Remark 2. Suppose $w \geq 0$ in Theorem 5.5, and we wish to consider only those (u', w') that have $w' \geq 0$. Then, according to the theorem, its final conditions must hold along with $cu(p) + dw(p) \geq 0$ for all $p \in P$. This might limit a, b, c, and d substantially. For example, for the case in Remark 1 we require $c = 0, d > 0$, and $a > 0$, but there is no restriction on b.

Proof of Theorem 5.5. Let the hypotheses of the theorem hold. Suppose first that $u' = au + bw$, $w' = cu + dw$, and $ad > bc$. Then

$$u'(p)w'(q) > u'(q)w'(p)$$

$$\Leftrightarrow [au(p) + bw(p)][cu(q) + dw(q)]$$

$$> [au(q) + bw(q)][cu(p) + dw(p)]$$

$$\Leftrightarrow (ad - bc)u(p)w(q) > (ad - bc)u(q)w(p)$$

$$\Leftrightarrow u(p)w(q) > u(q)w(p),$$

so $p > q \Leftrightarrow u'(p)w'(q) > u'(q)w'(p)$.

Conversely, suppose linear u' and w' satisfy $p > q \Leftrightarrow u'(p)w'(q) > u'(q)w'(p)$ for all $p, q \in P$. Let $\phi(p, q) = u(p)w(q) - u(q)w(p)$ and $\phi'(p, q) = u'(p)w'(q) - u'(q)w'(p)$. Then, by Theorem 4.1, there is a positive number λ such that $\phi' = \lambda\phi$. Hence for all $p, q \in P$,

$$\mu'(p)w'(q) - u'(q)w'(p) = \lambda[u(p)w(q) - u(q)w(p)].$$

Suppose first that $u'(x) = 0$ for some $x \in P$. Then $w'(x) \neq 0$ by Theorem 5.4 and, for all $p \in P$,

$$u'(p) = \lambda[u(p)w(x) - u(x)w(p)]/w'(x) = au(p) + bw(p),$$

where $a = \lambda w(x)/w'(x)$ and $b = -\lambda u(x)/w'(x)$. Since $u'(x) = 0$, nonempty $>$ requires $u'(y) \neq 0$ for some $y \in P$, so

$$w'(p) = -\{\lambda[u(p)w(y) - u(y)w(p)] - u'(p)w'(y)\}/u'(y)$$

$$= cu(p) + dw(p),$$

with c and d defined in context. Then $ad > bc$ by the procedure in the preceding paragraph. A similar result obtains if we presume that $w'(x) = 0$ for some $x \in P$.

Finally, suppose that $0 \notin u'(P)$ and $0 \notin w'(P)$. Then with $x > y$ for some x and y since $>$ is nonempty,

$$u'(y)[u'(p)w'(x) - w'(p)u'(x)]$$

$$= u'(y)\lambda[u(p)w(x) - w(p)u(x)],$$

$$u'(x)[u'(p)w'(y) - w'(p)u'(y)]$$

$$= u'(x)\lambda[u(p)w(y) - w(p)u(y)],$$

so, by subtraction,

$$u'(p)[u'(y)w'(x) - u'(x)w'(y)] = Au(p) + Bw(p).$$

Since $x > y$, the term in brackets is nonzero, and therefore we get $u'(p) = au(p) + bw(p)$ for all $p \in P$. A similar procedure gives $w'(p) = cu(p) + dw(p)$ for all $p \in P$. As before, $ad > bc$. ∎

5.6 EQUIVALENT AXIOM SETS

We now establish the equivalence of the three axiom sets for the weighted linear representation that were noted in Section 3.6. The axioms there that have not been used in the interim are

A3. $\{p > q, q > r\} \Rightarrow \alpha p + (1 - \alpha)r > q$ and $q > \beta p + (1 - \beta)r$
 for some α and β in $(0, 1)$.

C2($>$). $\{p > q, p \gtrsim r, 0 < \lambda < 1\} \Rightarrow p > \lambda q + (1 - \lambda)r$.
 $\{q > p, r \gtrsim p, 0 < \lambda < 1\} \Rightarrow \lambda q + (1 - \lambda)r > p$.

D2. $p \sim q \Rightarrow$ *for every $0 < \alpha < 1$ there is a $0 < \beta < 1$ such that, for all $r \in P$, $\alpha p + (1 - \alpha)r \sim \beta q + (1 - \beta)r$.*

E2. $p \sim q \Rightarrow$ *there is a $0 < \beta < 1$ such that, for all $r \in P$, $\frac{1}{2}p + \frac{1}{2}r \sim \beta q + (1 - \beta)r$.*

THEOREM 5.6. *Suppose the hypotheses of Theorem 5.1 hold. Then the following three sets of axioms are mutually equivalent:* $\{A1, A3, C2(>),$ $D2\}$, $\{A1(\sim), C1, C2, C3\}$, $\{C1, C2, E2\}$.

Proof. We note first that A3, D2, and E2 are necessary for the weighted linear representation. This follows for A3 from Theorems 1.4 and 5.3. For D2, let linear u and $w \geq 0$ satisfy the weighted linear representation and suppose that $p \sim q$ and $0 < \alpha < 1$. If $r \sim q$ for all $r \in P$ then D2 holds trivially (in the following display, the second equation reduces to $0 = 0$). Assume $r \not\sim q$ for some $r \in P$. Then

$$\alpha p + (1 - \alpha)r \sim \beta q + (1 - \beta)r$$

$$\Leftrightarrow u(\alpha p + (1 - \alpha)r)w(\beta q + (1 - \beta)r)$$

$$= u(\beta q + (1 - \beta)r)w(\alpha p + (1 - \alpha)r)$$

$$\Leftrightarrow \alpha(1 - \beta)[u(p)w(r) - u(r)w(p)]$$

$$= (1 - \alpha)\beta[u(q)w(r) - u(r)w(q)] \Leftrightarrow \beta$$

$$= \frac{\alpha[u(p)w(r) - u(r)w(p)]}{\alpha[u(p)w(r) - u(r)w(p)] + (1 - \alpha)[u(q)w(r) - u(r)w(q)]}.$$

The ratio for β is in $(0, 1)$ since $r \not\sim q \sim p$ implies that each term in brackets has the same nonzero sign. If $s \not\sim q$ also, then the preceding ratio does not change when r is replaced by s. To see this, cross multiply the two ratios, cancel equivalent terms, and use the fact that $p \sim q \Rightarrow u(p)w(q) = u(q)w(p)$ to conclude that the ratios are equal. Since $t \sim q$ also satisfies $\alpha p + (1 - \alpha)t \sim \beta q + (1 - \beta)t$, D2 follows. Since D2 $\Rightarrow$ E2, E2 is also necessary for the weighted linear representation.

With necessity established, Theorem 5.3 shows that $\{A1(\sim), C1, C2, C3\}$ implies the other two sets in Theorem 5.6. We complete the proof by showing that $\{C1, C2, E2\} \Rightarrow \{A1(\sim), C1, C2, C3\}$ and then that $\{A1, A3, C2(>), D2\} \Rightarrow \{C1, C2, E2\}$.

Assume first that C1, C2, and E2 hold. To verify $A1(\sim)$, suppose to the contrary that $p \sim q$, $q \sim r$, and $p > r$. Then C2 implies $p > \frac{1}{2}r + \frac{1}{2}q$ and $r \sim \frac{1}{2}r + \frac{1}{2}q$, so by C2 for all $0 < \beta < 1$, $\beta p + (1 - \beta)r > \frac{1}{2}r + \frac{1}{2}q$, which contradicts E2. Hence $p \sim q \sim r \Rightarrow p \sim r$. To verify C3, assume its hypotheses: $p > q > r$, $p > r$, and $q \sim \frac{1}{2}p + \frac{1}{2}r$. By E2 there is a $0 < \beta < 1$ such that, for all $x \in P$,

$$\tfrac{1}{2}q + \tfrac{1}{2}x \sim \beta(\tfrac{1}{2}p + \tfrac{1}{2}r) + (1 - \beta)x.$$

With $x = p$ and then $x = r$ we get $\lambda p + (1 - \lambda)r \sim \frac{1}{2}p + \frac{1}{2}q$ and $\lambda r + (1 - \lambda)p \sim \frac{1}{2}r + \frac{1}{2}q$ when $\lambda = \beta/2 + (1 - \beta)$. Suppose $\mu \neq \lambda$ and $\mu p + (1 - \mu)r \sim \frac{1}{2}p + \frac{1}{2}q$. Then, by $A1(\sim)$, $\lambda p + (1 - \lambda)r \sim \mu p + (1 - \mu)r$.

However, this gives a contradiction, since, with $p > r$, C2 allows $\lambda p + (1 - \lambda)r \sim \mu p + (1 - \mu)r$ only if $\lambda = \mu$. It follows that, for all γ in $(0, 1)$,

$$\gamma p + (1 - \gamma)r \sim \tfrac{1}{2}p + \tfrac{1}{2}q \Leftrightarrow \gamma r + (1 - \gamma)p \sim \tfrac{1}{2}r + \tfrac{1}{2}q,$$

the conclusion of C3.

Assume henceforth that A1, A3, C2($>$), and D2 hold. Since D2 $\Rightarrow$ E2, we need only consider C1 and C2. The only part of C2 not covered by C2($>$) is $(p \sim q, p \sim r) \Rightarrow p \sim \lambda q + (1 - \lambda)r$. Assume $p \sim q$ and $p \sim r$. Suppose for definiteness and contrary to the desired conclusion that $p > \lambda q + (1 - \lambda)r$. Then, by A1, $q > \lambda q + (1 - \lambda)r$ and $r > \lambda q + (1 - \lambda)r$, so, by C2($>$), $\lambda q + (1 - \lambda)r > \lambda q + (1 - \lambda)r$. But this contradicts asymmetry, so C2 holds.

To verify C1, suppose it fails with $p > q > r$ and $q \not\sim \alpha p + (1 - \alpha)r$ for all $0 < \alpha < 1$. It then follows from A3, C2, and A1 that there is a unique α^* in $(0, 1)$ such that $\alpha p + (1 - \alpha)r > q$ for all $\alpha > \alpha^*$, $q > \alpha p + (1 - \alpha)r$ for all $\alpha < \alpha^*$, and either $\alpha^* p + (1 - \alpha^*)r > q$ or $q > \alpha^* p + (1 - \alpha^*)r$. Whichever of the latter holds, a contradiction follows easily from A3. ∎

Since D2 was not used in the last two paragraphs to derive C1 and C2, it can be replaced in {A1, A3, C2($>$), D2} by E2.

5.7 EXTENSION FOR PROBABILITY MEASURES

Suppose S0, C4, and C5 of Section 4.8 hold in the context of the weighted linear representation with $\phi(p, q) = u(p)w(q) - u(q)w(p)$. Then, with the natural extensions of u, w, and ϕ for X, we have

$$u(p)w(q) - u(q)w(p) = \phi(p, q)$$

$$= \iint \phi(x, y)\, dp(x)\, dq(y)$$

$$= \iint [u(x)w(y) - u(y)w(x)]\, dp(x)\, dq(y)$$

$$= \int u(x)\, dp(x) \int w(y)\, dq(y) - \int u(y)\, dq(y) \int w(x)\, dp(x).$$

This gives the expectational form

$$p > q \Leftrightarrow \int u\, dp \int w\, dq > \int u\, dq \int w\, dp$$

for the weighted linear representation.

6 Applications for Choice Theory and Risk

Expected utility theory has been used extensively in diverse areas of decision theory and economic analysis. Recent investigations have demonstrated the efficacy of generalizations of expected utility in these areas as well as areas not well suited to the expected utility assumptions. This chapter presents results for SSB utility and weighted linear utility that illustrate their analytical and interpretational potential for an array of topics including choice theory with cyclic preferences, social choice theory, noncooperative games, multiattribute utility, mean value, stochastic dominance, and risk attitudes.

6.1 VON NEUMANN'S MINIMAX THEOREM

This chapter demonstrates the application of SSB utility theory to a variety of concerns and problems that have often been addressed from the more restrictive linear utility perspective of von Neumann and Morgenstern (1944). Our results also pertain to specializations of the SSB theory such as weighted linear utility when the conditions needed for such specializations hold. *It is assumed throughout that ϕ or ϕ_i is an SSB utility functional on the Cartesian product of a convex set of probability measures with itself.*

The next three sections focus on contexts that use von Neumann's minimax theorem (von Neumann, 1928; Kakutani, 1941; Fan, 1952; Nikaidô, 1954; Luce and Raiffa, 1957) to establish the existence of maximally preferred measures. Section 6.5 then proves the existence of Nash (1951) equilibria for noncooperative games in which players have SSB utilities. The final four sections consider generalizations of popular topics in expected utility, including multiattribute decomposition, stochastic dominance, and risk attitudes. Readers familiar with these subject areas will note that our analyses only begin to tap their potential.

For use in the next few sections we state an intermediate-level version of the minimax theorem as given in Nikaidô (1954). Other versions are noted in the preceding references and in Geraghty and Lin (1985), which discusses relaxations of linear structure and provides a useful bibliography. Readers unfamiliar with the notion of a linear topological space may consult a text such as Kelley (1955) or Kelley and Namioka (1963), or simply note that our ensuing applications deal only with finite-dimensional Euclidean spaces ($\mathbf{R}^n$) endowed with the usual topology (Fishburn, 1970a, pp. 35–37). A subset A of a linear topological space $\mathcal{L}$ is said to be *compact* if every collection of (open) sets in $\mathcal{L}$ whose union includes A has a finite subcollection whose union includes A. Let f denote a functional on $A_1 \times A_2$, where each A_i is a convex compact subset of a linear topological space $\mathcal{L}_i$. Then f is *quasi-concave in its first argument* if, for all $x_1, x_2 \in A_1$, $y \in A_2$, $c \in \mathbf{R}$, and $0 \leqslant \alpha \leqslant 1$,

$$[f(x_1, y) \geqslant c, f(x_2, y) \geqslant c] \Rightarrow f(\alpha x_1 + (1 - \alpha)x_2, y) \geqslant c;$$

f is *quasi-convex in its second argument* if, for all $x \in A_1$, $y_1, y_2 \in A_2$, $c \in \mathbf{R}$, and $0 \leqslant \alpha \leqslant 1$,

$$[f(x, y_1) \leqslant c, f(x, y_2) \leqslant c] \Rightarrow f(x, \alpha y_1 + (1 - \alpha)y_2) \leqslant c.$$

THEOREM 6.1 (von Neumann's minimax theorem). *Suppose A_i is a nonempty convex compact subset of a linear topological space $\mathcal{L}_i$ for $i = 1, 2$ and $f: A_1 \times A_2 \Rightarrow \mathbf{R}$ is continuous in each argument, quasi-concave in its first argument, and quasi-convex in its second argument. Then*

$$\max_{x \in A_1} \min_{y \in A_2} f(x, y) = \min_{y \in A_2} \max_{x \in A_1} f(x, y).$$

For Euclidean spaces ($\mathbf{R}^n$), continuity of f in its first argument has the usual meaning that if $x_i \rightarrow x$ then, for every $y \in A_2$, $f(x_i, y) \rightarrow f(x, y)$. Continuity in the second argument is defined similarly.

6.2 CHOICE WITH CYCLIC PREFERENCES

As first proved by Kreweras (1961) and, independently, Fishburn (1984c), SSB utility theory provides a nice resolution of the problem of choosing one alternative from a finite set when, due to cyclic preferences, every alternative in the set is less preferred than something else in the set (see Section 2.7). It says that there is a probability distribution p^* over the basic alternatives that is preferred or indifferent to every other such distribution, thus providing a basis for choice in terms of binary preferences. As before, we let P denote a convex set of probability measures or distributions and denote the convex hull of $Q \subseteq P$ by $H(Q)$.

THEOREM 6.2. *If Q is a nonempty finite subset of P, then there is a $p^* \in H(Q)$ such that $\phi(p^*, q) \geqslant 0$ for every $q \in H(Q)$.*

Proof. When $H(Q)$ is viewed as the simplex based on Q, the continuity, quasi-concavity, and quasi-convexity properties of Theorem 6.1 for ϕ on $H(Q) \times H(Q)$ follow immediately from bilinearity. Therefore the minimax theorem applies to give

$$\max_{p \in H(Q)} \min_{q \in H(Q)} \phi(p, q) = \min_{q \in H(Q)} \max_{p \in H(Q)} \phi(p, q) \quad \text{(minimax)}$$

$$= \min_{q} \max_{p} [-\phi(q, p)] \quad \text{(skew-symmetry)}$$

$$= -\max_{q} \min_{p} \phi(q, p) \quad \text{(algebra)}$$

$$= -\max_{p} \min_{q} \phi(p, q) \quad \text{(notation)}$$

so that $\max_p [\min_q \phi(p, q)] = 0$. Hence $\phi(p^*, q) \geq 0$ for some p^* and all q in $H(Q)$. ∎

Suppose $p \succ q \Leftrightarrow \phi(p, q) > 0$ as in the SSB representation. Then Theorem 6.2 guarantees that the *maximally preferred subset* of $H(Q)$, $\{p \in H(Q): p \succeq q$ for all $q \in H(Q)\}$, is never empty when Q is nonempty and finite. If $\succ$ is a weak order on $H(Q)$, as in the weighted linear theory, the maximally preferred subset is simply the convex hull of the $q \in Q$ that maximize preference over Q. In the general SSB case with $Q = \{r_1, \ldots, r_n\}$, it follows from bilinearity and

$$\{p \in H(Q) : \phi(p, q) \geq 0 \text{ for all } q \in H(Q)\}$$
$$= \{p \in H(Q) : \sum_i p(r_i)\phi(r_i, r_j) \geq 0 \text{ for } j = 1, \ldots, n\}$$

that the maximally preferred subset of $H(Q)$ is a polytope (Grünbaum, 1970; Rockafellar, 1970)—that is, the convex hull of a finite number of points in $H(Q)$.

Our next theorem shows that the existence of maximally preferred measures in an *arbitrary* nonempty subset $Q \subseteq P$ is tantamount to a slightly modified conclusion of the minimax theorem for Q by itself.

THEOREM 6.3. *Suppose* $\varnothing \subset Q \subseteq P$. *Then* $\phi(p^*, q) \geq 0$ *for some* p^* $\in Q$ *and all* $q \in Q$ *if and only if*

$$\max_{p \in Q} \inf_{q \in Q} \phi(p, q) = \min_{q \in Q} \sup_{p \in Q} \phi(p, q).$$

Proof. If the equality holds then the existence of a p^* as claimed follows as in the proof of the preceding theorem. Conversely, if $\phi(p^*, q) \geq 0$ for some p^* and all q in Q, with $\phi(p^*, p^*) = 0$, then $\sup_p \inf_q \phi(p, q) \geq 0$. But, since $\phi(p, p^*) \leq 0$ [i.e., $\phi(p^*, p) \geq 0$] and therefore $\inf_q \phi(p, q) \leq 0$ for all $p \in Q$, it follows that

$$\sup_{p} \inf_{q} \phi(p, q) = 0 = \inf_{q} \phi(p^*, q) = \max_{p} \inf_{q} \phi(p, q).$$

By skew-symmetry, $\min_q \sup_p \phi(p, q) = 0$. ∎

Fishburn (1984c) provides additional commentary on applications of Theorem 6.3 and choice by randomization when Q contains no maximally preferred alternative.

6.3 SOCIAL CHOICE LOTTERIES

Theorem 6.2 provides an appealing resolution to the problem of choosing an alternative from a nonempty finite set X on the basis of paired-comparison voting data when there is no clear majority winner because of cyclic majorities and/or tied votes. This resolution was first discussed by Kreweras (1965) and subsequently analyzed and generalized by Fishburn (1984d).

Assume that the voting data for X are summarized by a function v on $X \times X$ with $v(x, x) = 0$ and, when $x \neq y$, with $v(x, y)$ the number of voters who reveal a preference for x over y. Let the *strict majority* relation $>_M$ on X be defined by

$$x >_M y \quad \text{if } v(x, y) > v(y, x),$$

and call x a *majority candidate* if $y >_M x$ for no $y \in X \setminus \{x\}$. Even when voters reveal preferences based on weak orders, a majority candidate may fail to exist. If $X = \{x, y, z\}$ and there are three voters with voting orders $x >_1 y >_1 z$, $z >_2 x >_2 y$, and $y >_3 z >_3 x$, respectively, then $x >_M y >_M z >_M x$.

Beginning with Condorcet (1785), election of majority candidates has been widely advocated. The problem with majority choice comes where there is no majority candidate. Various nonlottery methods have been proposed to resolve such situations (Black, 1958; Sen, 1970; Schwartz, 1972; Fishburn, 1973a, 1977b), but there is no agreement on a best deterministic rule.

Others, including Zeckhauser (1969), Shepsle (1970), Fishburn (1973a), and Barbera and Sonnenschein (1978), consider social choice by lottery. This means that a probability distribution on X is used to choose the winning candidate. Most of these discussions are based on von Neumann–Morgenstern utilities for voters and/or for the electorate as a whole, and they are not well suited to resolution of the cyclic majorities' problem.

Kreweras's resolution effects a nice compromise between the possibility of no majority candidate and choice by lottery. Given v on $X \times X$, define skew-symmetric ϕ on $X \times X$ by

$$\phi(x, y) = v(x, y) - v(y, x).$$

Thus $\phi(x, y)$ is the signed vote differential between x and y, with $x >_M y \Leftrightarrow \phi(x, y) > 0$. Extend ϕ bilinearly to $P = P_X$,

$$\phi(p, q) = \sum \sum p(x)q(y)\phi(x, y),$$

and let $P^* = \{p \in P : \phi(p, q) \geqslant 0 \text{ for all } q \in P\}$. Since ϕ is an SSB functional on $P \times P$, we know by Theorem 6.2 that P^* is not empty. Moreover, as in the remarks following the theorem, P^* is a polytope in P. The basic proposal of Kreweras (1965) and Fishburn (1984d) is to choose a winner using a distribution in P^*.

This proposal satisfies several properties that are often considered desirable for social choice. We note two of these here. Others are discussed in Fishburn (1984a, pp. 81–83; 1984d). We say that a social choice procedure is *strongly Condorcet* (Smith, 1973) if, whenever X can be partitioned into nonempty A and B such that $a >_M b$ for all $(a, b) \in A \times B$, the social choice from X is in A. In addition, the procedure is *Pareto optimal* if, whenever $>_1, >_2, \ldots, >_n$ is a finite list of weak orders on X such that, for all $x, y \in X$,

$$\phi(x, y) = |\{i : x >_i y\}| - |\{i : y >_i x\}|,$$

y will never be the social choice from X when there is an x such that $x \gtrsim_i y$ for all i and $x >_i y$ for at least one y. The weak orders $>_i$ in such a list need not correspond to the voters' actual preference orders, if in fact they have weakly ordered preferences, and their number n need not be the number of voters. If there are several such lists that satisfy the vote-differential condition, then our Pareto optimality condition is to hold for each of them.

THEOREM 6.4. *Every social choice lottery procedure that uses a distribution in P^* to choose a winner is strongly Condorcet and Pareto optimal.*

Proof. For the strong Condorcet property, suppose that $\{A, B\}$ is a nontrivial partition of X with $a >_M b$, or $\phi(a, b) > 0$, for all $a \in A$ and all $b \in B$. We are to prove that $(p \in P^*, b \in B) \Rightarrow p(b) = 0$. Consider any lottery $p \in P$ for which $p(B) = \Sigma_B p(b) > 0$. If $p(A) = 0$, then clearly $\phi(a, p) = \Sigma_X p(x)\phi(a, x) > 0$ for every $a \in A$, so $p \notin P^*$. If $p(A) > 0$, let $q(a) = p(a)/p(A)$ for all $a \in A$ with $q(B) = 0$. Then

$$\phi(q, p) = \sum_{\{a,x \in A : \phi(a,x) > 0\}} \phi(a, x)[q(a)p(x) - q(x)p(a)]$$

$$+ \sum_{\{b,y \in B : \phi(b,y) > 0\}} \phi(b, y)[q(b)p(y) - q(y)p(b)]$$

$$+ \sum_{a \in A, b \in B} \phi(a, b)[q(a)p(b) - q(b)p(a)]$$

$$= 0 + 0 + \sum_{a,b} \phi(a, b)p(a)p(b)/p(A) > 0.$$

Therefore $\phi(q, p) > 0$, or $\phi(p, q) < 0$, so again $p \notin P^*$. Hence $p \in P^* \Rightarrow$ $p(B) = 0$.

For Pareto optimality, suppose $\succ_1, \ldots, \succ_n$ is a list of weak orders on X that satisfies the vote-differential condition for ϕ and that x Pareto dominates y: $x \succsim_i y$ for all i, $x \succ_i y$ for some i. We are to prove that $p \in P^* \Rightarrow p(y) = 0$. Suppose p is any lottery in P for which $p(y) > 0$. Note that $\phi(x, y) > 0$ and $\phi(x, a) \geq \phi(y, a)$ for every $a \in X \setminus \{x, y\}$. (The latter inequalities follow easily from Pareto dominance and the vote-differential condition under weak orders.)

Let q equal p except on $\{x, y\}$, where $q(x) = p(x) + p(y)$ and $q(y) = 0$. Then

$$\phi(q, p) = \phi(x, y)[p(x) + p(y)]p(y)$$

$$+ \sum_{a \in X \setminus \{x,y\}} \phi(x, a)\{[p(x) + p(y)]p(a) - p(a)p(x)\}$$

$$+ \sum_{a \in X \setminus \{x,y\}} \phi(y, a)[- p(a)p(y)]$$

$$= p(y)\{\phi(x, y)[p(x) + p(y)]$$

$$+ \sum_{a} p(a)[\phi(x, a) - \phi(y, a)]\} > 0.$$

Therefore $p \notin P^*$, so $p \in P^* \Rightarrow p(y) = 0$. $\blacksquare$

Observe that if the original definition for ϕ as the vote differential is replaced by

$$\phi(x, y) = f(v(x, y) - v(y, x)),$$

where $f(0) = 0, f(1) = 1, j > k \Rightarrow f(j) \geq f(k)$, and $f(-j) = -f(j)$ for all j, then Theorem 6.4 holds for P^* defined on the basis of the new ϕ, since no changes are needed in its proof. The lottery procedure with $f(j) = 1$ for all $j > 0$ is concerned only with whether $x >_M y, y >_M x$, or $v(x, y) = v(y, x)$, and pays no attention to the sizes of strict majorities.

6.4   CHOICE AMONG CHOICE CONTEXTS

This section illustrates the sequential application of the minimax theorem by considering choice among choice contexts. Suppose a two-stage decision process unfolds temporally with the selection of one of a number of finite subsets of alternatives X_1, X_2, . . . , X_n followed by a choice from the selected X_i. Under the lottery approach, one could adopt the precommitment strategy of choosing a probability distribution on $X = \bigcup X_i$ and then follow through with the $x \in X$ selected by that distribution. Such a strategy is guided by and justified with Theorem 6.2 in the SSB setting.

On the other hand, one might consider it desirable to use a two-step strategy that first selects an X_i and then chooses a probability distribution over the selected X_i to make the final choice. When this is done, one would naturally choose a maximally preferred p from the P_{X_i} for the selected X_i, but it may be unclear how X_i ought to be selected in the first step.

To approach this problem, Fishburn and LaValle (1986) consider choice among choice contexts, where the set of *contexts* **P** is defined by

$$\mathbf{P} = \{H(Q) : Q \text{ is a nonempty finite subset of } P_X\}.$$

In the preceding formulation we wish to choose one of the contexts $P_{X_1}, \ldots,$ P_{X_n}. To do this, we consider lotteries over contexts. Formally, convex combinations of contexts $\mathbf{p}, \mathbf{q} \in \mathbf{P}$ are defined by

$$\lambda\mathbf{p} + (1 - \lambda)\mathbf{q} = \{\lambda p + (1 - \lambda)q : p \in \mathbf{p}, q \in \mathbf{q}\},$$

$$0 \leqslant \lambda \leqslant 1,$$

and are easily seen to be in **P**. A natural definition of preference between contexts which ensures that the defined relation $>_0$ is asymmetric on **P** is provided by

$$\mathbf{p} >_0 \mathbf{q} \quad \text{if } p > q \text{ for some } p \in \mathbf{p} \text{ and all } q \in \mathbf{q}.$$

Assuming that ϕ on $P \times P$ represents $>$ as in Theorem 4.1, and defining Φ on $\mathbf{P} \times \mathbf{P}$ by

$$\Phi(\mathbf{p}, \mathbf{q}) = \max_{p \in \mathbf{p}} \min_{q \in \mathbf{q}} \phi(p, q),$$

we clearly see that, for all $\mathbf{p}, \mathbf{q} \in \mathbf{P}$,

$$\mathbf{p} >_0 \mathbf{q} \Leftrightarrow \Phi(\mathbf{p}, \mathbf{q}) > 0.$$

Because of this representation, which looks suspiciously like the usual SSB representation, we work with Φ in what follows.

Unlike ϕ on $P \times P$, Φ on $\mathbf{P} \times \mathbf{P}$ is not generally an SSB functional. However, it is skew-symmetric and has vestiges of bilinearity that appear as conclusions (c) and (d) in the following lemma.

LEMMA 6.1. *For all* $\mathbf{p}, \mathbf{q}, \mathbf{r} \in \mathbf{P}$ *and all* $0 \leqslant \lambda \leqslant 1$:

(a) $\Phi(\mathbf{p}, \mathbf{q}) = \min_{\mathbf{q}} \max_{\mathbf{p}} \phi(p, q)$.
(b) $\Phi(\mathbf{q}, \mathbf{p}) = - \Phi(\mathbf{p}, \mathbf{q})$.
(c) $\Phi(\lambda\mathbf{p} + (1 - \lambda)\mathbf{q}, \mathbf{r}) \geqslant \lambda\Phi(\mathbf{p}, \mathbf{r}) + (1 - \lambda)\Phi(\mathbf{q}, \mathbf{r})$.

(d) $\Phi(\lambda\mathbf{p} + (1 - \lambda)\mathbf{q}, \mathbf{r})$ *is continuous in* λ.

Proof. (a) This follows directly from Theorem 6.1, since ϕ on $\mathbf{p} \times \mathbf{q}$ has the requisite properties.

(b) Using (a) and skew-symmetry for ϕ, we get

$$\Phi(\mathbf{q}, \mathbf{p}) = \max_{\mathbf{q}} \min_{\mathbf{p}} \phi(q, p) = \min_{\mathbf{p}} \max_{\mathbf{q}} \phi(q, p)$$

$$= \min_{\mathbf{p}} \max_{\mathbf{q}} [-\phi(p, q)] = -\max_{\mathbf{p}} \min_{\mathbf{q}} \phi(p, q)$$

$$= -\Phi(\mathbf{p}, \mathbf{q}).$$

(c) Conclusion (c) follows from

$$\Phi(\lambda\mathbf{p} + (1 - \lambda)\mathbf{q}, \mathbf{r})$$

$$= \max_{\mathbf{p}, \mathbf{q}} \min_{\mathbf{r}} \phi(\lambda p + (1 - \lambda)q, r)$$

$$= \min_{\mathbf{r}} \max_{\mathbf{p}, \mathbf{q}} [\lambda\phi(p, r) + (1 - \lambda)\phi(q, r)]$$

$$= \min_{\mathbf{r}} [\lambda \max_{\mathbf{p}} \phi(p, r) + (1 - \lambda) \max_{\mathbf{q}} \phi(q, r)]$$

$$\geqslant \min_{\mathbf{r}} [\lambda \max_{\mathbf{p}} \phi(p, r)] + \min_{\mathbf{r}} [(1 - \lambda) \max_{\mathbf{q}} \phi(q, r)]$$

$$= \lambda\Phi(\mathbf{p}, \mathbf{r}) + (1 - \lambda)\Phi(\mathbf{q}, \mathbf{r}).$$

(d) Suppose $\mathbf{p} = H(\{p_1, \ldots, p_a\})$, $\mathbf{q} = H(\{q_1, \ldots, q_b\})$, and $\mathbf{r} = H(\{r_1, \ldots, r_c\})$. Let $\mathbf{p}$, $\mathbf{q}$, and $\mathbf{r}$ be represented by the corresponding simplexes in the Euclidean space with coordinate set $\{p_1, \ldots, r_c\}$. Also let f and g denote the continuous functions over $\mathbf{r}$ defined by $f(r) = \max_{\mathbf{p}} \phi(p, r)$ and $g(r) = \max_{\mathbf{q}} \phi(q, r)$. Then, as in the proof of (c),

$$\Phi(\lambda\mathbf{p} + (1 - \lambda)\mathbf{q}, \mathbf{r}) = \min_{\mathbf{r}} [\lambda f(r) + (1 - \lambda)g(r)].$$

It is easily seen that the right side of this expression is continuous in λ since $\lambda f(r) + (1 - \lambda)g(r)$ is jointly continuous in λ and r. ■

Although Φ is not an SSB functional, its properties in Lemma 6.1 are sufficient for application of Theorem 6.1 to show that for every nonempty finite set of contexts there is a $\mathbf{p}^*$ in the convex hull of those contexts such that $\Phi(\mathbf{p}^*, \mathbf{q}) \geqslant 0$ for every $\mathbf{q}$ in the convex hull.

THEOREM 6.5. *If* $\mathbf{Q}$ *is a nonempty finite subset of* $\mathbf{P}$, *then*

$$\max_{\mathbf{p}\in H(\mathbf{Q})} \min_{\mathbf{q}\in H(\mathbf{Q})} \Phi(\mathbf{p}, \mathbf{q}) = \min_{\mathbf{q}\in H(\mathbf{Q})} \max_{\mathbf{p}\in H(\mathbf{Q})} \Phi(\mathbf{p}, \mathbf{q}) = 0.$$

Proof. Suppose $\mathbf{Q} = \{\mathbf{p}_1, \ldots, \mathbf{p}_n\}$ and let $\alpha = (\alpha_1, \ldots, \alpha_n)$

represent $\Sigma \, \alpha_i \mathbf{p}_i$ in $H(\mathbf{Q})$, with $\Phi'(\alpha, \beta) = \Phi(\Sigma \, \alpha_i \mathbf{p}_i, \Sigma \, \beta_i \mathbf{p}_i)$. Parts (b), (c), and (d) of Lemma 6.1 imply that Φ' is continuous in each argument, quasi-concave in its first argument, and quasi-convex in its second argument. Hence, by Theorem 6.1, $\max_\alpha \min_\beta \Phi'(\alpha, \beta) = \min_\beta \max_\alpha \Phi'(\alpha, \beta)$. It then follows from skew-symmetry that $\max_\alpha \min_\beta \Phi'(\alpha, \beta) = 0$. ∎

Theorem 6.5 suggests two ways of selecting a context from $\{\mathbf{p}_1, \ldots, \mathbf{p}_n\}$ when one of these is required from the first step of a two-step strategy. The first way is to use a lottery $\mathbf{p}^*$ on $\{\mathbf{p}_1, \ldots, \mathbf{p}_n\}$ for which $\Phi(\mathbf{p}^*, \mathbf{q}) \geqslant 0$ for all lotteries $\mathbf{q}$ on $\{\mathbf{p}_1, \ldots, \mathbf{p}_n\}$. We refer to this as the *naive* strategy. The second way involves a look-ahead feature that acknowledges that once a $\mathbf{p}_i$ is selected the final choice will be made by some p_i in

$$m(\mathbf{p}_i) = \{p_i \in \mathbf{p}_i : \phi(p_i, q_i) \geqslant 0 \quad \text{for all } q_i \in \mathbf{p}_i\}.$$

For any $\mathbf{p} \in \mathbf{P}$ it is easily checked that $m(\mathbf{p}) \in \mathbf{P}$ and that $m(m(\mathbf{p})) = m(\mathbf{p})$. In view of this the second way, referred to as *sophisticated*, says to use a lottery $\mathbf{p}'$ on $\{m(\mathbf{p}_1), \ldots, m(\mathbf{p}_n)\}$ for which $\Phi(\mathbf{p}', \mathbf{q}') \geqslant 0$ for all lotteries $\mathbf{q}'$ on $\{m(\mathbf{p}_1), \ldots, m(\mathbf{p}_n)\}$ to determine the $\mathbf{p}_i$ or $m(\mathbf{p}_i)$ selected in the first step.

Fishburn and LaValle (1986) suggest that the sophisticated strategy may be preferable to the naive strategy in the two-step case, and they give a simple example showing that, when $>$ is intransitive, each of the precommitment, naive, and sophisticated strategies can give different results. They also note that if $>$ is a weak order, so the weighted linear model applies, then the three strategies are essentially equivalent.

6.5 NASH EQUILIBRIA IN NONCOOPERATIVE GAMES

Linear utility theory was developed for use in the theory of games by von Neumann and Morgenstern (1944) and has been widely adopted for game-theoretic analyses in the intervening years. Kreweras (1961) was among the first to show that certain results of game theory can be established using much weaker assumptions about players' utilities. In particular, using a proof exactly analogous to Nash's (1951) proof for the existence of equilibria in finite noncooperative games, he proved that every finite noncooperative game with SSB utilities for the players has a Nash equilibrium. This proof was rediscovered by Fishburn and Rosenthal (1986), who give an example of a game in which a player's equilibrium mixed strategy not only serves the usual strategic purpose of randomness vis-à-vis other players but also resolves the intrapersonal problem caused by cyclic preferences over pure strategies.

Although there are several theorems for the existence of equilibria when player's preferences are assumed to satisfy conditions that are weaker than those of the SSB theory (Mas-Colell, 1974; Shafer and Sonnenschein, 1975; Yannelis and Prabhakar, 1983; Toussaint, 1984), their proofs rely on fixed-point theorems that are more advanced than Brouwer's theorem used in the Nash-Kreweras proof.

THEOREM 6.6 (Brouwer's fixed-point theorem). *Let $S_n = \{x \in \mathbf{R}^n : \|x\| \leqslant 1\}$ denote the unit sphere in $\mathbf{R}^n$. If f is a continuous function from S_n into S_n, then $f(x) = x$ for some $x \in S_n$.*

Browder (1983) recounts historical developments involving this theorem and subsequent generalizations, and Milnor (1978) gives an elementary proof and references to other proofs. More advanced fixed-point theorems are discussed by Kakutani (1941), Fan (1952), and Smart (1974), among others.

To formulate Kreweras's theorem, assume there are $n \geqslant 2$ players and that player i has $m_i \in \{1, 2, \ldots\}$ pure strategies. Let $P_i = \{(p_{i1}, \ldots, p_{im_i}): p_{i\sigma} \geqslant 0, \Sigma_\sigma p_{i\sigma} = 1\}$, player's i's simplex of mixed strategies, and let $\pi_{i\sigma} = (0, \ldots, 0, 1$ in position $\sigma), 0, \ldots, 0)$ denote the σth pure strategy of i, so $p_i \in P_i$ can be written as $p_i = \Sigma_\sigma p_{i\sigma} \pi_{i\sigma} = (p_{i1}, \ldots, p_{im_i})$. The set of mixed strategy n-tuples for the players is $P^0 = P_1 \times \cdots \times P_n$. We let X denote the set of pure strategy n-tuples and take $P = P_X$. For convenience we write $(p_1, \ldots, p_{i-1}, t_i, p_{i+1}, \ldots, p_n)$ in P^0 as $(p; t_i)$ and observe that

$$(p; t_i) = \left(p; \sum_\sigma t_{i\sigma} \pi_{i\sigma} \right) = \sum_\sigma t_{i\sigma}(p; \pi_{i\sigma}).$$

Assume that for $i = 1, \ldots, n$, ϕ_i is an SSB functional on $P \times P$ that represents i's preference relation $>_i$ on P. For $p, q \in P^0$ [i.e., $p = (p_1, \ldots, p_n)$ and $q = (q_1, \ldots, q_n)$], we write $\phi_i(p, q)$ to denote $\phi_i(p', q')$ when p' and q' are the distributions in P induced by p and q, respectively, under the usual assumption of independence among players.

We refer to the foregoing situation as an *SSB game*. In the game, $p = (p_1, \ldots, p_n)$ in P^0 is said to be a *Nash equilibrium* if, for all i and all $t_i \in P_i$, $\phi_i(p, (p; t_i)) \geqslant 0$; that is, $p' \gtrsim_i (p; t_i)'$ for all i and t_i. At a Nash equilibrium, no player can increase his or her own preference by a unilateral change in strategy.

THEOREM 6.7. *Every SSB game has a Nash equilibrium.*

Proof. For each $p = (p_1, \ldots, p_n)$ in P^0 let $\tau_{i\sigma}(p) = \max\{0, \phi_i((p; \pi_{i\sigma}), p)\}$ for all i and σ. The $\tau_{i\sigma}$ are continuous in p. Define $T: P^0 \to P^0$ by $T(p) = p^*$, where

$$p_i^* = \left[p_i \sum_\sigma \tau_{i\sigma}(p) \pi_{i\sigma} \right] \bigg/ \left[1 + \sum_\sigma \tau_{i\sigma}(p) \right].$$

Since T is continuous, and since there exists a one-to-one continuous mapping from P^0 onto a unit sphere of suitable dimensionality, it follows from Theorem 6.6 that T has a fixed point (i.e., $T(p) = p$). We show that the fixed points of T are the Nash equilibria of the SSB game.

Suppose first that p is a Nash equilibrium. Then, for all i and σ, $\phi_i(p, (p; \pi_{i\sigma})) \geq 0$, so $\phi_i((p; \pi_{i\sigma}), p) \leq 0$ by skew-symmetry, and therefore $\tau_{i\sigma}(p) = 0$. Hence $p^* = T(p) = p$.

Observe that, given $p \in P^0$, for each i

$$0 = \phi_i(p, p) = \phi_i\left(\left(p; \sum_\sigma p_{i\sigma}\pi_{i\sigma}\right), p\right) = \sum_\sigma p_{i\sigma}\phi_i((p; \pi_{i\sigma}), p).$$

Therefore, there is a σ such that $p_{i\sigma} > 0$ and $\phi_i((p; \pi_{i\sigma}), p) \leq 0$, or $p_{i\sigma} > 0$ and $\tau_{i\sigma}(p) = 0$.

Now suppose p is a fixed point of T, so $p^* = p$. Then for the σ at the end of the preceding paragraph, $p_{i\sigma} = p_{i\sigma}^* = p_{i\sigma}/[1 + \Sigma_\mu \tau_{i\mu}(p)]$, which forces $\tau_{i\mu}(p)$ to 0 for all μ. This is true for each i. Hence, for all i and σ, $\tau_{i\sigma}(p) = 0$, so $\phi_i((p; \tau_{i\sigma}), p) \leq 0$, or $\phi_i(p, (p; \tau_{i\sigma})) \geq 0$. Since $\phi_i(p, (p; t_i)) = \Sigma_\sigma t_{i\sigma}\phi_i(p, (p; \tau_{i\sigma}))$, it follows that $\phi_i(p, (p; t_i)) \geq 0$ for all i and t_i, and hence that p is a Nash equilibrium. ∎

6.6 MULTIPLE ATTRIBUTES

Despite a great deal of research on decompositions of multiattribute linear utility functionals (Keeney and Raiffa, 1976, and other references in Section 1.7) and the aggregation of linear functionals, these topics are relatively open for nonlinear theories. One example of the latter topic is Chew's (1983) application of weighted linear utility to the measurement of income inequality; another example (Fishburn and Gehrlein, 1987) examines generalizations of Harsanyi's linear aggregation theorem (Harsanyi, 1955; Fishburn, 1984e) for SSB functionals.

In this section we prove a decomposition theorem for ϕ on P_X when $X = X_1 \times X_2$ and note its natural extension to more than two attributes along with its specialization when preferences are transitive. Additional comments are given by Fishburn (1984f), who identifies conditions that yield $\phi(p, q) = \phi_1(p_1, q_1) + \phi_2(p_2, q_2)$ in the two-attribute case.

Recall from (1.12) that when $X = X_1 \times \cdots \times X_n$ and p_i is the marginal distribution on X_i induced by p in $P = P_X$, the X_i are *value independent* if for all $p, q \in P$, $(p_i = q_i$ for $i = 1, \ldots, n) \Rightarrow p \sim q$. Given linear u on P, value independence implies $u(p) = u_1(p_1) + \cdots + u_n(p_n)$ with each u_i a linear functional on $P_i = P_{X_i}$. The situation for SSB utilities is not as simple.

THEOREM 6.8. *Suppose* $X = X_1 \times X_2$, ϕ *represents* $>$ *on* $P = P_X$ *as in Theorem 4.1, and the* X_i *are value independent. Then there are SSB functionals* ϕ_1 *on* $P_1 \times P_1$ *and* ϕ_2 *on* $P_2 \times P_2$ *and a bilinear functional* ρ *on* $P_1 \times P_2$ *such that, for all* p, $q \in P$,

$$\phi(p, q) = \phi_1(p_1, q_1) + \phi_2(p_2, q_2) + \rho(p_1, q_2) - \rho(q_1, p_2).$$

Moreover, with ϕ *fixed,* ϕ_1, ϕ_2, *and* ρ *are unique up to transformations*

$$\phi_1'(p_1, q_1) = \phi_1(p_1, q_1) + \tau_1(p_1) - \tau_1(q_1),$$

$$\phi_2'(p_2, q_2) = \phi_2(p_2, q_2) + \tau_2(p_2) - \tau_2(q_2),$$

$$\rho'(p_1, p_2) = \rho(p_1, p_2) - \tau_1(p_1) + \tau_2(p_2) + b,$$

where τ_1 *and* τ_2 *are linear functionals on* P_1 *and* P_2, *respectively, and* $b \in$ **R**.

This decomposition extends straightforwardly to $X = X_1 \times \cdots \times X_n$. Value independence in the *n*-attribute case gives

$$\phi(p, q) = \sum_{i=1}^{n} \phi_i(p_i, q_i) + \sum_{i<j} [\rho_{ij}(p_i, q_j) - \rho_{ij}(q_i, p_j)]$$

with each ϕ_i SSB and each ρ_{ij} bilinear. The proof method for Theorem 6.8 applies to the general case.

The transitive specialization of the theorem uses the modified weighted linear representation of Theorem 5.4 in Section 5.5.

THEOREM 6.9. *Suppose the hypotheses of Theorem 6.8 hold and that there are linear functionals* u *and* w *on* P *that do not vanish at the same point and satisfy* $p > q \Leftrightarrow u(p)w(q) > u(q)w(p)$ *for all* p, $q \in P$. *Then there are linear functionals* u_1 *and* w_1 *on* P_1 *and* u_2 *and* w_2 *on* P_2 *such that, for all* $p \in P$,

$$u(p) = u_1(p_1) + u_2(p_2),$$

$$w(p) = w_1(p_1) + w_2(p_2).$$

Moreover, with u *and* w *fixed, the* u_i *and* w_i *are unique up to transformations* $u_1' = u_1 + a$, $u_2' = u_2 - a$, $w_1' = w_1 + b$, *and* $w_2' = w_2 - b$, *where* a, $b \in$ **R**.

Value independence with $X = X_1 \times \cdots \times X_n$ in the setting of Theorem 6.9 gives $u(p) = \Sigma u_i(p_i)$ and $w(p) = \Sigma w_i(p_i)$.

We prove only the representation parts of the preceding theorems here. The uniqueness proofs can be found in Fishburn (1984f).

Representation Proof of Theorem 6.8. We begin with the observation that if p and p' have the same marginals, say (p_1, p_2), and if q and q' have the same marginals, say (q_1, q_2), then $\phi(p, q) = \phi(p', q')$. Assuming the hypotheses of this claim, value independence gives $\frac{1}{2}p + \frac{1}{2}q' \sim \frac{1}{2}p' + \frac{1}{2}q$. The SSB representation and bilinearity then imply

$$0 = 4\phi\left(\tfrac{1}{2}p + \tfrac{1}{2}q', \tfrac{1}{2}p' + \tfrac{1}{2}q\right)$$
$$= \phi(p, q) + \phi(q', q) + \phi(p, p') + \phi(q', p').$$

Value independence also gives $q' \sim q$ and $p \sim p'$; hence $\phi(q', q) = \phi(p, p') = 0$ and, by skew-symmetry, $\phi(p, q) = \phi(p', q')$.

As a consequence, ϕ depends only on the marginals, and we shall henceforth let (p_1, p_2) in $P_1 \times P_2$ denote the distribution $p \in P$ with $p(x_1, x_2) = p_1(x_1)p_2(x_2)$ for all $(x_1, x_2) \in X_1 \times X_2$. Fix $(a_1, a_2) \in X_1 \times X_2$ and let (a_1, a_2) stand for the degenerate distribution in P with sure outcome (a_1, a_2), and similarly for a_1 in P_1 and a_2 in P_2. By the preceding observation,

$$\phi\left(\tfrac{1}{2}(p_1, p_2) + \tfrac{1}{2}(a_1, a_2), \tfrac{1}{2}(q_1, q_2) + \tfrac{1}{2}(a_1, a_2)\right)$$
$$= \phi((\tfrac{1}{2}p_1 + \tfrac{1}{2}a_1, \tfrac{1}{2}p_2 + \tfrac{1}{2}a_2),$$
$$(\tfrac{1}{2}q_1 + \tfrac{1}{2}a_1, \tfrac{1}{2}q_2 + \tfrac{1}{2}a_2))$$
$$= \phi(\tfrac{1}{2}(p_1, a_2) + \tfrac{1}{2}(a_1, p_2), \tfrac{1}{2}(q_1, a_2) + \tfrac{1}{2}(a_1, q_2)).$$

Since the first and third ϕ terms here are equal, bilinearity and $\phi((a_1, a_2), (a_1, a_2)) = 0$ yield

$$\phi((p_1, p_2), (q_1, q_2)) = \phi((p_1, a_2), (q_1, a_2)) + \phi((a_1, p_2), (a_1, q_2))$$
$$+ \phi((p_1, a_2), (a_1, q_2)) + \phi((a_1, p_2), (q_1, a_2))$$
$$- \phi((p_1, p_2), (a_1, a_2)) - \phi((a_1, a_2), (q_1, q_2)).$$

Two similar applications of our initial observation give

$$\phi((p_1, p_2), (a_1, a_2)) = \phi((p_1, a_2), (a_1, a_2)) + \phi((a_1, p_2), (a_1, a_2)),$$
$$\phi((a_1, a_2), (q_1, q_2)) = \phi((a_1, a_2), (q_1, a_2)) + \phi((a_1, a_2), (a_1, q_2)).$$

Substitute these into the preceding equation and define

$$\phi_1(p_1, q_1) = \phi((p_1, a_2), (q_1, a_2)),$$
$$\phi_2(p_2, q_2) = \phi((a_1, p_2), (a_1, q_2)),$$
$$\rho(r_1, r_2) = \phi((r_1, a_2), (a_1, r_2)) - \phi((r_1, a_2),$$
$$(a_1, a_2)) - \phi((a_1, a_2), (a_1, r_2))$$

to obtain the decomposition displayed in the theorem.   ∎

Representation Proof of Theorem 6.9. Given the hypotheses of the theorem, let $\phi(p, q) = u(p)w(q) - u(q)w(p)$. Define ϕ_1, ϕ_2, and ρ on the basis of fixed (a_1, a_2) as in the preceding proof. When their defining right sides are decomposed with $\phi = uw - uw$ and the uw terms are rearranged in the representation of Theorem 6.8, we get

$$\phi(p, q) = [u_1(p_1) + u_2(p_2)][w_1(q_1) + w_2(q_2)]$$

$$- [u_1(q_1) + u_2(q_2)][w_1(p_1) + w_2(p_2)],$$

where $u_1(p_1) = u(p_1, a_2) - u(a_1, a_2)$, $u_2(p_2) = u(a_1, p_2)$, $w_1(p_1) = w(p_1, a_2) - w(a_1, a_2)$, and $w_2(p_2) = w(a_1, p_2)$.

By the initial observation of the preceding proof, u and w depend only on the marginals, and it follows that $u(p_1, p_2) = u(p_1, a_2) + u(a_1, p_2) - u(a_1, a_2) = u_1(p_1) + u_2(p_2)$ and similarly for w. ∎

6.7 MEAN VALUE AND CERTAINTY EQUIVALENCE

Throughout the rest of this chapter we assume that X is a nondegenerate interval in **R**. We will often view X as a monetary variable with preference increasing in $x \in X$.

The present section discusses a series of increasingly general notions of mean value, motivated in part by certainty equivalence in utility theory (Sections 1.6, 2.8, and 3.11). As will be evident, our focus on mean value constitutes a move away from specialized concerns of preference theory, but we make connections to this theory in process. Chew (1983) includes an excellent introduction to the topic.

It will be assumed that P is a convex set of countably additive probability measures on the usual Borel algebra of subsets of X (Halmos, 1950; Fishburn, 1970a, p. 131). We let m, with or without subscripts, denote a mapping from P into X and will interpret $m(p)$ as the mean value of p in a designated sense.

Three increasingly general notions of mean value are defined by

$$m_1(p) = \int_X x \, dp(x),$$

$$m_2(p) = f^{-1}\left[\int_X f(x) \, dp(x) \right],$$

$$m_3(p) = f^{-1}\left[\int_X f(x)g(x) \, dp(x) \Big/ \int_X g(x) \, dp(x) \right]$$

where $f: X \to \mathbf{R}$ is continuous and strictly monotonic and $g: X \to \mathbf{R}$ is continuous and nonvanishing except perhaps at a closed end point of X (Chew, 1983). m_1 is the *linear mean* (expected value), m_2 the *quasilinear mean,* and m_3 the *weighted quasilinear mean*. The quasilinear mean was axiomatically characterized by Nagumo (1930) and Kolmogorov (1930) for simple uniform measures and extended by de Finetti (1931a) to arbitrary simple measures. The weighted quasilinear mean was axiomatized by Chew (1983). Axioms similar to those of Chew and de Finetti will be noted shortly. The direction of f's monotonicity for m_2 and m_3 is immaterial. Indeed, m_2 and m_3 are unchanged when f is replaced by $-f$, or g by $-g$. More generally, m_2 is invariant only under nondegenerate linear transformations ($f \to af + b$; a, $b \in$ **R**; $a \neq 0$) of f, and m_3 is preserved only under paired transformations $\{f' = [af + b]/[cf + d]$, $g' = [cf + d]g\}$ with $ad \neq bc$ and $cf + d$ nonzero on the interior of X. Problems with the existence of $m_1(p)$ when X is unbounded can always be avoided by suitable boundedness conditions on f and g for m_2 and m_3 (Chew, 1983; Fishburn, 1970a, Chapter 10, 1982a, Chapter 3).

For utility theory, $m(p)$ is usually identified with an individual's certainty equivalent $c(p)$ for measure p in monetary contexts. $m_1 = c$ for expected value maximizers, $m_2 = c$ for a von Neumann–Morgenstern expected utility maximizer with increasing utility function $u = f$, and $m_3 = c$ for Chew's weighted linear utility representation with $g = w$ and $f = u/w$ (Section 3.6, Theorem 5.3).

In a further generalization of mean value that provides a correspondence to certainty equivalence in SSB utility theory, Fishburn (1986b) considers an implicit characterization of $m(p)$ as the unique solution of $\int_X h(x, m(p))\, dp(x) = 0$. This characterization presumes that h is skew-symmetric and satisfies the two additional properties of

Uniform Monotonicity: Either $h(x, y)$ increases in x for every $y \in X_0$ (interior of X) or $h(x, y)$ decreases in x for every $y \in X_0$.

Ratio Continuity: If $x \neq y$, then $h(x, t)/h(y, t)$ is continuous at $t = x$ and at all $t \neq y$ in X_0.

Depending on P, h might also satisfy a boundedness condition. The implicit characterization reduces to m_2 if $h(x, y) = f(x) - f(y)$, and to m_3 if $h(x, y) = [f(x) - f(y)]g(x)g(y)$. However, since m_3 does not presume the equivalent of uniform monotonicity in Chew's setting, his generalization is not strictly a special case of the implicit mean characterization. This appears true also for a different generalization considered in Chew (1984).

The implicit characterization is axiomatized in Fishburn (1986b) by seven axioms for $m: P \to X$ under the structural assumptions that P contains every one-point measure and is closed under conditional measures on intervals within X. We let $\lambda^* = (1 - \lambda)/\lambda$ for $0 < \lambda < 1$ and let $>_1$ be the first-degree stochastic dominance relation defined by $p >_1 q$ if $p(X \cap (-\infty, y]) \leqslant q(X \cap (-\infty, y])$ for all $y \in X$ with $<$ holding for at least one y. The axioms are, for all p, $q \in P$, all x, x_1, $\ldots$, $x_5 \in X$, all α, β, γ, δ, $\theta \in (0, 1)$, and all intervals $A \subseteq X$:

M1. Certainty Matching: $p(\{x\}) = 1 \Rightarrow m(p) = x$.

M2. Convexity: $m(p) = m(q) \Rightarrow m(\frac{1}{2}p + \frac{1}{2}q) = m(p)$.

M3. Betweenness: $m(p) < m(q) \Rightarrow m(p) < m(\alpha p + (1 - \alpha)q) < m(q)$.

M4. Continuity: $m(p) < x < m(q) \Rightarrow m(\lambda p + (1 - \lambda)q) = x$ *for some* $0 < \lambda < 1$.

M5. Dominance: $p >_1 q \Rightarrow m(p) > m(q)$.

M6. Cancellation: $[x_1 < x_2 < x_3 < x_4 < x_5, x_2 = m(\alpha x_1' + (1 - \alpha)x_3'), x_3 = m(\beta x_2' + (1 - \beta)x_4'), x_4 = m(\gamma x_3' + (1 - \gamma)x_5'), x_2 = m(\delta x_1' + (1 - \delta)x_4'), x_4 = m(\theta x_2' + (1 - \theta)x_5')] \Rightarrow \alpha*\beta*\gamma* = \delta*\theta*$, where x' denotes a one-point distribution.

M7. Truncation: $m(p) < x \Rightarrow m(p_{[y,\infty)\cap X}) \leqslant x$ *for some* $y \in X$; $x < m(p) \Rightarrow x \leqslant m(p_{(-\infty,y]\cap X})$ *for some* $y \in X$.

All of these hold for m_2, and all but M5 hold for m_3. The first five axioms are straightforward and, except perhaps for M5, seem like natural conditions on any reasonable notion of mean value. The cancellation axiom M6 is suggested directly by Lemma 4.12. It is needed for skew-symmetry and appears not to be replaceable by a simpler condition, although C3 (symmetry) sufficed in the SSB theory with its richer $P \times P$ structure. The truncation axiom M7 serves much the same purpose as truncation axioms considered in Sections 1.8 and 4.8.

The essential difference between m_2, m_3 and the implicit characterization lies in their independence axioms. We use M6 for the implicit case. The quasilinear independence axiom (cf. A2 in Section 1.4) is

$$m(p) = m(q) \Rightarrow m(\lambda p + (1 - \lambda)r) = m(\lambda q + (1 - \lambda)r),$$

and Chew's independence axiom for m_3 (cf. D2 in Section 5.6) says that

$$[m(p) = m(q) \neq m(r), m(\beta p + (1 - \beta)r) = m(\gamma q + (1 - \gamma)r)]$$
$$\Rightarrow m(\beta p + (1 - \beta)s) = m(\gamma q + (1 - \gamma)s) \quad \text{for all } s \in P.$$

The implicit form reduces to m_3 when this axiom is adopted, and m_3 reduces to m_2 when the quasilinear independence axiom is imposed.

The principal implications of M1–M7 are summarized in the following theorem (X_0 = interior of X).

THEOREM 6.10. *Suppose* $m:P \to X$. *Then* m *satisfies* M1–M7 *if and only if there is a skew-symmetric, uniformly monotonic, and ratio continuous* $h:X \times X \to \mathbf{R}$ *such that, for all* $(p, y) \in P \times X_0$, $\int h(x, y) dp(x)$ *exists and*

$$m(p) = y \Leftrightarrow \int_X h(x, y) \, dp(x) = 0.$$

Moreover, excepting h(a, b) and h(b, a) when X = [a, b], h' satisfies the representation in place of h if and only if h'(x, y) = kh(x, y) for some k ≠ 0 and all x, y ∈ X.

The proof (Fishburn, 1986b) is patterned after the SSB proof in Chapter 4 but is simpler. When the SSB representation holds, $c(p)$ is the solution of $\int \phi(x, c(p)) \, dp(x) = 0$. Hence in the SSB context, $m = c$ requires $h(x, y) = k\phi(x, y)$ for some $k \neq 0$. With $m = c$ in the SSB context, $m(p) > m(q)$ does not necessarily imply $p > q$, and $m(p) = m(q)$ does not entail $p \sim q$. In fact, preference reversals (Sections 2.8 and 3.11) in the general sense occur precisely when $p > q$ and $m(q) > m(p)$.

6.8   STOCHASTIC DOMINANCE

In Section 1.6 we noted that first ($>_1$) and second ($>_2$) degree stochastic dominance correspond to greater expected utility for increasing and increasing concave utility respectively. A similar result for SSB utility based on the behavior of $\phi(x, y)$ on its first argument will be proved shortly as Theorem 6.12.

We assume in this section that $P = P_X$ and, in this simple measures setting, will use Abel's formula for summation by parts,

$$\sum_{i=1}^{n} a_i b_i = \sum_{j=1}^{n-1} \left(\sum_{i=1}^{j} a_i \right) (b_j - b_{j+1}) + b_n \sum_{i=1}^{n} a_i \qquad (a_i, b_i \in \mathbf{R}),$$

in our ensuing proofs. Stochastic dominance analyses for more general probability measures and higher degrees of stochastic dominance are included in Fishburn (1976b, 1980b) for linear utility and in Chew (1983) for weighted linear utility. Machina (1982a) proves several results for the first- and second-degree relations in his nonlinear smooth utility context (Section 3.4) for probability distribution functions on $X = [0, M]$.

We also assume that $\phi(x, y) = \phi(p, q)$ when $p(x) = q(y) = 1$. Let Φ_1 be the class of all skew-symmetric ϕ on $X \times X$ that increase in the first argument for every fixed value of the second argument, and let Φ_2 be the class of functions in Φ_1 that are strictly concave in the first argument; that is, $(x \neq y, 0 < \lambda < 1) \Rightarrow \lambda\phi(x, z) + (1 - \lambda)\phi(y, z) < \phi(\lambda x + (1 - \lambda)y, z)$. It is natural in the monetary setting to assume that $\phi \in \Phi_1$. Moreover, so long as p and q have certainty equivalents $c(p)$ and $c(q)$ in the SSB case (which is ensured by continuity), we must have $c(p) > c(q)$ whenever $\phi \in \Phi_1$ and $p >_1 q$. In conjunction with our later theorem, this prohibits preference reversals between p and q whenever $p >_1 q$.

THEOREM 6.11. *For all* $\phi \in \Phi_1$ *that are continuous in the first argument, and all* $p, q \in P$,

$$p >_1 q \Rightarrow c(p) > c(q).$$

Proof. Assume $p >_1 q$ with $\phi \in \Phi_1$ continuous in its first argument, and let $x = c(p)$ and $y = c(q)$. Also let $x_1 < x_2 < \cdots < x_n$ be the support points of p and q and set $p_i = p(x_i)$, $q_i = q(x_i)$. [p^k denotes the kth cumulative of p, with $p_i^k = p^k(x_i)$.]

Suppose to the contrary of the theorem that $y \geqslant x$. Since $\phi \in \Phi_1$, $\phi(y, x_i) \geqslant \phi(x, x_i)$ and therefore $\phi(x_i, x) \geqslant \phi(x_i, y)$ for all i by skew-symmetry. Then, by the definition of c,

$$\sum_i q_i \phi(x_i, y) = 0 = \sum_i p_i \phi(x_i, x) \geqslant \sum_i p_i \phi(x_i, y),$$

so that $\Sigma (q_i - p_i)\phi(x_i, y) \geqslant 0$. It follows from Abel's formula that

$$\sum_{i=1}^n (q_i^1 - p_i^1)[\phi(x_i, y) - \phi(x_{i+1}, y)] \geqslant 0.$$

However, this is impossible since $\phi(x_i, y) - \phi(x_{i+1}, y) < 0$ for each i and $q_i^1 \geqslant p_i^1$ for all i with $q_i^1 > p_i^1$ for some i. ∎

Just as there is doubt about the general concavity of u for linear utility, we would not generally expect ϕ to be concave in its first argument in the SSB context. Our analysis of derivatives in the next section says more about this. However, $\phi \in \Phi_2$ does have nice implications for stochastic dominance.

THEOREM 6.12. *For all* $p, q \in P$,

$$p >_1 q \Leftrightarrow \phi(p, q) > 0 \text{ for all } \phi \in \Phi_1,$$

$$p >_2 q \Leftrightarrow \phi(p, q) > 0 \text{ for all } \phi \in \Phi_2.$$

Proof. Since $\phi(x, y) = u(x) - u(y)$ is a special case for ϕ, the linear utility stochastic dominance results say that if $\phi(p, q) > 0$ for all $\phi \in \Phi_j$ then $u(p) > u(q)$ for all u in the corresponding linear class and therefore $p >_j q$.

To prove the converses ($\Rightarrow$), let $x_1 < x_2 < \cdots < x_n$ be the support points of p and q. For notational convenience, take $p_i = p(x_i)$, $p_i^1 = p^1(x_i)$, $p_i^2 = p^2(x_i)$, $q_i = q(x_i)$, $q_i^1 = q^1(x_i)$, $q_i^2 = q^2(x_i)$, $v_{ij} = \phi(x_i, x_j)$. Then, using Abel's formula twice, we have

$$\phi(p, q) = \phi(p, q) - \phi(q, q)$$

$$= \sum_i (p_i - q_i) \sum_j q_j v_{ij}$$

$$= \sum_{i=1}^{n-1} (p_i^1 - q_i^1) \left[\sum_{j=1}^{n} q_j v_{ij} - \sum_{j=1}^{n} q_j v_{i+1,j} \right]$$

$$= \sum_{i=1}^{n-1} (q_i^1 - p_i^1) \sum_{j=1}^{n} q_j (v_{i+1,j} - v_{ij}) \qquad [>_1]$$

$$= \sum_{i=1}^{n-1} (q_i^1 - p_i^1)(x_{i+1} - x_i) \sum_{j=1}^{n} q_j \left(\frac{v_{i+1,j} - v_{ij}}{x_{i+1} - x_i} \right)$$

$$= \sum_{i=1}^{n-2} \left\{ \sum_{k=1}^{i} (q_k^1 - p_k^1)(x_{k+1} - x_k) \right\}$$

$$\cdot \sum_{j=1}^{n} q_j \left(\frac{v_{i+1,j} - v_{ij}}{x_{i+1} - x_i} - \frac{v_{i+2,j} - v_{i+1,j}}{x_{i+2} - x_{i+1}} \right)$$

$$+ \sum_{k=1}^{n-1} (q_k^1 - p_k^1)(x_{k+1} - x_k)$$

$$\cdot \sum_{j=1}^{n} q_j \left(\frac{v_{nj} - v_{n-1,j}}{x_n - x_{n-1}} \right)$$

$$= \sum_{i=1}^{n-2} (q_{i+1}^2 - p_{i+1}^2)$$

$$\cdot \sum_{j=1}^{n} q_j \left(\frac{v_{i+1,j} - v_{ij}}{x_{i+1} - x_i} - \frac{v_{i+2,j} - v_{i+1,j}}{x_{i+2} - x_{i+1}} \right)$$

$$+ (q_n^2 - p_n^2) \sum_{j=1}^{n} q_j \left(\frac{v_{nj} - v_{n-1,j}}{x_n - x_{n-1}} \right) .$$

The line identified by $[>_1]$ shows that $\phi(p, q) > 0$ if $p >_1 q$ and $\phi \in \Phi_1$, since then all its terms are nonnegative and at least one must be positive. The final expression implies $\phi(p, q) > 0$ if $p >_2 q$ and $\phi \in \Phi_2$, since then each $q_j^2 - p_j^2$ is nonnegative, at least one is positive, and every v term is positive. ∎

Several other SSB stochastic dominance results are noted in Fishburn (1984c, Section 5).

6.9   RISK ATTITUDES

We assume in this final section that $X = \mathbf{R}$ and that ϕ on $X \times X$ has continuous derivatives through the second order. We let $\phi_1(x, y) = \partial\phi(x, y)/\partial x$, $\phi_2(x, y) = \partial\phi(x, y)/\partial y$, $\phi_{11}(x, y) = \partial\phi_1(x, y)/\partial x$, $\phi_{12}(x, y) = \partial\phi_1(x, y)/\partial y$, and so forth. Skew-symmetry and the derivatives assumption imply

$$\phi_2(x, y) = -\phi_1(y, x),$$

$$\phi_{22}(x, y) = -\phi_{11}(y, x),$$

$$\phi_{21}(x, y) = \phi_{12}(x, y) = -\phi_{21}(y, x) = -\phi_{12}(y, x).$$

Because of these we focus on ϕ_1, ϕ_{11}, and ϕ_{12}. We comment on ϕ_1 and ϕ_{11} first and then examine the mixed derivative.

A main feature of SSB in comparison to linear utility is its much greater potential to reflect different risk attitudes. For example, each fixed y gives rise to a risk attitude profile for $\phi(\cdot, y)$ in terms of $\phi_1(\cdot, y)$ and $\phi_{11}(\cdot, y)$ in much the same way that $u^{(1)}$ and $u^{(2)}$ do this for the linear case discussed in Section 1.6. As y changes, these y-conditioned profiles can change in various ways that reflect different attitudes that depend on comparisons between x and the conditioning value of y. An example occurs when each $\phi(\cdot, y)$ is convex (risk seeking) for small x and concave (risk averse) for larger x with the inflection point between the two regions changing as y changes. In the linear case with $\phi(x, y) = u(x) - u(y)$, all y-conditioned profiles are identical.

With Δ a small positive amount, $\phi_1 > 0$, $\phi_1(x, y) - \phi_1(y, x) < 0$ and $\phi_{11}(x, y) < 0$ correspond to

$$\phi(x + \Delta, y) > \phi(x, y),$$

$$\phi(x, y) > \phi(x + \Delta, y + \Delta),$$

$$2\phi(x + \Delta, y) > \phi(x, y) + \phi(x + 2\Delta, y),$$

respectively. The first of these follows from $x > y \Rightarrow x \succ y$ if $x \leqslant y \leqslant x + \Delta$, but not otherwise. Hence the assumption that ϕ increases in its first argument entails more than the mere presumption that preference increases as x increases. Given $\phi_1 > 0$, the second inequality holds whenever $x > y$ if $\phi(x, y) > 0$ shrinks when the same positive amount is added to both x and y, thus indicating that the lottery-based differentials contract for equal differences in their arguments when the arguments get larger. If ϕ depends only on the difference between x and y then $\phi(x, y) = \phi(x + \Delta, y + \Delta)$ and $\phi_1(x, y) = \phi_1(y, x)$ for all x and y. Using x^* to denote the one-point measure with outcome x, we see that the third inequality is tantamount to

$$\phi(x + \Delta, y) > \phi(\tfrac{1}{2}x^* + \tfrac{1}{2}(x + 2\Delta)^*, y),$$

which expresses a notion of conditional risk aversion in the SSB setting.

The corresponding expression for a positive mixed derivative, $\phi_{12}(x, y) > 0$, is

$$\phi(x, y) + \phi(x + \Delta, y + \Delta) > \phi(x + \Delta, y) + \phi(x, y + \Delta).$$

But note also that $\phi_{12}(x, x) = 0$ since $\phi_{12}(x, y) + \phi_{12}(y, x) = 0$. The following theorem reveals important connections of ϕ_{12} to specializations of ϕ.

THEOREM 6.13. *For all* $x, y \in X$:

(a) $\phi_{12}(x, y) = -\phi_{11}(x, y)$ *if and only if ϕ depends only on $x - y$.*
(b) *If $>$ on P is a weak order, then* $\phi(x, y)\phi_{12}(x, y) = -\phi_1(x, y)\phi_1(y, x) + \phi_1(x, x)\phi_1(y, y).$
(c) $\phi_{12} \equiv 0$ *if and only if the linear utility representation holds.*

Proof. (a) Let $z = x - y$ and define v on $\mathbf{R}^2$ by $v(z, y) = \phi(x, y)$. By the chain rule with $\phi_1(x, y) = v_1(z, y) \, dz/dx = v_1(z, y)$,

$$\phi_{12}(x, y) = \left[\frac{\partial v_1(z, y)}{\partial z}\right]\frac{\partial z}{\partial y} + \left[\frac{\partial v_1(z, y)}{\partial y}\right]$$

$$= -v_{11}(z, y) + v_{12}(z, y) = -\phi_{11}(x, y) + v_{12}(z, y).$$

Therefore $\phi_{12} = -\phi_{11}$ if and only if $v_{12} \equiv 0$. If ϕ depends only on z so that $v(z, y) = v(z)$, then $v_{12} \equiv 0$. Conversely, suppose $v_{12} \equiv 0$. Then $v_1(z, y) = g(z)$ for some functional g. Let $G(z)$ be such that $dG(z)/dz = g(z)$. Then

$$\partial[v(z, y) - G(z)]/\partial z = v_1(z, y) - g(z) = 0,$$

and therefore there is a functional f such that

$$v(z, y) - G(z) = f(y) \qquad \text{for all } z \text{ and } y.$$

Hence, by the definition of v,

$$\phi(x, y) = G(x - y) + f(y) \qquad \text{for all } x \text{ and } y.$$

Let $y = x$. Then, since $\phi(x, x) = 0$, $f(x) = -G(0)$ for all x, so f is constant and ϕ depends solely on $x - y$.

(b) Suppose $\phi(x, y) = u(x)w(y) - u(y)w(x)$, as in the weighted linear model for weak order in the SSB setting. Then $\phi_{12}(x, y) = u'(x)w'(y) - u'(y)w'(x)$ [primes denote derivatives]. It follows that

$$\phi(x, y)\phi_{12}(x, y) + \phi_1(x, y)\phi_1(y, x)$$

$$= \phi(x, y)\phi_{12}(x, y) - \phi_1(x, y)\phi_2(x, y)$$

$$= [u(x)w(y) - u(y)w(x)][u'(x)w'(y) - u'(y)w'(x)]$$

$$- [u'(x)w(y) - u(y)w'(x)][u(x)w'(y) - u'(y)w(x)]$$

$$= [u(x)w'(x) - u'(x)w(x)][u(y)w'(y) - u'(y)w(y)]$$

$$= \phi_1(x, x)\phi_1(y, y).$$

(c) If $\phi(x, y) = u(x) - u(y)$, then $\phi_1(x, y) = u'(x)$ and $\phi_{12}(x, y) = 0$. Conversely, Suppose $\phi_{12} \equiv 0$. Then $\phi_1(x, y) = v(x)$ for some functional v. Let $V(x)$ have derivative $v(x)$. Then $\partial[\phi(x, y) - V(x)]/\partial x = 0$, and therefore there is a functional f such that $\phi(x, y) = V(x) + f(y)$ for all x and y. Since $\phi(y, y) = 0$, $f(y) = -V(y)$, and therefore $\phi(x, y) = V(x) - V(y)$. ∎

Fishburn (1984g) gives specific examples to illustrate parts (a) and (b) of Theorem 6.13. The example for (a) is

$$\phi(x, y) = 1 - \exp\{-(x - y)^2 - \sqrt{2}(x - y)\} \qquad \text{for } x \geqslant y.$$

For fixed y, $\phi(\cdot, y)$ begins convex and then changes to concave. The inflection point for y is at $x = y$. The example for (b) has

$$u(x) = -e^{-x} \qquad \text{and} \qquad w(x) = \pi/2 + \tan^{-1}(x).$$

In this case the region for $\phi_{11} > 0$ is a proper subregion of the $(-, -)$ quadrant with $\phi_{11} < 0$ elsewhere except on the region's boundary. In addition, $\phi_1 > 0$, and $\phi_{12}(x, y) > 0 \Leftrightarrow x > y$.

7 Additive Expected Utility

There are two standard formulations for theories of decision under uncertainty that represent preference between decision alternatives by expected utilities based on subjective probability as well as utility. The first is Savage's formulation in which an alternative is an act that assigns an outcome to each state in a set of states of the world. The second uses lottery acts, each of which assigns a simple lottery over outcomes to each state. This chapter explains these formulations in detail and then presents traditional normative theories of subjective probability and expected utility developed by Savage and others. Alternatives to the traditional theories are discussed in the next two chapters.

7.1 DECISION UNDER UNCERTAINTY

In the last three chapters of the book we extend ideas of earlier chapters to the realm of decision making under uncertainty in conjunction with new considerations involving subjective probability. The present chapter describes Savage's (1954) additive expected utility theory and related developments, including basic theory of subjective probability. Much of the work discussed here was completed by the mid-1960s. The next chapter raises questions about assumptions behind additive expected utility that were not addressed in Chapter 2. In parallel to Chapter 3, it then reviews generalizations of additive expected utility that, with a few exceptions, were developed since 1980. The final chapter concludes with detailed analyses of generalizations of Savage's theory that presume neither transitivity nor the reduction principle but adopt his sure-thing principle and the additivity of subjective probability.

Because Savage's theory is often referred to as ''subjective expected utility'' or simply ''expected utility,'' a word about our designation ''additive expected utility'' (which I have used to mean something else in Fishburn, 1970a) is in order. In the traditional designation, *subjective* refers to the additive subjective probability feature of Savage's representation. However, alternatives to Savage's theory have been proposed in the past few years that also use subjective probability and an expectation operation but do not require probabilities to be additive (see Sections 8.2 and 8.3). Because of this I now find it more suitable to use *additive* as a modifier for theories of decision under uncertainty that use additive subjective probability, and to employ *nonadditive* for ones that do not assume that subjective probability is necessarily additive.

In addition, various other modifiers will be used to identify whether a theory's representation uses an expectation operation and whether its formulation uses "extraneous" probabilities for scaling purposes to construct lotteries on outcomes or on acts. In this part of the book, *expected* utility refers only to a *formulation* like Savage's that is devoid of direct reference to probability of any sort. Thus, for Savage, we speak of "additive expected utility"; in the next chapter we encounter "nonadditive expected utility," "additive nonexpected intensive utility" (Allais), and so forth. The modification of Savage's theory considered in Section 7.6, which uses the extraneous scaling probability device but is otherwise the same as Savage's theory, is referred to as an "additive linear utility" theory, since the linear utility theory of von Neumann and Morgenstern is directly involved in its representation. Theories presented in the next chapter that also use extraneous scaling probabilities include "nonadditive linear utility" and "additive SSB utility."

As a final preliminary to our discussion of additive subjective probability and additive expected (linear) utility in this chapter, we outline the two formulations of decision under uncertainty alluded to in the preceding paragraph.

Savage's formulation begins with a set S of states of the world, or simply *states*, and a set X of consequences or *outcomes*. In Savage's approach, states are the carriers of uncertainty, and outcomes the carriers of value. The states in S are presumed to be mutually exclusive and collectively exhaustive so that exactly one state, the state that *obtains*, is the *true state*. The two states of a just-picked mushroom might be "harmless" and "poisonous." The decision maker is uncertain about which state is the true state, the identify of the the true state will not be known until after the decision has been taken (if ever), and the decision is presumed not to affect the state that obtains. Although the decision maker might conduct an experiment at some cost to learn more about which state is the true state, we shall not deal with experimentation as a separate feature of the decision process but note that it can be an implicit part of the formulation. Explicit treatments are available in Good (1950), Savage (1954), Schlaifer (1959), Raiffa and Schlaifer (1961), Raiffa (1968), Howard (1968), DeGroot (1970), LaValle (1978), and Hartigan (1983).

Subsets of states are called *events* by Savage, and event A is said to *obtain* if A contains the true state. We shall let $\mathcal{E}$ denote a Boolean algebra of events with $S \in \mathcal{E}$. The empty set $\varnothing$ is the *empty event*, and S is the *universal event*. Subjective probabilities will be assigned to the elements of $\mathcal{E}$, with $\pi(\varnothing) = 0$ and $\pi(S) = 1$ when π is a probability measure on $\mathcal{E}$. Throughout this chapter and in much of what follows, we take $\mathcal{E} = 2^S$, the set of all subsets of S. In this case, $\mathcal{E}$ is a Borel algebra.

For Savage the outcomes in X are to contain all value-relevant aspects of the situation at hand. A decision alternative, called an *act*, is a function from S into X. The outcome assigned by act f to state s is $f(s)$. Two acts are illustrated for an n-state S in Figure 7.1. Other illustrations appear in Figures 2.1 and 2.2. Act f is *constant* if $f(S) = \{x\}$ for some $x \in X$ and is *simple* if $f(S) = \{f(s):s \in S\}$ is finite.

Savage applies the preference relation $\succ$ to a set F of acts in his axioms. He assumes that F contains at least all simple acts and defines $\succ$ on X from $\succ$ on F through constant acts: $x \succ y$ if $f \succ g$ when $f(S) = \{x\}$ and $g(S) = \{y\}$. We assume later that $F = X^S$, the set of all functions from S into X, in describing his theory.

Our other formulation for decision under uncertainty is a lottery-acts modification of Savage's formulation, similar to those used by Anscombe and Aumann (1963) and Pratt et al. (1964). Let $P = P_X$, the set of all lotteries or simple probability distributions on X. The lottery-acts formulation replaces outcomes in a matrix like that of Figure 7.1 by lotteries on outcomes and defines a *lottery act* as a function $\mathbf{f}$ from S into P. The probabilities used in the $p \in P$ are to be thought of as extraneous scaling probabilities associated with events for precisely calibrated random devices such as roulette wheels or fair coins, which are imagined to be completely independent of the states in S. Thus, if $\mathbf{f}$ is chosen in the lottery-acts case and state s obtains, it remains to play out $\mathbf{f}(s)$ to determine the outcome.

In the lottery-acts formulation, $\succ$ is applied to a set $\mathbf{F}$ of lottery acts. Preferences between regular Savage acts in F are then defined from $\succ$ on $\mathbf{F}$ through degenerate lottery acts: $f \succ g$ if $\mathbf{f} \succ \mathbf{g}$ when $[\mathbf{f}(s)](f(s)) = [\mathbf{g}(s)](g(s)) = 1$ for every $s \in S$. We will assume that $\mathbf{F} = P^S$, the set of all possible lottery acts. In this case, as well as some other cases, $\mathbf{F}$ is convex under the statewise definition for $\lambda\mathbf{f} + (1 - \lambda)\mathbf{g}$. For each $s \in S$,

$$(\lambda\mathbf{f} + (1 - \lambda)\mathbf{g})(s) = \lambda\mathbf{f}(s) + (1 - \lambda)\mathbf{g}(s).$$

The technical advantage for the lottery-acts formulation comes from convexity, which allows us to formulate axioms such as $(\mathbf{f} \succ \mathbf{g}, 0 < \lambda < 1) \Rightarrow (\lambda\mathbf{f} + (1 - \lambda)\mathbf{h} \succ \lambda\mathbf{g} + (1 - \lambda)\mathbf{h})$, which has no meaning for Savage's formulation. At the same time, it can be criticized for including a notion of probability within the axioms. As several people have recognized, it is

FIGURE 7.1 $f(s_i) = x_i, g(s_i) = y_i$

$$
\begin{array}{c|cccc}
 & s_1 & s_2 & \cdots & s_n \\
\hline
f & x_1 & x_2 & \cdots & x_n \\
g & y_1 & y_2 & \cdots & y_n \\
\end{array}
$$

possible to embed the lottery idea within Savage's formulation by enlarging the state space S to include events generated by random devices. This would avoid direct reference to extraneous scaling probabilities in the axioms. However, it would also disguise the distinctive feature of randomization in the lottery-acts approach and nullify the use of convex combinations in the axioms.

7.2 ADDITIVE SUBJECTIVE PROBABILITY

This section and the next consider subjective probability in its own right based on a comparative probability relation $\succ_*$ on the event algebra $\mathcal{E}$. We read $A \succ_* B$ as A *is more probable than* B, and define $\sim_*$ and $\succsim_*$ in the usual ways as

$$A \sim_* B \quad \text{if not } (A \succ_* B) \text{ and not } (B \succ_* A),$$

$$A \succsim_* B \quad \text{if } A \succ_* B \text{ or } A \sim_* B.$$

Section 7.4 defines $\succ_*$ on $\mathcal{E}$ from $\succ$ on F after the fashion of de Finetti (1931b, 1964), Ramsey (1931), and Savage (1954), but until then we consider $(\mathcal{E}, \succ_*)$ apart from considerations of preference or choice.

We say that $(\mathcal{E}, \succ_*)$ has an *additive representation* if there is a probability measure π on $\mathcal{E}$ such that, for all $A, B \in \mathcal{E}$,

$$A \succ_* B \leftrightarrow \pi(A) > \pi(B).$$

When this holds, π *agrees* with $\succ_*$, and when it holds for exactly one probability measure, we say that $(\mathcal{E}, \succ_*)$ has a *unique* additive representation. This section considers only additive representations, which require $S \succ_*$ $\varnothing$ (nontriviality), $A \succsim_* \varnothing$ (nonnegativity), $A \supseteq B \Rightarrow A \succsim_* B$ (monotonicity), weak order for $\succ_*$ on $\mathcal{E}$, and various additivity conditions such as $[(A \cup B) \cap C = \varnothing, A \succ_* B] \Rightarrow A \cup C \succ_* B \cup C$. Weaker representations are surveyed in Fine (1973) and Fishburn (1986c), and several nonadditive representations will be introduced in Section 8.3.

Necessary and sufficient conditions for an additive representation for finite $\mathcal{E}$ were first presented by Kraft et al. (1959). With no loss of generality in this case let $S = \{1, 2, \ldots, n\}$ and $\mathcal{E} = 2^S$. For all $m \geq 2$ and all sequences $(A_1, \ldots, A_m)$ and $(B_1, \ldots, B_m)$ of events in $\mathcal{E}$, define $=_0$ on pairs of sequences by

$$(A_1, \ldots, A_m) =_0 (B_1, \ldots, B_m)$$

$$\text{if } |\{j : i \in A_j\}| = |\{j : i \in B_j\}| \text{ for all } i.$$

The import of this balance condition can be seen from the fact that if π with $\pi_i = \pi(\{i\})$ agrees with $\succ_*$ and if $(A_1, \ldots, A_m) =_0 (B_1, \ldots, B_m)$, then $\Sigma_j \pi(A_j) = \Sigma_j \Sigma_{i \in A_j} \pi_i = \Sigma_j \Sigma_{i \in B_j} \pi_i = \Sigma_j \pi(B_j)$, hence we cannot have $A_j \succsim_* B_j$ for all j and $A_j \succ_* B_j$ for at least one j.

THEOREM 7.1. *Suppose* $\mathcal{E} = 2^{\{1, \ldots, n\}}$. *Then* $(\mathcal{E}, \succ_*)$ *has an additive representation if and only if the following hold for all* A, A_j, $B_j \in \mathcal{E}$ *and all* $m \geq 2$:

F1. Nontriviality: $\{1, \ldots, n\} \succ_* \varnothing$.
F2. Nonnegativity: $A \succsim_* \varnothing$.
F3. Strong Additivity: $[(A_1, \ldots, A_m) =_0 (B_1, \ldots, B_m), A_j \succsim_* B_j$ *for* $j = 1, \ldots, m - 1] \Rightarrow$ *not* $(A_m \succ_* B_m)$.

Remarks. The strong additivity axiom F3 cannot in general be replaced by a simpler axiom that bounds m without regard to n. An agreeing π is not generally unique, since it is only required to satisfy a finite system of linear inequalities.

Proof. Necessity follows from our comments prior to the theorem. For sufficiency we are to show that F1, F2, and F3 imply that there are nonnegative numbers $\pi_1, \ldots, \pi_n$ that sum to 1 such that, for all $A, B \in \mathcal{E}$,

$$A \succ_* B \Rightarrow \sum_{i \in A} \pi_i > \sum_{i \in B} \pi_i,$$

$$A \sim_* B \Rightarrow \sum_{i \in A} \pi_i = \sum_{i \in B} \pi_i.$$

The resultant system of linear inequalities ($>$ for $\succ_*$, $\geq$ both ways for $\sim_*$) translates directly into a system like that in Theorem 4.3(a) where the coefficient vectors (the x_i) consist entirely of numbers in $\{0, 1, -1\}$. Because of this, if (a) is false, the r_i in (b) can be taken to be integers, and if (b) holds it translates back into the conclusion that F3 fails. Hence F3, by itself, implies that our system has a π_i solution without regard to sign. F2 then implies that each π_i is nonnegative, and F1 implies that $\Sigma \pi_i > 0$. Normalization completes the proof. ∎

We now consider Savage's axioms for an additive representation. These force S to be infinite and imply uniqueness. Because of this his axioms, in particular G5, are not wholly necessary for agreement but are considerably simpler than necessary and sufficient conditions for the general case (Chateauneuf and Jaffray, 1984).

THEOREM 7.2. *Suppose* $\mathcal{E} = 2^S$ *and that* $\succ_*$ *on* $\mathcal{E}$ *satisfies the following for all A, B, C* $\in \mathcal{E}$:

G1. $S \succ_* \varnothing$.
G2. $A \succsim_* \varnothing$.
G3. $\succ_*$ *on* $\mathcal{E}$ *is a weak order*.
G4. $[(A \cup B) \cap C = \varnothing] \Rightarrow (A \succ_* B \Leftrightarrow A \cup C \succ_* B \cup C)$.
G5. $A \succ_* B \Rightarrow$ *there is a finite partition of S such that* $A \succ_* B \cup E$ *for every member E of the partition*.

Then $(\mathcal{E}, \succ_*)$ *has a unique additive representation. Moreover, if* π *agrees with* $\succ_*$, *then for every* $A \in \mathcal{E}$ *and* $0 \leqslant \lambda \leqslant 1$ *there is a* $B \subseteq A$ *such that* $\pi(B) = \lambda\pi(A)$.

Savage's nonnecessary Archimedean axiom G5 turns out to have powerful implications as seen from uniqueness and the final conclusion of the theorem. Among other things, it leads to the condition that for every positive integer n there is an n-part uniform partition of S with $\pi(A) = 1/n$ for each member of the partition. This condition in its qualitative form ($\sim_*$) was used earlier by Bernstein (1917), de Finetti (1931b), and Koopman (1940) for related axiomatizations of the additive representation. Savage (1954, pp. 38–39) defends G5 with an argument which can be paraphrased as follows: If you consider A more probable than B, then surely there is an n and a coin of your own choosing such that you consider A more probable than the union of B and any particular sequence of heads and tails for n tosses of the coin. This gets rather close to the notion of extraneous random devices invoked in the lottery-acts formulation and suggests how we could enrich a finite S so that Savage's axioms could apply.

Although all of G1 through G5 are instrumental for the representation of Theorem 7.2, G4 is the crucial assumption behind π's additivity. Plausible failures of G4 will be noted in Section 8.1.

Because Theorem 7.2 is intimately involved in one of the generalizations of additive expected utility examined in Chapters 8 and 9, we shall outline its proof in the next section. Before doing that, we remark that Savage's agreeing π is finitely additive $[A \cap B = \varnothing \Rightarrow \pi(A \cup B) = \pi(A) + \pi(B)]$ but not generally countably additive (Section 1.8). Countable additivity does however follow from the addition of Villegas's (1964) *monotone continuity* axiom, which says that for all $A, B, A_1, A_2, \cdots$ in $\mathcal{E}$ for which $A_1 \subseteq A_2 \subseteq \cdots$,

$$\left(A = \bigcup A_i, B \succsim_* A_i \text{ for all } i \right) \Rightarrow B \succsim_* A.$$

Savage recognized the possibility of adding this to G1–G5, but declined to do so on the grounds that it lacked the same intuitive normative status as the other axioms. A recent analysis of the matter is given by Seidenfeld and Schervish (1983).

7.3 PROOF OF SAVAGE'S PROBABILITY THEOREM

We assume throughout this section that $\mathcal{E} = 2^S$ and that $\succ_*$ on $\mathcal{E}$ satisfies G1 through G5 of Theorem 7.2. To establish the existence of a unique π that agrees with $\succ_*$ and satisfies the final conclusion of the theorem, we begin with a series of implications of G1–G5.

LEMMA 7.1. *For all A, B, C, D $\in$ $\mathcal{E}$:*

(a) $B \subseteq C \Rightarrow S \succsim_* C \succsim_* B \succsim_* \varnothing.$
(b) $(A \sim_* B, A \cap C = \varnothing) \Rightarrow A \cup C \succsim_* B \cup C.$
(c) $(A \succ_* B, A \cap C = \varnothing) \Rightarrow A \cup C \succ_* B \cup C.$
(d) $(A \sim_* B, C \sim_* D, A \cap C = \varnothing) \Rightarrow A \cup C \succsim_* B \cup D.$
(e) $(A \succsim_* B, C \succ_* D, A \cap C = \varnothing) \Rightarrow A \cup C \succ_* B \cup D.$
(f) $(A \sim_* B, C \sim_* D, A \cap C = B \cap D = \varnothing) \Rightarrow A \cup C \sim_* B \cup D.$
(g) $A \succ_* \varnothing \Rightarrow A$ *can be partitioned into B and C for which* $B \succ_* \varnothing$ *and* $C \succ_* \varnothing.$
(h) $(A, B, $ *and C are mutually disjoint,* $A \cup C \succ_* B \succsim_* A) \Rightarrow$ *there is a* $D \subseteq C$ *for which* $D \succ_* \varnothing$ *and* $A \cup (C \setminus D) \succ_* B \cup D.$
(i) $(A \succ_* \varnothing, B \succ_* \varnothing, A \cap B = \varnothing) \Rightarrow B$ *can be partitioned into C and D such that* $A \cup C \succsim_* D \succsim_* C.$
(j) $A \succ_* \varnothing \Rightarrow A$ *can be partitioned into B and C with* $B \sim_* C.$
(k) $A \succ_* \varnothing \Rightarrow$ *for every* $n \in \{1, 2, \ldots\}$ *there is a* 2^n-*part partition of A such that* $\sim_*$ *holds between each two members of the partition.*

Proof. (a) Left to the reader.

(b) Assume $A \sim_* B$ and $A \cap C = \varnothing$. Since $B = (B \setminus C) \cup (B \cap C)$ and $B \cap (C \setminus B) = \varnothing$, G4 $\Rightarrow (B \setminus C) \cup (B \cap C) \cup (C \setminus B) \sim_* A \cup (C \setminus B)$, or $B \cup C \sim_* A \cup (C \setminus B)$. By (a), $A \cup C \succsim_* A \cup (C \setminus B)$. Hence, by G3, $A \cup C \succsim_* B \cup C$.

(c) Replace $\sim_*$ by $\succ_*$ in the proof of (b).

(d) Assume $A \sim_* B$, $C \sim_* D$, and $A \cap C = \varnothing$. Since $(D \setminus A) \cap A = \varnothing$, (b) $\Rightarrow A \cup D = A \cup (D \setminus A) \succsim_* B \cup (D \setminus A)$. Also, since $(A \setminus D) \cap C = \varnothing$, (b) $\Rightarrow C \cup (A \setminus D) \succsim_* D \cup (A \setminus D) = A \cup D$. By G3, $C \cup (A \setminus D) \succsim_* B \cup (D \setminus A)$. This, (b), (c), and $(A \cap D) \cap (C \cup A \setminus D) = \varnothing$ then imply $C \cup (A \setminus D) \cup (A \cap D) \succsim_* B \cup (D \setminus A) \cup (A \cap D)$, or $A \cup C \succsim_* B \cup D$.

(e) Replace $C \sim_* D$ in the preceding proof by $C \succ_* D$ and use (c).

(f) Assume $A \sim_* B$, $C \sim_* D$, and $A \cap C = B \cap D = \varnothing$. By (d), $A \cup C \succsim_* B \cup D$ and $B \cup D \succsim_* A \cup C$. Hence $A \cup C \sim_* B \cup D$.

(g) Assume $A \succ_* \varnothing$. G5 $\Rightarrow$ there is a partition $\{D_1, \ldots, D_m\}$ of S such that $A \succ_* D_i$ for each i. (a) $\Rightarrow D_i = (D_i \cap A) \cup (D_i \setminus A) \succsim_* D_i \cap A$. Hence $A \succ_* D_i \cap A$ for all i. If $D_i \cap A \sim_* \varnothing$ for each i, then (f) $\Rightarrow \cup_i(D_i \cap A) \sim_* \varnothing$, or $A \sim_* \varnothing$, a contradiction. If $D_i \cap A \succ_* \varnothing$ for only one i, say $i = 1$, then $A \sim_* D_1 \cap A$, which contradicts $A \succ_* D_1 \cap A$. Hence $D_i \cap A \succ_* \varnothing$ for at least two i, and the desired result follows from (e).

(h) Assume mutual disjointness and $A \cup C \succ_* B \succsim_* A$. (G3, G4) $\Rightarrow C \succ_* \varnothing$. Since $C \succ_* \varnothing$ and $A \cup C \succ_* B$, it follows from G5 that there is a $D_1 \subseteq C$ for which $D_1 \succ_* \varnothing$ and $A \cup C \succ_* B \cup D_1$. By (g) and G3, D_1 can be partitioned into D and D' with $D' \succsim_* D \succ_* \varnothing$, so $(C \setminus D) \cup D \cup A \succ_* D' \cup D \cup B$. G4 $\Rightarrow (C \setminus D) \cup A \succ_* B \cup D'$, and (G4, $D' \succsim_* D$) $\Rightarrow B \cup D' \succsim_* B \cup D$. Hence $A \cup (C \setminus D) \succ_* B \cup D$.

(i) Assume $A \succ_* \varnothing$, $B \succ_* \varnothing$, and $A \cap B = \varnothing$. If $A \succsim_* B$, the conclusion follows from (g). Assume $B \succ_* A$. G5 $\Rightarrow$ there is a partition $\{E_1, \ldots, E_n\}$ of B such that $A \succ_* E_i$ for each i. Assume for definiteness that $E_n \succsim_* \cdots \succsim_* E_1$ and let m be such that $\cup_1^{m+1} E_i \succsim_* \cup_{m+1}^n E_i \succsim_* \cup_1^m E_i$. Let $C = \cup_1^m E_i$ and $D = \cup_{m+1}^n E_i$. Then $C \cup E_{m+1} \succsim_* D \succsim_* C$. Since $A \succ_* E_{m+1}$, this and (G3, G4) imply $C \cup A \succ_* D$.

(j) & (k) Since (k) follows from (e) and (j), we complete the proof of the lemma by proving (j). Assume $A \succ_* \varnothing$. It follows from (g) that A can be partitioned into B_1, C_1, and D_1 such that $C_1 \cup D_1 \succsim_* B_1$ and $B_1 \cup D_1 \succsim_* C_1$. If one of these is $\sim_*$, the conclusion of (j) holds, so assume henceforth that both are $\succ_*$. Then $D_1 \succ_* \varnothing$. For definiteness take $C_1 \succsim_* B_1$. Then (h) $\Rightarrow$ there is a $C^2 \subseteq D_1$ such that $C^2 \succ_* \varnothing$ and $B_1 \cup (D_1 \setminus C^2) \succsim_* C_1 \cup C^2$. Hence $D_1 \setminus C^2 \succ_* \varnothing$ and, by (i), $D_1 \setminus C^2$ can be partitioned into B^2 and D_2 such that $C^2 \cup B^2 \succsim_* D_2 \succsim_* B^2$. Since $C_1 \succsim_* B_1$, G4 $\Rightarrow C_1 \cup D_2 \cup C^2 \succ_* C_1 \cup D_2 \succsim_* B_1 \cup B^2$. Let $B_2 = B_1 \cup B^2$ and $C_2 = C_1 \cup C^2$. We then get a partition $\{B_2, C_2, D_2\}$ of A for which

1. $C_2 \cup D_2 \succ_* B_2$ and $B_2 \cup D_2 \succ_* C_2$.
2. $B_1 \subseteq B_2$, $C_1 \subseteq C_2$, $D_2 \subseteq D_1$.
3. $D_1 \setminus D_2 \succsim_* D_2$.

By repeating this process, we get a sequence $\ldots, \{B_n, C_n, D_n\}, \ldots$ of three-part partitions of A such that, for each $n \geqslant 1$,

(1) $C_n \cup D_n \succ_* B_n$ and $B_n \cup D_n \succ_* C_n$.
(2) $B_n \subseteq B_{n+1}$, $C_n \subseteq C_{n+1}$, $D_{n+1} \subseteq D_n$.
(3) $D_n \setminus D_{n+1} \succsim_* D_{n+1}$.

Hence $D_n \succ_* \varnothing$ for all n, and D_n includes two disjoint events (D_{n+1} and

$D_n \setminus D_{n+1}$) each of which bears $\gtrsim_*$ to D_{n+1}. Hence, by (3) and (e), for any E_1 and E_2 such that $D_{n+1} \succ_* E_1$ and $D_{n+1} \succ_* E_2$, we have $D_n \succ_* E_1 \cup E_2$.

Now for any event G with $G \succ_* \varnothing$, $G \succ_* D_n$ for sufficiently large n. For example, if $D_n \gtrsim_* G$ then with $\{E_1, \ldots, E_m\}$ as in G5 for $G \succ_* \varnothing$ with $G \succ_* E_i$ for all i, $D_n \succ_* E_i$ for all i so that $D_{n-1} \succ_* E_1 \cap E_2$, $D_{n-1} \succ_* E_3 \cup E_4, \ldots$ and then $D_{n-2} \succ_* \cup_1^4 E_i, \ldots$ and so forth; hence, with n large, $D_1 \succ_* \cup_1^m E_i$, or $D_1 \succ_* S$, contrary to (a) and G3. Moreover, $\cap_{n=1}^{\infty} D_n \sim_* \varnothing$, for if $\cap D_n \succ_* \varnothing$ then $\cap D_n \succ_* D_m$ for large m, and this is false since $\cap D_n \subseteq D_m$.

Let

$$B = \bigcup_{n=1}^{\infty} B_n \quad \text{and} \quad C = \left(\bigcup_{n=1}^{\infty} C_n \right) \cup \left(\bigcap_{n=1}^{\infty} D_n \right)$$

$\{B, C\}$ is a partition of A since $(\cup B_n) \cap (\cup C_n) = (\cup B_n) \cap (\cap D_n) = (\cup C_n) \cap (\cap D_n) = \varnothing$. To verify $B \sim_* C$, note first that $C \sim_* \cup C_n$ since $\cap D_n \sim_* \varnothing$. Suppose $C \succ_* B$. Then $\cup C_n \succ_* B$ and, by (h), there is a $G \subseteq \cup C_n$ for which $G \succ_* \varnothing$ and

$$\left(\bigcup C_n \right) \setminus G \succ_* B \cup G.$$

Since $B \cap G = \varnothing$ and $B \gtrsim_* B_n$ (since $B_n \subseteq B$), G4 implies

$$B \cup G \gtrsim_* B_n \cup G.$$

For large n, $G \succ_* D_n$ so that, again by G4,

$$B_n \cup G \succ_* B_n \cup D_n.$$

Since $G \succ_* D_n \cap (\cup C_n)$ for large n and $\cup C_n = [(\cup C_n) \setminus G] \cup G = [(\cup C_n) \setminus D_n] \cup ((\cup C_n) \cap D_n)$, it follows by (e) for large n that

$$\left(\bigcup C_n \right) \setminus D_n \gtrsim_* \left(\bigcup C_n \right) \setminus G.$$

Finally, since $(\cup C_n) \setminus D_n \subseteq C_n$, (a) $\Rightarrow C_n \gtrsim_* (\cup C_n) \setminus D_n$. This and the four preceding displayed expressions yield $C_n \succ_* B_n \cup D_n$ by transitivity, which contradicts $B_n \cup D_n \succ_* C_n$ in (1). Therefore not ($C \succ_* B$). By a similar proof, not ($B \succ_* C$), and we conclude that $B \sim_* C$. ∎

We are now ready to prove

LEMMA 7.2. $(\mathcal{E}, \succ_*)$ *has a unique additive representation.*

Proof. Call a partition $\{A_1, \ldots, A_m\}$ of A a *uniform partition* when $A \succ_* \varnothing$ and $A_1 \sim_* A_2 \sim_* \cdots \sim_* A_m$. Let

$$C(r, 2^n) = \{A : A \text{ is the union of } r \text{ members of some}$$
$$2^n\text{-part uniform partition of } S\}.$$

We establish Lemma 7.2 by a series of steps.

Step 1. $[A, B \in C(r, 2^n)] \Rightarrow A \sim_* B$. First, if $A, B \in C(1, 2^n)$ and if $A \succ_* B$, it follows easily from Lemma 7.1(e) that $S \succ_* S$, a contradiction. Hence $A \sim_* B$ if $r = 1$. It follows from Lemma 7.1(f) that $A \sim_* B$ for all $r \leqslant 2^n$.

Step 2. $[A \in C(r, 2^n), B \in C(r2^m, 2^{n+m})] \Rightarrow A \sim_* B$. If $r = 1$ and not ($A \sim_* B$), step 1 and Lemma 7.1(e) give $S \succ_* S$. The desired conclusion then follows from Lemma 7.1(f).

Step 3. $[A \in C(r, 2^n), B \in C(t, 2^m)] \Rightarrow (A \succsim_* B \Leftrightarrow r/2^n \geqslant t/2^m)$. If $r/2^n = t/2^m$, then $r2^m = t2^n$, and, with $D \in C(r2^m, 2^{n+m})$ it follows from step 2 that $A \sim_* D$ and $D \sim_* B$; hence $A \sim_* B$. If $r2^m > t2^n$, then, with $D_1 \in C(r2^m, 2^{n+m})$ and $D_2 \in C(t2^n, 2^{n+m})$, we get $A \sim_* D_1$ and $B \sim_* D_2$. But clearly $D_1 \succ_* D_2$ when $r2^m > t2^n$. Therefore $A \succ_* B$.

Step 4. Given $A \in \mathcal{E}$ let $k(A, 2^n)$ be the *largest* integer $r \geqslant 0$ such that $A \succsim_* B$ when $B \in C(r, 2^n)$, and define

$$\pi(A) = \sup \{ k(A, 2^n)/2^n : n = 0, 1, 2, \cdots \}.$$

Clearly $\pi(\varnothing) = 0$, $\pi(S) = 1$, and $\pi \geqslant 0$. Moreover,

$$A \in C(r, 2^n) \Rightarrow \pi(A) = r/2^n.$$

To prove this, observe that if $A \in C(r, 2^n)$ then $\pi(A) \geqslant r/2^n$. If $\pi(A) > r/2^n$, then $A \succsim_* B$ for some $B \in C(t, 2^m)$ for which $t/2^m > r/2^n$. But this is impossible by step 3.

Step 5. $A \succsim_* B \Rightarrow \pi(A) \geqslant \pi(B)$ by the definition of π.

Step 6. π *is additive*. Take $A \cap B = \varnothing$. Then for each n there is a 2^n-part uniform partition of S such that $A \succsim_* A_n$, $B \succsim_* B_n$, A_n and B_n are unions of members of the partition, $A_n \cap B_n = \varnothing$, $A_n \in C(k(A, 2^n), 2^n)$ and $B_n \in C(k(B, 2^n), 2^n)$. Hence $A \cup B \succsim_* A_n \cup B_n$ by Lemma 7.1(d), (e), and $k(A \cup B, 2^n) \geqslant k(A, 2^n) + k(B, 2^n)$. Since for any A it is easily seen that $k(A, 2^n)/2^n$ does not decrease as n increases, it follows that

$$\pi(A) + \pi(B) \leqslant \pi(A \cup B).$$

If we now define $k^*(A, 2^n)$ as the *smallest* integer $r \geqslant 0$ for which $B \succsim_* A$ when $B \in C(r, 2^n)$, it readily follows from the fact that $\{r/2^n : r = 0, 1, \ldots, 2^n; n = 0, 1, \ldots \}$ is dense in $[0, 1]$ that $\inf \{k^*(A, 2^n)/2^n : n = 0, 1, \ldots \} = \sup \{k(A, 2^n)/2^n : n = 0, 1, \ldots \}$. A proof symmetric to that just completed then implies that

$$\pi(A \cup B) \leqslant \pi(A) + \pi(B).$$

Hence $A \cap B = \varnothing \Rightarrow \pi(A \cup B) = \pi(A) + \pi(B)$.

Step 7. $A \succ_* \varnothing \Rightarrow \pi(A) > 0$. Take $A \succ_* \varnothing$. By G5 there is a partition $\{A_1, \ldots, A_n\}$ of S for which $A \succ_* A_i$ for each i. Then step 5 $\Rightarrow \pi(A) \geqslant \pi(A_i)$, and additivity $\Rightarrow \pi(A) > 0$.

Step 8. $A \succ_* B \Rightarrow \pi(A) > \pi(B)$. Suppose $A \succ_* B$. Then, using G5, there is a $C \subseteq S$ for which $C \succ_* \varnothing$, $C \cap B = \varnothing$, and $A \succ_* C \cup B$. By steps 5 and 6, $\pi(A) \geqslant \pi(C) + \pi(B)$. By step 7, $\pi(C) > 0$. Hence $\pi(A) > \pi(B)$.

Steps 5 and 8 give $A \succ_* B \Leftrightarrow \pi(A) > \pi(B)$, and it is obvious that π as defined here in step 4 is the only probability measure on $\mathcal{E}$ that satisfies the additive representation. ∎

We conclude with the final assertion of Theorem 7.2.

LEMMA 7.3. $(A \in \mathcal{E}, 0 \leqslant \lambda \leqslant 1) \Rightarrow \pi(B) = \lambda\pi(A)$ *for some* $B \subseteq A$.

Proof. If $\pi(A) = 0$, the result is obvious, so assume that $\pi(A) > 0$. Let $\{A_1^1, A_2^1\}, \{A_1^2, \cdots, A_4^2\}, \ldots$ be a sequence of 2^n-part uniform partitions of A such that $\{A_{2i-1}^{n+1}, A_{2i}^{n+1}\}$ is a 2-part uniform partition of A_i^n. Given n, let $m = \sup\{j : \pi(\bigcup_{i=1}^j A_i^n) < \lambda\pi(A)\}$ so that

$$\pi\left(\bigcup_1^m A_i^n\right) + 2^{-n}\pi(A) \geqslant \lambda\pi(A),$$

and let $k = \inf\{j : \pi(\bigcup_{i=j}^{2^n} A_i^n) < (1 - \lambda)\pi(A)\}$ so that

$$\pi\left(\bigcup_k^{2^n} A_i^n\right) + 2^{-n}\pi(A) \geqslant (1 - \lambda)\pi(A).$$

Let $C_n = \bigcup_{i=1}^m A_i^n$ and $D_n = \bigcup_{i=k}^{2^n} A_i^n$ so that $C_1 \subseteq C_2 \subseteq \cdots$, $D_1 \subseteq D_2 \subseteq \cdots$, $C_n \cap D_n = \varnothing$ for all n, and $\pi(C_n) \geqslant \lambda\pi(A) - 2^{-n}\pi(A)$ and $\pi(D_n) \geqslant (1 - \lambda)\pi(A) - 2^{-n}\pi(A)$ for all n. Since $C_n \subseteq \bigcup C_n$ and $D_n \subseteq \bigcup D_n$, $\lambda\pi(A) \leqslant \pi(\bigcup C_n)$ and $(1 - \lambda)\pi(A) \leqslant \pi(\bigcup D_n)$. Moreover, $(\bigcup C_n) \cap (\bigcup D_n) = \varnothing$. Hence by additivity, Lemma 7.1(a) and the representation,

$$\pi\left(\bigcup C_n\right) + \pi\left(\bigcup D_n\right) = \pi\left(\left(\bigcup C_n\right) \cup \left(\bigcup D_n\right)\right) \leqslant \pi(A),$$

which requires $\pi(\bigcup C_n) = \lambda\pi(A)$ and $\pi(\bigcup D_n) = (1 - \lambda)\pi(A)$. ∎

7.4 ADDITIVE EXPECTED UTILITY

Although Ramsey (1931) outlined a version of additive expected utility about 25 years before Savage developed his own theory, Savage (1954) set forth the first completely worked out axiomatization of preference between uncertain acts for the additive expected utility representation

$$f \succ g \Leftrightarrow \int_S u(f(s))\, d\pi(s) > \int_S u(g(s))\, d\pi(s)$$

in which u is a utility function on the outcome set X and π is a finitely additive probability measure on the algebra of subsets of S. In addition to

Ramsey, Savage credits de Finetti (1964/1937) for his guidance on the treatment of subjective probability and von Neumann and Morgenstern (1944) for their linear utility theory. The next section shows how the linear utility representation emerges from Savage's axioms during the course of his proof for the additive expected utility representation.

Savage's work has motivated a few dozen subsequent axiomatizations of additive expected utility and related representations. These include basic modifications of the Ramsey–Savage theory (Suppes, 1956; Davidson and Suppes, 1956; Pfanzagl, 1967, 1968; Toulet, 1986), lottery-based theories (Anscombe and Aumann, 1963; Pratt et al., 1964, 1965; Fishburn, 1970a, 1982a), event-conditioned theories that do (Fishburn, 1973b) or do not (Luce and Krantz, 1971; Krantz et al., 1971, Chapter 8) have a lottery feature, and theories that avoid Savage's distinction between events and outcomes (Jeffrey, 1965, 1978; Bolker, 1967; Domotor, 1978). These are reviewed in detail by Fishburn (1981b). A review of more recent theories that depart substantially from standard treatments of subjective probability or utility appears in the next chapter.

The personalistic view of probability developed by Ramsey, de Finetti, and Savage holds that probability measures the confidence that a person has in the truth of a particular proposition as revealed by the extent to which he or she is prepared to act on it or to bet on its being true. Savage translates this into the comparative mode as follows. Let A and B be two events in $\mathcal{E}$, and let x and y be outcomes such that x is definitely preferred to y (i.e., $x \succ y$). Consider acts

f: get x if A obtains, y otherwise,

g: get x if B obtains, y otherwise.

Then the proposition "A obtains" is more probable than "B obtains" precisely when $f \succ g$. In other words if you would rather bet on A than B to receive a valuable prize when the event you choose contains the true state, then *for you* A is more probable than B.

Savage interprets the comparative probability relation $\succ_*$ of Section 7.2 in this way. Since $A \succ_* B$ is defined from $f \succ g$ of the preceding paragraph, we might just as well write $A \succ B$ and read this as "A is preferred to B." However, I will maintain $\succ_*$ and the comparative probability language since the distinction is sometimes useful.

A main purpose of Savage's axioms for $\succ$ on F is to give $\succ_*$ a precise meaning when its $f \succ g$ characterization is to hold for all $x \succ y$ when it holds for one such outcome pair, in such a way that G1 through G5 of Theorem 7.2 hold for $(\mathcal{E}, \succ_*)$. Once this has been done, relatively few additional assumptions are needed to obtain his additive expected utility representation.

To state his axioms, recall from Section 7.1 that $>$ is to be applied to F $= X^S$ with $x > y$ if $(f > g, f(S) = \{x\}, g(S) = \{y\})$ and similarly for $x > g, f > y$, and so forth. As usual, $\sim$ denotes the symmetric complement of $>$, and $\gtrsim_*$ is the union of $>$ and $\sim$. For all $f, g \in F$, all $x, y \in X$ and all $A \subseteq S$, we define

$$f =_A x \qquad \text{if } f(s) = x \text{ for all } s \in A,$$

$$f =_A g \qquad \text{if } f(s) = g(s) \text{ for all } s \in A,$$

$$A^c = S \setminus A, \qquad \text{the complement of } A \text{ in } S,$$

$$xAy \text{ as the } f \in F \text{ with } f =_A x \text{ and } f =_{A^c} y.$$

Savage's full definition of $\gtrsim_*$ on $\mathcal{E} = 2^S$ is

$$A \gtrsim_* B \text{ if } xAy > xBy \text{ for all } x, y \in X \text{ for which } x > y.$$

A subclass of *null events* $\mathfrak{N} \subseteq \mathcal{E}$ is defined by

$$A \in \mathfrak{N} \text{ if, for all } f, g \in F, f =_{A^c} g \Rightarrow f \sim g.$$

It will turn out that $A \in \mathfrak{N} \leftrightarrow A \sim_* \varnothing \leftrightarrow \pi(A) = 0$. In addition, for each event A we define a *conditional preference relation* $>_A$ on F by

$$f >_A g \text{ if, for all } f', g' \in F, (f' =_A f,$$

$$g' =_A g, f' =_{A^c} g') \Rightarrow f' > g'.$$

This reflects the part of Savage's representation which says that preference between f and g depends only on those states for which $f(s) \neq g(s)$. The definitions of $\gtrsim_A$ and $\sim_A$ are similar to that for $>_A$ with $f' > g'$ replaced by $f' \gtrsim g'$ and $f' \sim g'$ respectively.

Savage's axioms are, for all $f, g, f', g' \in F$, all $x, y, x', y' \in X$, and all $A, B \subseteq S$:

P1. $>$ *on F is a weak order.*
P2. $(f =_A f', g =_A g', f =_{A^c} g, f' =_{A^c} g') \Rightarrow (f > g \leftrightarrow f' > g')$.
P3. $(A \notin \mathfrak{N}, f =_A x, g =_A y) \Rightarrow (f >_A g \leftrightarrow x > y)$.
P4. $(x > y, x' > y') \Rightarrow (xAy > xBy \leftrightarrow x'Ay' > x'By')$.
P5. $z > w$ *for some* $z, w \in X$.
P6. $f > g \Rightarrow$ [*given* x, *there is a finite partition of S such that, for every member E of the partition,* $(f' =_E x, f' =_{E^c} f) \Rightarrow f' > g$, *and* $(g' =_E x, g' =_{E^c} g) \Rightarrow f > g'$].
P7. $(f >_A g(s) \text{ for all } s \in A) \Rightarrow f \gtrsim_A g$; $(f(s) >_A g \text{ for all } s \in A) \Rightarrow f \gtrsim_A g$.

P1 is a typical ordering axiom, P2 says that preference between f and g should not depend on those states for which $f(s) = g(s)$, and P3 says that conditional preference between degenerate conditional acts on nonnull events corresponds to preference between consequences in an obvious way. P4 gives consistency to $\succ_*$ for different consequence pairs with $x \succ y$, P5 is Savage's nontriviality postulate, and P6, his Archimedean axiom, asserts that for any $f \succ g$ and $x \in X$ one can modify f or g on "small pieces" of S that cover S finitely in such a way that $f \succ g$ after any such change to x on a "small piece."

The final axiom, P7, is a dominance condition that plays no role in the derivation of π by way of Theorem 7.2 or in the construction of u for the additive expected utility representation for all *simple* acts. It is used only in extending the representation to other acts and, in the process, implies that u is bounded. If one were to replace F by the set of simple acts and delete P7 then the following representation/uniqueness theorem of Savage remains valid without the stipulation that u is bounded. Further technical comments on P7 are given by Seidenfeld and Schervish (1983) and Toulet (1986).

THEOREM 7.3. *Suppose* P1 *through* P7 *hold for* $\succ$ *on* $F = X^S$, *and* $\succ_*$ *on* $\mathcal{E} = 2^S$ *is as defined before. Then* $(\mathcal{E}, \succ_*)$ *has a unique additive representation with the properties of its agreeing probability measure* π *as specified in Theorem* 7.2 *along with, for all* $A \in \mathcal{E}$, $A \in \mathfrak{N} \Leftrightarrow \pi(A) = 0$; *and there is a bounded functional* u *on* X *such that, for all* $f, g \in F$, $f \succ g \Leftrightarrow \int_S u(f(s))\, d\pi(s) > \int_S u(g(s))\, d\pi(s)$. *Moreover,* u *is unique up to positive linear transformations.*

We conclude this section with comments on Savage's axioms and their implications before discussing the proof of Theorem 7.3 in the next section.

Several implications of Savage's representation are especially important for connections to Chapters 2, 8, and 9. We consider the reduction principle first. For any simple act f let π_f denote the probability distribution on X induced by π through f:

$$\pi_f(x) = \pi(\{s \in S : f(s) = x\}) \qquad \text{for all } x \in X.$$

The final property of Theorem 7.2 is easily seen to imply that $P = P_X = \{\pi_f : f \text{ is a simple act in } F\}$. Two versions of the reduction principle discussed at length in Chapter 2 are, for all simple $f, f', g, g' \in F$:

Reduction principle: $(\pi_f = \pi_{f'}, \pi_g = \pi_{g'}) \Rightarrow (f \succ g \Leftrightarrow f' \succ g')$.

Identity reduction principle: $\pi_f = \pi_g \Rightarrow f \sim g$.

As before, the reduction principle asserts that (at least for simple acts) preference between acts depends only on their probability distributions over the outcomes. The identity reduction principle, based on P1–P6, is Theorem 5.2.1 in Savage (1954) and Theorem 14.3 in Fishburn (1970a). It and P1 obviously imply the reduction principle.

The reduction principle is more or less similar to conditions of invariance (Section 2.2) in Tversky and Kahneman (1986), extensionality in Arrow (1982), and reduction of compound lotteries in Allais (1953, 1979b) and Luce and Raiffa (1957). We consider it further in the next chapter.

Other important implications involve P2 and P3, which Savage refers to as the *sure-thing principle*. One such implication is the

Substitution principle: $(f =_A f', g =_A g', f =_{A^c} x =_{A^c} g,$
$f' =_{A^c} y =_{A^c} g') \Rightarrow (f > g \Leftrightarrow f' > g'),$

which is a weakening of P2 that we alluded to earlier (Section 2.5) as "Savage's independence principle." It is also referred to as the "sure-thing principle" even though it entails only part of {P2, P3}.

Savage also associated the notion of statewise dominance with his sure-thing principle. Three versions of dominance principle are:

Simple dominance principle: $(\{A_1, \ldots, A_n\}$ is a partition of $S, f =_{A_i} x_i$ and $g =_{A_i} y_i$ for all $i, x_i \succsim y_i$ for all $i) \Rightarrow f \succsim g$; if, in addition, $x_i > y_i$ for some $A_i \notin \mathfrak{N}$, then $f > g$.

Monotone dominance principle: $(f(s) \succsim g(s)$ for all $s \in S) \Rightarrow f \succsim g$.

Conditional dominance principle: $(A \cap B = \varnothing, f \succsim_A g, f \succsim_B g) \Rightarrow f \succsim_{A \cup B} g$; if, in addition, $f >_A g$, then $f >_{A \cup B} g$.

Savage introduces his discussion of the sure-thing principle with an example like the conditional dominance principle (with $A \cup B = S$) and says that "except possibly for the assumption of simple ordering, I know of no other extralogical principle governing decisions that finds such ready acceptance" (1954, p. 21). A few pages later he proves that P1, P2, and P3 imply the simple dominance principle and notes that one could use such a principle as a basic axiom in place of P3. The monotone dominance principle, which Schmeidler (1984) refers to simply as monotonicity, is the natural extension of the first part of the simple principle to arbitrary acts. This extension appears to depend on much more than P1–P3, and the related assertion $(f(s) > g(s)$ for all $s) \Rightarrow f > g$ does *not* follow from P1–P7 when π is not countably additive (Fishburn, 1970a, p. 213; Savage, 1954, p. 78).

The conditional dominance principle has a different nature than the other two since it makes no reference to preference between outcomes. In fact, it follows from P1 and the definitions.

LEMMA 7.4. P1 $\Rightarrow$ *conditional dominance principle*.

Proof. Given $A \cap B = \varnothing, f \succsim_A g$, and $f \succsim_B g$, let h be any other act. Also let $f', k, g' \in F$ be such that

$$f' =_A f, \quad f' =_B f, \quad f' =_{(A \cup B)^c} h,$$

$$k =_A g, \quad k =_B f, \quad k =_{(A \cup B)^c} h,$$

$$g' =_A g, \quad g' =_B g, \quad g' =_{(A \cup B)^c} h.$$

Then, by the definitions of $\gtrsim_A$ and $\gtrsim_B$, $f' \gtrsim k$ and $k \gtrsim g'$, so $f' \gtrsim g'$ by P1. Since h is arbitrary, $f \gtrsim_{A \cup B} g$. If $f >_A g$ also, then $f' > k \gtrsim g'$, so $f' > g'$ by P1 and $f >_{A \cup B} g$ by the definition of $>_{A \cup B}$. ∎

The next two chapters discuss a generalization of Savage's theory that drops P1 but uses the conditional dominance principle. As far as I can tell, the principle is independent of P2–P6. Section 9.3 notes that P7 is unsuitable for the generalization.

7.5 COMMENTS ON SAVAGE'S REPRESENTATION PROOF

In this section we comment on the proof of Theorem 7.3, omitting most of the details which are available in Savage (1954) and Fishburn (1970a, Chapter 14). In Ramsey's (1931) earlier approach, outcome utilities were scaled first with the use of simple 50-50 lotteries for bisection based on an "ethically neutral proposition" with subjective probability $\frac{1}{2}$. Given u, Ramsey then assessed π by indifference between simple acts. For example, if $x > y > z$ and $xAz \sim y$, then $\pi(A)u(x) + [1 - \pi(A)]u(z) = u(y)$, so $\pi(A) = [u(y) - u(z)]/[u(x) - u(z)]$.

Savage reverses Ramsey's approach by first obtaining π by way of Theorem 7.2. He then obtains u by showing that the identity reduction principle holds and that the von Neumann–Morgenstern linear utility axioms hold for $P = \{\pi_f : f \text{ is a simple act in } F\}$. This gives u by way of Theorem 1.3 and, as a consequence, shows that the additive expected utility representation holds for all simple acts in F.

P7 is not used thus far. The next step, which appears only in Fishburn (1970a, Section 14.5) since Savage did not realize earlier that his axioms imply boundedness, adds P7 to show that u on X is bounded. The final step, essentially carried out by Savage, proves that the representation holds for all acts in F.

For later reference and to demonstrate the approach to Theorem 7.2, we note that its additive representation for subjective probability via Savage's axioms for $>$ on F requires no more than two outcomes in X. Let

$$F_{xy} = \{f \in F : f(S) \subseteq \{x, y\}\}$$

and for the following lemma, given $x > y$, define $>_*$ on $\mathcal{E} = 2^S$ by

$$A >_* B \quad \text{if } xAy > xBy.$$

LEMMA 7.5. *Suppose* $x > y$ *and* P1, P2, P3, *and* P6 *hold for* $>$ *on* F_{xy}. *Then* $(\mathcal{E}, >_*)$ *has a unique additive representation whose agreeing* π *satisfies the final conclusion of Theorem 7.2.*

Proof. Let the hypotheses of the lemma hold. In view of Theorem 7.2 we show that G1–G5 hold.

G1. Immediate from $x \succ y$.

G2. If $A \in \mathfrak{N}$, then $xAy \sim x\varnothing y$; hence $A \sim_* \varnothing$. If $A \notin \mathfrak{N}$, then P3 and $x \succ y$ give $(xAy) \succ_A (x\varnothing y)$; hence $xAy \succ x\varnothing y$ by the definition of $\succ_A$. Therefore $A \succ_* \varnothing$. This shows that $A \in \mathfrak{N} \Leftrightarrow A \sim_* \varnothing$.

G3. By P1, $\succ_*$ is asymmetric. For negative transitivity use P1 to get [not $(A \succ_* B)$, not $(B \succ_* C)$] $\Rightarrow (xBy \succsim xAy, xCy \succsim xBy) \Rightarrow (xCy \succsim xAy) \Rightarrow$ not $(A \succ_* C)$.

G4. Assume $(A \cup B) \cap C = \varnothing$. Then, using $A \cup B$ in P2, $A \succ_* B \Leftrightarrow xAy \succ xBy \Leftrightarrow x(A \cup C)y \succ x(B \cup C)y \Leftrightarrow A \cup C \succ_* B \cup C$.

G5. Given $A \succ_* B$ (i.e., $xAy \succ xBy$), use P6 to conclude from the $f \succ g'$ part that there is a finite partition of S such that $xAy \succ x(B \cup E)y$; hence $A \succ_* B \cup E$, for every member E of the partition. ∎

Axiom P5 ensures at least one outcome pair with $x \succ y$, and P4 guarantees that we get the same π for all pairs $x \succ y$ and that $\succ_*$ defined prior to Lemma 7.5 is identical to its definition in the preceding section.

As indicated earlier, the next task is to prove that the identify reduction principle $\pi_f = \pi_g \Rightarrow f \sim g$ for simple acts follows from P1–P6. Then, with $\succ$ defined on the convex set $P = \{\pi_f : f \text{ is a simple act in } F\}$ by

$$p \succ q \quad \text{if } f \succ g \text{ whenever } \pi_f = p \text{ and } \pi_g = q,$$

we show that A1–A3 hold for $\succ$ on P. This is trivial for A1, given P1 and the reduction principle, but requires a bit more work for A2 ($p \succ q \Rightarrow \lambda p + (1 - \lambda)r \succ \lambda q + (1 - \lambda)r$) and A3 ($p \succ q \succ r \Rightarrow \alpha p + (1 - \alpha)r \succ q \succ \beta p + (1 - \beta)r$ for some $\alpha, \beta \in (0, 1)$). As a consequence of Theorem 1.3 we then obtain u on X, unique up to positive linear transformations, such that $f \succ g \Leftrightarrow \int u(f(s)) \, d\pi(s) > \int u(g(s)) \, d\pi(s)$ for all simple $f, g \in F$.

To show that u is bounded when P7 is added, we first state two lemmas whose simple proofs are left to the reader. (Hint for Lemma 7.6: see Lemma 7.4.)

LEMMA 7.6. (P1, $\{A_1, \ldots, A_n\}$ *is a partition of* $A, f \succsim_{A_i} g$ *for* $i = 1, \ldots, n$) $\Rightarrow f \succsim_A g$; *if, in addition,* $f \succ_{A_i} g$ *for some i, then* $f \succ_A g$.

LEMMA 7.7. (P1, P2, P7, $f \succ_A x$ *and* $g \succ_A x$ *for all* $x \in X$) $\Rightarrow f \sim_A g$; (P1, P2, P7, $x \succ_A f$, *and* $x \succ_A g$ *for all* $x \in X$) $\Rightarrow f \sim_A g$.

Given u as above, we now prove

LEMMA 7.8. (P1–P7) $\Rightarrow u$ *on* X *is bounded.*

Proof. Given P1–P7, suppose u on X is unbounded above. Using the final conclusion of Theorem 7.2, construct a sequence $B_1, B_2, \ldots$ of mutually disjoint events in S with $\pi(B_n) = 2^{-n}$ for $n = 1, 2, \ldots$. If $\bigcup_n B_n$ does not exhaust S add $S \setminus \bigcup B_n$ to B_1. Take $u(x_n) \geq 2^n$ for each n. Let

$$f =_{B_n} x_n \qquad \text{for } n = 1, 2, \ldots$$

so that $\int u(f(s))\, d\pi(s) = \infty$. Consider any outcome $x \in X$. Then for some $y \in \{x_1, x_2, \ldots\}$,

$$u(x) < \int \min\{u(f(s)), u(y)\}\, d\pi(s).$$

Let f' equal f on $\{s : y \geq f(s)\}$ and y on $\{s : f(s) > y\}$ so that f' is simple and has $\int u(f')\, d\pi$ equal to the right side of the preceding inequality. Thus, by the representation for simple acts, $f' > x$. Moreover, $f \geq f'$ by Lemma 7.6 since P7 implies that $f \geq_{\{s : f(s) > y\}} f'$. Hence $f > x$, and this holds for every $x \in X$.

Next, let $z \in X$ be such that $u(z) > u(x_1)$. Take $g =_{B_1} z$ and $g =_{B_1^c} f$. As in the preceding paragraph, $g > x$ for every x and therefore $f \sim g$ by Lemma 7.7. But $g >_{B_1} f$ since $z > x_1$ and $\pi(B_1) > 0$, and $g \sim_{B_1^c} f$ since g and f are identical on B_1^c. Hence $g > f$ by Lemma 7.6, so we obtain a contradiction.

It follows that u is bounded above. A symmetric proof shows that u is bounded below. ∎

The final step in the proof of Theorem 7.3 is to show that the additive expected utility representation holds for all acts in F. To do this we divide F into three subsets as follows:

f is *big* if $f > x$ for every $x \in X$.
f is *normal* if $x \geq f \geq y$ for some $x, y \in X$.
f is *little* if $x > f$ for every $x \in X$.

Also, with no loss of generality, let $\inf u(X) = 0$ and $\sup u(X) = 1$, as allowed by P5, Lemma 7.8, and uniqueness up to positive linear transformations.

Consider normal acts first. If f is normal, it can be shown that $f \sim p$ for some $p \in P = P_X$, where $f \sim p$ means that $f \sim g$ for every simple g with $\pi_g = p$. Then by the use of bounding lemmas for the integration, we get

$$f \sim p \Rightarrow \int_S u(f(s))\, d\pi(s) = \sum_X u(x)p(x).$$

Along with $\int u(g(s))\, d\pi(s) = \Sigma\, u(x)p(x)$ for $\pi_g = p$ from the simple acts part of the proof, plus P1, it follows that the representation holds for all normal acts.

If there are big acts then these are all indifferent by Lemma 7.7. Moreover it can be shown that

f is big $\Rightarrow u(x) < 1$ for all $x \in X$;
$\pi(\{s : u(f(s)) \geq 1 - \delta\}) = 1$ for all $\delta > 0$;
$\int u(f(s))\, d\pi(s) = 1$.

Hence all big acts have the same expected utility, which exceeds the expected utility of all normal acts.

A symmetric proof shows that if there are little acts then they are all indifferent, have the same expected utility 0, and the expected utility of every normal act exceeds 0.

7.6 ADDITIVE LINEAR UTILITY

To consider the lottery-acts approach with $P = P_X$ as part of the axiomatic structure, we continue to assume that $\mathcal{E} = 2^S$ and, similar to $F = X^S$ in the preceding sections, will take $\mathbf{F} = P^S$ for our set of lottery acts. As noted earlier, convex combinations of lottery acts are defined statewise: $(\lambda \mathbf{f} + (1 - \lambda)\mathbf{g})(s) = \lambda \mathbf{f}(s) + (1 - \lambda)\mathbf{g}(s)$. Substantial weakenings of the structure presumed here, including more general algebras $\mathcal{E}$, the use of mixture sets for P, and minimal overlap among the outcomes that can occur under different states, are examined in detail by Pratt et al. (1964, 1965) and Fishburn (1970a, 1982a).

The most important point we can make about our lottery-acts formulation is that, since $\mathbf{F}$ is convex, virtually all axioms from earlier chapters for $>$ on P can be used for $>$ on $\mathbf{F}$. For example, we could begin with the linear utility axioms A1, A2, and A3 for $>$ on $\mathbf{F}$, or the SSB axioms C1, C2, and C3, or some other set. Axioms that make explicit use of the state structure can then be added to obtain subjective probabilities or, short of that, to induce a representation for $>$ on $\mathbf{F}$ that goes beyond what is possible without such axioms.

This section and the next adopt the linear utility approach for $(\mathbf{F}, >)$. Other possibilities are considered in the next two chapters. We shall consider three increasingly restricted axiom sets for $(\mathbf{F}, >)$, beginning with $\{A1, A2, A3\}$ and ending with axioms that imply the full additive linear utility representation

$$\mathbf{f} > \mathbf{g} \Leftrightarrow \int_S u(\mathbf{f}(s)) \, d\pi(s) > \int_S u(\mathbf{g}(s)) \, d\pi(s)$$

in which π is a unique additive probability measure on $\mathcal{E}$ and u is a linear functional on P that is unique up to positive linear transformations. The intermediate set will generate π and u for the additive linear representation on the subset of simple lottery acts, that is, those $\mathbf{f}$ for which $\mathbf{f}(S)$ is finite. The proofs of ensuing theorems appear in the next section.

Our first theorem shows that A1, A2, and A3 by themselves imply a linear utility decomposition over any finite partition of S. It is to be understood that each A_i in a partition $\{A_1, \ldots, A_n\}$ is nonempty and that, given $\{A_1, \ldots, A_n\}$, $\mathbf{F}'$ denotes the $\mathbf{f} \in \mathbf{F}$ that are constant on each member of the partition. That is, $\mathbf{f} \in \mathbf{F}$ is in $\mathbf{F}'$ if and only if there are $p_i \in P$

such that $\mathbf{f} =_{A_i} p_i$ for $i = 1, \ldots, n$. Our notation throughout the section will be analogous to the notation of Section 7.4 with F replaced by $\mathbf{F}$ and X replaced by P. Thus $\mathbf{f} =_A p$ means that $\mathbf{f}(s) = p$ for all $s \in A$, $p A q$ is the $\mathbf{f}$ for which $\mathbf{f} =_A p$ and $\mathbf{f} =_{A^c} q$, $A \in \mathfrak{N}$ if $\mathbf{f} =_{A^c} \mathbf{g} \Rightarrow \mathbf{f} \sim \mathbf{g}$ for all $\mathbf{f}, \mathbf{g} \in \mathbf{F}$, and so forth.

THEOREM 7.4. *Suppose* $\succ$ *on* $\mathbf{F} = P^S$ *satisfies the following for all* $\mathbf{f}$, $\mathbf{g}, \mathbf{h} \in \mathbf{F}$ *and all* $0 < \lambda < 1$:

A1. $\succ$ *on* $\mathbf{F}$ *is a weak order.*
A2. $\mathbf{f} \succ \mathbf{g} \Rightarrow \lambda \mathbf{f} + (1 - \lambda)\mathbf{h} \succ \lambda \mathbf{g} + (1 - \lambda)\mathbf{h}$.
A3. $\mathbf{f} \succ \mathbf{g} \succ \mathbf{h} \Rightarrow \alpha \mathbf{f} + (1 - \alpha)\mathbf{h} \succ \mathbf{g}$ *and* $\mathbf{g} \succ \beta \mathbf{f} + (1 - \beta)\mathbf{h}$ *for some* α *and* β *in* $(0, 1)$.

Then for each finite partition $\{A_1, \ldots, A_n\}$ *of* S *there are linear functionals* $u_1, \ldots, u_n$ *on* P *such that, for all* $\mathbf{f}, \mathbf{g} \in \mathbf{F}'$, *with* $\mathbf{f} =_{A_i} p_i$ *and* $\mathbf{g} =_{A_i} q_i$ *for* $i = 1, \ldots, n$,

$$\mathbf{f} \succ \mathbf{g} \Leftrightarrow \sum_{i=1}^{n} u_i(p_i) > \sum_{i=1}^{n} u_i(q_i).$$

Moreover, linear u_i *that satisfy this representation for the given partition are unique up to similar positive linear transformations.*

The uniqueness conclusion means that if linear u_i satisfy the representation for F' then so do linear u_i' if and only if there are real numbers $a, b_1, \ldots, b_n$ with $a > 0$ such that $u_i' = au_i + b_i$ for each i. The *similar* means that the same scale factor $a > 0$ is used for each i.

The decomposition in the representation of Theorem 7.4 hints at the emergence of weighting factors $\pi_i \geq 0$ for different i so that $u_i = \pi_i u$ for a common u on P. This is accomplished by one additional axiom, S2, which is a direct counterpart to Savage's conditional preference postulate P3. We also use a nontriviality axiom, S1, which corresponds to P5, to get a unique π.

THEOREM 7.5. *Suppose the hypotheses of Theorem 7.4 hold along with the following for all* $A \subseteq S$, *all* $\mathbf{f}, \mathbf{g} \in \mathbf{F}$, *and all* $p, q \in P$:

S1. $p' \succ q'$ *for some* $p', q' \in P$.
S2. $(A \notin \mathfrak{N}, \mathbf{f} =_A p, \mathbf{g} =_A q, \mathbf{f} =_{A^c} \mathbf{g}) \Rightarrow (\mathbf{f} \succ \mathbf{g} \Leftrightarrow p \succ q)$.

Then there is a unique additive probability measure π *on* $\mathcal{E}$, *with* $A \in \mathfrak{N} \Leftrightarrow \pi(A) = 0$, *and a linear functional* u *on* P, *unique up to positive linear transformations, such that, for all simple* $\mathbf{f}, \mathbf{g} \in \mathbf{F}$,

$$\mathbf{f} \succ \mathbf{g} \Leftrightarrow \int_S u(\mathbf{f}(s)) \, d\pi(s) > \int_S u(\mathbf{g}(s)) \, d\pi(s).$$

No restrictions are imposed on π beyond those stated in the theorem. In particular, it need not satisfy the final conclusion of Theorem 7.2; in fact, S can be any nonempty set in the lottery-acts theory. This greater generality by comparison to Savage's π is caused by the use of P in the present axioms. As with $x > y$ in Savage's case, $p > q$ here is defined in terms of constant lottery acts: $p > q$ if $\mathbf{f} > \mathbf{g}$ when $\mathbf{f}(S) = \{p\}$ and $\mathbf{g}(S) = \{q\}$.

The extension of the additive linear representation to all lottery acts uses an axiom similar to Savage's P7 without the conditionality feature.

THEOREM 7.6. *Suppose the hypotheses of Theorem 7.5 hold along with the following for all* $\mathbf{f}, \mathbf{g} \in \mathbf{F}$:

S3. $(\mathbf{f} > \mathbf{g}(s) \text{ for all } s \in S) \Rightarrow \mathbf{f} \gtrsim \mathbf{g}; (\mathbf{f}(s) > \mathbf{g} \text{ for all } s \in S) \Rightarrow \mathbf{f} \gtrsim \mathbf{g}.$

Then there are π *on* $\mathcal{E}$ *and* u *on* P *with the properties noted in the conclusion of Theorem 7.5 such that, for all* $\mathbf{f}, \mathbf{g} \in \mathbf{F}, \mathbf{f} > \mathbf{g} \Leftrightarrow \int u(\mathbf{f}(s)) \, d\pi(s) > \int u(\mathbf{g}(s)) \, d\pi(s)$. *Moreover, given this representation:*

(a) *Every* $\mathbf{f} \in \mathbf{F}$ *is bounded; that is, there are real numbers c and d that can depend on* $\mathbf{f}$ *such that* $\pi(\{s: c \leqslant u(\mathbf{f}(s)) \leqslant d\}) = 1$.

(b) u *is bounded if there is a denumerable partition of S such that* $\pi(A) > 0$ *for every member of the partition.*

Other than nonconstancy (S1), linearity, and (b), there are no restrictions on u. If S happens to be finite, then S3 is redundant since the complete representation is covered by Theorem 7.5.

7.7 ADDITIVE LINEAR UTILITY PROOFS

Since A1, A2, and A3 are presumed for $(\mathbf{F}, >)$ in the theorems of the preceding section, it follows from Theorem 1.3 that there is a linear u on $\mathbf{F}$, unique up to positive linear transformations, such that for *all* $\mathbf{f}, \mathbf{g} \in \mathbf{F}, \mathbf{f} > \mathbf{g}$ $\Leftrightarrow u(\mathbf{f}) > u(\mathbf{g})$. We intend to define u on P by $u(p) = u(\mathbf{f})$ when $\mathbf{f}(S) = \{p\}$, but will work only with u on $\mathbf{F}$ for the time being.

Proof of Theorem 7.4. Let $\{A_1, \ldots, A_n\}$ be a partition of S, and for convenience write $\mathbf{f}$ in $\mathbf{F}'$ as $(p_1, \ldots, p_n)$ when $\mathbf{f} =_{A_i} p_i$ for each i. Fix $\mathbf{h}$ $= (r_1, \ldots, r_n)$ in $\mathbf{F}'$, and let $\mathbf{p}_i = (r_1, \ldots, r_{i-1}, p_i, r_{i+1}, \ldots, r_n)$ for all $p_i \in P$. Then, with $\mathbf{f} = (p_1, \ldots, p_n)$, $(1/n)\mathbf{f} + ((n-1)/n)\mathbf{h} = \Sigma_i (1/n)\mathbf{p}_i$. Therefore, by the linearity of u on $\mathbf{F}$, $u(\mathbf{f}) + (n-1)u(\mathbf{h}) = \Sigma_i u(\mathbf{p}_i)$. Define u_i on P by

$$u_i(p_i) = u(\mathbf{p}_i) - [(n-1)/n]u(\mathbf{h}).$$

Then summation over i gives $\Sigma_i u_i(p_i) = \Sigma_i u(\mathbf{p}_i) - (n-1)u(\mathbf{h})$ and therefore

$$u(\mathbf{f}) = \sum_i u_i(p_i), \qquad \mathbf{f} = (p_1, \ldots, p_n).$$

This verifies the representation of Theorem 7.4 so long as each u_i is linear. To show this let $\mathbf{q}_i = (r_1, \ldots, r_{i-1}, q_i, r_{i+1}, \ldots, r_n)$. Then, by the preceding result,

$$u(\lambda \mathbf{p}_i + (1 - \lambda)\mathbf{q}_i) = u_i(\lambda p_i + (1 - \lambda)q_i) + \sum_{j \neq i} u_j(r_j).$$

In addition,

$$u(\lambda \mathbf{p}_i + (1 - \lambda)\mathbf{q}_i) = \lambda u(\mathbf{p}_i) + (1 - \lambda)u(\mathbf{q}_i)$$

$$= \lambda u_i(p_i) + (1 - \lambda)u_i(q_i) + \sum_{j \neq i} u_j(r_j),$$

and therefore $u_i(\lambda p_i + (1 - \lambda)q_i) = \lambda u_i(p_i) + (1 - \lambda)u_i(q_i)$.

If u_i' satisfy the representation along with the u_i, then, letting $u'(\mathbf{f}) = \Sigma$ $u_i'(p_i)$ when $\mathbf{f} = (p_1, \ldots, p_n)$, we get $u' = au + b$ with $a > 0$. Holding p_j fixed for all $j \neq i$ gives $u_i' = au_i + b_i$. The "converse" obviously holds. ∎

Proof of Theorem 7.5. Assume the hypotheses of the theorem, including S1 and S2. We first prove

LEMMA 7.9. *Given a partition* $\{A_1, \ldots, A_n\}$ *of S, there is a linear functional* v *on P, unique up to positive linear transformations, and unique* $\rho_i \geqslant 0$ *with* $\Sigma_{i=1}^n \rho_i = 1$ *and* $\rho_i = 0 \Leftrightarrow A_i \in \mathfrak{N}$ *such that, for all* $\mathbf{f}$ $= (p_1, \ldots, p_n)$ *and* $\mathbf{g} = (q_1, \ldots, q_n)$ *in* $\mathbf{F}'$,

$$\mathbf{f} > \mathbf{g} \Leftrightarrow \sum_{i=1}^n \rho_i v(p_i) > \sum_{i=1}^n \rho_i v(q_i).$$

Proof. Let $K = \{i: i \in \{1, \ldots, n\} \text{ and } A_i \notin \mathfrak{N}\}$. By S1 and the preceding proof, $K \neq \varnothing$. In view of S1, S2, and the representation of Theorem 7.4, which we assume here, the representation of Lemma 7.9 requires $\rho_i > 0 \Leftrightarrow A_i \notin \mathfrak{N} \Leftrightarrow i \in K$.

If $K = \{i\}$, the lemma's conclusion follows with $\rho_i = 1$, $\rho_j = 0$ for each $j \neq i$, and $v = u_i$.

Suppose henceforth that $|K| \geqslant 2$. For all $i, j \in K$, it follows from S2 that $u_i(p) > u_i(q) \Leftrightarrow u_j(p) > u_j(q)$ for all $p, q \in P$. Fix $p_0 \in P$. The uniqueness property for linear utility implies that for all $i, j \in K$ there is a unique $a_{ij} > 0$ such that

$$u_i(p) - u_i(p_0) = a_{ij}(u_j(p) - u_j(p_0)) \qquad \text{for all } p \in P.$$

Fix $k \in K$ and define ρ and v by

$$\rho_i = 0 \qquad \text{for all } i \notin K,$$

$$\rho_i = a_{ik} \Big/ \sum_{j \in K} a_{jk} \qquad \text{for all } i \in K,$$

$$v(p) = [u_i(p) - u_i(p_0)]/\rho_i \qquad \text{for all } p \in P \text{ and all } i \in K.$$

To show that v is well defined, we need to prove that

$$u_i(p) - u_i(p_0) = \frac{a_{ik}}{a_{jk}} [u_j(p) - u_j(p_0)] \qquad \text{when } i, j \in K.$$

But this follows easily from the first equation above for a_{ij} and the fact that each u_i for $i \in K$ is not constant on P. Substitution of $\rho_i v(p) + u_i(p_0)$ for $u_i(p)$ into the representation of Theorem 7.4 then gives the representation of the lemma.

The uniqueness properties in the lemma follow easily from those of Theorem 7.4. ∎

We now continue with the proof of Theorem 7.5, designating finite partitions $\{A_1, \ldots, A_n\}$ and $\{B_1, \ldots, B_m\}$ of S by α and β, respectively.

For any finite partition $\{A_1, \ldots, A_n\}$ of S it follows from Lemma 7.9 that there are nonnegative numbers $\pi_\alpha(A_1), \ldots, \pi_\alpha(A_n)$ that sum to 1 with $\pi_\alpha(A_i) = 0 \Leftrightarrow A_i \in \mathfrak{N}$, and a linear functional v_α on P such that, for all $\mathbf{f} = (p_1, \ldots, p_n)$ and $\mathbf{g} = (q_1, \ldots, q_n)$ in $\mathbf{F}_\alpha = \mathbf{F}'$,

$$\mathbf{f} > \mathbf{g} \Leftrightarrow \sum \pi_\alpha(A_i) v_\alpha(p_i) > \sum \pi_\alpha(A_i) v_\alpha(q_i).$$

Moreover, the $\pi_\alpha(A_i)$ are unique, and v_α is unique up to positive linear transformations.

Consider any other partition $\{B_1, \ldots, B_m\}$ of S, with a similar representation using $\pi_\beta(B_i)$ instead of $\pi_\alpha(A_i)$ and v_β instead of v_α. Since the constant lottery acts give $p > q \Leftrightarrow v_\alpha(p) > v_\alpha(q) \Leftrightarrow v_\beta(p) > v_\beta(q)$, v_β must be a positive linear transformation of v_α. We can therefore drop the partition designator on v with no loss in generality to replace the preceding displayed representation by

$$\mathbf{f} > \mathbf{g} \Leftrightarrow \sum \pi_\alpha(A_i) v(p_i) > \sum \pi_\alpha(A_i) v(q_i),$$

with v unique up to positive linear transformations.

Consider any event A. Suppose A is a member of both $\{A_1, \ldots, A_n\}$ and $\{B_1, \ldots, B_m\}$. Then, by the preceding representation,

$$\pi_\alpha(A)v(p) + [1 - \pi_\alpha(A)]v(q) > \pi_\alpha(A)v(p') + [1 - \pi_\alpha(A)]v(q')$$

$$\Leftrightarrow \pi_\beta(A)v(p) + [1 - \pi_\beta(A)]v(q) > \pi_\beta(A)v(p')$$

$$+ [1 - \pi_\beta(A)]v(q')$$

for all $p, q, p', q' \in P$ since all pAq are in both $\mathbf{F}_\alpha$ and $\mathbf{F}_\beta$. It then follows from the representation for the partition $\{A, A^c\}$ that $\pi_\alpha(A) = \pi_\beta(A)$. Hence, with $\pi(\varnothing) = 0$ and $\pi(S) = 1$, we can drop the partition designator on π to obtain

$$\mathbf{f} > \mathbf{g} \Leftrightarrow \sum \pi(A_i)v(p_i) > \sum \pi(A_i)v(q_i).$$

Finite additivity for π is easily demonstrated using partitions $\{A, B, (A \cup B)^c\}$ and $\{A \cup B, (A \cup B)^c\}$ with $A \cap B = \emptyset$ in an analysis similar to that just completed. Clearly, π is unique.

Finally, to show that the additive linear representation holds for all simple $\mathbf{f}, \mathbf{g} \in \mathbf{F}$, suppose $\mathbf{f} = (p_1, \ldots, p_n)$ for partition $\{A_1, \ldots, A_n\}$ and $\mathbf{g} = (q_1, \ldots, q_m)$ for partition $\{B_1, \ldots, B_m\}$. When the preceding representation is applied to the partition $\{A_i \cap B_j : 1 \leq i \leq n, 1 \leq j \leq m, A_i \cap B_j \neq \emptyset\}$, we get

$$\mathbf{f} > \mathbf{g} \Leftrightarrow \sum_i \sum_j \pi(A_i \cap B_j)v(p_i) > \sum_i \sum_j \pi(A_i \cap B_j)v(q_j).$$

Finite additivity reduces the inequality to $\Sigma_i \pi(A_i)v(p_i) > \Sigma_j \pi(B_j)v(q_j)$ to obtain the additive linear representation. ∎

Proof of Theorem 7.6. Assume the hypotheses of the theorem, and let π and u (on P) be as specified in Theorem 7.5. Also let u on $\mathbf{F}$ be as specified in the opening paragraph of this section. Since the specialization of this u on constant lottery acts must be a positive linear transformation of v in the preceding proof, we can presume that u on P for Theorem 7.5 is identical to the noted specialization of u on $\mathbf{F}$. With the definition of $\mathbf{f}$ bounded as in Theorem 7.6(a), the proof of the theorem will be completed by proving the following four lemmas.

LEMMA 7.10. $u(\mathbf{f}) = \int u(\mathbf{f}(s)) \, d\pi(s)$ *for all bounded* $\mathbf{f}$.

LEMMA 7.11. u *on* P *is bounded if there is a denumerable partition of* S *such that* $\pi(A) > 0$ *for every member of the partition.*

LEMMA 7.12. *If for each* $n \in \{1, 2, \ldots\}$ *there is an n-part partition of* S *every member of which has* $\pi(A) > 0$, *then there is a denumerable partition with this property.*

LEMMA 7.13. *If the hypotheses of Lemma 7.12 are false, then all lottery acts are bounded.*

Remark. Lemma 7.11 is conclusion (b) of Theorem 7.6 and Lemmas 7.11–7.13 say that all $\mathbf{f} \in \mathbf{F}$ are bounded. This, Lemma 7.10, and $\mathbf{f} > \mathbf{g} \Leftrightarrow u(\mathbf{f}) > u(\mathbf{g})$ by the opening paragraph of this section show that the additive linear representation holds for all lottery acts.

Proof of Lemma 7.10. We show first that if $\pi(A) = 1$, and if $c = \inf\{u(\mathbf{f}(s)) : s \in A\}$ and $d = \sup\{u(\mathbf{f}(s)) : s \in A\}$ are finite, then $c \leq u(\mathbf{f}) \leq d$. Given these hypotheses let $\mathbf{g} =_A \mathbf{f}$ along with $c \leq u(\mathbf{g}(s)) \leq d$ for all $s \in A^c$. Since $A^c \in \mathfrak{N}$, $\mathbf{g} \sim \mathbf{f}$ and $u(\mathbf{g}) = u(\mathbf{f})$. Suppose to the contrary of $c \leq u(\mathbf{g}) \leq d$ that $d < u(\mathbf{g})$. Take $q' \in P$ with $c \leq u(q') \leq d$ and let $\mathbf{g}' =_S q'$. Also let $\mathbf{h} = \lambda \mathbf{g} + (1 - \lambda)\mathbf{g}'$ with $\lambda < 1$ but near enough to 1 so that $d <$

$u(\mathbf{h}) = \lambda u(\mathbf{g}) + (1 - \lambda)u(\mathbf{g}') < u(\mathbf{g})$. Then $\mathbf{g} \succ \mathbf{h}$. But since $u(\mathbf{h}) > d \geqslant u(\mathbf{g}(s))$ for all s, $\mathbf{h} \succ \mathbf{g}(s)$ for all s, so $\mathbf{h} \succsim \mathbf{g}$ by S3 for a contradiction. Therefore $u(\mathbf{g}) \leqslant d$. By a symmetric proof, $c \leqslant u(\mathbf{g})$.

Assume that $\mathbf{f}$ is bounded with A, c, and d as in the preceding paragraph. If $c = d$, then $u(\mathbf{f}) = \int u(\mathbf{f}(s))\, d\pi(s)$ is immediate. Assume henceforth that $c < d$, and with no loss of generality let $c = 0$ and $d = 1$. Define $\mathbf{g}$ as in the preceding paragraph so that $u(\mathbf{g}) = u(\mathbf{f})$ and, as is easily proved, $\int u(\mathbf{g}(s))\, d\pi(s) = \int u(\mathbf{f}(s))\, d\pi(s)$. We show $u(\mathbf{g}) = \int u(\mathbf{g}(s))\, d\pi(s)$.

Ignoring empty sets, let $\{A_1, \ldots, A_n\}$ be the partition of S defined by

$$A_1 = \{s : 0 \leqslant u(\mathbf{g}(s)) \leqslant 1/n\},$$

$$A_i = \{s : (i - 1)/n < u(\mathbf{g}(s)) \leqslant i/n\}, \qquad i = 2, \ldots, n,$$

and let $p_i \in P$ be such that $(i - 1)/n \leqslant u(p_i) \leqslant i/n$ for each i. Let

$$\mathbf{h}_i =_{A_i} \mathbf{g}, \quad \mathbf{h}_i =_{A_i^c} p_i \qquad \text{for } i = 1, \ldots, n,$$

$$\mathbf{h}_0 = \sum_i \left(\frac{1}{n}\right) \mathbf{h}_i,$$

$$\mathbf{k} =_{A_i} \sum_{j \neq i} \left(\frac{1}{n-1}\right) p_j \qquad \text{for } i = 1, \ldots, n.$$

Then, when $s \in A_i$,

$$\mathbf{h}_0(s) = \sum_i \left(\frac{1}{n}\right) \mathbf{h}_i(s) = \left(\frac{1}{n}\right) \mathbf{g}(s)$$

$$+ \left(\frac{n-1}{n}\right) \sum_{j \neq i} \left(\frac{1}{n-1}\right) p_j,$$

and therefore $\mathbf{h}_0 = (1/n)\mathbf{g} + [(n - 1)/n]\mathbf{k}$. Hence, by linearity and the definition of $\mathbf{h}_0$,

$$u(\mathbf{g}) = \sum_{i=1}^{n} u(\mathbf{h}_i) - (n - 1)u(\mathbf{k}).$$

Since $\mathbf{k}$ is simple,

$$u(\mathbf{k}) = \sum_i u\left(\sum_{j \neq i} \left[\frac{1}{n-1}\right] p_j\right) \pi(A_i)$$

$$= \left(\frac{1}{n-1}\right) \sum_i \left[\sum_{j \neq i} u(p_j)\right] \pi(A_i).$$

When this is substituted into the preceding expression for $u(\mathbf{g})$, we get

$$u(\mathbf{g}) = \sum_i u(\mathbf{h}_i) - \sum_i \sum_{j \neq i} u(p_j) \pi(A_i).$$

By the bounds on $u(p_i)$, the first paragraph of this proof, and the definition of $\mathbf{h}_i$,

$$(i - 1)/n \leqslant u(\mathbf{h}_i) \leqslant i/n \qquad \text{for } i = 1, \ldots, n.$$

Since $0 = \inf\{u(\mathbf{g}(s)){:}s \in S\}$ and $1 = \sup\{u(\mathbf{g}(s)){:}s \in S\}$, the p_i can be selected so that either

$$u(p_1) = 1/n, \qquad u(p_i) = (i - 1)/n \quad \text{for } i > 1$$

or

$$u(p_i) = i/n \quad \text{for } i < n, \qquad u(p_n) = (n - 1)/n.$$

Applying the first of these and $(i - 1)/n \leqslant u(\mathbf{h}_i)$ to the final equation in the preceding paragraph, we get

$$u(\mathbf{g}) \geqslant \sum_{i=1}^{n} \left(\frac{i - 1}{n} \right) \pi(A_i) - \frac{1}{n},$$

and applying the second and $u(\mathbf{h}_i) \leqslant i/n$ to the same equation, we get

$$u(\mathbf{g}) \leqslant \sum_{i=1}^{n} \left(\frac{i}{n} \right) \pi(A_i) + \frac{1}{n}.$$

By the definition of expectation,

$$\sum \left(\frac{i - 1}{n} \right) \pi(A_i) \leqslant \int u(\mathbf{g}(s)) \, d\pi(s) \leqslant \sum \left(\frac{i}{n} \right) \pi(A_i),$$

so that $|u(\mathbf{g}) - \int u(\mathbf{g}(s)) \, d\pi(s)| \leqslant 2/n$ for all n. Therefore $u(\mathbf{g}) = \int u(\mathbf{g}(s)) \, d\pi(s)$. ∎

Proof of Lemma 7.11. Let $\mathbf{A}$ be a denumerable partition of S with $\pi(A) > 0$ for all $A \in \mathbf{A}$. By working from a largest $\pi(A)$ on down, we get a sequence $A_1, A_2, \ldots$ with $\{A_1, A_2, \ldots\} = \mathbf{A}$ and $\pi(A_1) \geqslant \pi(A_2) \geqslant \cdots$.

Contrary to the conclusion that u on P is bounded, suppose it is unbounded above. By a linear transformation we can assume $[0, \infty) \subseteq u(P)$. Let $p_i \in P$ satisfy

$$u(p_i) = 1/\pi(A_i) \qquad \text{for } i = 1, 2, \cdots.$$

Also let $\mathbf{f} = _{A_i} p_i$ for all i, and let $\mathbf{g}_n$ be constant on each A_i for $i \leqslant n$ and on $\bigcup_{i > n} A_i$ with

$$u(\mathbf{g}_n(s)) = 1/\pi(A_n) - 1/\pi(A_i) \qquad \text{for } s \in A_i \text{ and } i \leqslant n,$$

$$u(\mathbf{g}_n(s)) = 0 \qquad\qquad \text{for } s \in \bigcup_{i > n} A_i.$$

Since each $\mathbf{g}_n$ is simple,

$$u(\mathbf{g}_n) = \sum_{i=1}^{n} \left[\frac{1}{\pi(A_n)} - \frac{1}{\pi(A_i)} \right] \pi(A_i)$$

$$= \frac{1}{\pi(A_n)} \sum_{i=1}^{n} \pi(A_i) - n.$$

Moreover, $u(\frac{1}{2}\mathbf{f}(s) + \frac{1}{2}\mathbf{g}_n(s)) = 1/2\pi(A_n)$ for all $s \in \bigcup_{i \leqslant n} A_i$, and $u(\frac{1}{2}\mathbf{f}(s) + \frac{1}{2}\mathbf{g}_n(s)) \geqslant 1/2\pi(A_n)$ for all $s \in \bigcup_{i > n} A_i$. Therefore, by the first paragraph of the proof of Lemma 7.10, $u(\frac{1}{2}\mathbf{f} + \frac{1}{2}\mathbf{g}_n) \geqslant 1/2\pi(A_n)$, which by linearity and the preceding equation for $u(\mathbf{g}_n)$ yield

$$u(\mathbf{f}) \geqslant \frac{1}{\pi(A_n)} \left[1 - \sum_{i=1}^{n} \pi(A_i) \right] + n \geqslant n \qquad \text{for } n = 1, 2, \cdots.$$

But this requires $u(\mathbf{f})$ to be infinite, contrary to the conclusion of Theorem 1.3. Hence u on P is bounded above. A symmetric proof shows that u on P is bounded below. ∎

Proof of Lemma 7.12. Given the hypotheses of the lemma, let $\mathbf{A}_n$ for each $n \geqslant 2$ be an n-part partition of S each member of which has $\pi(A) > 0$. Define a new set of partitions recursively as follows: $\mathbf{B}_2 = \mathbf{A}_2$ and for $n \geqslant 3$,

$$\mathbf{B}_n = \{A \cap B : A \in \mathbf{A}_n, B \in \mathbf{B}_{n-1}, A \cap B \neq \varnothing\}.$$

It is easily seen that $\mathbf{B}_n$ has n or more positive-probability members and that $\mathbf{B}_{n+1}$ is as fine as $\mathbf{B}_n$; that is, $B \in \mathbf{B}_{n+1} \Rightarrow C \in \mathbf{B}_n$ for some $C \supseteq B$. For each $A \in \mathbf{B}_2$ let $N_n^1(A)$ be the number of members of $\mathbf{B}_n$ ($n > 2$) that are included in A and have positive probability. With $\mathbf{B}_2 = \{A, A^c\}$ it follows that $N_n^1(A) + N_n^1(A^c) \geqslant n$ for all $n \geqslant 3$. Thus, as n gets large at least one of $N_n^1(A)$ and $N_n^1(A^c)$ approaches infinity. Let A_1 be a member of $\mathbf{B}_2$ for which $N_n^1(A_1) \to \infty$ and let $B_1 = A_1^c$. Then $\pi(B_1) > 0$ and B_1 will be the first element in our desired denumerable partition.

Next, let m be such that $\mathbf{B}_m$ has more than one subset of A_1 with positive probability. For each $A \subseteq A_1$ with $A \in \mathbf{B}_m$ let $N_n^2(A)$ be the number of members of $\mathbf{B}_n$ ($n > m$) that are included in A and have positive probability. Let $\mathbf{A} = \{A : A \subseteq A_1, A \in \mathbf{B}_m\}$. Then $\Sigma_\mathbf{A} N_n^2(A) = N_n^1(A_1)$, and therefore $N_n^2(A) \to \infty$ as $n \to \infty$ for some $A \in \mathbf{A}$. Let A_2 be such an A and let $B_2 =$

$A_1 \cap A_2^c$. Then $\pi(B_2) > 0$ and $\{B_1, B_2, A_2\}$ is a partition of S with $N_n^2(A_2)$ $\to \infty$.

Continuation gives a denumerable sequence $B_1, B_2, B_3, \ldots$ of mutually disjoint events with $\pi(B_i) > 0$ for all i. ■

Proof of Lemma 7.13. Given the hypotheses of the lemma, let $m = \max\{n$: there is a partition of S with n members for which $\pi(A) > 0\}$.

With no loss of generality let $u(y) = 0$ for a $y \in X$. Contrary to the conclusion of the lemma, suppose that $\mathbf{g}$ is unbounded above. Define $\mathbf{f}$ from $\mathbf{g}$ by replacing each x for which $\mathbf{g}(s)(x) > 0$ and $u(x) < 0$ by y, for every s. Then $u(\mathbf{f}(s)) \geqslant 0$ for all s, and $\mathbf{f}$ is unbounded above. Hence, for every $n \geqslant 1$, $\pi(\{s:u(\mathbf{f}(s)) \geqslant n\}) > 0$. By the preceding paragraph, this π quantity can change no more than m times as n increases. Hence there is an N and $\alpha > 0$ such that

$$\pi(\{s : u(\mathbf{f}(s)) \geqslant n\}) = \alpha \quad \text{for all } n \geqslant N.$$

Let $u(p_i) = i$ for $i = 1, 2, \ldots$, let $\mathbf{g}_n =_{\{s:u(\mathbf{f}(s))\geqslant n\}} \mathbf{f}$ and $\mathbf{g}_n =_{\{s:u(\mathbf{f}(s))<n\}} p_n$, and let $\mathbf{h}_n =_{\{s:u(\mathbf{f}(s))\geqslant n\}} p_n$ and $\mathbf{h}_n =_{\{s:u(\mathbf{f}(s))<n\}} \mathbf{f}$. Also let $\mathbf{p}_n$ denote the constant lottery act with $\mathbf{p}_n(s) = p_n$ for all s. Then $\frac{1}{2}\mathbf{f} + \frac{1}{2}\mathbf{p}_n = \frac{1}{2}\mathbf{g}_n + \frac{1}{2}\mathbf{h}_n$ and

$$u(\mathbf{f}) + n = u(\mathbf{g}_n) + u(\mathbf{h}_n) \quad \text{for all } n \geqslant 1.$$

Since $\mathbf{h}_n$ is bounded, Lemma 7.10 gives $u(\mathbf{h}_n) = \int u(\mathbf{h}_n(s)) \, d\pi(s) \geqslant n\alpha$ for all $n \geqslant N$. Since $\mathbf{g}_n(s) > p_{n-1}$ for all s, S3 implies $\mathbf{g}_n \succsim p_{n-1}$ so that $u(\mathbf{g}_n) \geqslant n - 1$ for all n. Then, by the preceding displayed equation,

$$u(\mathbf{f}) \geqslant n\alpha - 1 \quad \text{for all } n \geqslant N,$$

which contradicts finiteness of $u(\mathbf{f})$. Hence, $\mathbf{g}$ is not unbounded above. Similarly, it must be bounded below. ■

The hypotheses of Lemma 7.13 do not imply that π is a simple probability measure (Fishburn, 1970a, p. 188).

7.8 SUMMARY

Savage's theory of decision under uncertainty is based on axioms for preference between functions (acts) $f, g, \ldots$ from a set S of states of the world into a set X of outcomes. His additive expected utility representation is

$$f > g \Leftrightarrow \int_S u(f(s)) \, d\pi(s) > \int_S u(g(s)) \, d\pi(s),$$

where u is a bounded utility functional on X and π is a finitely additive probability measure on the algebra of all subsets of S. His axioms imply that S is infinite and π is unique. Subjective probability is based on preference: $\pi(A) > \pi(B)$ if and only if, when x is preferred to y, the act that yields x if A

obtains and y otherwise is preferred to the act that yields x if B obtains and y otherwise.

Another formulation uses functions (lottery acts) $\mathbf{f}$, $\mathbf{g}$, . . . from S into the set P of simple probability distributions on X and views the probabilities for P as extraneous scaling probabilities independent of S. When the von Neumann–Morgenstern axioms for preference on the set of lottery acts are supplemented by other independence and dominance axioms, we obtain the additive linear utility representation

$$\mathbf{f} > \mathbf{g} \Leftrightarrow \int_S u(\mathbf{f}(s)) \, d\pi(s) > \int_S u(\mathbf{g}(s)) \, d\pi(s),$$

where u is a linear functional on P and π is a unique probability measure on the subsets of S. Because of the lottery feature, no further restrictions apply to S or π in this case.

8 Generalizations of Additive Expected Utility

Prior to about 1980, the main alternative to Savage's additive expected utility theory and the additive linear theory of Anscombe and Aumann was Allais's additive nonexpected intensive utility theory for decision under uncertainty. Since that time, several new alternatives have been developed to accommodate violations of independence, substitution, reduction, and transitivity. Most of these either assume that subjective probability is additive but preferences need not be transitive, or that preferences are transitive and subjective probability need not be additive. This chapter reviews these theories after discussing violations of traditional axioms and representations for nonadditive probability.

8.1 CRITIQUE OF ADDITIVE EXPECTED UTILITY

Chapter 2 presented an array of plausible violations of the von Neumann–Morgenstern expected utility theory that focused on the independence axiom ($p \succ q \Rightarrow \lambda p + (1 - \lambda)r \succ \lambda q + (1 - \lambda)r$), transitivity, and the use of nontransformed outcome probabilities in numerical representations of preference. Many of those violations apply also to Savage's additive expected utility of Section 7.4 and the additive linear model of Section 7.6. Other challenges to these states theories arise directly from the states formulation. They are concerned primarily with the reduction principle, the independence or substitution principle (P2) part of Savage's sure-thing principle, and the approach to subjective probability developed by Ramsey, de Finetti, and Savage.

This section further illustrates these challenges. The next section then discusses nonadditive subjective probability, and the remainder of the chapter reviews theories designed to accommodate observed violations of the theories in the preceding chapter.

We have already discussed aspects of the reduction principle in Chapter 2. Another example is provided by Figure 8.1 with dollar payoffs and 10

FIGURE 8.1   Payoff matrix

STATE PROBABILITIES

	0.1	0.1	0.1	0.1	0.1	0.1	0.1	0.1	0.1	0.1
f	10	20	30	40	50	60	70	80	90	100
g	20	30	40	50	60	70	80	90	100	10

equally likely states. By the identity reduction principle of Section 7.4, $f \sim g$ since $\pi_f = \pi_g$. This is defended by the claim that, once an act has been chosen, the only thing that should matter is that act's probabilities for the outcomes. This claim sees f and g as effectively identical. Hence they ought to be equally attractive.

One argument against the reduction principle involves a comparative evaluation position that asserts that alignments of outcomes under events as well as outcome probabilities themselves can affect choices in reasonable ways. An example of this (Tversky, 1975; Loomes and Sugden, 1982; Bell, 1982) focuses on the regret/rejoicing a person might experience by learning that one could have done better/worse if one had chosen differently. Some people may prefer g to f for Figure 8.1 because g gives a greater return than f in 9 of the 10 states, reasoning that if the final state obtains it is merely a case of bad luck. Others may prefer f to g because they would experience great regret if they choose g and the final state obtains, but would not be troubled by losing out on the $10 difference in the other nine cases under selection of f.

A connection to stochastic dominance arises from one change in Figure 8.1. Suppose $g > f$, and $h = g$ except that h's final outcome is $9 instead of $10. It may well be true that $h > f$. This violates the *combination* of the reduction principle and first-degree stochastic dominance, which yield $f > h$ by way of $\pi_f >_1 \pi_h$. Note, however, that $h > f$ does *not* violate the dominance principles discussed near the end of Section 7.4.

Reduction also has intimate ties to transitivity. Consider the lottery acts of Figure 8.2. Suppose there is a preference cycle $p > q > r > p$ on the three lotteries. Since **f** is preferred to **g** under each state, the obvious dominance conclusion for lottery acts is **f** > **g**. But the reduction principle requires **f** $\sim$ **g** since their overall probability distributions on outcomes are identical. If we insist on the statewise dominance principle but allow preference cycles in P, the reduction principle must be rejected. Or, to put it the other way around, dominance and reduction virtually force transitivity.

We now turn to independence and substitution as seen by Allais and then Ellsberg. Figure 8.3 shows Savage's (1954, p. 103) event-dependent arrangement of the alternatives used in Section 2.5 to illustrate the common consequence effect. Allais (1953, p. 526; 1979a, p. 89) used as a similar

FIGURE 8.2   Lottery acts

STATE PROBABILITIES

	1/3	1/3	1/3
f	p	q	r
g	q	r	p

FIGURE 8.3   Savage's payoff matrix

TICKET NUMBERS FOR 100-TICKET
LOTTERY. ONE TO BE DRAWN AT RANDOM.

		1	2-11	12-100
SITUATION 1	f	$ 500,000	$ 500,000	$ 500,000
	g	0	$ 2,500,000	$ 500,000
SITUATION 2	f'	$ 500,000	$ 500,000	0
	g'	0	$ 2,500,000	0

arrangement described graphically. However, when he confronted Savage with comparisons like those of Situations 1 and 2 at the 1952 Paris colloquium on decision under uncertainty, Allais presented the situations in the event-free mode of Section 2.5. Since both accepted the reduction principle, this would presumably not affect choices, although we now know from framing effects that it can. In any event Savage, like many others, initially preferred f to g and g' to f' in the event-free mode, but later, after viewing them in the way of Figure 8.3, changed to $f' > g'$ along with $f > g$ to avoid the obvious clash with the substitution principle.

Savage, among others, felt that such arrangements would convince (most?) people of the compelling nature of the substitution principle and, by implication from the reduction principle, of the reasonableness of the von Neumann–Morgenstern independence axiom. However, Allais's original contention to the contrary has been well supported by later experiments (MacCrimmon, 1968; Slovic and Tversky, 1974; MacCrimmon and Larsson, 1979). Moreover, violations of substitution persist when subjects are instructed in the arguments of Allais and Savage before they make their choices.

As already mentioned in Section 3.3, Allais's resolution to his acceptance of reduction, weak order, and stochastic dominance in conjunction with his rejection of independence and substitution is a representation that avoids an expectational form. He does, however, subscribe to additive subjective probability for decision under uncertainty, but with a very different interpretation (1979b, pp. 469–73) than the personalistic one adopted by Savage. In particular, he rejects the preference-based definition of $\succ_*$ in the preceding chapter (1979b, pp. 510–14) not only because it clashes with what he believes is the correct approach to the assessment of subjective probability (see Section 8.4) but also because it is at variance with his refutation of the substitution principle.

The latter point was emphasized by Ellsberg (1961), who used the notion of event ambiguity to construct examples that challenge Savage's substitution principle and the closely related additivity axiom G4 of Theorem 7.2. Figure 8.4 gives a case in point. Suppose an urn is filled with 90 balls, 30 of which are red (R) and 60 of which are black (B) and yellow (Y) in an unknown mixture. One ball is to be drawn at random with a payoff of either $0 or $1,000 depending on the act selected and the color of the drawn ball. Ellsberg claimed, and many subsequent experiments have verified, that a high proportion of subjects prefer f to g and prefer g' to f', in direct violation of the substitution principle. The preference $f \succ g$ seems to arise from the specificity of R relative to B, or, equivalently, from the ambiguity of B relative to R, since exactly 30 balls are known to be red while an unknown number from 0 to 60 are black. The preference $g' \succ f'$ depends on the same phenomenon: Exactly 60 balls are black or yellow, whereas an unknown number from 30 to 90 are red or yellow. One might say that $f \succ g$ and $g' \succ f'$ demonstrate a preference for specificity, or an aversion to ambiguity, which is something quite different than the concept of risk aversion discussed in Section 1.6.

According to Savage's definition of $\succ_*$, $f \succ g \Rightarrow R \succ_* B$, and $g' \succ f'$ $\Rightarrow B \cup Y \succ_* R \cup Y$. Hence if we subscribe to these preferences and Savage's definition, π cannot be additive since it would yield $\pi(R) > \pi(B)$ from $R \succ_* B$ and $\pi(B) > \pi(R)$ from $B \cup Y \succ_* R \cup Y$.

Raiffa (1961) gives a critique of Ellsberg (1961) that is consistent with Savage's position. Subsequent discussants of ambiguity include Sherman (1974), Franke (1978), Gärdenfors and Sahlin (1982), and Einhorn and Hogarth (1985, 1986). Segal (1987) presents a two-stage decision model designed to accommodate ambiguity.

8.2 NONADDITIVE SUBJECTIVE PROBABILITY

A variety of alternatives to the additive probability theory of Section 7.2 have been proposed to accommodate noncomparability of incommensurable events, imprecise or vague judgment, ambiguity, failures of additivity, and intransitivities. Some of these treat $\succ_*$ from an intuitional viewpoint (Keynes, 1921; Koopman, 1940; Good, 1950; Adams, 1965; Fine, 1973; Suppes, 1974; Shafer, 1976; Walley and Fine, 1979; Fishburn, 1986c, 1986f), and others define $\succ_*$ from preferences or choices (Savage, 1954; Smith, 1961,

FIGURE 8.4   Ellsberg's urn

	30 BALLS	60 BALLS	
	R	B	Y
f	\$ 1000	\$ 0	\$ 0
g	\$ 0	\$ 1000	\$ 0
f'	\$ 1000	\$ 0	\$ 1000
g'	\$ 0	\$ 1000	\$ 1000

1965; Heath and Sudderth, 1972; Schmeidler, 1984; Gilboa, 1987; Fishburn, 1983c, 1986d).

In some cases full additivity is retained but weak order is relaxed to partial order to obtain a one-way representation of the form $A \succ_* B \Rightarrow \pi(A) > \pi(B)$ or perhaps $A \succsim_* B \Rightarrow \pi(A) \geq \pi(B)$. Examples include Savage (1954), Kraft et al. (1959), Adams (1965), Fishburn (1969, 1975b), Narens (1974), and Wakker (1981).

Another approach that is designed to accommodate vague judgment and may or may not involve additivity uses upper and lower probability functions on $\mathcal{E}$. We denote these by π^* and π_* respectively, with $\pi^* \geq \pi_*$. According to Dempster (1968), upper and lower probabilities go back at least to Boole (1854). It is generally assumed that $\pi_*(\varnothing) = \pi^*(\varnothing) = 0$, $\pi_*(S) = \pi^*(S) = 1$, and that π_* and π^* are *monotonic;* that is, $A \subseteq B \Rightarrow [\pi_*(A) \leq \pi_*(B), \pi^*(A) \leq \pi^*(B)]$. Many authors, including Koopman (1940) and Good (1962) from an intuitive viewpoint, Smith (1961, 1965) from an adaptation of de Finetti's (1964) fair-bets approach, and Dempster (1967, 1968), also assume the following:

> *complementary symmetry*: $\pi_*(A) + \pi^*(A^c) = 1$.
> *superadditivity of π_**: $A \cap B = \varnothing \Rightarrow \pi_*(A) + \pi_*(B) \leq \pi_*(A \cup B)$.
> *subadditivity of π^**: $A \cap B = \varnothing \Rightarrow \pi^*(A \cup B) \leq \pi^*(A) + \pi^*(B)$.

These functions are usually taken to characterize $\succ_*$ in the sense that, for all $A, B \in \mathcal{E}$,

$$A \succ_* B \Leftrightarrow \pi_*(A) > \pi^*(B),$$

or, if we think of $[\pi_*(A), \pi^*(A)]$ as the *probability interval* for A, $A \succ_* B$ if and only if A's probability interval everywhere exceeds B's probability interval. It may or may not be true that $\pi_* \leq \pi \leq \pi^*$ for some additive measure π on $\mathcal{E}$.

Additional comments on related models are given in Fishburn (1986f). This paper provides axiomatizations of interval and semiorder representations for $(\mathcal{E}, \succ_*)$ that range from the case in which only monotonicity is presumed for π_* and π^* to cases that assume complementary symmetry, superadditivity, and subadditivity, and $\pi_* \leqslant \pi \leqslant \pi^*$ for an additive π.

Davidson and Suppes (1956), Schmeidler (1984), and Gilboa (1987) axiomatize preference between acts or lottery acts to obtain a single probability measure that represents $\succ_*$ in the weak-order manner of Section 7.2 and is monotonic *but not necessarily additive*. To distinguish their measure from additive π, denote it by σ with $\sigma(\varnothing) = 0$, $\sigma(S) = 1$, and $A \subseteq B \Rightarrow \sigma(A) \leqslant \sigma(B)$. Davidson and Suppes's finite-sets theory entails

complementary additivity: $\sigma(A) + \sigma(A^c) = 1$,

which presumes the complementarity axiom $A \succ_* B \leftrightarrow B^c \succ_* A^c$. Gilboa (1985a) presents a cogent argument for complementary additivity in the nonadditive expected utility theories of Schmeidler (1984) and Gilboa (1987), although it is not presumed by their axioms.

The latter theories were designed to accommodate ambiguity and failures of the substitution principle as discussed in the preceding section. Other probability models for ambiguity have been proposed by Einhorn and Hogarth (1985) and Fishburn (1986d) among others. The descriptive approach of Einhorn and Hogarth begins with an initial assessment p_A of the probability of A, then adjusts it to account for ambiguity by means of nonnegative parameters θ and β to yield

$$\sigma(A) = p_A + \theta(1 - p_A - p_A^\beta).$$

For example, in Figure 8.4 one might begin with $p_B = \frac{1}{3}$ and end up with $\sigma(B) = 0.31$. Here θ is the basic ambiguity parameter ($\theta = 0$ for no ambiguity), and β accounts for ambiguity aversion ($\beta < 1$), neutrality ($\beta = 1$), or ambiguity seeking ($\beta > 1$). Their model satisfies complementary additivity if $\theta = 0$ or $\beta = 1$.

The model in Fishburn (1986d) is

$$\sigma(A) = \pi(A) - \pi(A)\tau(A^c) - \pi(A^c)\tau(A),$$

where π is an additive probability measure and τ is an additive unsigned measure that can take on negative as well as positive values. This model does not satisfy monotonicity naturally, but that can be imposed. The τ measure is designed to account for ambiguity. The model does not generally satisfy complementary additivity, but its correction for ambiguity, namely $- \pi(A)\tau(A^c) - \pi(A^c)\tau(A)$, is the same for both A and A^c.

A different approach to ambiguity is axiomatized in Fishburn (1983c,

1983d) in ways suggested by SSB utility theory. The representation is

$$A \succ_* B \Leftrightarrow \rho(A, B) > 0,$$

where ρ is a skew-symmetric functional on $\mathcal{E} \times \mathcal{E}$, $\rho(S, \varnothing) = 1$, $A \supseteq B \Rightarrow$ $\rho(A, B) \geq 0$ (monotonicity), and

$$A \cap B = \varnothing \Rightarrow \rho(A \cup B, C) + \rho(\varnothing, C) = \rho(A, C) + \rho(B, C).$$

The last property, called *conditional additivity,* is a first-order generalization of the usual additivity property $A \cap B = \varnothing \Rightarrow \pi(A \cup B) + \pi(\varnothing) = \pi(A) + \pi(B)$. Positive ρ values for Figure 8.4 that agree with ambiguity aversion and $f \succ g$, $g' \succ f'$, are $\rho(R, B) = \rho(R, Y) = 0.02$, $\rho(R, \varnothing) = 0.38$, $\rho(B, \varnothing) = \rho(Y, \varnothing) = 0.31$. These and $\rho(B, Y) = 0$ completely determine ρ with the use of skew-symmetry and conditional additivity.

8.3 GENERALIZATIONS OF ADDITIVE EXPECTED UTILITY

Our basic classification of generalizations of additive expected utility and additive linear utility uses three dichotomies: additive versus nonadditive subjective probability, transitive (weak order) versus nontransitive preference, and regular Savage acts versus lottery acts. These give eight basic categories as follows:

   I. Additive, transistive, regular acts
     A. Expected (Ramsey, 1931; Savage, 1954)
     B. Nonexpected intensive (Allais, 1953, 1979a, b)
     C. Expected disappointment (Loomes and Sugden, 1986)
  II. Additive, transitive, lottery acts
     A. Linear (Anscombe and Aumann, 1963)
 III. Additive, nontransitive, regular acts
     A. Expected regret (Bell, 1982; Loomes and Sugden, 1982, 1987)
     B. Skew-symmetric additive (Fishburn,1986e)
  IV. Additive, nontransitive, lottery acts
     A. SSB (Fishburn, 1984b; Fishburn and LaValle, 1987a)
   V. Nonadditive, transitive, regular acts
     A. Expected finite (Davidson and Suppes, 1956)
     B. Expected (Gilboa, 1987)
     C. Biexpected (Luce and Narens, 1985)
  VI. Nonadditive, transitive, lottery acts
     A. Linear (Schmeidler, 1984)
 VII. Nonadditive, nontransitive, regular acts
VIII. Nonadditive, nontransitive, lottery acts

A. Basic SSB (Fishburn, 1984b)
B. Conditionally additive (Fishburn, 1983c)
C. Modified SSB (Fishburn, 1986d).

As seen by the citation dates, most of these not already discussed in Chapter 7 are very recent, and one category (**VII**) is, to the best of my knowledge, presently empty. Unlike the listing in Chapter 3, no distinction is made for the Archimedean aspect since all theories cited above have real-valued representations.

There are a few major differences in regard to the treatment of utility and probability. The theories in **IB, IC,** and **IIIA** measure outcome utility in the riskless intensive manner of Bernoulli described in Chapters 1–3. The rest base utility measurement on preference between acts or lottery acts by natural extensions of the approaches described in Chapter 7. A similar division obtains for the measurement of subjective probability. In particular, Allais assesses probability apart from the specific acts at hand, Bell (1982) and Loomes and Sugden (1982, 1986, 1987) simply take additive state probabilities as given, however they might be assessed, and the others derive subjective probability from their preference axioms.

Most of these theories were proposed in a normative spirit. The axiomatic style used for **IA** and **IIA** has been successfully applied to **IIIB, IVA, VA-B, VIA, VIIIA,** and **VIIIB,** and **IIA** has been used to axiomatize so-called state dependent utilities (Fishburn, 1970, Chapter 13; Karni et al., 1983; Karni, 1985). Only partial axiomatizations exist for **VC** and **VIIIC.** The others (Allais, Loomes and Sugden, Bell) do not have comparable axiomatizations because of their different treatment of utility and probability.

The rest of the chapter describes the generalizations in varying detail except for **VA** (see Fishburn, 1981b). We begin with Allais's additive nonexpected intensive theory and its expected disappointment specialization in Loomes and Sugden (1986), followed by the additive expected regret theory of Loomes and Sugden (1982, 1987) and Bell (1982). Fishburn's SSA (skew-symmetric additive) theory is described in Section 8.6, followed by the additive SSB theory in Section 8.7. These are fully developed in the next chapter.

The final four sections discuss nonadditive theories, beginning with Schmeidler's linear theory in Section 8.8. Gilboa's regular-acts version of Schmeidler's theory is outlined in Section 8.9. We then conclude with sketches of the Luce–Narens model and the models in the final category.

8.4 ADDITIVE NONEXPECTED INTENSIVE UTILITY

The basic elements of Allais's approach to decision under uncertainty were described in Section 3.3 with the exception of his treatment of subjective probability. Allais (1979b, pp. 469–73) believes that so-called objective probability is most accurately modeled by the classical notion of equally likely cases operationalized by a reference urn with N identical balls (except say for a different number on each). Our intuition that the probability of drawing one of n designated balls is n/N is supported by long-run relative frequency of sampling with replacement. To assess your subjective probability of event $A \subseteq S$, vary n until you feel that the likelihood that A obtains is the same as the objective probability of drawing one of n designated balls from the urn. Corrections may ne needed to assure additivity, but if S is finite and N is large, the state probabilities can be assessed simultaneously (use all the balls) to assure additivity.

Once additive subjective probabilities are assessed, they are used as the probabilities for the distributions p, q, $\ldots$ by way of the reduction principle.We then have $p \succ q \Leftrightarrow V(p) > V(q)$, with

$$V(p) = \sum v(x)p(x) + \alpha(p^*),$$

where v denotes riskless intensive utility, p^* is the probability distribution induced by p on the differences $v(x) - \sum v(x)p(x)$, and α is a functional on such distributions.

A similar theory presented by Loomes and Sugden (1986) replaces $\alpha(p^*)$ by an expectation that involves a concept of disappointment/elation. For S finite let $\pi(s)$ denote the probability of state s and let $f(s)$ be the outcome for act f when s obtains, as in Savage's formulation. Then with $v(f)$ $= \sum \pi(s)v(f(s)) =$ the expected value of riskless intensive utility for f, Loomes and Sugden consider

$$V(f) = v(f) + \sum \pi(s)\beta[v(f(s)) - v(f)],$$

where β is a disappointment/elation functional on differences between outcome utilities and their mean $v(f)$. The basic intuition for β is that it has the same sign as its argument: If $v(f(s)) - v(f) > 0$, then one is elated by doing better than the mean, but if $v(f(s)) < v(f)$, then there is disappointment. I refer to their representation as an *additive expected disappointment* model, since it uses additive probability and an expectational form for V, that is, $V(f) = \sum \pi(s)\{v(f(s)) + \beta[v(f(s)) - v(f)]\}$. If β is linear in its argument with $\beta(d) = \lambda d$, then V reduces to the acts-formulation correspondent of Bernoullian expected utility. A somewhat different notion of disappointment is discussed by Bell (1985).

8.5 EXPECTED REGRET THEORY

Prior to their work on disappointment, Loomes and Sugden (1982) and Bell (1982) formulated models for preference comparisons between acts that incorporate a concept of regret/rejoicing. Their original papers focused on monetary outcomes, but this was generalized to arbitrary outcomes in Loomes and Sugden (1987).

The most general form of the *additive expected regret* representation can be written as

$$f > g \Leftrightarrow \int_S \phi(f(s), g(s)) \, d\pi(s) > 0,$$

where ϕ is a skew-symmetric functional on $X \times X$. As in the preceding section, utility is based on the Bernoullian riskless intensity notion. In the present case, this is coupled with an adjustment for regret/rejoicing that *jointly* involves f and g and is therefore quite different than the disappointment/elation notion. The concept of regret is designed to accommodate the experience of choosing f from $\{f, g\}$ and, when s obtains, of getting $f(s)$ rather than $g(s)$. If f is chosen and $f(s) > g(s)$, one might rejoice at one's good fortune, but one could experience regret if $g(s) > f(s)$. One explicit form for ϕ is

$$\phi(x, y) = v(x) - v(y) + \gamma[v(x) - v(y)],$$

where γ is a functional for which $\gamma(-d) = -\gamma(d)$, $\gamma(0) = 0$, and $\gamma(d) > 0$ if $d > 0$.

Given $>$ on F defined from the additive expected regret representation, it is easily seen that $>$ on F satisfies all of Savage's necessary axioms (i.e., P1–P4 of Section 7.4), except for P1. In particular, there can be preference cycles and the reduction principle does not generally hold. Thus, first-degree stochastic dominance can be violated when the reduction principle is used to obtain π_f and π_g separately for f and g. On the other hand, expected regret theory is fully consistent with Savage's sure-thing principle, P2 and P3, and with the substitution and the dominance principles near the end of Section 7.4.

Loomes and Sugden (1987) note that the additive expected regret representation reduces to the SSB representation of Section 3.9 and Chapter 4 for pairs of stochastically independent acts. For convenience assume that S is finite. We then say that f and g are *stochastically independent* if, for all $x, y \in X$,

$$\pi(\{s \in S : (f(s), g(s)) = (x, y)\}) = \pi_f(x)\pi_g(y).$$

When f and g are stochastically independent,

$$\int_S \phi(f(s), g(s)) \, d\pi(s) = \sum_x \sum_y \phi(x, y)\pi_f(x)\pi_g(y),$$

which is the expectational form of the SSB representation for distributions $p = \pi_f$ and $q = \pi_g$. As a consequence, the reduction principle does hold for pairs of stochastically independent acts, and first-degree stochastic dominance also holds for such acts. But both can fail otherwise. See Sections 2.2 and 2.5 for further remarks on independence versus interdependence.

8.6 SSA UTILITY THEORY

The second theory of category **III,** Fishburn's (1986e) skew-symmetric additive theory, has the same representation $f > g \Leftrightarrow \int \phi(f(s), g(s)) \, d\pi(s)$ > 0 as the additive expected regret theory but is interpreted very differently. The main difference is that utility is not based on the riskless intensity approach or on explicit regret/rejoicing but is derived from axioms for $>$ on F as in Savage's theory. Similarly, π is deduced from the axioms in precisely the same way that Savage obtains π, by way of Lemma 7.5 and Theorem 7.2.

Given π as in Theorem 7.2, ϕ on $X \times X$ is scaled through indifference comparisons of the form $xAw \sim yAz$. According to the SSA representation,

$$xAw \sim yAz \Rightarrow \pi(A)\phi(x, y) = [1 - \pi(A)]\phi(z, w).$$

Thus, if $x > y$ and $z > w$, we determine $A \subseteq S$ at which $xAw \sim yAz$ to specify the relationship between $\phi(x, y)$ and $\phi(z, w)$.

We make only one major change and two minor changes in Savage's six basic axioms to obtain the SSA representation for all simple acts in F. The major change weakens the ordering axiom P1 by not assuming transitivity except on subsets of F whose acts are confined to two outcomes. The first minor change is to add the conditional dominance principle as an explicit axiom (P2*) since it no longer follows from the weakened P1; see Lemma 7.4. The other minor change is to strengthen Savage's Archimedean axiom P6 to a form suitable for the SSA approach.

To specify these changes precisely, let F_{xy} denote the set of all $f \in F$ for which $f(s) \in \{x, y\}$ for all $s \in S$. Then, with the definitions as in Section 7.4, we have the following for all $f, g, f', g' \in F$, all $x, y \in X$, and all $A, B \subseteq S$:

P1*. $>$ *on F is asymmetric;* $>$ *on F_{xy} is a weak order.*
P2*. $(A \cap B = \varnothing, f \succsim_A g, f \succsim_B g) \Rightarrow f \succsim_{A \cup B} g; (A \cap B = \varnothing, f$ $>_A g, f \succsim_B g) \Rightarrow f >_{A \cup B} g.$
P6*. $f > g \Rightarrow$ [*given x, y, there is a finite partition of S such that, for every member E of the partition,* $(f' =_E x \text{ or } f' =_E f, g'$ $=_E y \text{ or } g' =_E g, f' =_{E^c} f, g' =_{E^c} g) \Rightarrow f' > g'$].

Section 9.2 proves that P1*, P2, P2*, P3, P4, P5, and P6* imply the SSA representation for all simple acts with π unique and ϕ unique up to multiplication by a positive constant. All but P6* are necessary for the representation, and we adhere to Savage's sure-thing principle and his approach to subjective probability, which entails the part of weak order retained by P1*. The only basic change from Savage is the deletion of transitivity throughout F and, as a consequence, the denial of the reduction principle. If *either* transitivity or reduction is restored, the SSA representation reduces to Savage's additive expected utility representation (Theorem 9.2). Comments on extension of the SSA representation to all acts appear in Section 9.3.

8.7 ADDITIVE SSB UTILITY

The additive SSB theory from Fishburn (1984b) and Fishburn and LaValle (1987a) bears the same relationship to the SSA theory that the additive linear theory of Section 7.6 bears to Savage's additive expected utility theory. In particular, it uses the lottery-acts approach with $F = P^S$ and replaces the SSA representation by

$$\mathbf{f} > \mathbf{g} \Leftrightarrow \int_S \phi(\mathbf{f}(s), \mathbf{g}(s)) \, d\pi(s) > 0,$$

where ϕ is an SSB functional on $P \times P$.

As might be expected by analogy with additive linear utility, the additive SSB theory applies C1, C2, and C3 (Section 4.1 or 3.6) to $>$ on F and then adds axioms that are necessary and sufficient for the existence of a unique additive probability measure π on $\mathcal{E} = 2^S$ for the representation. As before, the use of P allows S to be any nonempty set, and no special conditions apply to π apart from additivity.

Three axioms beyond C1–C3 are used for the simple lottery acts part of the additive SSB representation. They are described more fully in Section 9.4 and consist of a nontriviality axiom and two independence axioms. The first independence axiom says that $pAr > qAr \Leftrightarrow pBr > qBr$ for nonnull A, B $\subseteq S$. This essentially allows the derivation of probability coefficients for each finite partition of S. The other independence axiom is a specialized version of the Herstein–Milnor (1953) independence axiom B2 of Section 1.5 applied to $>$ on F. In conjunction with C1–C3, the second independence axiom implies the decomposition

$$\phi(\mathbf{f}, \mathbf{g}) = \sum_{i=1}^{n} \phi(\mathbf{f}A_i p, \mathbf{g}A_i p)$$

for any finite partition $\{A_1, \cdots, A_n\}$ of S and any fixed $p \in P$, where $\mathbf{f}Ap$ denotes the lottery act that equals $\mathbf{f}$ on A and is constant at p throughout A^c. Given the lottery-acts formulation, the axioms are necessary as well as sufficient for the simple lottery-acts version of the additive SSB representation, with one exception, namely that only the specializations of the axioms to simply lottery acts are needed. The complete axioms are necessary for the general representation, which also requires other assumptions as specified in Section 9.6. Just as the SSA representation of the preceding section reduces to Savage's additive expected utility representation when transitivity (P1) is restored, the additive SSB representation reduces to the additive linear representation if it is assumed that $>$ on $\mathbf{F}$ is a weak order, provided that $0 < \pi(A) < 1$ for some event A; see Theorem 9.6 near the end of Section 9.4. If π is degenerate, say $\pi(\{s\}) = 1$ for some $s \in S$, then the imposition of weak order only reduces it to the weighted linear representation of Section 3.6 and Chapter 5.

8.8 NONADDITIVE LINEAR UTILITY

The first broad generalization of additive expected–linear utility designed to accommodate failures of the substitution principle and Ellsberg's ambiguity problem through the use of nonadditive probability in an expectational representation was developed by David Schmeidler in the early 1980s. The theories in the preceding three sections satisfy substitution and do not resolve Ellsberg's problem, while Allais avoids the substitution principle with a nonexpectational representation and additive probability.

Schmeidler (1984) presents his theory in the lottery-acts formulation of Sections 7.1 and 7.6. Gilboa (1987) subsequently axiomatized Schmeidler's model in the Savage-acts format as described in the next section. Since their representations are based on Choquet's (1955) definition of expectation with respect to a monotonic but not necessarily additive probability measure σ on $\mathcal{E}$, we say a word about this first. We assume for simplicity that $\mathcal{E} = 2^S$. Additional discussions of Choquet integration with relationships to decision under uncertainty are provided by Schmeidler (1986) and Gilboa (1985a, b).

Given a functional w on S and a monotonic probability measure σ on $\mathcal{E}$, $\int w \, d\sigma$ is defined by

$$\int_S w(s) \, d\sigma(s) = \int_{c=0}^{\infty} \sigma(\{s \in S : w(s) \geqslant c\}) \, dc$$

$$- \int_{c=-\infty}^{0} [1 - \sigma(\{s \in S : w(s) \geqslant c\})] \, dc,$$

provided that the right side is not $\infty - \infty$, in which case $\int w \, d\sigma$ is undefined. The integrals on the right side are ordinary Riemann integrals with integrands ordered in the positive and negative domains so that they are monotonic (decreasing for $+$, increasing for $-$). When w is constant on each member of a finite partition $\{A_1, \cdots, A_n\}$ of S, say with

$$w(s) = c_i \quad \text{for all } s \in A_i \quad (i = 1, \ldots, n),$$

arranged so that $c_1 > c_2 > \cdots > c_n$, then evaluation of the defined integral yields

$$\int w \, d\sigma = \sum_{i=1}^{n-1} (c_i - c_{i+1}) \sigma \left(\bigcup_{j=1}^{i} A_j \right) + c_n.$$

Apart from the indexing of the w values, this is identical to the form for $V(p)$ used in the basic decumulative representation of Section 3.5 (Quiggin, 1982).

Schmeidler (1984) uses four axioms plus a nontriviality condition, including A1 and A3 for $\succ$ on **F** (or a subset thereof) and a weakening of the independence axiom A2. This weakening, which is the crucial step that allows failures of the substitution principle, uses the following definition of comonotonicity between lottery acts. We say that **f**, **g** $\in P^S$ are *comonotonic* if there do not exist s and t in S such that $\mathbf{f}(s) \succ \mathbf{f}(t)$ and $\mathbf{g}(t) \succ \mathbf{g}(s)$. In other words, $\mathbf{f}(s) \succeq \mathbf{f}(t)$ whenever $\mathbf{g}(s) \succ \mathbf{g}(t)$, and $\mathbf{g}(s) \succeq \mathbf{g}(t)$ whenever $\mathbf{f}(s) \succ \mathbf{f}(t)$. Comonotonicity is a very restrictive hypothesis. For example, under the lottery acts specialization to ordinary acts for Figures 8.1 and 8.4, **f** and **g** are *not* comonotonic in any of Figures 8.1, 8.2, and 8.4.

Schmeidler's axioms, applied to all **f**, **g**, **h** $\in$ **F** (or a subset thereof) and all $0 < \lambda < 1$, are:

A1. $\succ$ *is a weak order.*

A2*. (**f**, **g**, *and* **h** *are mutually comonotonic,* **f** $\succ$ **g**) $\Rightarrow$ $\lambda \mathbf{f} + (1 - \lambda)\mathbf{h} \succ \lambda \mathbf{g} + (1 - \lambda)\mathbf{h}$.

A3. **f** $\succ$ **g** $\succ$ **h** $\Rightarrow$ $\alpha \mathbf{f} + (1 - \alpha)\mathbf{h} \succ \mathbf{g}$ *and* **g** $\succ \beta \mathbf{f} + (1 - \beta)\mathbf{h}$ *for some* α *and* β *in* $(0, 1)$.

S1*. **f**' $\succ$ **g**' *for some* **f**', **g**'.

S2*. (**f**(s) $\succeq$ **g**(s) *for all* $s \in S$) $\Rightarrow$ **f** $\succeq$ **g**.

The nontriviality axiom is obviously S1* (cf. S1 in Theorem 7.5), and S2* is the monotone dominance principle for lottery acts.

THEOREM 8.1. *Suppose* A1, A2*, A3, S1*, *and* S2* *hold on the set of simple lottery acts. Then there is a unique monotonic probability measure* σ *on* $\mathcal{E}$ *and a linear functional* u *on* P, *unique up to positive linear transformations, such that, for all simple lottery acts* **f** *and* **g**,

$$\mathbf{f} \succ \mathbf{g} \Leftrightarrow \int_S u(\mathbf{f}(s)) \, d\sigma(s) > \int_S u(\mathbf{g}(s)) \, d\sigma(s).$$

Schmeidler also notes that the conclusion of the theorem implies its five axioms. Its proof in Schmeidler (1984) begins with the fact that A1, A2*, and A3 imply A1, A2, and A3 on P, considered as the set of constant lottery acts. This gives u on P by way of Theorem 1.3. The remainder of the proof is then devoted to establishing the existence of σ as asserted. A result from Schmeidler (1986) is used in this part of his proof.

The extension of his nonadditive linear utility representation to nonsimple acts is examined by Schmeidler (1984, 1986). Call $f \in F$ *bounded* if there are $p, q \in P$ such that $p \succeq f(s) \succeq q$ for all $s \in S$. He then proves the following.

THEOREM 8.2. *If $\succ$ on the set of simple lottery acts satisfies A1, A2*, A3, and S2*, then it has a unique extension to the set of bounded lottery acts that satisfies the same axioms on those acts. Moreover, if the extended $\succ$ is not empty, then there are σ and u as in Theorem 8.1 such that $f \succ g \Leftrightarrow \int u(f(s)) \, d\sigma(s) > \int u(g(s)) \, d\sigma(s)$ for all bounded lottery acts.*

Additional results for the representations of Schmeidler and Gilboa are developed by Wakker (1986).

8.9 NONADDITIVE EXPECTED UTILITY

The Savage-acts correspondent of Schmeidler's representation is the *nonadditive expected utility representation*

$$f \succ g \Leftrightarrow \int_S u(f(s)) \, d\sigma(s) > \int_S u(g(s)) \, d\sigma(s),$$

where u is a functional on X and σ is a monotonic probability measure on $\mathcal{E} = 2^S$. Gilboa (1987) axiomatizes this representation in Savage's fashion for $F = X^S$ and notes carefully just how he is changing P1–P7 for the more general model.

Unlike the SSA situation of Section 8.6 which requires only a few changes in Savage's axioms, at least for simple acts, Gilboa retains only P1 in its original form. Because of his extensive changes, I shall note only those that involve P2–P4; see Gilboa's paper for his modifications of P5–P7. To avoid confusion with Section 8.6, double asterisks will be used for Gilboa's changes even though this work preceded and motivated Fishburn (1986e).

Comonotonicity between acts is defined by analogy to Schmeidler's definition. For convenience, extend the notation xAy to xAf as the act f' for which $f' =_A x$ and $f' =_{A^c} f$. Gilboa replaces $\{P2, P3, P4\}$ by two axioms, applied to all $f, g, f', g' \in F$, all $x, y, z, w \in X$, and all $A, B \subseteq S$:

P2**. *If xAf, yAf, zAg, and wAg are mutually comonotonic; if xBf', yBf', zBg' and wBg' are mutually comonotonic; and if $x \succ y, z \succ w, xAf \succeq xBf', yAf \sim yBf'$, and $wAg \sim wBg'$, then $zAg \succeq zBg'$.*
P3**. *$x \succ y \Rightarrow xAf \succeq yAf$.*

The latter axiom is an appealing weakening of Savage's P3. The former, P2**, is Gilboa's replacement for the P2 part of the sure-thing principle, designed to avoid implication of the substitution principle. It also embodies aspects of P4 with its pairs of outcomes and two events, and implies P4 in the presence of P1. Unfortunately, P2** has little direct intuitive appeal. Gilboa notes that if the comonotonicity hypotheses of P2** are removed, then it essentially says that an improvement from y to x $(x > y)$ that swings the indifference $yAf \sim yBf'$ in A's favor, to $xAf \succsim xBf'$, cannot be reversed by a similar change from w to z when $z > w$; that is, we cannot also then have $wAg \sim wBg'$ and $zBg' > wAg$. However, this unrestricted form is too strong for the nonadditive expected utility representation. When the comonotonicity restrictions are added, the resultant P2** becomes necessary for the representation.

Gilboa (1987) proves that P1, P2**, P3** and his replacements for P5–P7 hold if and only if there is a monotonic probability measure σ on $\mathcal{E}$ and a bounded functional u on X that satisfy the nonadditive expected utility representation for all $f, g \in F$ along with, for all $A \subseteq B$ and all $0 < \lambda < 1$,

$$\sigma(C) = \lambda\sigma(A) + (1 - \lambda)\sigma(B) \qquad \text{for some } A \subseteq C \subseteq B,$$

and for which σ is unique and u is unique up to positive linear transformations. Unlike the proofs developed elsewhere for related representations (Savage, 1954; Anscombe and Aumann, 1963; Schmeidler, 1984; Fishburn, 1984b, 1986e), Gilboa's cannot draw directly on the von Neumann–Morgenstern linear utility theorem or Savage's additive probability measure and therefore requires a new approach.

In a sequel, Gilboa (1985a) makes a case for the complementary additivity condition

$$\sigma(A) + \sigma(A^c) = 1 \qquad \text{for all } A \subseteq S,$$

for Schmeidler's representation and his own, neither of which presumes this condition. Part of his case deals with technical aspects of Choquet integration. For example, within the context of his representation, it may seem reasonable to require that maximization with the form $\int u \, d\sigma$ should be equivalent to minimization with the form $\int (-u) \, d\sigma$, but this turns out to be true in general if and only if σ satisfies complementary additivity. He also develops a condition for $>$ on F that is tantamount to complementary additivity within the setting of his other axioms, and later suggests that a consistent theory for conditional probability arises only when σ is fully additive.

8.10 NONADDITIVE BIEXPECTED UTILITY

Luce and Narens (1985) develop a model for decision under uncertainty that illustrates how their analysis of concatenation structures in measurement theory might be applied to the decision area. Because their formulation differs somewhat from those of Chapter 7 and the other generalizations of the present chapter, I shall first give a paraphrased version of their theory in Savage's setting and then explain their approach.

As usual, let xAy denote the act with outcome x if A obtains and outcome y otherwise, and let $\mathfrak{F}_0 = X \times \mathcal{E} \times X$, the set of all such acts. We then say that $(\mathfrak{F}_0, \succ)$ has a *nonadditive biexpected utility representation* if there is a functional u on $\mathfrak{F}_0$, with $u(x)$ defined as $u(xSx)$, and monotonic probability measures σ^+ and σ^- on $\mathcal{E}$ such that, for all $xAy, zBw \in \mathfrak{F}_0$,

$$xAy \succ zBw \Leftrightarrow u(xAy) > u(zBw)$$

and

$$u(xAy) = u(x)\sigma^+(A) + u(y)[1 - \sigma^+(A)] \qquad \text{if } x \succ y,$$
$$= u(x) \qquad\qquad\qquad\qquad\qquad\quad \text{if } x \sim y,$$
$$= u(x)\sigma^-(A) + u(y)[1 - \sigma^-(A)] \qquad \text{if } y \succ x.$$

The novel feature of this representation is its use of two monotonic measures whose applications depend on preference between the outcomes as well as on $\mathcal{E}$. It reduces to a special case of Gilboa's representation with $\sigma^+ = \sigma^-$ if and only if the complementarity condition $xAy \sim yA^cx$ holds throughout $\mathfrak{F}_0$. My designation "nonadditive biexpected utility" attempts to maintain consistency with the general terminology of this chapter and Chapter 7. Necessary axioms for the representation include weak order, $(A \subseteq B, x \succ y) \Rightarrow xBy \succsim xAy$, $(A \subseteq B, y \succ x) \Rightarrow xAy \succsim xBy$, $(x \succ z, y \succ w) \Rightarrow xAy \succ zAw$, and $(x \succ y, z \succ w, xAy \succ xBy) \Rightarrow zAw \succ zBw$.

The approach of Luce and Narens applies $\succ$ to a set $\mathfrak{F}$ that is built up recursively from elements in $X \times \mathcal{E}_0 \times X$, where $\mathcal{E}_0$ is a family of events that is not generally assumed to be a Boolean algebra and, as a technical convenience, omits $\varnothing$ and S. I shall denote elements in $\mathfrak{F}$ as $\mathbf{x}A\mathbf{y}$, where $\mathbf{x}$ and $\mathbf{y}$ are outcomes in X, or simple acts of the form $\mathbf{x} = zBw$, or more complex entities obtained recursively from $X \times \mathcal{E}_0 \times X$. In an expression like $(zBw)Ay$, A and B are interpreted as statistically independent; the gamble based on A is carried out first and then, if A obtains, the zBw gamble is carried out. A similar interpretation applies to the two instances of A in $xA(zAy)$. Although this is awkward for the states setting, it fits nicely with the measurement theory in their paper.

Luce and Narens refer to their basic utility representation for $(\mathfrak{F}, \succ)$ as the *dual bilinear utility representation*. It consists of a functional u on $\mathfrak{F}$ and functionals σ^+ and σ^- from $\mathcal{E}_0$ into $(0, 1)$ such that, for all $\mathbf{x}A\mathbf{y}, \mathbf{z}B\mathbf{w} \in \mathfrak{F}$,

$$\mathbf{x}A\mathbf{y} \succ \mathbf{z}B\mathbf{w} \Leftrightarrow u(\mathbf{x}A\mathbf{y}) > u(\mathbf{z}B\mathbf{w})$$

and

$$u(\mathbf{x}A\mathbf{y}) = u(\mathbf{x})\sigma^+(A) + u(\mathbf{y})[1 - \sigma^+(A)] \qquad \text{if } \mathbf{x} > \mathbf{y},$$
$$= u(\mathbf{x}) \qquad\qquad\qquad\qquad \text{if } \mathbf{x} \sim \mathbf{y},$$
$$= u(\mathbf{x})\sigma^-(A) + u(\mathbf{y})[1 - \sigma^-(A)] \qquad \text{if } \mathbf{y} > \mathbf{x}.$$

This representation is approached from a scale-theoretic viewpoint in Luce and Narens (1985, p. 59), and its preference axioms are discussed by Luce (1984).

The dual bilinear utility representation does not presume that σ^+ and σ^- are monotonic, but this is readily supplied by assuming $\mathbf{x} \succeq \mathbf{y} \Leftrightarrow \mathbf{x}A\mathbf{y} \succeq \mathbf{x}B\mathbf{y}$ whenever $B \subseteq A$. Separately, their representation satisfies complementary symmetry in the form $\sigma^+(A) + \sigma^-(A^c) = 1$ if and only if $\mathbf{x}A\mathbf{y} \sim \mathbf{y}A^c\mathbf{x}$, provided that $\mathcal{E}_0$ is closed under complementation. These and other specializations are discussed in some detail by Luce and Narens.

I have glossed over a few of the finer points in their paper and urge interested readers to consult the original. Of special interest is their discussion of accommodation of the Allais and Ellsberg phenomena and their demonstration that the prospect theory model of Kahneman and Tversky (1979) is a special case of the dual bilinear model under a suitable translation of the Kahneman–Tversky structure into their own format.

8.11   NONADDITIVE, NONTRANSITIVE THEORIES

We conclude our review of generalizations of additive expected utility by commenting on three representations that accommodate Ellsberg's ambiguity problem partly through nonadditive subjective probability without assuming that preferences are transitive.

The first theory, the basic SSB theory of category **VIII**, applies the SSB axioms C1, C2, and C3 to $>$ on **F**, as in the initial part of the axiomatization for the additive SSB theory outlined in Section 8.7. It uses no other axioms and does not yield an unambiguous monotonic probability measure. However, its representation, which is described in Theorem 9.4, involves a partial decomposition over states.

Our second theory provides a preference-based axiomatization of the conditionally additive skew-symmetric functional ρ on $\mathcal{E} \times \mathcal{E}$ described in Section 8.2. The axiomatization is based on only two outcomes, x and y with $x > y$, takes $\mathcal{E}$ as a Boolean algebra of subsets of S, and applies $>$ to the set **G** of modified simple lottery acts defined by

$$\mathbf{G} = \{\mathbf{f} : \mathcal{E} \to [0, 1] : \mathbf{f}(A) > 0 \text{ for no more than a}$$
$$\text{finite number of } A \in \mathcal{E}, \sum \mathbf{f}(A) = 1\}.$$

Thus each $\mathbf{f}$ assigns a "probability" $\mathbf{f}(A)$ to every event A in $\mathcal{E}$. We interpret $\mathbf{f}$ as an option that yields the preferred outcome x with probability

$$\sum_{\{A \in \mathcal{E}: s \in A\}} \mathbf{f}(A) \qquad \text{when state } s \text{ obtains,}$$

and yields y with complementary probability $1 - \Sigma\ \{\mathbf{f}(A):s \in A\}$ when s obtains. The probabilities used in the definition of $\mathbf{G}$ are viewed as extraneous scaling probabilities, and it is easily seen that each $\mathbf{f} \in \mathbf{G}$ corresponds to a simple lottery act as that term has been used previously. Moreover, $\mathbf{G}$ is a convex set.

For convenience, let $\mathbf{f}_A$ denote the element in $\mathbf{G}$ that assigns probability 1 to event $A \in \mathcal{E}$. Then, in the manner of Savage, we define $\succ_*$ on $\mathcal{E}$ by

$$A \succ_* B \qquad \text{if } \mathbf{f}_A \succ \mathbf{f}_B.$$

In terms of prior notation $\mathbf{f}_A = xAy$ and $\mathbf{f}_B = xBy$. The axioms for $(\mathbf{G}, \succ)$ consist of the SSB axioms C1–C3 along with the following for all $A, B \in \mathcal{E}$ and all $\mathbf{f}, \mathbf{g} \in \mathbf{G}$:

H1. $\mathbf{f}_S \succ \mathbf{f}_\varnothing$.
H2. $A \supseteq B \Rightarrow \mathbf{f}_A \succsim \mathbf{f}_B$.
H3. $(\Sigma\ \{\mathbf{f}(C):s \in C\} = \Sigma\ \{\mathbf{g}(C): s \in C\} \text{ for all } s \in S) \Rightarrow \mathbf{f} \sim \mathbf{g}$.

The first two of these are obvious nontriviality and monotonicity conditions. H3 says that if $\mathbf{f}$ and $\mathbf{g}$ have the same probability of yielding the preferred outcome in every possible state then $\mathbf{f} \sim \mathbf{g}$.

Fishburn (1983c) proves that C1–C3 and H1–H3 hold for $(\mathbf{G}, \succ)$ if and only if there is a unique SSB functional ρ on $\mathbf{G} \times \mathbf{G}$ such that, for all $\mathbf{f}, \mathbf{g} \in \mathbf{G}$,

$$\mathbf{f} \succ \mathbf{g} \Leftrightarrow \rho(\mathbf{f}, \mathbf{g}) > 0,$$

and such that ρ on $\mathcal{E} \times \mathcal{E}$, defined by $\rho(A, B) = \rho(\mathbf{f}_A, \mathbf{f}_B)$, is monotonic, conditionally additive, and has $\rho(S, \varnothing) = 1$. By the preceding definition of $\succ_*$, $A \succ_* B \Leftrightarrow \rho(A, B) > 0$.

There seem to be two main problems with the conditionally additive theory. The first concerns C2. To illustrate, suppose an urn contains 100 black (B) and red (R) balls in an unknown mixture. Let $\mathbf{f} = \frac{1}{2}\mathbf{f}_\varnothing + \frac{1}{2}\mathbf{f}_S$, so $\mathbf{f}$ yields x with probability $\frac{1}{2}$ regardless of which ball is drawn. Ellsberg's analysis suggests that many people will have $\mathbf{f} \succ \mathbf{f}_B$ and $\mathbf{f} \succ \mathbf{f}_R$. Then C2 requires $\mathbf{f} \succ \frac{1}{2}\mathbf{f}_B + \frac{1}{2}\mathbf{f}_R$. But, by H3, $\mathbf{f} \sim \frac{1}{2}\mathbf{f}_B + \frac{1}{2}\mathbf{f}_R$ since the mixture yields x with probability $\frac{1}{2}$ regardless of which ball is drawn. Hence there are limits on the extent to which this approach accommodates ambiguity aversion.

The second problem concerns the extension of the theory to a general outcome set X. I have been unable to devise a natural extension that avoids the implication that subjective probability is additive as in the additive SSB utility theory of Sections 8.7 and 9.4. Again I suspect that the problem lies in unrestricted application of the convexity axiom C2.

The third representation designed to accommodate ambiguity, failures of the substitution principle, and intransitivities was developed in the lottery-acts setting (Fishburn, 1986d) but can also be expressed with Savage acts for category **VII**. In the latter setting with $F = X^S$ and S finite, the model is

$$f > g \Leftrightarrow V(f, g) > 0$$

with

$$V(f, g) = \sum_s \pi(s)\phi(f(s), g(s))$$

$$- \sum_{s \in S} \sum_{t \in S} \pi(s)\tau(t)[|\phi(f(s), f(t))| - |\phi(g(s), g(t))|],$$

where each $\pi(s) \geqslant 0$, $\Sigma \pi(s) = 1$, $\tau(s) \in \mathbf{R}$, and ϕ is a skew-symmetric functional on $X \times X$, or on $P \times P$ (with bilinearity) in the lottery-acts case. If $\tau \equiv 0$, this reduces to the SSA representation for regular acts and to the additive SSB representation for lottery acts.

In the general case the $\pi(s)$ behave exactly like additive subjective probabilities but are confounded by the other state function τ, which is designed to accommodate ambiguity. When $>_*$ is defined by $A >_* B$ if $xAy > xBy$ whenever $x > y$, it is easily seen that the model implies $S >_* \emptyset$, $>_*$ is a weak order on $\mathcal{E} = 2^S$, and, for all $A, B \in \mathcal{E}$,

$$A >_* B \Leftrightarrow \sigma(A) > \sigma(B),$$

where

$$\sigma(A) = \pi(A) - \pi(A)\tau(A^c) - \pi(A^c)\tau(A)$$

as in the penultimate paragraph of Section 8.2. As indicated there, $>_*$ is not naturally monotonic, but this can be assumed if desired.

Although neither the regular nor lottery-acts version of the V representation has been axiomatized, a few necessary conditions are noted in Fishburn (1986d) for the lottery-acts version. These include C1–C3 on the set of constant lottery acts (where the term in τ vanishes) and the correspondent of Savage's P4. Moreover, the representation has appealing uniqueness properties in this case, with ϕ unique up to multiplication by a positive constant, unique π, and, except for a few special cases, unique τ.

The representation also has some undesirable implications from a normative perspective unless its functions are constrained in certain ways. In connection with the potential nonmonotonicity of $>_*$, the model does not naturally imply that $pAq \gtrsim pBq$ whenever $A \supseteq B$ and $p > q$. In addition, because of the way it deals with ambiguity through within-act variability, it is possible to violate the simple dominance principle or the monotone dominance principle of Section 7.4.

FIGURE 8.5   Expected utility theories with states

	REGULAR ACTS	LOTTERY ACTS
ADDITIVE, TRANSITIVE	SAVAGE (1954)	ANSCOMBE AND AUMANN (1963)
NONADDITIVE, TRANSITIVE	GILBOA (1987)	SCHMEIDLER (1984)
ADDITIVE, NONTRANSITIVE	FISHBURN (1986e)	FISHBURN (1984b)
NONADDITIVE, NONTRANSITIVE	?	FISHBURN (1983c, 1984b)

Finally, I note that if ϕ in the lottery-acts case is decomposable in the linear utility manner as $\phi(p, q) = u(p) - u(q)$, then it can be shown that the representation reduces to a special case of Schmeidler's (1984) model of Section 8.8, provided that $(A \supseteq B, p > q) \Rightarrow pAq \succsim pBq$ is assumed.

8.12 SUMMARY

Generalizations of the additive expected or linear utility theories of Savage, Anscombe and Aumann, and others can be conveniently classified according to whether they use additive subjective probability, whether they assume transitivity, and whether they are based on regular Savage acts or lottery acts. A few generalizations adopt the Bernoulli–Allais riskless intensity approach for utility measurement, but most derive utilities from simple preference comparisons between acts or lottery acts.

The three main additive representations developed to date are Allais's transitive nonexpected form, the skew-symmetric expectational form for regular acts in the regret theories of Bell and Loomes–Sugden and the SSA theory of Fishburn, and the additive SSB representation for the lottery-acts formulation. The latter theories do not assume that preferences are transitive.

The primary nonadditive representations that have been satisfactorily axiomatized thus far are Schmeidler's nonadditive linear representation for lottery acts and Gilboa's corresponding nonadditive, expected utility representation for regular acts. Both assume transitivity and can account for Ellsberg's ambiguity phenomenon. Figure 8.5 identifies initial contributions for theories that have been more or less satisfactorily axiomatized in the simple preference comparisons style of von Neumann–Morgenstern and Savage.

9 Additive Nontransitive Nonlinear Utility

As noted in the preceding chapter, Savage's additive expected utility theory and the corresponding additive linear utility theory have been generalized to avoid transitivity and the reduction principle while retaining additive subjective probability. This chapter proves that the resultant SSA (skew-symmetric additive) and additive SSB representations follow from the axioms of Chapter 7 with various modifications appropriate to these more general representations. It also shows how the new representations reduce to their correspondents in Chapter 7 when transitivity is restored.

9.1 SKEW-SYMMETRIC ADDITIVE UTILITY

This chapter examines in detail the SSA (skew-symmetric additive) representation

$$f > g \Leftrightarrow \int_S \phi(f(s), g(s))\, d\pi(s) > 0$$

that generalizes Savage's additive expected utility representation of Section 7.4, and the additive SSB representation

$$\mathbf{f} > \mathbf{g} \Leftrightarrow \int_S \phi(\mathbf{f}(s), \mathbf{g}(s))\, d\pi(s) > 0$$

that generalizes the additive linear representation of Section 7.6. This section and the next two focus on the SSA theory; the rest of the chapter considers extensions of the SSB theory of Chapter 4 to the states setting.

The definitions and notation of Chapter 7 apply throughout the present chapter unless noted otherwise. In particular, we take $F = X^S$, $\mathbf{F} = P^S$, and $\mathcal{E} = 2^S$, with P the set of all simple probability distributions on X. Also, $F_{xy} = \{f \in F{:}f(S) \subseteq \{x, y\}\}$, the set of all acts whose outcomes are confined to $\{x, y\}$, xAy is the act that yields x if A obtains ($f =_A x$) and y if A does not obtain ($f =_{A^c} y$), and $A >_* B$ if $xAy > xBy$ for all $x, y \in X$ for which $x > y$.

For convenience we recall the basic SSA axioms, which apply to all f, g, f', $g' \in F$, all x, y, x', $y' \in X$, and all A, $B \subseteq S$:

P1*. $>$ on F is asymmetric; $>$ on F_{xy} is a weak order.

P2. $(f =_A f', g =_A g', f =_{A^c} g, f' =_{A^c} g') \Rightarrow (f > g \leftrightarrow f' > g')$.

P2*. $(A \cap B = \varnothing, f \succsim_A g, f \succsim_B g) \Rightarrow f \succsim_{A \cup B} g$; $(A \cap B = \varnothing, f \succ_A g, f \succsim_B g) \Rightarrow f \succ_{A \cup B} g$.

P3. $(A \notin \mathfrak{N}, f =_A x, g =_A y) \Rightarrow (f \succ_A g \leftrightarrow x > y)$.

P4. $(x > y, x' > y') \Rightarrow (xAy > xBy \leftrightarrow x'Ay' > x'By')$.

P5. $z > w$ for some z, $w \in X$.

P6*. $f > g \Rightarrow$ [given x, y, there is a finite partition of S such that, for every member E of the partition, $(f' =_E x$ or $f' =_E f, g' =_E y$ or $g' =_E g, f' =_{E^c} f, g' =_{E^c} g) \Rightarrow f' > g'$].

It is easily seen that all axioms except the Archimedean condition P6* are necessary for the SSA representation. Our basic SSA theorem shows that these axioms are sufficient for the representation confined to simple acts.

THEOREM 9.1. *Suppose* P1*, P2, P2*, P3, P4, P5, *and* P6* *hold for* $>$ *on* $F = X^S$ *with* $\succ_*$ *on* $\mathcal{E} = 2^S$ *as defined above. Then* $(\mathcal{E}, \succ_*)$ *has a unique additive representation with the properties of its agreeing probability measure* π *as specified in Theorem 7.2 along with, for all A* $\in \mathcal{E}, A \in \mathfrak{N} \leftrightarrow \pi(A) = 0$; *and there is a skew-symmetric functional* ϕ *on* $X \times X$ *such that, for all simple f, g* $\in F, f > g \leftrightarrow \int_S \phi(f(s), g(s)) d\pi(s) > 0$. *Moreover,* ϕ *is unique up to similarity transformations.*

The proof of the theorem, which begins with Theorem 7.2 and Lemma 7.5, is completed in the next section. Section 9.3 then discusses the extension of the SSA form to nonsimple acts in F. We note there that Savage's P7 is unsuitable for the extension and suggest other axioms that are presumed by the extension, including the monotone dominance principle, but do not provide a complete resolution of the extension problem.

We conclude the present section with the observation that full transitivity (P1), which obviously reduces the SSA representation for simple acts to Savage's additive expected utility representation, is tantamount to the identity reduction principle of Sections 7.4 and 8.1.

THEOREM 9.2. *Given the representation of Theorem* 9.1, P1 *holds for* $>$ *on the set of simple acts in F if and only if the identity reduction principle* $(\pi_f = \pi_g \Rightarrow f \sim g)$ *holds.*

Proof. It suffices to consider only simple acts. If the representation of Theorem 9.1 holds along with P1, we obtain Savage's representation, which implies the identity reduction principle; see Section 7.5 for comments. Conversely, if the representation of Theorem 9.1 holds in conjunction with the identity reduction principle, then with $\{A, B, C\}$ a three-part uniform partition of S as follows from the final conclusion of Theorem 7.2, we get $f \sim g$ when $(f =_A x, f =_B y, f =_C z)$ and $(g =_A y, g =_B z, g =_C x)$, and therefore $\phi(x, y)/3 + \phi(y, z)/3 + \phi(z, x)/3 = 0$, or

$$\phi(x, y) + \phi(y, z) + \phi(z, x) = 0$$

for all $x, y, z \in X$. Fix $x_0 \in X$ and define u on X by $u(x) = \phi(x, x_0)$. Then, by the preceding equation and skew-symmetry, take $z = x_0$ to get

$$\phi(x, y) = u(x) - u(y).$$

Substitution of this in the SSA representation gives Savage's representation, so P1 holds. ∎

9.2 SSA UTILITY PROOF

The following easy consequences of P1*, P2 and the definitions preceding Savage's axioms in Section 7.4 will be used without special mention throughout this section:

$(f > g, f =_{Ac} g) \Rightarrow f >_A g.$
$(f \sim g, f =_{Ac} g) \Rightarrow f \sim_A g.$
$(f \gtrsim g, f =_{Ac} g) \Rightarrow f \gtrsim_A g.$
$A \in \mathfrak{N} \Leftrightarrow (f' \sim_A g' \text{ for all } f', g' \in F).$
$>_A$ is asymmetric.
$\sim_A$ is symmetric and reflexive.
$f \sim_A g \Leftrightarrow [\text{not } (f >_A g) \text{ and not } (g >_A f)].$
$f \gtrsim_A g \Leftrightarrow (f \sim_A g \text{ or } f >_A g).$

We assume henceforth in this section that the hypotheses of Theorem 9.1 hold. Lemma 7.5 and the paragraph following its proof give π for Theorem 9.1, so we focus henceforth on the construction of skew-symmetric ϕ on $X \times X$ that satisfies the SSA representation for all simple acts in F. All acts used henceforth in this section are presumed to be simple.

Our construction of ϕ is based directly on the fact that if the SSA representation holds, then

$$xAw \sim yAz \Rightarrow \pi(A)\phi(x, y) = \pi(A^c)\phi(z, w).$$

To prepare for our subsequent definition of ϕ and the SSA representation verification, we first prove a series of lemmas. The crucial ones are Lemmas 9.7 and 9.9.

LEMMA 9.1. *$(f(s) \gtrsim g(s)$ for all $s \in S) \Rightarrow f \gtrsim g$. If, in addition, $\{s:f(s) > g(s)\} \notin \mathfrak{N}$, then $f > g$.*

Remark. This is similar to the monotone dominance principle. As noted earlier, it applies here only to *simple* acts.

Proof. Partition S into events on which $(f(s), g(s))$ is constant. Then P3, the definition of $\mathfrak{N}$, and a series of applications of P2* give the desired conclusions. ∎

LEMMA 9.2. $(A \sim_* B, A \cap B = \varnothing, f =_A x, f =_B y, g =_A y, g =_B x)$ $\Rightarrow f \sim_{A \cup B} g$.

Proof. If $x > y$ or $y > x$, the conclusion follows from the definitions. If $x \sim y$, use Lemma 9.1. ∎

LEMMA 9.3. $(A \sim_* C, B \sim_* D; A, B, C,$ *and* D *are mutually disjoint;* $f =_A x, f =_B w, g =_A y, g =_B z; f' =_C x, f' =_D w, g' =_C y, g' =_D z) \Rightarrow$ $(f >_{A \cup B} g \Leftrightarrow f' >_{C \cup D} g')$.

Proof. Given the hypotheses, define simple h, k in part by

$$h =_A x, \quad h =_B w, \quad h =_C y, \quad h =_D z,$$

$$k =_A y, \quad k =_B z, \quad k =_C x, \quad k =_D w.$$

By Lemma 9.2, $h \sim_{A \cup C} k$ and $h \sim_{B \cup D} k$. Hence P2* implies $h \sim_{A \cup B \cup C \cup D} k$. Again by P2*, $h >_{A \cup B} k \Leftrightarrow k >_{C \cup D} h$, which is the desired conclusion of the lemma. ∎

For the next lemma and later define

$$\Lambda_0 = \{k/2^n : n = 1, 2, \ldots ; k = 1, \ldots, 2^n\}.$$

LEMMA 9.4. $(A \cap B = \varnothing, C \subseteq A, D \subseteq B; \lambda \in \Lambda_0, \pi(C) = \lambda \pi(A),$ $\pi(D) = \lambda \pi(B); f =_A x, f =_B w, g =_A y, g =_B z) \Rightarrow (f >_{A \cup B} g \Leftrightarrow f >_{C \cup D} g)$.

Proof. If $\lambda = \frac{1}{2}$, then by Lemma 9.3 and P2*, $f >_{C \cup D} g \Leftrightarrow f >_{(A \setminus C) \cup (B \setminus D)} g \Leftrightarrow f >_{A \cup B} g$. Successive bisections of C and D, and so forth, using the final property for π in Theorem 7.2, lead to the conclusion whenever $\lambda \in \{\frac{1}{2}, \frac{1}{4}, \frac{1}{8}, \ldots\}$. The same conclusion for every $\lambda \in \Lambda_0$ then follows from the second implication in the first paragraph of this section and successive applications of P2*. ∎

Our next lemma, which extends Lemma 9.3, gives a key property of preference invariance under equally likely events.

LEMMA 9.5. $(A \sim_* C, B \sim_* D, A \cap B = C \cap D = \varnothing; f =_A x, f =_B w, g =_A y, g =_B z; f' =_C x, f' =_D w, g' =_C y, g' =_D z) \Rightarrow (f >_{A \cup B} g \Leftrightarrow f' >_{C \cup D} g')$.

Proof. According to Lemma 9.4, it suffices to prove Lemma 9.5 under the assumption that $\pi(A) + \pi(B) \leq \frac{1}{3}$, since otherwise $A, B, C,$ and D in the present case can be 'reduced' by the same factor under successive bisection. Given $\pi(A) + \pi(B) \leq \frac{1}{3}$, hence $\pi(C) + \pi(D) \leq \frac{1}{3}$, let $E = (A \cup B \cup C \cup D)^c$ so that $\pi(E) \geq \frac{1}{3}$. Choose $E_1, E_2 \subseteq E$ with $E_1 \cap E_2 = \varnothing$ so that

$\pi(E_1) = \pi(A) = \pi(C)$ and $\pi(E_2) = \pi(B) = \pi(D)$. Then, by Lemma 9.3 with $h =_{E_1} x$, $h =_{E_2} w$, $k =_{E_1} y$, $k =_{E_2} z$, we have

$$f \succ_{A \cup B} g \Leftrightarrow h \succ_{E_1 \cup E_2} k,$$
$$f' \succ_{C \cup D} g' \Leftrightarrow h \succ_{E_1 \cup E_2} k,$$

and therefore $f \succ_{A \cup B} g \Leftrightarrow f' \succ_{C \cup D} g'$. ∎

LEMMA 9.6. $(x \succ y, z \succ w, A \cap B = \varnothing, B \notin \mathfrak{N}, xAw \succsim yAz) \Rightarrow$ $x(A \cup B)w \succ y(A \cup B)z$.

Proof. Let $C = (A \cup B)^c$, $f = xAw$, and $g = yAz$. Assume $f \succsim g$ as in the hypotheses. If $g \succsim_{A \cup C} f$, then, since $g \succ_B f$ (by $z \succ w$, $B \notin \mathfrak{N}$, and P3), P2* implies $g \succ f$, a contradiction. Hence $f \succ_{A \cup C} g$. Let $f' =_{A \cup C} f$, g' $=_{A \cup C} g$, $f' =_B x$, and $g' =_B y$ so that $f' = x(A \cup B)w$ and $g' = y(A \cup B)z$. Since $f' \succ_{A \cup C} g'$ by $f \succ_{A \cup C} g$, and $f' \succ_B g'$ by $x \succ y$ and P3, P2* implies $f' \succ g'$. ∎

LEMMA 9.7. *If* $x \succ y$ *and* $z \succ w$, *then there is a unique* $\lambda \in (0, 1)$ *such that, for all* $A \in \mathcal{E}$,

$$\pi(A) > \lambda \Leftrightarrow xAw \succ yAz,$$

$$\pi(A) = \lambda \Leftrightarrow xAw \sim yAz,$$

$$\pi(A) < \lambda \Leftrightarrow yAz \succ xAw.$$

Proof. Assume $x \succ y$ and $z \succ w$. Consider xAw and yAz. By Lemma 9.5, preference between xAw and yAz depends only on $\pi(A)$ and not on A's specific identity. Hence, when $\pi(A) = \alpha$, we write $x\alpha w$ and $y\alpha z$ in place of xAw and yAz, respectively. By Lemma 9.6, $(\mu > \lambda, x\lambda w \succ y\lambda z) \Rightarrow x\mu w \succ y\mu z$, and $(\mu < \lambda, y\lambda z \succ x\lambda w) \Rightarrow y\mu z \succ x\mu w$. Moreover, $x1w \succ y1z$ and $y0z \succ x0w$. According to P6* with outcome pair (w, z) when $(f, g) = (x, y)$, and outcome pair (y, x) when $(f, g) = (z, w)$, we get $x\lambda w \succ y\lambda z$ for some $\lambda < 1$, and $y\lambda z \succ x\lambda w$ for some $\lambda > 0$. It follows that there is a unique $\lambda' \in (0, 1)$ such that

$$\lambda > \lambda' \Rightarrow x\lambda w \succ y\lambda z,$$

$$\lambda < \lambda' \Rightarrow y\lambda z \succ x\lambda w.$$

If either $x\lambda'w \succ y\lambda'z$ or $y\lambda'z \succ x\lambda'w$, then a similar application of P6* yields a contradiction of Lemma 9.6 with $\{f, g\} = \{x\lambda'w, y\lambda'z\}$ in the hypotheses of P6*. Hence $x\lambda'w \sim y\lambda'z$. ∎

Henceforth we use the notation $x\alpha y$ for $(xAy, \pi(A) = \alpha)$ as justified by Lemma 9.5.

LEMMA 9.8. $(C \cap D = \varnothing, 0 < \lambda < 1, \pi(C) = \lambda\pi(A), \pi(D) = \lambda\pi(A^c), f =_C x, f =_D w, g =_C y, g =_D z) \Rightarrow (xAw \succ yAz \Leftrightarrow f \succ_{C \cup D} g)$.

Proof. This follows from Lemmas 9.4 and 9.5 for all $\lambda \in \Lambda_0$, and it holds for all $0 < \lambda < 1$ by Lemma 9.1 and the definitions unless $(x \succ y, z \succ w)$ or $(y \succ x, w \succ z)$. Assume henceforth that $(x \succ y, z \succ w)$, $0 < \lambda < 1$, and $\lambda \notin \Lambda_0$. Also let $\alpha = \pi(A)$.

Suppose $x\alpha w \succ y\alpha z$. Then, by Lemma 9.7, there is a positive $\beta < \alpha$ such that $x\beta w \succ y\beta z$. Given such a β, choose $\lambda_0 \in \Lambda_0$ so that $\lambda < \lambda_0$, $\lambda_0\beta < \lambda\alpha$, and $\lambda(1 - \alpha) < \lambda_0(1 - \beta)$. Let C_0 and D_0 be disjoint events for which $C_0 \subset C$, $D_0 \subset D$, $\pi(C_0) = \lambda_0\beta$, and $\pi(D_0) = \lambda_0(1 - \beta)$. Also let simple acts h and k have $h =_{C_0} x$, $h =_{D_0} w$, $k =_{C_0} y$, and $k =_{D_0} z$. Then, since $x\beta w \succ y\beta z$ and since Lemma 9.8 holds for λ_0, $h \succ_{C_0 \cup D_0} k$. Two applications of Lemma 9.6 (first replacing D_0 by D, then C_0 by C) for its straightforward modification to the conditional case then yield $f \succ_{C \cup D} g$.

A converse proof that uses the same basic method shows that $f \succ_{C \cup D} g$ $\Rightarrow x\alpha w \succ y\alpha z$. ∎

In our final lemma we use the notation

$$\pi^0(A) = \pi(A)/\pi(A^c) \qquad \text{for all } A \in \mathcal{E} \text{ for which } \pi(A^c) > 0.$$

LEMMA 9.9. *Suppose $x, y, z, w, t, v \in X$; $A, B, C \in \mathcal{E}$; $x \succ y, z \succ w$, $t \succ v$, and*

$$xAw \sim yAz$$

$$zBv \sim wBt$$

$$tCy \sim vCx.$$

Then $\pi^0(A)\pi^0(B)\pi^0(C) = 1$.

Proof. Given the hypotheses, let $\alpha = \pi(A)$, $\beta = \pi(B)$, and $\gamma = \pi(C)$. By Lemma 9.7, α, β, and γ are in $(0, 1)$. Also let $\lambda = \beta/(\beta + 1 - \alpha)$ and let $\{A, B, C, D\}$ be a four-part partition of S with $\pi(A) = \lambda\alpha$, $\pi(B) = \lambda(1 - \alpha)$, $\pi(C) = (1 - \lambda)\beta$, and $\pi(D) = (1 - \lambda)(1 - \beta)$. Let (f, g) equal (x, y), (w, z), (z, w), and (v, t) on A, B, C, and D, respectively.

By Lemma 9.8, $f \sim_{A \cup B} g$ and $f \sim_{C \cup D} g$, so $f \sim g$ by P2*. Since $\lambda(1 - \alpha) = (1 - \lambda)\beta$ by the definition of λ, $f \sim_{B \cup C} g$, so again by P2*, $f \sim_{A \cup D} g$. Hence, by Lemma 9.8,

$$x[\lambda\alpha/(\lambda\alpha + (1 - \lambda)(1 - \beta))]v$$
$$\sim y[(1 - \lambda)(1 - \beta)/(\lambda\alpha + (1 - \lambda)(1 - \beta))]t.$$

Then Lemma 9.7 gives $\lambda\alpha/(\lambda\alpha + (1 - \lambda)(1 - \beta)) = 1 - \gamma$, which reduces to $\alpha\beta\gamma/[(1 - \alpha)(1 - \beta)(1 - \gamma)] = 1$. ∎

Proof of Theorem 9.1. Given π by way of Lemma 7.5 and Theorem 7.2, define ϕ on $X \times X$ as follows. Fix $x_0, y_0 \in X$ with $x_0 \succ y_0$ as guaranteed by P5, and let $\phi_0 = \phi(x_0, y_0)$ be any positive number. Then take

$$\phi(z, w) = 0 \qquad \text{if } z \sim w,$$

$$\phi(z, w) = \pi^0(A)\phi_0 \qquad \text{if } z > w \text{ and } x_0 A w \sim y_0 A z,$$

$$\phi(z, w) = -\phi(w, z) \qquad \text{if } w > z.$$

Given ϕ_0, it should be clear that ϕ must be defined in this way if it is to be skew-symmetric and satisfy the SSA representation.

By Lemma 9.7, ϕ is well defined. (When $(z, w) = (x_0, y_0)$, we have $\pi^0(A) = 1$ at indifference.) Moreover, ϕ is unique up to multiplication by a positive constant since the only freedom in its definition is the value chosen for ϕ_0, and if this changes to ϕ_0' then ϕ changes to $\phi' = (\phi_0'/\phi_0)\phi$. In addition, Lemma 9.9 assures us that the same ϕ is obtained (up to a similarity transformation) regardless of which (x_0, y_0) is used for the definition. For example, if $x_0 > y_0$, $x_1 > y_1$, and $\phi(x_1, y_1)$ is obtained from $\phi(x_0, y_0)$ by

$$\phi(x_1, y_1) = \pi^0(D)\phi(x_0, y_0) \qquad \text{with } x_0 D y_1 \sim y_0 D x_1,$$

and if $\phi(z, w)$ for $z > w$ is scaled against each of (x_0, y_0) and (x_1, y_1) by

$$\phi(z, w) = \pi^0(A)\phi(x_0, y_0), \qquad x_0 A w \sim y_0 A z,$$

$$\phi(z, w) = \pi^0(B)\phi(x_1, y_1), \qquad x_1 B w \sim y_1 B z,$$

then the same value of $\phi(z, w)$ obtains for both equations if and only if $\pi^0(A)\phi(x_0, y_0) = \pi^0(B)\phi(x_1, y_1)$; that is, $\pi^0(A) = \pi^0(B)\pi^0(D)$, which follows from Lemma 9.9 by a rearrangement of terms.

Given simple acts f and g, let $\{A_1, \ldots, A_n\}$ be the smallest-cardinality partition of S such that (f, g) is constant on each member of the partition with

$$(f(s), g(s)) = (x_i, y_i) \qquad \text{for all } s \in A_i,$$

$$\alpha_i = \pi(A_i),$$

$i = 1, \ldots, n$, and $\Sigma \alpha_i = 1$. Fix $t \in X$. Successively replace each (x_i, y_i) by (t, t) for all $A_i \in \mathfrak{N}$ and the $A_i \notin \mathfrak{N}$ at which $x_i \sim y_i$. By P2* and P3, this does not change the preference or indifference between f and g, and it clearly has no affect on the sign of $\int \phi(f, g) \, d\pi$.

With f and g thus modified, assume for definiteness that $A_1, \ldots, A_m (m \leq n)$ are the members of the partition for which $\alpha_i > 0$ and not $(x_i \sim y_i)$. If $m = 0$, then $f = g$; hence $f \sim g$, and $\int \phi(f, g) \, d\pi = 0$. If $m \geq 1$ and $x_i > y_i$ for each $i \leq m$, Lemma 9.1 gives $f > g$, and clearly $\int \phi(f, g) \, d\pi > 0$.

Suppose $x_i > y_i$ and $y_j > x_j$ for some $i, j \leq m$. Take $(i, j) = (1, 2)$ for definiteness. By Lemmas 9.7–9.9 there is a unique number $r > 0$ such that

$$\phi(y_2, x_2) = r\phi(x_1, y_1),$$

and $f' \sim_{C \cup D} g'$ whenever $\pi(C)/\pi(D) = r, f' =_C x_1, f' =_D x_2, g' =_C y_1,$ and $g' =_D y_2$. If $\alpha_1/\alpha_2 = r$, then $f \sim_{A_1 \cup A_2} g$ and, by P2*, we can replace both (x_1, y_1) and (x_2, y_2) by (t, t) without changing the preference or indifference between f and g thus modified. Moreover,

$$\alpha_1 \phi(x_1, y_1) + \alpha_2 \phi(x_2, y_2) = 0$$

$$= (\alpha_1 + \alpha_2)\phi(t, t) \quad \text{on } A_1 \cup A_2.$$

On the other hand, if $\alpha_1/\alpha_2 > r$, then by Theorem 7.2 there is a $B_1 \subset A_1$ with $\pi(B_1) = \alpha_2 r$; hence $f \sim_{B_1 \cup A_2} g$. In this case we replace (x_1, y_1) on B_1 and (x_2, y_2) on A_2 by (t, t) without changing preference or indifference between f and g. Here $(f(s), g(s))$ remains at (x_1, y_1) on $A_1 \setminus B_1$ and, on $B_1 \cup A_2$, $\alpha_2 r \phi(x_1, y_1) + \alpha_2 \phi(x_2, y_2) = 0 = (\alpha_2 r + \alpha_2)\phi(t, t)$. Similar changes with A_1 and A_2 interchanged are made when $\alpha_1/\alpha_2 < r$.

The applicable changes of the preceding two paragraphs eliminate at least one of (x_1, y_1) and (x_2, y_2) completely, replacing it by (t, t). So long as there are $x_i > y_i$ and $y_j > x_j$ with positive probabilities for the modified f and g, we repeat the procedure. Eventually either both f and g have outcome t on all of S, with $f \sim g$ and $\int \phi(f, g) \, d\pi = 0$ for the original and modified f and g, or positive-probability events remain that all have $x_i > y_i$ or all have $y_i > x_i$. If $x_i > y_i$ in the latter case, we get $f > g$ and $\int \phi(f, g) \, d\pi > 0$ for the original and modified forms of f and g. Similarly, if only $y_i > x_i$ is left, then $g > f$ and $\int \phi(g, f) \, d\pi > 0$.

Thus $f > g \Leftrightarrow \int \phi(f, g) \, d\pi > 0$ for all simple f and g in F.   ■

9.3   EXTENSION FOR NONSIMPLE ACTS

Extension of the SSA representation to nonsimple acts in $F = X^S$ when X is infinite is more complex than extensions for separable representations (Sections 1.8, 7.5, and 7.6) and nonseparable representations based on lotteries (Sections 5.8 and 9.6). The complexity is due to the nonseparability of ϕ on $X \times X$, the fact that $\phi(X \times X)$ can be any skew-symmetric subset of **R** subject to boundedness (see below), and, unlike the additive SSB extension of Section 9.6, the fact that we do not start with an SSB functional or some other numerical representation with nice uniqueness properties for $>$ on $F \times F$. As a consequence, I shall only comment on aspects of extension and leave open the question of conditions beyond those of Theorem 9.1 that are necessary and sufficient for the SSA representation for all acts.

Our first observation is that, quite apart from the cardinality of X, Savage's extension axiom

P7. $(f >_A g(s) \text{ for all } s \in A) \Rightarrow f \succsim_A g; (f(s) >_A g \text{ for all } s \in A) \Rightarrow f \succsim_A g,$

is unsuitable for the SSA representation. To see why, let $\pi(B) = \frac{1}{2}$, $f = xBw$, $g = yBz$, and suppose that

$$\phi(x, y) + \phi(w, y) > 0 > \phi(x, y),$$

$$\phi(x, z) + \phi(w, z) > 0 > \phi(w, z),$$

which is certainly consistent with the representation. Then with $A = S$ in P7, the SSA representation gives $f > g(s)$ for all $s \in S$ (by the > 0 inequalities), hence $f \gtrsim g$ by P7. But the representation also gives $g > f$ since, by the $0 >$ inequalities, $y > x$ and $z > w$.

We focus henceforth on two conditions that *are* necessary for the SSA representation within the context of Theorem 9.1 but are not implied by the axioms of that theorem when X is infinite. They are two hold for all f, g, f', $g' \in F$, all $x, y \in X$, and all $A \in \mathcal{E}$.

> P8. $(A \sim_* A^c, f(s)Ag'(s) \gtrsim g(s)Af'(s)$ for all $s \in S$, $f' \gtrsim g') \Rightarrow f \gtrsim g$; if, in addition, $f' > g'$, then $f > g$.
>
> P9. $(f > g, x > y) \Rightarrow$ [*there is a finite partition of S such that, for every member E of the partition*, $(f' =_E f, g' =_E g, f' =_{E^c} y, g' =_{E^c} x) \Rightarrow g' > f'$].

Axiom P8 is a state-by-state dominance axiom which with the use of π and ϕ in Theorem 9.1 translates into

$$[\phi(f(s), g(s)) \geq \phi(f'(s), g'(s)) \text{ for all } s \in S, f' \gtrsim g'] \Rightarrow f \gtrsim g,$$

along with $f > g$ when $f' > g'$. By taking $f' =_S x$ and $g' =_S x$, P8 yields

> P8*. $(f(s) \gtrsim g(s)$ for all $s \in S) \Rightarrow f \gtrsim g$,

which is the monotone dominance principle of Section 7.4.

The other new axiom, P9, is a sort of upside-down Archimedean axiom. It says that if $f > g$ and if f and g are changed to constant y and x, respectively, on a high-probability subset of S, with $x > y$, then the modified g will be preferred to the modified f. A few facts about the new axioms are summarized in

THEOREM 9.3. *Suppose the SSA representation $f > g \Leftrightarrow \int \phi(f(s), g(s)) \, d\pi(s) > 0$ holds for all $f, g \in F$ with π as in Theorem 7.2 and ϕ a skew-symmetric functional on $X \times X$. Then ϕ on $X \times X$ is bounded and P8 and P9 hold.*

Alternatively, suppose the axioms and representational conclusions of Theorem 9.1 hold. Then P8* and P9 imply that ϕ on $X \times X$ is bounded.

Proof. Assume the hypotheses of the first part. Then ϕ on $X \times X$ must be bounded, for otherwise it is easy to construct acts for which $\int \phi(f, g) \, d\pi$ is infinite or undefined. The hypotheses of P8 preceding $f' \gtrsim g'$ imply $\phi(f(s),$

$g(s)) \geqslant \phi(f'(s), g'(s))$ for all $s \in S$. Hence if $f' \gtrsim (>) g'$, then $\int \phi(f', g') \, d\pi \geqslant (>) 0$, so $\int \phi(f, g) \, d\pi \geqslant (>) 0$ and $f \gtrsim (>) g$. For P9, suppose $f > g$ and $x > y$. Let $\alpha = \phi(x, y) > 0$. Then, using the final property of Theorem 7.2 and the boundedness of ϕ, S can be partitioned into a finite number of events such that, for each event E, $\int_E \phi(f, g) \, d\pi < [1 - \pi(E)]\alpha$. Hence $\int \phi(f', g') \, d\pi = \int_E \phi(f, g) \, d\pi - [1 - \pi(E)]\alpha < 0$, so, using skew-symmetry, $g' > f'$.

For the second part of the theorem let the axioms of Theorem 9.1 hold with π and ϕ as specified therein. Contrary to the conclusion, suppose ϕ is unbounded. We then construct a denumerable partition $\{A_1, A_2, \ldots\}$ of S with $\pi(A_i) = 2^{-i}$ for each i along with acts f and g for which $f =_{A_i} x_i$ and $g =_{A_i} y_i$ with $\phi(x_i, y_i) \geqslant 2^i$ for each i. By P2* and P8*, $f > g$, and of course $\int \phi(f, g) \, d\pi = \infty$. Given $x > y$, there must be an E in the partition of S that satisfies the conclusion of P9 for which $\int_E \phi(f, g) \, d\pi = \infty$. Given such an E and $g' > f'$ as in the conclusion of P9, indifference tradeoffs as in the proof of Theorem 9.1 that match parts of E^c (where $g' = x$ and $f' = y$) against subevents of E (where $f' = x_i$ and $g' = y_i$) must eliminate all of (x, y) on E^c, replacing it by (t, t), with $g' > f'$ after the changes. However, the modified f' and g' satisfy the hypotheses of P8*, which yields $f' \gtrsim g'$, a contradiction. Therefore ϕ on $X \times X$ must be bounded. ∎

Suppose P8 and P9 hold along with the axioms of Theorem 9.1. Then, since ϕ is bounded, the expectation $\int \phi(f, g) \, d\pi$ is finite and well defined for all $f, g \in F$. To verify the SSA representation for all acts, we would like to show that $\int \phi(f, g) \, d\pi > 0 \Rightarrow f > g$ and $\int \phi(f, g) \, d\pi = 0 \Rightarrow f \sim g$. These appear easy to verify in some cases but not others. For example, given $\int \phi(f, g) \, d\pi > 0$, if we can construct simple f' and g' such that the hypotheses of P8 hold and $\int \phi(f', g') \, d\pi > 0$, then $f' > g'$ and therefore $f > g$. On the other hand, suppose $\inf\{\phi(x, y):x > y\} = 1$, $\phi(x, y)$ never equals 1, and f and g are such that, for all $\delta > 0$, $\pi(\{s:1 < \phi(f(s), g(s)) < 1 + \delta\}) = 1$. Then the only obvious conclusion from P8, or P8*, is $f \gtrsim g$. An additional condition, such as $[\phi(f(s), g(s)) \geqslant c$ for all $s \in S$ and some $c > 0] \Rightarrow f > g$, seems to be needed to obtain $f > g$ here, but I can see no natural way to formulate this as an axiom or to obtain it from other appealing axioms.

9.4 ADDITIVE SSB UTILITY

In the rest of this chapter we examine the additive SSB representation, $\mathbf{f} > \mathbf{g} \Leftrightarrow \int \phi(\mathbf{f}(s), \mathbf{g}(s)) \, d\pi(s) > 0$, discussed in Section 8.7, after noting its basic SSB precursor in Theorem 9.4. The present section states theorems that roughly parallel Theorems 7.4 and 7.5 for additive linear utility, then proves that the imposition of transitivity on a nontrivial additive SSB model reduces it to an additive linear model. Proofs of the initial theorems in the section are given in the next section. The final two sections of the chapter consider the extension of the additive SSB model to all lottery acts in $\mathbf{F} = P^S$. The definitions and notations of Section 7.6 apply throughout.

Our first theorem identifies the decompositional effects on ϕ on $\mathbf{F} \times \mathbf{F}$ of the basic SSB axioms for $>$ on $\mathbf{F}$.

THEOREM 9.4. *Suppose* $>$ *on* $\mathbf{F} = P^S$ *satisfies the following for all* $\mathbf{f}$, $\mathbf{g}$, $\mathbf{h} \in \mathbf{F}$ *and all* $0 < \lambda < 1$:

C1. $\mathbf{f} > \mathbf{g} > \mathbf{h} \Rightarrow \mathbf{g} \sim \alpha \mathbf{f} + (1 - \alpha) \mathbf{h}$ *for some* $0 < \alpha < 1$;

C2. $(\mathbf{f} > \mathbf{g}, \mathbf{f} \gtrsim \mathbf{h}) \Rightarrow \mathbf{f} > \lambda \mathbf{g} + (1 - \lambda)\mathbf{h}$; $(\mathbf{f} \sim \mathbf{g}, \mathbf{f} \sim \mathbf{h}) \Rightarrow \mathbf{f} \sim \lambda \mathbf{g} + (1 - \lambda)\mathbf{h}$; $(\mathbf{g} > \mathbf{f}, \mathbf{h} \gtrsim \mathbf{f}) \Rightarrow \lambda \mathbf{g} + (1 - \lambda)\mathbf{h} > \mathbf{f}$;

C3. $(\mathbf{f} > \mathbf{g} > \mathbf{h}, \mathbf{f} > \mathbf{h}, \mathbf{g} \sim \frac{1}{2}\mathbf{f} + \frac{1}{2}\mathbf{h}) \Rightarrow [\lambda \mathbf{f} + (1 - \lambda)\mathbf{h} \sim \frac{1}{2}\mathbf{f} + \frac{1}{2}\mathbf{g}$ $\Leftrightarrow \lambda \mathbf{h} + (1 - \lambda)\mathbf{f} \sim \frac{1}{2}\mathbf{h} + \frac{1}{2}\mathbf{g}]$.

Then there is an SSB functional ϕ *on* $\mathbf{F} \times \mathbf{F}$, *unique up to similarity transformations, such that* $\mathbf{f} > \mathbf{g} \Leftrightarrow \phi(\mathbf{f}, \mathbf{g}) > 0$ *for all* $\mathbf{f}, \mathbf{g} \in \mathbf{F}$. *Given such a* ϕ, *and given any finite partition* $\{A_1, \ldots, A_n\}$ *of* S *with* $n \geq 2$, *there are bilinear functionals* ϕ_{ij} *on* $P \times P$ *and linear functionals* u_i *on* P *for all* $i, j \in \{1, \ldots, n\}$ *such that*

$$\phi_{ij}(p, q) = -\phi_{ji}(q, p) \quad \text{for all } i, j \text{ and all } p, q \in P,$$

and such that for all $\mathbf{f}, \mathbf{g} \in \mathbf{F}'$, *with* $\mathbf{f} =_{A_i} p_i$ *and* $\mathbf{g} =_{A_i} q_i$ *for* $i = 1, \cdots, n$,

$$\phi(\mathbf{f}, \mathbf{g}) = \sum_{i=1}^{n} \sum_{j=1}^{n} \phi_{ij}(p_i, q_j) - (n - 1) \sum_{i=1}^{n} [u_i(p_i) - u_i(q_i)].$$

Moreover, with ϕ *fixed, bilinear* ϕ_{ij}' *and linear* u_i' *satisfy these equations in place of the* ϕ_{ij} *and* u_i *if and only if there are linear functionals* τ_{ij} *on* P *and real numbers* c_i *for all* $i, j \in \{1, \ldots, n\}$ *such that, for all* i, j *and all* $p, q \in P$,

$$\phi_{ij}'(p, q) = \phi_{ij}(p, q) + \tau_{ij}(p) - \tau_{ji}(q),$$

$$u_i'(p) = u_i(p) + c_i + \frac{1}{n - 1} \sum_{j=1}^{n} \tau_{ij}(p).$$

The first conclusion of the theorem is simply a restatement of the conclusions of Theorem 4.1. As might be expected for the SSB case, the decomposition of ϕ for $\mathbf{F}'$ (set of lottery acts constant on each member of the partition $\{A_1, \ldots, A_n\}$) is somewhat more involved than the linear decomposition $u = \Sigma u_i$ implied by Theorem 7.4 in the additive linear setting. The condition $\phi_{ij}(p, q) = -\phi_{ji}(q, p)$ implies that ϕ_{ii} is skew-symmetric hence SSB, but it does not entail skew-symmetry for ϕ_{ij} when $i \neq j$. The linear term in the decomposition for $\phi(\mathbf{f}, \mathbf{g})$ arises in a natural way during the proof but could be incorporated into the ϕ_{ii} term to yield the simpler-looking

$\phi(\mathbf{f}, \mathbf{g}) = \Sigma_i \Sigma_j \phi_{ij}(p_i, q_j)$. In the proof we fix $t \in P$ and define the ϕ_{ij} and u_i by

$$\phi_{ij}(p, q) = \phi(pA_i t, qA_j t),$$

$$u_i(p) = \phi(pA_i t, tA_i t) = \phi_{ii}(p, t).$$

The uniqueness conclusions of Theorem 9.4 reflect the fact that uniqueness for additive bilinear forms must involve linear additions, just as uniqueness for additive linear forms involves the addition of constants.

Three more axioms are used to obtain π on $\mathcal{E} = 2^S$ and the additive SSB representation for all *simply* lottery acts. Because of technical aspects of the present axiomatization, *we define* $\mathfrak{N}$ *here by* $A \in \mathfrak{N}$ *if for all* $p, q, r \in P$, $pAr \sim qAr$. The axioms apply to all $\mathbf{f}, \mathbf{g}, \mathbf{h} \in \mathbf{F}$, all $p, q, r \in P$, all $A, B, C \subseteq S$, and all $0 \leqslant \lambda \leqslant 1$:

T1. $S \notin \mathfrak{N}$.

T2. $A, B \notin \mathfrak{N} \Rightarrow (pAr > qAr \Leftrightarrow pBr > qBr)$.

T3. $(A, B, and C are mutually disjoint, A \cup B \cup C = S, \mathbf{f} =_A \mathbf{g}, \mathbf{g} =_B \mathbf{h}, \mathbf{h} =_C \mathbf{f}, \mathbf{f} \sim \lambda\mathbf{g} + (1 - \lambda)\mathbf{h}) \Rightarrow \frac{1}{2}\mathbf{f} + \frac{1}{2}\mathbf{h} \sim \frac{1}{2}(\lambda\mathbf{g} + (1 - \lambda)\mathbf{h}) + \frac{1}{2}\mathbf{h}$.

Axiom T1 is a nontriviality condition that ensures uniqueness of π. T2 is an independence axiom that mirrors aspects of Savage's sure-thing principle, especially P3, and S2 in Theorem 7.5. Its necessity for the additive SSB representation follows from the correspondences $pAr > qAr \Leftrightarrow \pi(A)\phi(p, q) > 0$ and $pBr > qBr \Leftrightarrow \pi(B)\phi(p, q) > 0$.

Axiom T3 is a sort of cyclic independence condition that is tailored to the SSB lottery-acts setting. The structure of its hypotheses prior to $\mathbf{f} \sim \lambda\mathbf{g} + (1 - \lambda)\mathbf{h}$ is illustrated in Figure 9.1. For convenience let $\phi_E(\mathbf{f}', \mathbf{g}') = \int_E \phi(\mathbf{f}'(s), \mathbf{g}'(s)) d\pi(s)$ for all $E \in \mathcal{E}$ and all $\mathbf{f}', \mathbf{g}' \in \mathbf{F}$. If the additive SSB representation holds along with $A \cap B = \varnothing$, $C = (A \cup B)^c$, $\mathbf{f} =_A \mathbf{g}, \mathbf{g} =_B \mathbf{h}$, and $\mathbf{h} =_C \mathbf{f}$, then

$\phi(\mathbf{f}, \mathbf{g}) + \phi(\mathbf{g}, \mathbf{h}) + \phi(\mathbf{h}, \mathbf{f})$

$= \phi_B(\mathbf{f}, \mathbf{g}) + \phi_C(\mathbf{f}, \mathbf{g}) + \phi_A(\mathbf{g}, \mathbf{h}) + \phi_C(\mathbf{g}, \mathbf{h})$

$\quad + \phi_A(\mathbf{h}, \mathbf{f}) + \phi_B(\mathbf{h}, \mathbf{f})$

$= [\phi_B(\mathbf{f}, \mathbf{g}) + \phi_B(\mathbf{g}, \mathbf{f})] + [\phi_C(\mathbf{f}, \mathbf{g}) + \phi_C(\mathbf{g}, \mathbf{f})] + [\phi_A(\mathbf{g}, \mathbf{h})$

$\quad + \phi_A(\mathbf{h}, \mathbf{g})]$

$= 0.$

The necessity of T3 for the full additive SSB representation follows from this observation. Suppose the representation holds along with the hypotheses of

FIGURE 9.1   Hypotheses of T3

	A	B	C
f	a	y	c
g	a	b	z
h	x	b	c

T3. Then $\phi(\mathbf{f}, \lambda\mathbf{g} + (1 - \lambda)\mathbf{h}) = 0$ and, using $\phi(\mathbf{f}, \mathbf{g}) + \phi(\mathbf{g}, \mathbf{h}) + \phi(\mathbf{h}, \mathbf{f}) = 0$,

$$\phi(\mathbf{f}, \mathbf{h}) + \phi(\mathbf{h}, \lambda\mathbf{g} + (1 - \lambda)\mathbf{h}) = \phi(\mathbf{f}, \mathbf{h}) + \lambda\phi(\mathbf{h}, \mathbf{g})$$

$$= \phi(\mathbf{f}, \mathbf{h}) + \lambda[\phi(\mathbf{f}, \mathbf{g}) + \phi(\mathbf{h}, \mathbf{f})] = \phi(\mathbf{f}, \lambda\mathbf{g} + (1 - \lambda)\mathbf{h}) = 0.$$

Therefore

$$0 = \tfrac{1}{4}[\phi(\mathbf{f}, \lambda\mathbf{g} + (1 - \lambda)\mathbf{h}) + \phi(\mathbf{f}, \mathbf{h}) + \phi(\mathbf{h}, \lambda\mathbf{g} + (1 - \lambda)\mathbf{h})]$$

$$= \phi(\tfrac{1}{2}\mathbf{f} + \tfrac{1}{2}\mathbf{h}, \tfrac{1}{2}(\lambda\mathbf{g} + (1 - \lambda)\mathbf{h}) + \tfrac{1}{2}\mathbf{h}),$$

so $\tfrac{1}{2}\mathbf{f} + \tfrac{1}{2}\mathbf{h} \sim \tfrac{1}{2}(\lambda\mathbf{g} + (1 - \lambda)\mathbf{h}) + \tfrac{1}{2}\mathbf{h}$.

T3 alone has powerful implications for ϕ on $\mathbf{F} \times \mathbf{F}$ in the context of Theorem 9.4. We extend our notation slightly as follows: given $\mathbf{f} \in \mathbf{F}, p \in P$, and $A \in \mathcal{E}$, let $\mathbf{f}Ap$ denote the lottery act $\mathbf{f}'$ for which $\mathbf{f}' =_A \mathbf{f}$ and $\mathbf{f}' =_{A_c} p$.

LEMMA 9.10. *Suppose ϕ on $\mathbf{F} \times \mathbf{F}$ is an SSB functional and, for all $\mathbf{f}$, $\mathbf{g} \in \mathbf{F}, \mathbf{f} > \mathbf{g} \Leftrightarrow \phi(\mathbf{f}, \mathbf{g}) > 0$. If T3 holds then for all $\mathbf{f}, \mathbf{g} \in \mathbf{F}$, all $p \in P$, and every partition $\{A_1, \ldots, A_n\}$ of S,*

$$\phi(\mathbf{f}, \mathbf{g}) = \sum_{i=1}^{n} \phi(\mathbf{f}A_ip, \mathbf{g}A_ip).$$

The addition of T1 and T2 then yields π and the additive SSB representation for simple lottery acts.

THEOREM 9.5. *Suppose $>$ on $\mathbf{F} = P^S$ satisfies the hypotheses of Theorem 9.4 along with T1, T2, and T3. Also let SSB ϕ on $\mathbf{F} \times \mathbf{F}$ satisfy the SSB representation for $>$ on $\mathbf{F}$, and define ϕ on $P \times P$ by $\phi(p, q) = \phi(\mathbf{f}, \mathbf{g})$ when $\mathbf{f} =_S p$ and $\mathbf{g} =_S q$. Then there is a unique additive probability measure π on $\mathcal{E} = 2^S$ such that, for all $A \in \mathcal{E}$ and all simple $\mathbf{f}, \mathbf{g} \in \mathbf{F}$,*

$$A \in \mathfrak{N} \Leftrightarrow \pi(A) = 0,$$

$$\phi(\mathbf{f}, \mathbf{g}) = \int_S \phi(\mathbf{f}(s), \mathbf{g}(s)) \, d\pi(s).$$

We conclude this section with an observation from Fishburn and LaValle (1987b) on transitivity before turning to the proofs of Lemma 9.10 and Theorems 9.4 and 9.5 in the next section. The point of the observation is that, when π is not completely trivial, each of transitivity and independence reduces the additive SSB representation to the additive linear representation of Section 7.6. Hence, unlike the situation for weighted linear utility in Section 5.3, where transitivity for the basic SSB representation yields a model intermediate between the linear and SSB models, the imposition of transitivity on the additive SSB representation does not yield a model that lies strictly between this representation and the additive linear representation.

We use the Herstein–Milnor independence axiom of Section 1.5 along with the transitive indifference axiom:

A1($\sim$). $\sim$ *on* **F** *is transitive.*
B2. *For all* **f, g, h** $\in$ **F**, **f** $\sim$ **g** $\Rightarrow \frac{1}{2}$**f** $+ \frac{1}{2}$**h** $\sim \frac{1}{2}$**g** $+ \frac{1}{2}$**h**.

THEOREM 9.6. *Suppose that the additive* SSB *representation* **f** $>$ **g** $\Leftrightarrow \int \phi(\mathbf{f}(s), \mathbf{g}(s)) \, d\pi(s) > 0$ *holds for all* **f, g** $\in$ **F** *with* π *and* ϕ *as in Theorem 9.5. Suppose also that* $0 < \pi(A) < 1$ *for some* $A \in \mathcal{E}$. *Then* A1($\sim$) *holds if and only if* B2 *holds, and either axiom implies that* (**F**, $>$) *has an additive linear representation.*

Proof. Assume the hypotheses. We show that each of A1($\sim$) and B2 reduces the representation to the additive linear representation. Since A1($\sim$) and B2 are implied by the latter representation, they are equivalent under the hypotheses of the theorem.

Suppose first that B2 holds. Then B2 holds for $\sim$ on P, and, since $\{C1, C2, B2\}$ holds for $>$ on P, it follows from Theorem 1.4 and the equivalence between $\{A1, A2, A3\}$ and $\{B1, B2, B3\}$ that $\phi(p, q) = u(p) - u(q)$ for linear u on P. Substitution in the additive SSB representation then gives the additive linear representation.

Suppose henceforth that A1($\sim$) holds. It then follows from Theorem 5.3 that there are linear functionals u and w on **F** with $w \geq 0$, $w > 0$ on $\{$g:**f** $>$ **g** $>$ **h** for some **f, h** $\in$ **F**$\}$, and, for all **f, g** $\in$ **F**,

$$\phi(\mathbf{f}, \mathbf{g}) = u(\mathbf{f})w(\mathbf{g}) - u(\mathbf{g})w(\mathbf{f}).$$

Our hypotheses (π unique) imply that **f** $>$ **g** $>$ **h** for some lottery acts in **F**.

Given $0 < \pi(A) < 1$, Let $\lambda = \pi(A)$ and consider simple lottery acts of the form pAq, which we write as (p, q) for convenience. By the additive SSB representation,

$$\phi((p_1, p_2), (q_1, q_2)) = \lambda\phi(p_1, q_1) + (1 - \lambda)\phi(p_2, q_2).$$

Therefore, by the decomposition of the preceding paragraph with $u(p) = u(\mathbf{f})$ and $w(p) = w(\mathbf{f})$ when $\mathbf{f} =_S p$,

$$(*) \qquad u(p_1, p_2)w(q_1, q_2) - u(q_1, q_2)w(p_1, p_2)$$
$$= \lambda[u(p_1)w(q_1) - u(q_1)w(p_1)]$$
$$+ (1 - \lambda)[u(p_2)w(q_2) - u(q_2)w(p_2)].$$

Set $q_1 = q_2 = q$ in this to get

$$u(p_1, p_2)w(q) - u(q)w(p_1, p_2)$$
$$= \lambda[u(p_1)w(q) - u(q)w(p_1)]$$
$$+ (1 - \lambda)[u(p_2)w(q) - u(q)w(p_2)]$$
$$= w(q)u(\lambda p_1 + (1 - \lambda)p_2) - u(q)w(\lambda p_1 + (1 - \lambda)p_2).$$

Hence, for all $q, p_1, p_2 \in P$,

$$w(q)[u(p_1, p_2) - u(\lambda p_1 + (1 - \lambda)p_2)]$$
$$= u(q)[w(p_1, p_2) - w(\lambda p_1 + (1 - \lambda)p_2)].$$

Since $>$ is not empty on $\mathbf{F}$, it is not empty on P. Therefore $u(q)/w(q)$ takes on all values in some nondegenerate real interval as q ranges over the part of P on which $w(q) > 0$. The preceding equation then requires $u(p_1, p_2) - u(\lambda p_1 + (1 - \lambda)p_2) = w(p_1, p_2) - w(\lambda p_1 + (1 - \lambda)p_2) = 0$ for all $p_1, p_2 \in P$. Hence

$$u(p_1, p_2) = u(\lambda p_1 + (1 - \lambda)p_2) \qquad \text{for all } p_1, p_2 \in P,$$
$$w(p_1, p_2) = w(\lambda p_1 + (1 - \lambda)p_2) \qquad \text{for all } p_1, p_2 \in P.$$

When these are used on the left side of $(*)$ with linear expansions, we get

$$[\lambda u(p_1) + (1 - \lambda)u(p_2)][\lambda w(q_1) + (1 - \lambda)w(q_2)]$$
$$- [\lambda u(q_1) + (1 - \lambda)u(q_2)][\lambda w(p_1) + (1 - \lambda)w(p_2)]$$
$$= \lambda[u(p_1)w(q_1) - u(q_1)w(p_1)]$$
$$+ (1 - \lambda)[u(p_2)w(q_2) - u(q_2)w(p_2)].$$

Set $p_2 = q_2 = r$ here and rearrange to obtain

$$\lambda(1 - \lambda)[u(p_1)w(r) + u(r)w(q_1) - u(q_1)w(r) - u(r)w(p_1)]$$
$$= \lambda(1 - \lambda)[u(p_1)w(q_1) - u(q_1)w(p_1)].$$

Then cancel $\lambda(1 - \lambda)$ to get

$$[u(p_1) - u(q_1)]w(r) - [w(p_1) - w(q_1)]u(r)$$
$$= u(p_1)w(q_1) - u(q_1)w(p_1)$$

for all $r, p_1, q_1 \in P$.

To complete the proof for A1($\sim$), suppose first that there are $p, q \in P$ such that $w(p) = w(q)$ and $u(p) \neq u(q)$. Then, by the preceding equation,

$$[u(p) - u(q)]w(r) = w(p)[u(p) - u(q)];$$

hence $w(r) = w(p)$ for all r. Since w is constant on P, say with value $w_0 \neq 0$, the additive SSB expression for ϕ reduces to $\phi(\mathbf{f}, \mathbf{g}) = \int [v(\mathbf{f}(s)) - v(\mathbf{g}(s))] \, d\pi(s)$ with $v(p) = w_0 u(p)$.

Contrary to the case of the preceding paragraph, suppose that $w(p) = w(q) \Rightarrow u(p) = u(q)$ for all $p, q \in P$. Then, by a slight generalization of Theorem 1.1 proved in Fishburn (1984e), there are real numbers a and b such that

$$u(p) = aw(p) + b \qquad \text{for all } p \in P.$$

But then $u(p)w(q) - u(q)w(p) = b[w(q) - w(p)]$ with $b \neq 0$ since $>$ on P is not empty. This reduces the additive SSB expression to $\phi(\mathbf{f}, \mathbf{g}) = \int [v(\mathbf{f}(s)) - v(\mathbf{g}(s))] \, d\pi(s)$ with $v(p) = -bw(p)$.   ■

9.5   ADDITIVE SSB PROOFS

Since C1, C2, and C3 are presumed by Lemma 9.10 and the theorems of the preceding section for $>$ on $\mathbf{F}$, we assume throughout the present section that ϕ on $\mathbf{F} \times \mathbf{F}$ is an SSB functional with $\mathbf{f} > \mathbf{g} \Leftrightarrow \phi(\mathbf{f}, \mathbf{g}) > 0$ for all $\mathbf{f}, \mathbf{g} \in \mathbf{F}$, as justified by the proof of Theorem 4.1 with P replaced by F throughout, since that proof depended only on P's convexity and not its specific structure in terms of probability measures. We begin with the representation proof for Theorem 9.4, followed by its uniqueness proof, and we then consider Lemma 9.10 and Theorem 9.5.

Representation Proof of Theorem 9.4. Let ϕ on $\mathbf{F} \times \mathbf{F}$ be as noted, let $\{A_1, \ldots, A_n\}$ be a partition of S, and fix t in P. Define ϕ_{ij} on $P \times P$ and u_i on P for all $i, j \in \{1, \ldots, n\}$ by

$$\phi_{ij}(p, q) = \phi(pA_i t, qA_j t),$$
$$u_i(p) = \phi(pA_i t, t),$$

where $\mathbf{t} =_S t$. The SSB properties of ϕ imply that each ϕ_{ij} is bilinear, each u_i

is linear, and $\phi_{ij}(p, q) = -\phi_{ji}(q, p)$. For example,

$$\phi_{ij}(\lambda p + (1 - \lambda)q, r) = \phi((\lambda p + (1 - \lambda)q)A_it, rA_jt)$$
$$= \phi(\lambda(pA_it) + (1 - \lambda)(qA_it), rA_jt)$$
$$= \lambda\phi(pA_it, rA_jt) + (1 - \lambda)\phi(qA_it, rA_jt)$$
$$= \lambda\phi_{ij}(p, r) + (1 - \lambda)\phi_{ij}(q, r).$$

To verify the decompositional form for $\mathbf{f}, \mathbf{g} \in \mathbf{F}'$, let $\mathbf{f} =_{A_i} p_i$ and $\mathbf{g} =_{A_i} q_i$ for each i and observe first that

$$\frac{1}{n + 1}\mathbf{f} + \sum_{j=1}^{n} \frac{1}{n + 1}(q_jA_jt) = \frac{1}{n + 1}\mathbf{g} + \sum_{i=1}^{n} \frac{1}{n + 1}(p_iA_it)$$

$$\frac{1}{n}\mathbf{f} + \frac{n - 1}{n}\mathbf{t} = \sum_{i=1}^{n} \frac{1}{n}(p_iA_it)$$

$$\frac{1}{n}\mathbf{g} + \frac{n - 1}{n}\mathbf{t} = \sum_{j=1}^{n} \frac{1}{n}(q_jA_jt).$$

The properties of ϕ and the definitions for the ϕ_{ij} and u_i then yield

$$0 = \phi\left(\frac{1}{n + 1}\mathbf{f} + \sum_{j} \frac{1}{n + 1}(q_jA_jt), \frac{1}{n + 1}\mathbf{g}\right.$$

$$\left. + \sum_{i} \frac{1}{n + 1}(p_iA_it)\right)$$

$$= (n + 1)^{-2}\left[\phi(\mathbf{f}, \mathbf{g}) + \sum_{i} \phi(\mathbf{f}, p_iA_it) + \sum_{j} \phi(q_jA_jt, \mathbf{g})\right.$$

$$\left. - \sum_{i}\sum_{j} \phi_{ij}(p_i, q_j)\right]$$

$$= (n + 1)^{-2}\left[\phi(\mathbf{f}, \mathbf{g}) + (n - 1)\sum_{i} \phi(p_iA_it, \mathbf{t})\right.$$

$$\left. - (n - 1)\sum_{j} \phi(q_jA_jt, \mathbf{t}) - \sum_{i}\sum_{j} \phi_{ij}(p_i, q_j)\right]$$

$$= (n + 1)^{-2}\left[\phi(\mathbf{f}, \mathbf{g}) - \sum_{i}\sum_{j} \phi_{ij}(p_i, q_j)\right.$$

$$+ (n - 1) \left(\sum_i u_i(p_i) - \sum_j u_j(q_j) \right) \bigg]$$

which give the desired result.   ■

Uniqueness Proof of Theorem 9.4. With ϕ fixed and partition $\{A_1, \ldots, A_n\}$ given, assume that the ϕ_{ij} and u_i are as specified in the initial conclusions of the theorem. If the ϕ'_{ij} and u'_i are as specified at the end of the theorem, it is easily checked that they satisfy the initial conclusions in place of the ϕ_{ij} and u_i.

Assume henceforth that the ϕ'_{ij} and u'_i satisfy the initial conclusions in place of the ϕ_{ij} and u_i. We are to show that there are linear τ_{ij} on P and constants c_i that satisfy the equations at the end of the theorem. To verify the penultimate equation, fix $t \in P$ and define τ_{ij} by

$$\tau_{ij}(p) = \sum_{k \neq j} [\phi_{ik}(p, t) - \phi'_{ik}(p, t)] - (n - 1)$$

$$\cdot [u_i(p) - u'_i(p) - u_i(t) + u'_i(t)].$$

Since each term on the right side is linear in p, τ_{ij} is a linear functional. Using the decompositional form and noting that $\phi_{kh}(t, t) + \phi_{hk}(t, t) = 0$, we have

$$\phi(pA_it, qA_jt) = \phi_{ij}(p, q) + \sum_{k \neq j} \phi_{ik}(p, t) + \sum_{k \neq i} \phi_{kj}(t, q)$$

$$- (n - 1)[u_i(p) + u_j(t) - u_i(t) - u_j(q)].$$

Since the same equation holds with primes on the right side, we conclude that

$$\phi'_{ij}(p, q) = \phi_{ij}(p, q) + \sum_{k \neq j} \phi_{ik}(p, t) - \sum_{k \neq j} \phi_{ik}(p, t)$$

$$- (n - 1)[u_i(p) - u'_i(p) - u_i(t) + u'_i(t)]$$

$$- \sum_{k \neq i} \phi_{jk}(q, t)$$

$$+ \sum_{k \neq i} \phi'_{jk}(q, t) + (n - 1)[u_j(q) - u'_j(q)$$

$$- u_j(t) + u'_j(t)]$$

$$= \phi_{ij}(p, q) + \tau_{ij}(p) - \tau_{ji}(q).$$

To verify the final equation of the theorem, use the decompositional form to get

$$\phi(pA_it, t) = \sum_k \phi_{ik}(p, t) + \sum_{k \neq i} \phi_{ki}(t, t) - (n - 1)[u_i(p) - u_i(t)].$$

Since the same equation holds with primes on the right,

$$
0 = \sum_k [\phi_{ik}(p, t) - \phi'_{ik}(p, t)] - (n - 1)[u_i(p) - u'_i(p)]
$$

$$
- u_i(t) + u'_i(t)] + \sum_{k \neq i} [\phi_{ki}(t, t) - \phi'_{ki}(t, t)]
$$

$$
= \frac{1}{n - 1} \sum_j \sum_{k \neq j} [\phi_{ik}(p, t) - \phi'_{ik}(p, t)] - (n - 1)[u_i(p) - u'_i(p)]
$$

$$
- u_i(t) + u'_i(t)] + \sum_{k \neq i} [\phi_{ki}(t, t) - \phi'_{ki}(t, t)]
$$

$$
= \frac{1}{n - 1} \sum_j [\tau_{ij}(p) + (n - 1)\{u_i(p) - u'_i(p) - u_i(t) + u'_i(t)\}]
$$

$$
- (n - 1)[u_i(p) - u'_i(p) - u_i(t) + u'_i(t)]
$$

$$
+ \sum_{k \neq i} [\phi_{ki}(t, t) - \phi'_{ki}(t, t)]
$$

$$
= \frac{1}{n - 1} \sum_j \tau_{ij}(p) + [u_i(p) - u'_i(p) - u_i(t) + u'_i(t)]
$$

$$
+ \sum_{k \neq i} [\phi_{ki}(t, t) - \phi'_{ki}(t, t)].
$$

Let c_i denote the sum of the terms in the last expression that do not contain p. Then $u'_i(p) = u_i(p) + c_i + (n - 1)^{-1}\Sigma_j \tau_{ij}(p)$.   ∎

Proof of Lemma 9.10. Given ϕ on $\mathbf{F} \times \mathbf{F}$, assume that T3 holds. We prove first that if $A \in \mathcal{E} \setminus \{\varnothing, S\}$ and $\{\mathbf{f}_1, \mathbf{f}_2, \mathbf{f}_3\} = \{\mathbf{f}Ap, \mathbf{g}A^c p, \mathbf{p}\}$, where $\mathbf{p} =_S p$, then

$$
\phi(\mathbf{f}_1, \mathbf{f}_2) + \phi(\mathbf{f}_2, \mathbf{f}_3) + \phi(\mathbf{f}_3, \mathbf{f}_1) = 0.
$$

Given $A \in \mathcal{E} \setminus \{\varnothing, S\}$, there is clearly some permutation $\mathbf{f}_1, \mathbf{f}_2, \mathbf{f}_3$ of $\mathbf{f}Ap$, $\mathbf{g}A^c p, \mathbf{p}$ and some $\mu \in [0, 1]$ such that $\mathbf{f}_1 \sim \mu\mathbf{f}_2 + (1 - \mu)\mathbf{f}_3$. Then $\phi(\mathbf{f}_1, \mu\mathbf{f}_2 + (1 - \mu)\mathbf{f}_3) = 0$, so linearity in the second argument gives

$$
\mu[\phi(\mathbf{f}_1, \mathbf{f}_2) - \phi(\mathbf{f}_1, \mathbf{f}_3)] = -\phi(\mathbf{f}_1, \mathbf{f}_3).
$$

Also, by T3, $\frac{1}{2}\mathbf{f}_1 + \frac{1}{2}\mathbf{f}_3 \sim \frac{1}{2}(\mu\mathbf{f}_2 + (1 - \mu)\mathbf{f}_3) + \frac{1}{2}\mathbf{f}_3$, and $\phi(\cdot, \cdot) = 0$, bilinearity, skew-symmetry, and $\phi(\mathbf{f}_1, \mu\mathbf{f}_2 + (1 - \mu)\mathbf{f}_3) = 0$ give

$$
\mu\phi(\mathbf{f}_2, \mathbf{f}_3) = \phi(\mathbf{f}_1, \mathbf{f}_3).
$$

When this is added to the preceding equation, we get $\mu[\phi(\mathbf{f}_1, \mathbf{f}_2) + \phi(\mathbf{f}_2, \mathbf{f}_3) + \phi(\mathbf{f}_3, \mathbf{f}_1)] = 0$, so the desired result holds if $\mu > 0$. If $\mu = 0$, simply interchange $\mathbf{f}_2$ and $\mathbf{f}_3$ throughout the preceding derivation to obtain the desired result.

Continuing with $A \notin \{\varnothing, S\}$, observe that

$$\tfrac{1}{3}\mathbf{f} + \tfrac{1}{3}(\mathbf{g}Ap) + \tfrac{1}{3}(\mathbf{g}A^{c}p) = \tfrac{1}{3}\mathbf{g} + \tfrac{1}{3}(\mathbf{f}Ap) + \tfrac{1}{3}(\mathbf{f}A^{c}p),$$

$$\tfrac{1}{2}\mathbf{f} + \tfrac{1}{2}\mathbf{p} = \tfrac{1}{2}(\mathbf{f}Ap) + \tfrac{1}{2}(\mathbf{f}A^{c}p),$$

$$\tfrac{1}{2}\mathbf{g} + \tfrac{1}{2}\mathbf{p} = \tfrac{1}{2}(\mathbf{g}Ap) + \tfrac{1}{2}(\mathbf{g}A^{c}p).$$

When $\phi(\cdot, \cdot) = 0$ is expanded bilinearly for each of these and substitutions are made in the first from the other two, we get

$$\phi(\mathbf{f}, \mathbf{g}) + \phi(\mathbf{f}Ap, \mathbf{p}) + \phi(\mathbf{f}A^{c}p, \mathbf{p}) + \phi(\mathbf{p}, \mathbf{g}Ap) + \phi(\mathbf{p}, \mathbf{g}A^{c}p)$$

$$+ \phi(\mathbf{g}Ap, \mathbf{f}Ap) + \phi(\mathbf{g}A^{c}p, \mathbf{f}A^{c}p) + \phi(\mathbf{g}Ap, \mathbf{f}A^{c}p)$$

$$+ \phi(\mathbf{g}A^{c}p, \mathbf{f}Ap) = 0.$$

But, by the result of the preceding paragraph,

$$\phi(\mathbf{f}Ap, \mathbf{p}) + \phi(\mathbf{p}, \mathbf{g}A^{c}p) + \phi(\mathbf{g}A^{c}p, \mathbf{f}Ap) = 0,$$

$$\phi(\mathbf{f}A^{c}p, \mathbf{p}) + \phi(\mathbf{p}, \mathbf{g}Ap) + \phi(\mathbf{g}Ap, \mathbf{f}A^{c}p) = 0.$$

Therefore

$$\phi(\mathbf{f}, \mathbf{g}) = \phi(\mathbf{f}Ap, \mathbf{g}Ap) + \phi(\mathbf{f}A^{c}p, \mathbf{g}A^{c}p).$$

If $n = 1$, the conclusion of the lemma is obvious; otherwise, use the result just proved to obtain

$$\phi(\mathbf{f}, \mathbf{g}) = \phi(\mathbf{f}A_1p, \mathbf{g}A_1p) + \phi(\mathbf{f}A_1^{c}p, \mathbf{g}A_1^{c}p)$$

$$= \phi(\mathbf{f}A_1p, \mathbf{g}A_1p) + \phi(\mathbf{f}A_2p, \mathbf{g}A_2p)$$

$$+ \phi(\mathbf{f}(A_1 \cup A_2)^{c}p, \mathbf{g}(A_1 \cup A_2)^{c}p)$$

$$\vdots$$

$$= \sum \phi(\mathbf{f}A_ip, \mathbf{g}A_ip). \qquad \blacksquare$$

Proof of Theorem 9.5. Assume the hypotheses of the theorem (C1–C3, T1–T3, ϕ) along with the result of Lemma 9.10. We consider first a partition $\{A_1, \ldots, A_n\}$ of S. Let $K = \{i : i \in \{1, \ldots, n\}$ and $A_i \notin \mathfrak{N}\}$. By T1 and the definition of $\mathfrak{N}$ in the preceding section, $p \succ q$ for some $p, q \in P$. The representation of Lemma 9.10 then implies that $K \neq \varnothing$, and it follows from T2 that, with $t \in P$ fixed, $\phi(pA_it, qA_it)$ is identically 0 for all $p, q \in P$ if and only if $i \notin K$, and for all $i, j \in K$ there is a unique $a_{ij} > 0$ such that $\phi(pA_it, qA_it) = a_{ij}\phi(pA_jt, qA_jt)$ for all $p, q \in P$. The latter conclusion follows from the uniqueness property for SSB utilities. With normalization as in the proof of Lemma 7.9, it follows that there are unique $\rho_i \geqslant 0$ that sum to

1 with $\rho_i = 0 \leftrightarrow A_i \in \mathfrak{N}$, and a similarity transformation ϕ' on $P \times P$ of ϕ on $P \times P$ as defined in Theorem 9.5 such that, for all $\mathbf{f}$ and $\mathbf{g}$ of the form $\mathbf{f} =_{A_i} p_i$ and $\mathbf{g} =_{A_i} q_i$, $\phi(\mathbf{f}, \mathbf{g}) = \Sigma \rho_i \phi'(p_i, q_i)$. The use of constant lottery acts gives $\phi' = \phi$ on $P \times P$.

Thus, every partition α of the form $\{A_1, \ldots, A_n\}$ has unique nonnegative $\pi_\alpha(A_i)$ that sum to 1 with $\pi_\alpha(A_i) = 0 \leftrightarrow A_i \in \mathfrak{N}$ such that, for all $\mathbf{f}$ and $\mathbf{g}$ as before,

$$\phi(\mathbf{f}, \mathbf{g}) = \sum \pi_\alpha(A_i)\phi(p_i, q_i).$$

If A is in both α and β then $\phi(pAr, qAr) = \pi_\alpha(A)\phi(p, q) = \pi_\beta(A)\phi(p, q)$, and it follows that we can drop the partition designator on π. Additivity for disjoint A and B follows from $\pi(A \cup B)\phi(p, q) = [\pi(A) + \pi(B)]\phi(p, q)$, and intersection of partitions gives the desired form for $\phi(\mathbf{f}, \mathbf{g})$ for all simple $\mathbf{f}, \mathbf{g} \in \mathbf{F}$. ∎

9.6   ADDITIVE SSB EXTENSION

We assume the hypotheses and conclusions of Theorem 9.5 *throughout the rest of this chapter.* It is assumed also that S is infinite, for otherwise Theorem 9.5 characterizes the additive SSB representation fully.

Three axioms will be used to extend the additive SSB representation by way of $\phi(\mathbf{f}, \mathbf{g}) = \int \phi(\mathbf{f}(s), \mathbf{g}(s)) \, d\pi \, (s)$ to all lottery acts. The second and third are to hold for all $\mathbf{f}, \mathbf{g}, \mathbf{f}', \mathbf{g}' \in \mathbf{F}$.

T4.   *For each positive integer n there is an n-part partition of S each member of which is not null.*

T5. $[\phi(\mathbf{f}(s), \mathbf{g}(s)) \geqslant \phi(\mathbf{f}'(s), \mathbf{g}'(s))$ *for all* $s \in S, \mathbf{f}' \sim \mathbf{g}'] \Rightarrow \mathbf{f} \succcurlyeq \mathbf{g}$.

T5*. $(\mathbf{f}(s) \succcurlyeq \mathbf{g}(s)$ *for all* $s \in S) \Rightarrow \mathbf{f} \succcurlyeq \mathbf{g}$.

The first of these is not necessary for the representation but is generous in the types of π measures it allows and is considerably weaker than Savage's requirements for π mentioned in Theorem 7.2. Our main use of T4 is its implication from Lemma 7.12 that there is a denumerable partition of S each member of which has positive probability.

Axioms T5 and T5*, which are clearly necessary for the representation, are similar to aspects of P8 and P8* in Section 9.3. T5*, which is identical to Schmeidler's S2* in Section 8.8, is implied by T5 (set $\mathbf{f}' = \mathbf{g}'$) and is the direct image of P8* for lottery acts. It is a very appealing assumption. T5 seems less appealing but is still intuitively attractive. Its obvious deficiency from a foundational perspective is its direct use of ϕ. This can be easily removed, as in P8, if $\pi(A) = \frac{1}{2}$ for some $A \subseteq S$, and we might assume such an A as does Ramsey (1931). Short of that, ϕ can be replaced in T5 by appropriate conditions on $\succsim$, but this seems awkward and adds nothing to its intuitive interpretation.

Although I do not have an example to the contrary, it appears that T4 and T5* are not sufficient for the full extension. However, they do allow several interesting conclusions. As before, $\mathbf{p} =_S p$.

THEOREM 9.7. *Suppose T4 and T5* hold. Then for all* $\mathbf{f}, \mathbf{g} \in \mathbf{F}$ *and all* $p \in P$:

(a) ϕ *on* $P \times P$ *is bounded.*
(b) $\inf_S \phi(\mathbf{f}(s), p) \leqslant \phi(\mathbf{f}, \mathbf{p}) \leqslant \sup_S \phi(\mathbf{f}(s), p)$.
(c) *If at least one of* $\mathbf{f}$ *and* $\mathbf{g}$ *is simple, then* $\phi(\mathbf{f}, \mathbf{g}) = \int \phi(\mathbf{f}(s), \mathbf{g}(s)) \, d\pi(s)$.
(d) ϕ *on* $\mathbf{F} \times \mathbf{F}$ *is bounded.*

The problem in extending (c) to all $\mathbf{f}$ and $\mathbf{g}$ without the use of T5 is directly related to the need to show that

$$\inf_S \phi(\mathbf{f}(s), \mathbf{g}(s)) \leqslant \phi(\mathbf{f}, \mathbf{g}) \leqslant \sup_S \phi(\mathbf{f}(s), \mathbf{g}(s)),$$

for without this we cannot conclude that $\phi(\mathbf{f}, \mathbf{g}) = \int \phi(\mathbf{f}(s), \mathbf{g}(s)) \, d\pi(s)$. This generalization of (b) will be noted in Lemma 9.20 to follow from T4 and T5. The lemma is then used to prove

THEOREM 9.8. *Suppose T4 and T5 hold. Then, in addition to the conclusions of Theorem 9.7,* $\phi(\mathbf{f}, \mathbf{g}) = \int \phi(\mathbf{f}(s), \mathbf{g}(s)) \, d\pi(s)$ *for all* $\mathbf{f}, \mathbf{g} \in \mathbf{F}$.

9.7 EXTENSION PROOFS

We assume the hypotheses and conclusions of Theorem 9.5 along with T4 (not needed for Lemmas 9.11 and 9.12) and T5*. Throughout this section, $\{A_1, A_2, \ldots\}$ with $\pi(A_1) \geqslant \pi(A_2) \geqslant \cdots$ and $\pi(A_i) > 0$ for all i is a denumerable partition of S (Lemma 7.12). The conclusions of Theorem 9.7 will be established by a series of lemmas. T5 is assumed later in the section for the proof of Theorem 9.8. As usual, $\mathbf{f}, \mathbf{g} \in \mathbf{F}$, $p, r \in P$, and $\mathbf{p} =_S p$.

LEMMA 9.11. *Let* $a = \inf_S \phi(\mathbf{f}(s), p)$. *Then* $a \leqslant \phi(\mathbf{f}, \mathbf{p})$ *if* $a = 0$ *or if* $(a > 0, p > r$ *for some* $r)$ *or if* $(a < 0, r > p$ *for some* $r)$.

LEMMA 9.12. *Let* $b = \sup_S \phi(\mathbf{f}(s), p)$. *Then* $\phi(\mathbf{f}, \mathbf{p}) \leqslant b$ *if* $b = 0$ *or if* $(b > 0, p > r$ *for some* $r)$ *or if* $(b < 0, r > p$ *for some* $r)$.

Proof. We prove Lemma 9.12; the proof of Lemma 9.11 is similar. If $b = \infty$, then there is nothing to prove, so assume b is finite. If $b = 0$ then $p \succsim \mathbf{f}(s)$ for all s, so $\mathbf{p} \succsim \mathbf{f}$ by T5*, and therefore $\phi(\mathbf{f}, \mathbf{p}) \leqslant 0$.

Suppose next that $b > 0$ and $p \succ r$. Define λ by $\lambda b + (1 - \lambda)\phi(r, p) = 0$. By the SSB properties and the definition of b,

$$\phi(\lambda \mathbf{f}(s) + (1 - \lambda)r, p) = \lambda\phi(\mathbf{f}(s), p) + (1 - \lambda)\phi(r, p)$$

$$= \lambda\phi(\mathbf{f}(s), p) - \lambda b \leqslant \lambda b - \lambda b = 0$$

for all s. T5* implies $\mathbf{p} \succeq \lambda \mathbf{f} + (1 - \lambda)\mathbf{r}$. Hence $\lambda b = (1 - \lambda)\phi(p, r) \geqslant \lambda\phi(\mathbf{f}, \mathbf{p})$, so $b \geqslant \phi(\mathbf{f}, \mathbf{p})$.

Finally, suppose $b < 0$ and $r \succ p$. Define λ again by $\lambda b + (1 - \lambda)\phi(r, p) = 0$. Then $\phi(\lambda \mathbf{f}(s) + (1 - \lambda)r, p) = \lambda\phi(\mathbf{f}(s), p) - \lambda b \leqslant 0$, so $\mathbf{p} \succeq \lambda \mathbf{f} + (1 - \lambda)\mathbf{r}$. As before, $\phi(\mathbf{f}, \mathbf{p}) \leqslant b$. ∎

LEMMA 9.13. *If $r \succ p$ for some r, then ϕ is bounded below on $P \times \{p\}$.*

LEMMA 9.14. *If $p \succ r$ for some r, then ϕ is bounded above on $P \times \{p\}$.*

Proof. We prove Lemma 9.14; the proof of Lemma 9.13 is similar. Given $p \succ r$, suppose to the contrary of Lemma 9.14 that ϕ is unbounded above on $P \times \{p\}$. Then $[0, \infty) \subseteq \phi(P \times \{p\})$. Choose $p_i \in P$ for each i so that $\phi(p_i, p) = 1/\pi(A_i)$ and define $\mathbf{f}$ by $\mathbf{f} =_{A_i} p_i$ for each i. Let $\mathbf{g}_n$ be a simple lottery act in $\mathbf{F}$ that is constant on each A_i for $i \leqslant n$ with

$$\phi(\mathbf{g}_n(s), p) = \pi(A_n)^{-1} - \pi(A_i)^{-1} \qquad \text{for all } s \in A_i,$$

and that has $\mathbf{g}_n(s) = p$ for all $s \in (A_1 \cup \cdots \cup A_n)^c$. Then, by Theorem 9.5,

$$\phi(\mathbf{g}_n, \mathbf{p}) = \sum_{i=1}^{n} \pi(A_i)[\pi(A_n)^{-1} - \pi(A_i)^{-1}]$$

$$= \pi(A_n)^{-1} \sum_{i \leqslant n} \pi(A_i) - n.$$

Note also that for $s \in A_i$, $i \leqslant n$,

$$\phi((\tfrac{1}{2}\mathbf{f} + \tfrac{1}{2}\mathbf{g}_n)(s), p) = \tfrac{1}{2}\phi(p_i, p) + \tfrac{1}{2}\phi(\mathbf{g}_n(s), p) = \tfrac{1}{2}\pi(A_n)^{-1},$$

and for $s \in A_i$, $i > n$,

$$\phi((\tfrac{1}{2}\mathbf{f} + \tfrac{1}{2}\mathbf{g}_n)(s), p) = \tfrac{1}{2}\pi(A_i)^{-1} \geqslant \tfrac{1}{2}\pi(A_n)^{-1}.$$

Hence $\inf_s \phi((\tfrac{1}{2}\mathbf{f} + \tfrac{1}{2}\mathbf{g}_n)(s), p) = \tfrac{1}{2}\pi(A_n)^{-1} > 0$, and, since $p \succ r$ by hypothesis, it follows from Lemma 9.11 that $\phi(\tfrac{1}{2}\mathbf{f} + \tfrac{1}{2}\mathbf{g}_n, \mathbf{p}) \geqslant \tfrac{1}{2}\pi(A_n)^{-1}$. Therefore

$$\phi(\mathbf{f}, \mathbf{p}) \geqslant \pi(A_n)^{-1} - \phi(\mathbf{g}_n, \mathbf{p})$$

$$= \pi(A_n)^{-1} - \pi(A_n)^{-1} \sum_{i \leqslant n} \pi(A_i) + n \geqslant n.$$

Consequently, $\phi(\mathbf{f}, \mathbf{p}) \geqslant n$ for all n, a contradiction, and therefore ϕ on $P \times \{p\}$ is bounded above. ∎

LEMMA 9.15 [Theorem 9.7(a)]. *ϕ on $P \times P$ is bounded.*

Proof. Suppose to the contrary that ϕ *on* $P \times P$ is unbounded, so $\phi(P \times P) = (-\infty, \infty)$. For definiteness let p_i and q_i for $i = 1, 2, \ldots$ satisfy $\phi(p_i, q_i) = \pi(A_i)^{-1}$. Also take $\mathbf{f} =_{A_i} p_i$ and $\mathbf{g} =_{A_i} q_i$. We shall obtain the contradiction that $\phi(\mathbf{f}, \mathbf{g})$ is infinite.

Fix r with $q > r > p$ for some $p, q \in P$. Define simple $\mathbf{f}_n$ and $\mathbf{g}_n$ by

$$\mathbf{f}_n =_{A_i} p_i \quad \text{for } i \leqslant n; \qquad \mathbf{f}_n(s) = r \quad \text{otherwise,}$$

$$\mathbf{g}_n =_{A_i} q_i \quad \text{for } i \leqslant n; \qquad \mathbf{g}_n(s) = r \quad \text{otherwise.}$$

Then by Theorem 9.5,

$$\phi(\mathbf{f}_n, \mathbf{g}_n) = \sum_{i=1}^n \pi(A_i)[\pi(A_i)^{-1}] = n.$$

In addition, note that $(\frac{1}{2}\mathbf{f} + \frac{1}{2}\mathbf{g}_n)(s) = (\frac{1}{2}\mathbf{g} + \frac{1}{2}\mathbf{f}_n)(s)$ for all $s \in A_1 \cup \cdots \cup A_n$ and that, for all $s \in (A_1 \cup \cdots \cup A_n)^c$,

$$\phi((\tfrac{1}{2}\mathbf{f} + \tfrac{1}{2}\mathbf{g}_n)(s), (\tfrac{1}{2}\mathbf{g} + \tfrac{1}{2}\mathbf{f}_n)(s))$$

$$= \phi(\tfrac{1}{2}p_i + \tfrac{1}{2}r, \tfrac{1}{2}q_i + \tfrac{1}{2}r)$$

$$= \tfrac{1}{4}[\phi(p_i, q_i) + \phi(p_i, r) + \phi(r, q_i)]$$

when $s \in A_i$. Since $\phi(p_i, q_i) \to \infty$ and since ϕ is bounded on $P \times \{r\}$ by Lemmas 9.13 and 9.14, it follows that there is an N such that

$$\phi(p_i, q_i) + \phi(p_i, r) + \phi(r, q_i) > 0 \qquad \text{for all } i \geqslant N.$$

This N does not depend on the particular n under consideration. Hence for all $n \geqslant N$,

$$(\tfrac{1}{2}\mathbf{f} + \tfrac{1}{2}\mathbf{g}_n)(s) \succsim (\tfrac{1}{2}\mathbf{g} + \tfrac{1}{2}\mathbf{f}_n)(s) \qquad \text{for all } s \in S.$$

Then, by T5*, $\tfrac{1}{2}\mathbf{f} + \tfrac{1}{2}\mathbf{g}_n \succsim \tfrac{1}{2}\mathbf{g} + \tfrac{1}{2}\mathbf{f}_n$ whenever $n \geqslant N$, so

$$\phi(\mathbf{f}, \mathbf{g}) \geqslant \phi(\mathbf{f}_n, \mathbf{g}) + \phi(\mathbf{f}_n, \mathbf{f}) + \phi(\mathbf{g}, \mathbf{g}_n)$$

$$= n + \phi(\mathbf{f}_n, \mathbf{f}) + \phi(\mathbf{g}, \mathbf{g}_n) \qquad \text{for } n \geqslant N.$$

We claim that $\phi(\mathbf{f}_n, \mathbf{f})$ and $\phi(\mathbf{g}, \mathbf{g}_n)$ are bounded. Consider $(\mathbf{f}, \mathbf{f}_n)$, which equals (p_i, p_i) on A_i for $i \leqslant n$ and (p_i, r) on all A_i for $i > n$. Since $\phi(x, r)$ is bounded on $P \times \{r\}$ by Lemmas 9.13 and 9.14, let

$$a = \inf\{\phi(x, r) : x \in P\}, \qquad b = \sup\{\phi(x, r) : x \in P\}$$

with a and b finite. If $b \leqslant 0$, then $\phi(\mathbf{f}, \mathbf{f}_n) \leqslant 0$ by T5*. If $b > 0$, define λ by $\lambda b + (1 - \lambda)\phi(p, r) = 0$, let $\mathbf{f}' =_{A_i} p_i$ for $i \leqslant n$, and $\mathbf{f}'(s) = \lambda p_i + (1 -$

$\lambda)p$ otherwise; observe that $\phi(\mathbf{f}'(s), \mathbf{f}_n(s)) \leqslant 0$ for all s, and thus conclude from T5* that $\phi(\mathbf{f}', \mathbf{f}_n) \leqslant 0$. Since

$$\phi(\mathbf{f}', \mathbf{f}_n) = \phi\left(\lambda\mathbf{f} + (1 - \lambda) \begin{Bmatrix} p_i & \text{for } i \leqslant n \\ p & \text{for } i > n \end{Bmatrix}, \mathbf{f}_n\right)$$

$$= \lambda\phi(\mathbf{f}, \mathbf{f}_n) + (1 - \lambda) \left[1 - \sum_{i \leqslant n} \pi(A_i)\right] \phi(p, r),$$

it follows that

$$\phi(\mathbf{f}, \mathbf{f}_n) \leqslant \left[1 - \sum_{i \leqslant n} \pi(A_i)\right] \phi(r, p) \frac{1 - \lambda}{\lambda} = b \left[1 - \sum_{i \leqslant n} \pi(A_i)\right].$$

Hence, $\phi(\mathbf{f}, \mathbf{f}_n) \leqslant \max\{0, b\}$. By a similar proof, $\min\{0, a\} \leqslant \phi(\mathbf{f}, \mathbf{f}_n)$.

Thus $\phi(\mathbf{f}_n, \mathbf{f})$ and $\phi(\mathbf{g}, \mathbf{g}_n)$ are bounded as n gets large. Since $\phi(\mathbf{f}, \mathbf{g}) \geqslant n + \phi(\mathbf{f}_n, \mathbf{f}) + \phi(\mathbf{g}, \mathbf{g}_n)$ for $n \geqslant N$, we obtain the contradiction that $\phi(\mathbf{f}, \mathbf{g})$ is infinite. ∎

LEMMA 9.16 [Theorem 9.7(b)]. $\inf_S \phi(\mathbf{f}(s), p) \leqslant \phi(\mathbf{f}, \mathbf{p}) \leqslant \sup_S \phi(\mathbf{f}(s), p)$.

Proof. We show $\phi(\mathbf{f}, \mathbf{p}) \leqslant \sup_S \phi(\mathbf{f}(s), p) = b$, where b is finite by Lemma 9.15. The only cases not already covered by Lemma 9.12 are ($b > 0$, $r \gtrsim p$ for all $r \in P$) and ($b < 0$, $p \gtrsim r$ for all $r \in P$).

Suppose first that $b > 0$, $r \gtrsim p$ for all r, and let $t \in P$ satisfy $t > p$. Such a t is guaranteed by $b > 0$. Let $c = \sup_S \phi(\mathbf{f}(s), t)$. For all $0 < \lambda < 1$, $\sup_S \phi(\mathbf{f}(s), \lambda t + (1 - \lambda)p) \leqslant \lambda c + (1 - \lambda)b$. Since $t > \lambda t + (1 - \lambda)p > p$, it follows from Lemma 9.12 that

$$\phi(\mathbf{f}, \lambda t + (1 - \lambda)\mathbf{p}) = \lambda\phi(\mathbf{f}, \mathbf{t}) + (1 - \lambda)\phi(\mathbf{f}, \mathbf{p})$$

$$\leqslant \lambda c + (1 - \lambda)b.$$

Let λ approach 0 to conclude that $\phi(\mathbf{f}, \mathbf{p}) \leqslant b$.

Suppose next that $b < 0$, $p \gtrsim r$ for all r, and let t satisfy $p > t$. Let $c = \sup_S \phi(\mathbf{f}(s), t)$ so, for $0 < \lambda < 1$, $\sup_S \phi(\mathbf{f}(s), \lambda t + (1 - \lambda)p) \leqslant \lambda c + (1 - \lambda)b$. Since $p > \lambda t + (1 - \lambda)p > t$, Lemma 9.12 yields

$$\phi(\mathbf{f}, \lambda t + (1 - \lambda)\mathbf{p}) = \lambda\phi(\mathbf{f}, \mathbf{t}) + (1 - \lambda)\phi(\mathbf{f}, \mathbf{p})$$

$$\leqslant \lambda c + (1 - \lambda)b,$$

and again $\phi(\mathbf{f}, \mathbf{p}) \leqslant b$. ∎

LEMMA 9.17. $\phi(\mathbf{f}, \mathbf{p}) = \int_S \phi(\mathbf{f}(s), p) \, d\pi(s)$.

Proof. This proof mimics our later proof of Theorem 9.8 with $\mathbf{g}$ there replaced by $\mathbf{p}$ and with Lemma 9.20 replaced by Lemma 9.16. ∎

LEMMA 9.18 [Theorem 9.7(c)]. $\phi(\mathbf{f}, \mathbf{g}) = \int_S \phi(\mathbf{f}(s), \mathbf{g}(s))\, d\pi(s)$ *if* $\mathbf{g}$ *is simple.*

Proof. Assume that $\mathbf{g} =_{B_i} p_i$ for a partition $\{B_1, \ldots, B_n\}$ of S. By Lemma 9.10, for each $x \in P$,

$$\phi(\mathbf{f}, \mathbf{g}) = \sum_{i=1}^{n} \phi(\mathbf{f}B_i x, p_i B_i x).$$

Consider $\phi(\mathbf{f}B_1 x, p_1 B_1 x)$. Write $\mathbf{f}B_1 x$ as $(\mathbf{f}, x, \ldots, x)$ and $p_1 B_1 x$ as $(p_1, x, \ldots, x)$, where the jth positions refer to B_j. By Lemma 9.10,

$$\phi((\mathbf{f}, x, \ldots, x), (p_1, x, \ldots, x))$$
$$= \phi((\mathbf{f}, p_1, x, \ldots, x), (p_1, p_1, x, \ldots, x))$$
$$\quad + \phi((p_1, x, p_1, \ldots, p_1), (p_1, x, p_1, \ldots, p_1))$$
$$= \phi((\mathbf{f}, p_1, x, \ldots, x), (p_1, p_1, x, \ldots, x))$$
$$= \phi((\mathbf{f}, p_1, p_1, x, \ldots, x), (p_1, p_1, p_1, x, \ldots, x))$$
$$\vdots$$
$$= \phi((\mathbf{f}, p_1, \ldots, p_1), (p_1, p_1, \ldots, p_1)).$$

Hence, by Lemma 9.17, $\phi(\mathbf{f}B_1 x, p_1 B_1 x) = \int_{B_1} \phi(\mathbf{f}(s), p_1)\, d\pi(s)$. Since a similar expression holds for each B_i,

$$\phi(\mathbf{f}, \mathbf{g}) = \sum_i \int_{B_i} \phi(\mathbf{f}(s), p_i)\, d\pi(s) = \int_S \phi(\mathbf{f}(s), \mathbf{g}(s))\, d\pi(s). \quad \blacksquare$$

LEMMA 9.19 [Theorem 9.7(d)]. ϕ *on* $\mathbf{F} \times \mathbf{F}$ *is bounded.*

Proof. Assume $\sup \phi(P \times P) = 1$ for definiteness. Let $p, q \in P$ satisfy $\phi(p, q) > \frac{7}{9}$. For any $\mathbf{f}, \mathbf{g} \in \mathbf{F}$,

$$16\phi(\tfrac{1}{4}\mathbf{f}(s) + \tfrac{3}{4}r, \tfrac{1}{4}\mathbf{g}(s) + \tfrac{3}{4}p)$$
$$= \phi(\mathbf{f}(s), \mathbf{g}(s)) + 3\phi(r, \mathbf{g}(s)) + 3\phi(\mathbf{f}(s), p) + 9\phi(r, p) < 0$$

since the first three terms sum to 7 or less and the last is smaller than -7. It follows from T5* that $\phi(\mathbf{f}, \mathbf{g}) \leqslant 3\phi(\mathbf{g}, r) + 3\phi(p, \mathbf{f}) + 9\phi(p, r) \leqslant 3 + 3 + 9$ (by Lemma 9.17), so $\phi(\mathbf{f}, \mathbf{g}) \leqslant 15$. Since $\mathbf{f}$ and $\mathbf{g}$ are arbitrary, $-15 \leqslant \phi(\mathbf{f}, \mathbf{g})$ by skew-symmetry, so ϕ on $\mathbf{F} \times \mathbf{F}$ is bounded. $\quad \blacksquare$

T5 *is assumed henceforth.*

LEMMA 9.20. $\inf_S \phi(\mathbf{f}(s), \mathbf{g}(s)) \leqslant \phi(\mathbf{f}, \mathbf{g}) \leqslant \sup_S \phi(\mathbf{f}(s), \mathbf{g}(s))$.

Proof. Let A be an event in $\mathcal{E}$ for which $0 < \pi(A) < 1$ as guaranteed by Theorem 9.5 and T4. By T1 and Theorem 9.7(a), (d), we assume with no loss of generality that sup $\phi(P \times P) = 1$, sup $\phi(\mathbf{F} \times \mathbf{F}) = K \geq 1$, and K is finite. Choose $y, z \in P$ with $\phi(y, z) \geq \frac{1}{2}$, and let $x = \frac{1}{2}y + \frac{1}{2}z$ so that $\phi(x, z) = \phi(y, x) > \frac{1}{4}$. Also let λ be any positive real number that does not exceed $\min\{\pi(A), \pi(A^c)\}/4K$.

Given $\mathbf{f}, \mathbf{g} \in \mathbf{F}$, let $\mathbf{g}_0 = \lambda\mathbf{g} + (1 - \lambda)\mathbf{f}$, so $\phi(\mathbf{f}, \mathbf{g}_0) = \lambda\phi(\mathbf{f}, \mathbf{g})$ and, for all s, $\phi(\mathbf{f}(s), \mathbf{g}_0(s)) = \lambda\phi(\mathbf{f}(s), \mathbf{g}(s))$. We show that the conclusion of the lemma holds for $(\mathbf{f}, \mathbf{g}_0)$, so it must also hold for $(\mathbf{f}, \mathbf{g})$.

By Lemma 9.10,

$$\phi(\mathbf{f}, \mathbf{g}_0) = \phi(\mathbf{f}Ax, \mathbf{g}_0Ax) + \phi(\mathbf{f}A^cx, \mathbf{g}_0A^cx)$$

with $\phi(\mathbf{f}Ax, \mathbf{g}_0Ax) = \lambda\phi(\mathbf{f}Ax, \mathbf{g}Ax)$ and $\phi(\mathbf{f}A^cx, \mathbf{g}_0A^cx) = \lambda\phi(\mathbf{f}A^cx, \mathbf{g}A^cx)$. Therefore

$$\max\{|\phi(\mathbf{f}Ax, \mathbf{g}_0Ax)|, |\phi(\mathbf{f}A^cx, \mathbf{g}_0A^cx)|\} \leq \min\{\pi(A), \pi(A^c)\}/4.$$

It follows from the construction of x that there are p and r in P such that $\pi(A^c)\phi(p, x) = \phi(\mathbf{f}Ax, \mathbf{g}_0Ax)$ and $\pi(A)\phi(r, x) = \phi(\mathbf{f}A^cx, \mathbf{g}_0A^cx)$, so that

$$\phi(\mathbf{f}, \mathbf{g}_0) = \pi(A)\phi(r, x) + \pi(A^c)\phi(p, x).$$

Moreover, Lemma 9.10 and Theorem 9.5 imply

$$\phi(\mathbf{f}Ax, \mathbf{g}_0Ap) = \phi(\mathbf{f}Ax, \mathbf{g}_0Ax) + \phi(xA^cx, pA^cx)$$

$$= \phi(\mathbf{f}Ax, \mathbf{g}_0Ax) + \pi(A^c)\phi(x, p) = 0,$$

$$\phi(\mathbf{f}A^cx, \mathbf{g}_0A^cx) = \phi(\mathbf{f}A^cx, \mathbf{g}_0A^cx) + \phi(xAx, rAx)$$

$$= \phi(\mathbf{f}A^cx, \mathbf{g}_0A^cx) + \pi(A)\phi(x, r) = 0,$$

and therefore $\mathbf{f}Ax \sim \mathbf{g}_0Ap$ and $\mathbf{f}A^cx \sim \mathbf{g}_0A^cr$.

We apply T5 to each of these $\sim$ statements to obtain the desired sup conclusion. (The inf conclusion is proved similarly.) It follows from our constructions that there are y' and z' in P such that

$$\phi(y', x) = \sup_A \phi(\mathbf{f}(s), \mathbf{g}_0(s)),$$

$$\phi(z', x) = \sup_{A^c} \phi(\mathbf{f}(s), \mathbf{g}_0(s)).$$

The first of these is used with $\mathbf{f}Ax \sim \mathbf{g}_0Ap$ in T5 to yield $y'Ax \gtrsim xAp$. Hence, by Theorem 9.5,

$$\phi(y'Ax, xAp) = \pi(A)\phi(y', x) + \pi(A^c)\phi(x, p) \geq 0,$$

or

$$\pi(A) \sup_A \phi(\mathbf{f}(s), \mathbf{g}_0(s)) \geq \pi(A^c)\phi(p, x).$$

Similarly, the defining equation for z' used with $\mathbf{f}A^c x \sim \mathbf{g}_0 A^c r$ in T5 yields

$$\pi(A^c) \sup_{A^c} \phi(\mathbf{f}(s), \mathbf{g}_0(s)) \geqslant \pi(A)\phi(r, x).$$

Therefore

$$\sup_{S} \phi(\mathbf{f}(s), \mathbf{g}_0(s))$$

$$= \pi(A) \sup_{S} \phi(\mathbf{f}(s), \mathbf{g}_0(s)) + \pi(A^c) \sup_{S} \phi(\mathbf{f}(s), \mathbf{g}_0(s))$$

$$\geqslant \pi(A) \sup_{A} \phi(\mathbf{f}(s), \mathbf{g}_0(s)) + \pi(A^c) \sup_{A^c} \phi(\mathbf{f}(s), \mathbf{g}_0(s))$$

$$\geqslant \pi(A^c)\phi(p, x) + \pi(A)\phi(r, x)$$

$$= \phi(\mathbf{f}, \mathbf{g}_0). \quad \blacksquare$$

Proof of Theorem 9.8. Given $\mathbf{f}, \mathbf{g} \in \mathbf{F}$, let

$$a = \inf_{S} \phi(\mathbf{f}(s), \mathbf{g}(s)), \qquad b = \sup_{S} \phi(\mathbf{f}(s), \mathbf{g}(s)).$$

If $a = b$, then $\phi(\mathbf{f}, \mathbf{g}) = a$ by Lemma 9.20, and $\int \phi(\mathbf{f}(s), \mathbf{g}(s)) \, d\pi(s) = a$, so the desired conclusion holds.

Assume henceforth that $a < b$. For a given $n \in \{1, 2, \ldots\}$ let

$$B_1 = \{s : a \leqslant \phi(\mathbf{f}(s), \mathbf{g}(s)) \leqslant a + (b - a)/n\},$$

$$B_i = \{s : a + (b - a)(i - 1)/n < \phi(\mathbf{f}(s), \mathbf{g}(s)) \leqslant a + (b - a)i/n\},$$

$$2 \leqslant i \leqslant n.$$

By Lemma 9.10,

$$\phi(\mathbf{f}, \mathbf{g}) = \sum_{i=1}^{n} \phi(\mathbf{f}B_i x, \mathbf{g}B_i x), \qquad x \in P.$$

Consider one term in this sum where $B_i \neq \varnothing$ and let $a_i = a + (b - a)(i - 1)/n$ and $b_i = a + (b - a)i/n$. For every $p, r \in P$ for which $a_i \leqslant \phi(p, r) \leqslant b_i$, Lemma 9.20 implies that $a_i \leqslant \phi(\mathbf{f}B_i p, \mathbf{g}B_i r) \leqslant b_i$. By Lemma 9.10 and Theorem 9.5,

$$\phi(\mathbf{f}B_i p, \mathbf{g}B_i r) = \phi(\mathbf{f}B_i x, \mathbf{g}B_i x) + \phi(pB_i^c x, rB_i^c x)$$

$$= \phi(\mathbf{f}B_i x, \mathbf{g}B_i x) + \pi(B_i^c)\phi(p, r).$$

Take $\phi(p, r)$ close to a_i and then close to b_i to get

$$\pi(B_i)a_i - 1/n^2 \leqslant \phi(\mathbf{f}B_i x, \mathbf{g}B_i x) \leqslant \pi(B_i)b_i + 1/n^2.$$

Since $\phi(\mathbf{f}, \mathbf{g}) = \Sigma \, \phi(\mathbf{f}B_i x, \mathbf{g}B_i x)$, it follows that

$$\sum_{i=1}^{n} \pi(B_i) \left[a + \frac{i-1}{n} (b - a) \right] - \frac{1}{n} \leqslant \phi(\mathbf{f}, \mathbf{g})$$

$$\leqslant \sum_{i=1}^{n} \pi(B_i) \left[a + \frac{i}{n} (b - a) \right] + \frac{1}{n} \, .$$

Moreover, by definition of expected value,

$$\sum_{i=1}^{n} \pi(B_i) \left[a + \frac{i-1}{n} (b - a) \right] \leqslant \int_{S} \phi(\mathbf{f}(s), \mathbf{g}(s)) \, d\pi(s)$$

$$\leqslant \sum_{i=1}^{n} \pi(B_i) \left[a + \frac{i}{n} (b - a) \right] \, .$$

Hence $|\phi(\mathbf{f}, \mathbf{g}) - \int \phi(\mathbf{f}(s), \mathbf{g}(s)) \, d\pi(s)| \leqslant (b - a + 1)/n$. Let $n \to \infty$ to obtain the desired conclusion. ∎

References

Adams, E. W. (1965). Elements of a theory of inexact measurement. *Philosophy of Science* **32**, 205–28.

Allais, M. (1953). Le comportement de l'homme rationnel devant le risque: Critique des postulats et axiomes de l'école américaine. *Econometrica* **21**, 503–46.

Allais, M. (1979a). The foundations of a positive theory of choice involving risk and a criticism of the postulates and axioms of the American school. *Expected Utility Hypotheses and the Allais Paradox* (ed. M. Allais and O. Hagen), pp. 27–145. Dordrecht, Holland: Reidel. Translation of "Fondements d'une theorie positive des choix comportant un risque et critique des postulats et axiomes de l'école américaine," *Colloques Internationaux du Centre National de la Recherche Scientifique. XL. Econométrie*, Paris, 1953, pp. 257–332.

Allais, M. (1979b). The so-called Allais paradox and rational decisions under uncertainty. *Expected Utility Hypotheses and the Allais Paradox* (ed. M. Allais and O. Hagen), pp. 437–681. Dordrecht, Holland: Reidel.

Allais, M. (1986). *The General Theory of Random Choices in Relation to the Invariant Cardinal Utility Function and the Specific Probability Function*. Dordrecht, Holland: Reidel (in press).

Allen, B. (1987). Smooth preferences and the approximate expected utility hypothesis. *Journal of Economic Theory* **41**, 340–55.

Alt, F. (1936). Über die Messbarkeit des Nutzens. *Zeitschrift für Nationaloekonomie* **7**, 161–69. English translation: On the measurement of utility. *Preferences, Utility, and Demand* (ed. J. S. Chipman, L. Hurwicz, M. K. Richter, and H. F. Sonnenschein), pp. 424–31. New York: Harcourt Brace Jovanovich, 1971.

Anscombe, F. J. and Aumann, R. J. (1963). A definition of subjective probability. *Annals of Mathematical Statistics* **34**, 199–205.

Armstrong, W. E. (1939). The determinateness of the utility function. *Economic Journal* **49**, 453–67.

Armstrong, W. E. (1948). Uncertainty and the utility function. *Economic Journal* **58**, 1-10.

Armstrong, W. E. (1950). A note on the theory of consumer's behaviour. *Oxford Economic Papers* **2**, 119–22.

Arrow, K. J. (1958). Bernoulli utility indicators for distributions over arbitrary spaces.

Technical Report **57**, Department of Economics, Stanford University, Stanford.

Arrow, K. J. (1974). *Essays in the Theory of Risk Bearing*. Amsterdam: North-Holland.

Aumann, R. J. (1962). Utility theory without the completeness axiom. *Econometrica* **30**, 445–62; **32** (1964), 210–12.

Barbera, S. and Sonnenschein, H. (1978). Preference aggregation with randomized social orderings. *Journal of Economic Theory* **18**, 244–54.

Baumol, W. J. (1958). The cardinal utility which is ordinal. *Economic Journal* **68**, 665–72.

Bawa, V. S. (1982). Stochastic dominance: a research bibliography. *Management Science* **28**, 698–712.

Bell, D. (1982). Regret in decision making under uncertainty. *Operations Research* **30**, 961–81.

Bell, D. E. (1983). Risk premiums for decision regret. *Management Science* **29**, 1156–66.

Bell, D. E. (1985). Disappointment in decision making under uncertainty. *Operations Research* **33**, 1–27.

Bernard, G. (1986). A discussion of the present state of utility theory (FUR II, Venice, 1984). *Theory and Decision* **20**, 173–88.

Bernoulli, D. (1954). Exposition of a new theory on the measurement of risk. *Econometrica* **22**, 23–36. Translated by L. Sommer from "Specimen theoriae novae de mensura sortis," *Commentarii Academiae Scientiarum Imperialis Petropolitanae* **5** (1738), 175–92.

Bernstein, S. N. (1917). On the axiomatic foundations of probability theory (in Russian). *Soobshcheniya i Protokolȳ Khar'kovskago Matematicheskago Obshchestva* **15**, 209–74.

Black, D. (1958). *The Theory of Committees and Elections*. Cambridge: Cambridge University Press.

Blackwell, D. and Girshick, M. A. (1954). *Theory of Games and Statistical Decisions*. New York: Wiley.

Bolker, E. D. (1966). Functions resembling quotients of measures. *Transactions of the American Mathematical Society* **124**, 292–312.

Bolker, E. D. (1967). A simultaneous axiomatization of utility and subjective probability. *Philosophy of Science* **34**, 333–40.

Boole, G. (1854). *An Investigation of the Laws of Thought*. New York: Dover (1958).

Browder, F. E. (1983). Fixed point theory and nonlinear problems. *Bulletin of the American Mathematical Society* **9**, 1–39.

Budescu, D. and Weiss, W. (1985). Reflection of transitive and intransitive preference: a test of prospect theory. IPDM Report 29, University of Haifa, Israel.

Chateauneuf, A. and Jaffray, J.-Y. (1984). Archimedean qualitative probabilities. *Journal of Mathematical Psychology* **28**, 191–204.

Chew, S. H. (1982). A mixture set axiomatization of weighted utility theory. Discussion Paper 82-4, College of Business and Public Administration, University of Arizona, Tucson.

Chew, S. H. (1983). A generalization of the quasilinear mean with applications to the measurement of income inequality and decision theory resolving the Allais paradox. *Econometrica* **51**, 1065–92.

Chew, S. H. (1984). An axiomatization of the rank dependent quasilinear mean generalizing the Gini mean and the quasilinear mean. Preprint, Department of Political Economy, Johns Hopkins University, Baltimore.

Chew, S. H. (1985). From strong substitution to very weak substitution: mixture-monotone utility theory and semi-weighted utility theory. Preprint, Department of Political Economy, Johns Hopkins University, Baltimore.

Chew, S. H., Karni, E. and Safra, Z. (1987). Risk aversion in the theory of expected utility with rank-dependent probabilities. *Journal of Economic Theory* **42**, 370–81.

Chew, S. H. and MacCrimmon, K. R. (1979). Alpha-nu choice theory: a generalization of expected utility theory. Working Paper 669, Faculty of Commerce and Business Administration, University of British Columbia, Vancouver.

Chew, S. H. and Waller, W. S. (1986). Empirical tests of weighted utility theory. *Journal of Mathematical Psychology* **30**, 55–72.

Chipman, J. S. (1960). The foundations of utility. *Econometrica* **28**, 193–224.

Chipman, J. S. (1971). Consumption theory without transitive indifference. *Preferences, Utility, and Demand* (ed. J. S. Chipman, L. Hurwicz, M. K. Richter, and H. F. Sonnenschein), pp. 224–53. New York: Harcourt Brace Jovanovich.

Choquet, G. (1955). Theory of capacities. *Annales de l'Institut Fourier* **5**, 131–295.

Cohen, M., Jaffray, J. Y., and Said, T. (1985). Individual behavior under risk and under uncertainty: an experimental study. *Theory and Decision* **18**, 203–28.

Condorcet, Marquis de (1785). Essai sur l'application de l'analyse á la probabilité des décisions rendues á la pluralité des voix. Paris.

Davidson, D. and Suppes, P. (1956). A finitistic axiomatization of subjective probability and utility. *Econometrica* **24**, 264–75.

Davis, J. M. (1958). The transitivity of preferences. *Behavioral Science* **3**, 26–33.

Debreu, G. (1960). Topological methods in cardinal utility theory. *Mathematical Methods in the Social Science, 1959* (ed. K. J. Arrow, S. Karlin, and P. Suppes), pp. 16–26. Stanford: Stanford University Press.

Debreu, G. (1972). Smooth preferences. *Econometrica* **40**, 603–15; **44** (1976), 831–32.

de Finetti, B. (1931a). Sul concetto di media. *Giornale dell'Instituto Italiano degli Attuari* **2**, 369–96.

de Finetti, B. (1931b). Sul significato soggettivo della probabilitá. *Fundamenta Mathematicae* **17**, 298–329.

de Finetti, B. (1964). Foresight: its logical laws, its subjective sources. *Studies in Subjective Probability* (ed. H. E. Kyburg and H. E. Smokler), pp. 93–158. New York: Wiley. Translated by H. E. Kyburg from "La prévision: ses lois logiques, ses sources subjectives," *Annales de l'Institut Henri Poincaré* **7** (1937), 1–68.

DeGroot, M. H. (1970). *Optimal Statistical Decisions*. New York: McGraw-Hill.

Dekel, E. (1986). An axiomatic characterization of preferences under uncertainty: weakening the independence axiom. *Journal of Economic Theory* **40**, 304–18.

Dempster, A. P. (1967). Upper and lower probabilities induced by a multivalued mapping. *Annals of Mathematical Statistics* **38**, 325–39.

Dempster, A. P. (1968). A generalization of Bayesian inference. *Journal of the Royal Statistical Society, Series B* **30**, 205–47.

Domotor, Z. (1978). Axiomatization of Jeffrey utilities. *Synthese* **39**, 165–210.

Edgeworth, F. Y. (1881). *Mathematical Psychics*. London: Kegan Paul.

Edwards, W. (1953). Probability-preferences in gambling. *American Journal of Psychology* **66**, 349–64.

Edwards, W. (1954a). The theory of decision making. *Psychological Bulletin* **51**, 380–417.

Edwards, W. (1954b). The reliability of probability preferences. *American Journal of Psychology* **67**, 68–95.

Edwards, W. (1954c). Probability preferences among bets with differing expected values. *American Journal of Psychology* **67**, 56–67.

Edwards, W. (1961). Behavioral decision theory. *Annual Review of Psychology* **12**, 473–98.

Edwards, W. (1968). Conservatism in human information processing. *Formal Representation of Human Judgment* (ed. B. Kleinmuntz), pp. 17–52. New York: Wiley.

Einhorn, H. J. and Hogarth, R. M. (1985). Ambiguity and uncertainty in probabilistic inference. *Psychological Review* **92**, 433–61.

Einhorn, H. J. and Hogarth, R. M. (1986). Decision making under ambiguity. *Journal of Business* **59**, S225–50.

Ellsberg, D. (1961). Risk, ambiguity, and the Savage axioms. *Quarterly Journal of Economics* **75**, 643–69.

Fan, K. (1952). Fixed-point and minimax theorems in locally convex topological linear spaces. *Proceedings of the National Academy of Sciences* (U.S.A.) **38** 121–26.

Farquhar, P. H. (1977). A survey of multiattribute utility theory and applications. *TIMS Studies in the Management Sciences* **6**, 59–89.

Farquhar, P. H. (1978). Interdependent criteria in utility analysis. *Multiple Criteria Problem Solving* (ed. S. Zionts), pp. 131–80. Berlin: Springer-Verlag.

Fine, T. (1973). *Theories of Probability*. New York: Academic Press.

Fishburn, P. C. (1965). Independence in utility theory with whole product sets. *Operations Research* **13**, 28–45.

Fishburn, P. C. (1967). Bounded expected utility. *Annals of Mathematical Statistics* **38**, 1054–60.

Fishburn, P. C. (1969). Weak qualitative probability on finite sets. *Annals of Mathematical Statistics* **40**, 2118–26.

Fishburn, P. C. (1970a). *Utility Theory for Decision Making*. New York: Wiley.

Fishburn, P. C. (1970b). Intransitive indifference in preference theory: a survey. *Operations Research* **18**, 207–28.

Fishburn, P. C. (1971a). A study of lexicographic expected utility. *Management Science* **17**, 672–78.

Fishburn, P. C. (1971b). One-way expected utility with finite consequence spaces. *Annals of Mathematical Statistics* **42**, 572–77.

Fishburn, P. C. (1972). Alternative axiomatizations of one-way expected utility. *Annals of Mathematical Statistics* **43**, 1648–51.

Fishburn, P. C. (1973a). *The Theory of Social Choice*. Princeton: Princeton University Press.

Fishburn, P. C. (1973b). A mixture-set axiomatization of conditional subjective expected utility. *Econometrica* **41**, 1–25.

Fishburn, P. C. (1974). Lexicographic orders, utilities, and decision rules: a survey. *Management Science* **20**, 1442–1471.

Fishburn, P. C. (1975a). Unbounded expected utility. *Annals of Statistics* **3**, 884–96.

Fishburn, P. C. (1975b). Weak comparative probability on infinite sets. *Annals of Probability* **3**, 889–93.

Fishburn, P. C. (1976a). Cardinal utility: an interpretive essay. *International Review of Economics and Business* **23**, 1102–14.

Fishburn, P. C. (1976b). Continua of stochastic dominance relations for bounded probability distributions. *Journal of Mathematical Economics* **3**, 295–311.

Fishburn, P. C. (1977a). Multiattribute utilities in expected utility theory. *Conflicting Objectives in Decisions* (ed. D. E. Bell, R. L. Keeney and H. Raiffa), pp. 172–94. New York: Wiley.

Fishburn, P. C. (1977b). Condorcet social choice functions. *SIAM Journal on Applied Mathematics* **33**, 469–89.

Fishburn, P. C. (1978a). A survey of multiattribute/multicriterion evaluation theories. *Multiple Criteria Problem Solving* (ed. S. Zionts), pp. 181–224. Berlin: Springer-Verlag.

Fishburn, P. C. (1978b). On Handa's "new theory of cardinality utility" and the maximization of expected return. *Journal of Political Economy* **86**, 321–24.

Fishburn, P. C. (1979). On the nature of expected utility. *Expected Utility Hypotheses and the Allais Paradox* (ed. M. Allais and O. Hagen), pp. 243–57. Dordrecht, Holland: Reidel.

Fishburn, P. C. (1980a). Lexicographic additive differences. *Journal of Mathematical Psychology* **21**, 191–218.

Fishburn, P. C. (1980b). Continua of stochastic dominance relations for unbounded probability distributions. *Journal of Mathematical Economics* **7**, 271–85.

Fishburn, P. C. (1981a). An axiomatic characterization of skew-symmetric bilinear functionals, with applications to utility theory. *Economics Letters* **8**, 311–13.

Fishburn, P. C. (1981b). Subjective expected utility: a review of normative theories. *Theory and Decision* **13**, 139–99.

Fishburn, P. C. (1982a). *The Foundations of Expected Utility*. Dordrecht, Holland: Reidel.

Fishburn, P. C. (1982b). A note on linear utility. *Journal of Economic Theory* **27**, 444–46.

Fishburn, P. C. (1982c). Nontransitive measurable utility. *Journal of Mathematical Psychology* **26**, 31–67.

Fishburn, P. C. (1983a). Transitive measurable utility. *Journal of Economic Theory* **31**, 293–317.

Fishburn, P. C. (1983b). Utility functions on ordered convex sets. *Journal of Mathematical Economics* **12**, 221–32.

Fishburn, P. C. (1983c). Ellsberg revisited: a new look at comparative probability. *Annals of Statistics* **11**, 1047–59.

Fishburn, P. C. (1983d). A generalization of comparative probability on finite sets. *Journal of Mathematical Psychology* **27**, 298–310.

Fishburn, P. C. (1984a). SSB utility theory: an economic perspective. *Mathematical Social Sciences* **8**, 63–94.

Fishburn, P. C. (1984b). SSB utility theory and decision-making under uncertainty. *Mathematical Social Sciences* **8**, 253–85.

Fishburn, P. C. (1984c). Dominance in SSB utility theory. *Journal of Economic Theory* **34**, 130–48.

Fishburn, P. C. (1984d). Probabilistic social choice based on simple voting comparisons. *Review of Economic Studies* **51**, 683–92.

Fishburn, P. C. (1984e). On Harsanyi's utilitarian cardinal welfare theorem. *Theory and Decision* **17**, 21–28.

Fishburn, P. C. (1984f). Multiattribute nonlinear utility theory. *Management Science* **30**, 1301–10.

Fishburn, P. C. (1984g). Elements of risk analysis in non-linear utility theory. *INFOR* **22**, 81–97.

Fishburn, P. C. (1985a). *Interval Orders and Interval Graphs.* New York: Wiley.

Fishburn, P. C. (1985b). Nontransitive preference theory and the preference reversal phenomenon. *International Review of Economics and Business* **32**, 39–50.

Fishburn, P. C. (1986a). Ordered preference differences without ordered preferences. *Synthese* **67**, 361–68.

Fishburn, P. C. (1986b). Implicit mean value and certainty equivalence. *Econometrica* **54**, 1197–1205.

Fishburn, P. C. (1986c). The axioms of subjective probability. *Statistical Science* **1**, 345–55.

Fishburn, P. C. (1986d). A new model for decisions under uncertainty. *Economics Letters* **21**, 127–30.

Fishburn, P. C. (1986e). Nontransitive measurable utility for decision under uncertainty. AT&T Bell Laboratories, Murray Hill, NJ.

Fishburn, P. C. (1986f). Interval models for comparative probability on finite sets. *Journal of Mathematical Psychology* **30**, 221–42.

Fishburn, P. C. and Gehrlein, W. V. (1987). Aggregation theory for SSB utility functionals. *Journal of Economic Theory* **42**, 352–62.

Fishburn, P. C. and Keeney, R. L. (1975). Generalized utility independence and some implications. *Operations Research* **23**, 928–40.

Fishburn, P. C. and Kochenberger, G. A. (1979). Two-piece von Neumann-Morgenstern utility functions. *Decision Sciences* **10**, 503–18.

Fishburn, P. C. and LaValle, I. H. (1986). Context-dependent choice with nonlinear and nontransitive utilities. *Econometrica* (in press).

Fishburn, P. C. and LaValle, I. H. (1987a). A nonlinear, nontransitive and additive-probability model for decisions under uncertainty. *Annals of Statistics* **15**, 830–44.

Fishburn, P. C. and LaValle, I. H. (1987b). Transitivity is equivalent to independence for states-additive SSB utilities. *Journal of Economic Theory* (in press).

Fishburn, P. C. and Rosenthal, R. W. (1986). Noncooperative games and nontransitive preferences. *Mathematical Social Sciences* **12**, 1–7.

Fisher, I. (1892). Mathematical investigations in the theory of values and prices. *Transactions of Connecticut Academy of Arts and Sciences* **9**, 1–124.

Flood, M. M. (1951–52). A preference experiment. The Rand Corporation Papers P-256, P-258, and P-263.

Franke, G. (1978). Expected utility with ambiguous probabilities and "irrational" parameters. *Theory and Decision* **9**, 267–83.

Friedman, M. and Savage, L. J. (1948). The utility analysis of choices involving risk. *Journal of Politcal Economy* **56**, 279–304.

Frisch, R. (1926). Sur un problème d'économie pure. *Norsk Matematisk Forenings Skrifter* **16**, 1–40. English translation: On a problem in pure economics. *Preferences, Utility, and Demand* (ed. J. S. Chipman, L. Hurwicz, M. K. Richter, and H. F. Sonnenschein), pp. 386–423. New York: Harcourt Brace Jovanovich, 1971.

Gärdenfors, P. and Sahlin, N.-E. (1982). Unreliable probabilities, risk taking, and decision making. *Synthese* **53**, 361–86.

Georgescu-Roegen, N. (1936). The pure theory of consumer's behavior. *Quarterly Journal of Economics* **50**, 545–93. Reprinted in Georgescu-Roegen (1966).

Georgescu-Roegen, N. (1954). Choice, expectations, and measurability. *Quarterly Journal of Economics* **58**, 503–34. Reprinted in Georgescu-Roegen (1966).

Georgescu-Roegen, N. (1958). Threshold in choice and the theory of demand. *Econometrica* **26**, 157–68. Reprinted in Georgescu-Roegen (1966).

Georgescu-Roegen, N. (1966). *Analytical Economics: Issues and Problems.* Cambridge, MA: Harvard University Press.

Geraghty, M. A. and Bor-Luh Lin (1985). Minimax theorems without linear structure. *Linear and Multilinear Algebra* **17**, 171–80.

Gilboa, I. (1985a). Duality in non-additive expected utility theory. Working Paper 7-85, Foerder Institute for Economic Research, Tel-Aviv University, Ramat Aviv, Israel.

Gilboa, I. (1985b). Subjective distortions of probabilities and non-additive probabilities. Working Paper 18-85, Foerder Institute for Economic Research, Tel-Aviv University, Ramat Aviv, Israel.

Gilboa, I. (1986). A combination of expected utility and maxmin decision criteria. Working Paper 12-86, Foerder Institute for Economic Research, Tel-Aviv University, Ramat Aviv, Israel.

Gilboa, I. (1987). Expected utility with purely subjective non-additive probabilities. *Journal of Mathematical Economics* **16**, 65–88.

Gilboa, I. and Schmeidler, D. (1986). Maxmin expected utility with a non-unique prior. Working Paper 16-86, Foerder Institute for Economic Research, Tel-Aviv University, Ramat Aviv, Israel.

Goldman, A. J. (1956). Resolution and separation theorems for polyhedral convex sets. *Linear Inequalities and Related Systems, Annals of Mathematics Studies 38* (ed. H. W. Kuhn and A. W. Tucker), pp. 41–51. Princeton: Princeton University Press.

Goldstein, W. and Einhorn, H. J. (1985). A theory of preference reversals. Preprint, Graduate School of Business, University of Chicago.

Good, I. J. (1950). *Probability and the Weighing of Evidence.* London: Griffin.

Good, I. J. (1962). Subjective probability as the measure of a non-measurable set. *Logic, Methodology and Philosophy of Science* (ed. E. Nagel, P. Suppes, and A. Tarski), pp. 319–29. Stanford: Stanford University Press.

Gossen, H. H. (1854). *Entwickelung der Gesetze des menschlichen Verkehrs, und der daraus fliessenden Regeln für menschliches Handeln.* Braunschweig: Vieweg and Sohn.

Grayson, C. J. (1960). *Decisions under Uncertainty: Drilling Decisions by Oil and Gas Operators.* Cambridge, MA: Harvard University.

Grether, D. M. and Plott, C. R. (1979). Economic theory of choice and the preference reversal phenomenon. *American Economic Review* **69**, 623–38.

Grünbaum, B. (1970). Polytopes, graphs, and complexes. *Bulletin of the American Mathematical Society* **76**, 1131–1201.

Hagen, O. (1972). A new axiomatization of utility under risk. *Teorie A Metoda* **4**, 55–80.

Hagen, O. (1979). Towards a positive theory of preferences under risk. *Expected Utility Hypotheses and the Allais Paradox* (ed. M. Allais and O. Hagen), pp. 271–302. Dordrecht, Holland: Reidel.

Halmos, P. R. (1950). *Measure Theory.* New York: Van Nostrand.

Handa, J. (1977). Risk, probabilities and a new theory of cardinal utility. *Journal of Politcal Economy* **85**, 97–122.

Harsanyi, J. C. (1955). Cardinal welfare, individualistic ethics, and interpersonal comparisons of utility. *Journal of Political Economy* **63**, 309–21.

Hartigan, J. A. (1983). *Bayes Theory.* New York: Springer-Verlag.

Hausner, M. (1954). Multidimensional utilities. *Decision Processes* (ed. R. M. Thrall, C. H. Coombs, and R. L. Davis), pp. 167–80. New York: Wiley.

Hausner, M. and Wendel, J. G. (1952). Ordered vector spaces. *Proceeding of the American Mathematical Society* **3**, 977–82.

Heath, D. C. and Sudderth, W. D. (1972). On a theorem of de Finetti, oddsmaking, and game theory. *Annals of Mathematical Statistics* **43**, 2072–77.

Hershey, J. C. and Schoemaker, P. J. H. (1980). Prospect theory's reflection hypothesis: a critical examination. *Organizational Behavior and Human Performance* **25**, 395–418.

Herstein, I. N. and Milnor, J. (1953). An axiomatic approach to measurable utility. *Econometrica* **21**, 291–97.

Hicks, J. R. and Allen, R. G. D. (1934). A reconsideration of the theory of value: I, II. *Economica* **1**, 52–75, 196–219.

Howard, R. A. (1968). The foundations of decision analysis. *IEEE Transactions on System Science and Cybernetics* **SSC-4**, 211–19.

Jeffrey, R. C. (1965). *The Logic of Decision.* New York: McGraw-Hill.

Jeffrey, R. C. (1978). Axiomatizing the logic of decision. *Foundations and Applications of Decision Theory, Vol. 1: Theoretical Foundations* (ed. C. A. Hooker, J. J. Leach, and E. F. McClennan), pp. 227–31. Dordrecht, Holland: Reidel.

Jensen, N. E. (1967). An introduction to Bernoullian utility theory. I. Utility functions. *Swedish Journal of Economics* **69**, 163–83.

Jevons, W. S. (1871). *The Theory of Political Economy*. London: Macmillan.

Kahneman, D., Slovic, P., and Tversky, A. (eds.) (1982). *Judgement under Uncertainty: Heuristics and Biases*. Cambridge: Cambridge University Press.

Kahneman, D. and Tversky, A. (1972). Subjective probability: a judgment of representativeness. *Cognitive Psychology* **3**, 430–54.

Kahneman, D. and Tversky, A. (1979). Prospect theory: an analysis of decision under risk. *Econometrica* **47**, 263–91.

Kahneman, D. and Tversky, A. (1984). Choices, values and frames. *American Psychologist* **39**, 341–50.

Kakutani, S. (1941). A generalization of Brouwer's fixed point theorem. *Duke Mathematical Journal* **8**, 457–59.

Kannai, Y. (1963). Existence of a utility in infinite dimensional partially ordered spaces. *Israel Journal of Mathematics* **1**, 229–34.

Karmarkar, U. S. (1978). Subjectively weighted utility: a descriptive extension of the expected utility model. *Organizational Behavior and Human Performance* **21**, 61–72.

Karni, E. (1985). *Decision Making under Uncertainty: The Case of State-Dependent Preferences*. Cambridge, MA: Harvard University Press.

Karni, E. and Safra, Z. (1987). "Preference reversal" and the observability of preferences by experimental methods. *Econometrica* **55**, 675–85.

Karni, E., Schmeidler, D. and Vind, K. (1983). On state dependent preferences and subjective probabilities. *Econometrica* **51**, 1021–32.

Kauder, E. (1965). *A History of Marginal Utility Theory*. Princeton: Princeton University Press.

Keeney, R. L. (1968). Quasi-separable utility functions. *Naval Research Logistics Quarterly* **15**, 551–65.

Keeney, R. L. and Raiffa, H. (1976). *Decisions with Multiple Objectives: Preferences and Value Tradeoffs*. New York: Wiley.

Kelley, J. L. (1955). *General Topology*. New York: American Book Company.

Kelley, J. L. and Namioka, I. (1963). *Linear Topological Spaces*. Princeton: Van Nostrand.

Keynes, J. M. (1921). *A Treatise on Probability*. New York: Macmillan. Torchbook edition, 1962.

Kolmogorov, A. (1930). Sur la notion de la moyenne. *Rendiconti Accademia dei Lincei* **12**, 338–91.

Koopman, B. O. (1940). The axioms and algebra of intuitive probability. *Annals of Mathematics* **41**, 269–92.

Kraft, C. H., Pratt, J. W., and Seidenberg, A. (1959). Intuitive probability on finite sets. *Annals of Mathematical Statistics* **30**, 408–19.

Krantz, D. H., Luce, R. D., Suppes, P., and Tversky, A. (1971). *Foundations of Measurement, Volume I*. New York: Academic Press.

Kreweras, G. (1961). Sur une possibilité de rationaliser les intransitivités. *La Décision,* Colloques Internationaux du Centre National de la Recherche Scientifique, pp. 27–32. Paris: Editions du Centre National de la Recherche Scientifique.

Kreweras, G. (1965). Aggregation of preference orderings. *Mathematics and Social Sciences I* (compiled by S. Sternberg et al.), pp. 73–79. Paris: Mouton.

Kuhn, H. W. (1956). Solvability and consistency for linear equations and inequalities. *American Mathematical Monthly* **63**, 217–32.

Lange, O. (1934). The determinateness of the utility function. *Review of Economic Studies* **1**, 218–24.

LaValle, I. H. (1978). *Fundamentals of Decision Analysis.* New York: Holt, Rinehart and Winston.

Ledyard, J. O. (1971). A pseudo-metric space of probability measures and the existence of measurable utility. *Annals of Mathematical Statistics* **42**, 794–98.

Libby, R. and Fishburn, P. C. (1977). Behavioral models of risk taking in business decisions: a survey and evaluation. *Journal of Accounting Research* **15**, 272–92.

Lichtenstein, S. and Slovic, P. (1971). Reversals of preferences between bids and choices in gambling decisions. *Journal of Experimental Psychology* **89**, 46–55.

Lichtenstein, S. and Slovic, P. (1973). Response-induced reversals of preferences in gambling: an extended replication in Las Vegas. *Journal of Experimental Psychology* **101**, 16–20.

Lindman, H. R. (1971). Inconsistent preferences among gambles. *Journal of Experimental Psychology* **89**, 390–97.

Loeve, M. (1960). *Probability Theory,* 2nd ed. Princeton: Van Nostrand.

Loomes, G. and Sugden, R. (1982). Regret theory: an alternative theory of rational choice under uncertainty. *Economic Journal* **92**, 805–24.

Loomes, G. and Sugden, R. (1983). A rationale for preference reversal. *American Economic Review* **73**, 428–32.

Loomes, G. and Sugden, R. (1986). Disappointment and dynamic consistency in choice under uncertainty. *Review of Economic Studies* **53**, 271–82.

Loomes, G. and Sugden, R. (1987). Some implications of a more general form of regret theory. *Journal of Economic Theory* **41**, 270–87.

Luce, R. D. (1956). Semiorders and a theory of utility discrimination. *Econometrica* **24**, 178–91.

Luce, R. D. (1978). Lexicographic tradeoff structures. *Theory and Decisions* **9**, 187–93.

Luce, R. D. (1984). Existence of dual bilinear representations. Preprint, Harvard University, Cambridge, MA.

Luce, R. D. and Krantz, D. H. (1971). Conditional expected utility. *Econometrica* **39**, 253–71.

Luce, R. D. and Narens, L. (1985). Classification of concatenation measurement structures according to scale type. *Journal of Mathematical Psychology* **29**, 1–72.

Luce, R. D. and Raiffa, H. (1957). *Games and Decisions.* New York: Wiley.

Luce, R. D. and Suppes, P. (1965). Preference, utility, and subjective probability. *Handbook of Mathematical Psychology, III* (ed. R. D. Luce, R. R. Bush, and E. Galanter), pp. 249–410. New York: Wiley.

MacCrimmon, K. R. (1968). Descriptive and normative implications of the decision-theory postulates. *Risk and Uncertainty* (ed. K. Borch and J. Mossin), pp. 3–32. New York: Macmillan.

MacCrimmon, K. R. and Larsson, S. (1979). Utility theory: axioms versus "paradoxes." *Expected Utility Hypotheses and the Allais Paradox* (ed. M. Allais and O. Hagen), pp. 333–409. Dordrecht, Holland: Reidel.

Machina, M. J. (1982a). "Expected utility" analysis without the independence axiom. *Econometrica* **50**, 277–323.

Machina, M. J. (1982b). A stronger characterization of declining risk aversion. *Econometrica* **50**, 1069–79.

Machina, M. J. (1983a). The economic theory of individual behavior toward risk: theory, evidence and new directions. Technical Report 433, Center for Research on Organizational Efficiency, Stanford University, Stanford.

Machina, M. J. (1983b). Generalized expected utility analysis and the nature of observed violations of the independence axiom. *Foundations of Utility and Risk Theory with Applications* (ed. B. Stigum and F. Wenstøp). Dordrecht, Holland: Reidel.

Machina, M. J. (1984). Temporal risk and the nature of induced preferences. *Journal of Economic Theory* **33**, 199–231.

Machina, M. J. (1985). Stochastic choice functions generated from deterministic preferences over lotteries. *Economic Journal* **95**, 575–94.

Machina, M. J. and Neilson, W. S. (1987). The Ross characterization of risk aversion: strengthening and extension. *Econometrica* **55**, 1139–49.

Manski, C. F. (1977). The structure of random utility models. *Theory and Decision* **8**, 229–54.

Marschak, J. (1950). Rational behavior, uncertain prospects, and measurable utility. *Econometrica* **18**, 111–41. Errata, 1950, p. 312.

Marshall, A. (1890). *Principles of Economics.* London: Macmillan.

Mas-Colell, A. (1974). An equilibrium existence theorem without complete or transitive preferences. *Journal of Mathematical Economics* **1**, 237–46.

May, K. O. (1954). Intransitivity, utility, and the aggregation of preference patterns. *Econometrica* **22**, 1–13.

McNeil, B. J., Pauker, S. G., Sox, H. C., Jr., and Tversky, A. (1982). On the elicitation of preferences for alternative therapies. *New England Journal of Medicine* **306**, 1259–62.

Menger, C. (1871). *Grundsätze der Volkswirthschaftslehre.* Vienna: W. Braumuller. English translation: *Principles of Economics.* Glencoe, IL: Free Press, 1950.

Menger, K. (1967). The role of uncertainty in economics. *Essays in Mathematical Economics* (ed. M. Shubik), pp. 211–31. Princeton, NJ: Princeton University Press. Translated by W. Schoellkopf from "Das Unsicherheitsmoment in der Wertlehre," *Zeitschrift für Nationaloekonomie* **5** (1934), pp. 459–85.

Milnor, J. (1978). Analytic proofs of the "hairy ball theorem" and the Brouwer fixed point theorem. *American Mathematical Monthly* **85**, 521–24.

Morrison, D. G. (1967). On the consistency of preferences in Allais' paradox. *Behavioral Science* **12**, 373–83.

Morrison, H. W. (1962). Intransitivity of paired comparison choices. Ph.D. Dissertation, University of Michigan, Ann Arbor.

Mosteller, F. and Nogee, P. (1951). An experimental measure of utility. *Journal of Political Economy* **59**, 371–404.

Nagumo, M. (1930). Uber eine klasse der mittelwerte. *Japan Journal of Mathematics* **7**, 71–79.

Nakamura, Y. (1984). Nonlinear measurable utility analysis. Ph.D. Dissertation, University of California, Davis.

Nakamura, Y. (1985). Weighted linear utility. Preprint, Department of Precision Engineering, Osaka University, Osaka, Japan.

Narens, L. (1974). Measurement without Archimedean axioms. *Philosophy of Science* **41**, 374–93.

Narens, L. (1985). *Abstract Measurement Theory*. Cambridge, MA: MIT Press.

Nash, J. (1951). Non-cooperative games. *Annals of Mathematics* **54**, 286–95.

Nikaidô, H. (1954). On von Neumann's minimax theorem. *Pacific Journal of Mathematics* **4**, 65–72.

Pareto, V. (1906). *Manuale di Economia Politica, con una Intraduzione alla Scienza Sociale.* Milan: Società Editrice Libraria.

Payne, J. W. (1973). Alternative approaches to decision making under risk: moments versus risk dimensions. *Psychological Bulletin* **80**, 435–53.

Payne, J. W. and Braunstein, M. L. (1971). Preferences among gambles with equal underlying distributions. *Journal of Experimental Psychology* **87**, 13–18.

Pfanzagl, J. (1967). Subjective probability derived from the Morgenstern–von Neumann utility concept. *Essays in Mathematical Economics* (ed. M. Shubik), pp. 237–51. Princeton: Princeton University Press.

Pfanzagl, J. (1968). *Theory of Measurement.* New York: Wiley.

Pinter, C. C. (1971). *Set Theory.* Reading, MA: Addison-Wesley.

Pollak, R. A. (1967). Additive von Neumann–Morgenstern utility functions. *Econometrica* **35**, 485–94.

Pommerehne, W. W., Schneider, F., and Zweifel, P. (1982). Economic theory of choice and the preference reversal phenomenon: a reexamination. *American Economic Review* **72**, 569–74.

Pratt, J. W. (1964). Risk aversion in the small and in the large. *Econometrica* **32**, 122–36.

Pratt, J. W., Raiffa, H., and Schlaifer, R. (1964). The foundations of decision under uncertainty: an elementary exposition. *Journal of the American Statistical Association* **59**, 353–75.

Pratt, J. W., Raiffa, H., and Schlaifer, R. (1965). *Introduction to Statistical Decision Theory.* New York: McGraw-Hill.

Preston, M. G. and Baratta, P. (1948). An experimental study of the auction value of an uncertain outcome. *American Journal of Psychology* **61**, 183–93.

Quiggin, J. (1982). A theory of anticipated utility. *Journal of Economic Behavior and Organization* **3**, 323–43.

Raiffa, H. (1961). Risk, ambiguity, and the Savage axioms: comment. *Quarterly Journal of Economics* **75**, 690–94.

Raiffa, H. (1968). *Decision Analysis: Introductory Lectures on Choice under Uncertainty.* Reading, MA: Addison-Wesley.

Raiffa, H. and Schlaifer, R. (1961). *Applied Statistical Decision Theory*. Boston: Harvard Graduate School of Business Administration.

Ramsey, F. P. (1931). Truth and probability. *The Foundations of Mathematics and Other Logical Essays*, pp. 156–98. London: Routledge and Kegan Paul. Reprinted in *Studies in Subjective Probability* (ed. H .E. Kyburg and H. E. Smokler), pp. 61–92. New York: Wiley, 1964.

Reilly, R. J. (1982). Preference reversal: further evidence and some suggested modifications in experimental design. *American Economic Review* **72**, 576–84.

Richter, M. K. (1971). Rational choice. *Preferences, Utility, and Demand* (ed. J. S. Chipman, L. Hurwicz, M. K. Richter, and H. F. Sonnenschein), pp. 29–58. New York: Harcourt Brace Jovanovich.

Rockafellar, R .T. (1970). *Convex Analysis*. Princeton: Princeton University Press.

Ross, S. (1981). Some stronger measures of risk aversion in the small and the large with applications. *Econometrica* **49**, 621–38.

Rubin, J. E. (1967). *Set Theory for the Mathematician*. San Fransicso: Holden-Day.

Samuelson, P. A. (1977). St. Petersburg paradoxes: defanged, dissected, and historically described. *Journal of Economic Literature* **15**, 24–55.

Savage, L. J. (1954). *The Foundations of Statistics*. New York: Wiley.

Schlaifer, R. (1959). *Probability and Statistics for Business Decisions*. New York: McGraw-Hill.

Schmeidler, D. (1984). Subjective probability and expected utility without additivity. Preprint 84, Institute for Mathematics and Its Applications, University of Minnesota, Minneapolis.

Schmeidler, D. (1986). Integral representation without additivity. *Proceedings of the American Mathematical Society* **97**, 255–61.

Schoemaker, P. J. H. (1980). *Experiments on Decisions under Risk*. Boston: Martinus Nijhoff.

Schwartz, T. (1972). Rationality and the myth of the maximum. *Noûs* **6**, 97–117.

Segal, U. (1984). Nonlinear decision weights with the independence axiom. Working Paper 353, Department of Economics, University of California, Los Angeles.

Segal, U. (1987). The Ellsberg paradox and risk aversion: an anticipated utility approach. *International Economic Review* **28**, 175–202.

Seidenfeld, T. and Schervish, M. J. (1983). A conflict between finite additivity and avoiding Dutch Book. *Philosophy of Science* **50**, 398–412.

Sen, A. K. (1970). *Collective Choice and Social Welfare*. San Francisco: Holden-Day.

Sen, A. (1985). Rationality and uncertainty. *Theory and Decision* **18**, 109–27.

Shafer, G. (1976). *A Mathematical Theory of Evidence*. Princeton: Princeton University Press.

Shafer, W. and Sonnenschein, H. (1975). Equilibrium in abstract economies without ordered preferences. *Journal of Mathematical Economics* **2**, 345–48.

Shepsle, K. A. (1970). A note on Zeckhauser's "Majority rule with lotteries on alternatives": the case of the paradox of voting. *Quarterly Journal of Economics* **84**, 705–9.

Sherman, R. (1974). The psychological difference between ambiguity and risk. *Quarterly Journal of Economics* **88**, 166–69.

Skala, H. J. (1975). *Non-Archimedean Utility Theory*. Dordrecht, Holland: Reidel.

Slovic, P. and Lichtenstein, S. (1968). The relative importance of probabilities and payoffs in risk taking. *Journal of Experimental Psychology* **78**, 1–18.

Slovic, P. and Lichtenstein, S. (1983). Preference reversals: a broader perspective. *American Economic Review* **73**, 596–605.

Slovic, P. and Tversky, A. (1974). Who accepts Savage's axiom? *Behavioral Science* **19**, 368–73.

Slutsky, E. (1915). Sulla teoria del bilancio del consumatore. *Giornale degli Economisti e Rivista di Statistica* **51**, 1–26.

Smart, D. R. (1974). *Fixed Point Theorems*. Cambridge, MA: Cambridge University Press.

Smith, C. A. B. (1961). Consistency in statistical inference and decision. *Journal of the Royal Statistical Society, Series B* **23**, 1–37.

Smith, C. A. B. (1965). Personal probability and statistical analysis. *Journal of the Royal Statistical Society, Series A* **128**, 469–99.

Smith, J. H. (1973). Aggregation of preferences with variable electorate. *Econometrica* **41**, 1027–41.

Stevens, S. S. (1946). On the theory of scales of measurement. *Science* **103**, 677–80.

Stigler, G. J. (1950). The development of utility theory: I, II. *Journal of Political Economy* **58**, 307–27, 373–96.

Stigum, B. P. and Wenstøp, F. (eds.) (1983). *Foundations of Utility and Risk Theory with Applications*. Dordrecht, Holland: Reidel.

Strotz, R. H. (1953). Cardinal utility. *American Economic Review* **43**, 384–97.

Sugden, R. (1985). Regret, recrimination and rationality. *Theory and Decision* **19**, 77–99.

Suppes, P. (1956). The role of subjective probability and utility in decision making. *Proceedings of the Third Berkeley Symposium on Mathematical Statistics and Probability, 1954–1955*, **5**, 61–73.

Suppes, P. (1974). The measurement of belief. *Journal of the Royal Statistical Society, Series B* **36**, 160–91.

Thrall, R. M. (1954). Applications of multidimensional utility theory. *Decision Processes* (ed. R. M. Thrall, C. H. Coombs, and R. L. Davis), pp. 181–86. New York: Wiley.

Toulet, C. (1986). An axiomatic model of unbounded utility functions. *Mathematics of Operations Research* **11**, 81–94.

Toussaint, S. (1984). On the existence of equilibria in economies with infinitely many commodities and without ordered preferences. *Journal of Economic Theory* **33**, 98–115.

Tversky, A. (1969). Intransitivity of preferences. *Psychological Review* **76**, 31–48.

Tversky, A. (1972a). Elimination by aspects: a theory of choice. *Psychological Review* **79**, 281–99.

Tversky, A. (1972b). Choice by elimination. *Journal of Mathematical Psychology* **9**, 341–67.

Tversky, A. (1975). A critique of expected utility theory: descriptive and normative considerations. *Erkenntnis* **9**, 163–73.

Tversky, A. and Kahneman, D. (1973). Availability: a heuristic for judging frequency probability. *Cognitive Psychology* **5**, 207–32.

Tversky, A. and Kahneman, D. (1981), The framing of decisions and the psychology of choice. *Science* **211**, 453–58.

Tversky, A. and Kahneman, D. (1986). Rational choice and the framing of decisions. *Rational Choice* (ed. R. M. Hogarth and M. W. Reder), pp. 67–94. Chicago: University of Chicago Press.

Villegas, C. (1964). On qualititive probability σ-algebras. *Annals of Mathematical Statistics* **35**, 1787–96.

von Neumann, J. (1928). Zur theorie der gesellschaftsspiele. *Mathematische Annalen* **100**, 295–320.

von Neumann, J. and Morgenstern, O. (1944). *Theory of Games and Economic Behavior*. Princeton, NJ: Princeton Univeristy Press; 2nd ed. 1947; 3rd ed. 1953.

Wakker, P. (1981). Agreeing probability measures for comparative probability structures. *Annals of Statistics* **9**, 658–62.

Wakker, P. P. (1986). *Representations of Choice Situations*. Catholic University, Nijmegen, Holland.

Walley, P. and Fine, T. L. (1979). Varieties of modal (classificatory) and comparative probability. *Synthese* **41**, 321–74.

Walras, L. (1874). *Eléments d'economie politique pure*. Lausanne: Corbas.

Whitmore, G. A. and Findlay, M. C. (eds.) (1978). *Stochastic Dominance*. Lexington, MA: Heath.

Yaari, M. E. (1986). Univariate and multivariate comparisons of risk aversion: a new approach. *Essays in Honor of Kenneth J. Arrow* (ed. W. W. Heller, R. Starr, and D. Starrett). Cambridge: Cambridge University Press.

Yaari, M. E. (1987). The dual theory of choice under risk. *Econometrica* **55**, 95–115.

Yannelis, N. C. and Prabhakar, N. D. (1983). Existence of maximal elements and equilibria in linear topological spaces. *Journal of Mathematical Economics* **12**, 233–45.

Zeckhauser, R. (1969). Majority rule with lotteries on alternatives. *Quarterly Journal of Economics* **83**, 696–703.

Index